LAFAYETTE
BETWEEN THE AMERICAN
AND THE
FRENCH REVOLUTION
(1783-1789)

LAFAYETTE
BETWEEN THE AMERICAN
AND THE
FRENCH REVOLUTION
(1783-1789)

By

LOUIS GOTTSCHALK

THE UNIVERSITY OF CHICAGO PRESS
CHICAGO & LONDON

THE UNIVERSITY OF CHICAGO PRESS, CHICAGO & LONDON
The University of Toronto Press, Toronto 5, Canada

Midway Reprint   1974

To

WILLIAM LINN WESTERMANN
Historian, Teacher, Friend

PREFACE

THIS is the fourth of a series of studies on the life and times of Lafayette. It takes him through a period of about six years—from the end of the War of American Independence in 1783 to the threshold of the French Revolution in 1789. The hero of this volume, inasmuch as the narration of events is focused upon him, is, of course, Lafayette. But he is not the most admirable character in it. The noblest figures are those of George Washington and Vergennes, who have already assumed heroic stature in the earlier volumes of this series, and Thomas Jefferson.

How thoroughly those men influenced Lafayette and, through him, the political development of France during this period has never been told before. These six years occupy only sixty-three pages (pp. 98–161) in Étienne Charavay's *Le général La Fayette 1757–1834* (Paris, 1898) and considerably less in other biographies. Their crucial significance as the years of passage from boyhood to manhood, from revolution in rehearsal in America to revolution in earnest in France, from a seldom rivaled success as a subordinate to a leadership that was doomed to disaster, has hitherto been largely neglected.

A few words are called for regarding the quotations in this volume. I have in some instances modified the orthography, punctuation, and capitalization of the originals where clarity might otherwise have been sacrificed to exactitude. Sometimes, although I have quoted from the manuscripts, I have nevertheless been satisfied to give the best printed collection as my source in the footnotes. In such instances, my version may vary slightly from the version cited. When the variant readings are more than slight, however, I have usually indicated them.

In this, as in the earlier volumes in the series, the list of persons to whom I am indebted would be a formidable one if I were to thank them all by name. I limit myself—as far as libraries are concerned—to mentioning the staff of the University of Chicago Library, whom I have exploited mercilessly; that of the Library of Congress, who have unfailingly met all my demands for help and materials; that of the Newberry Library, where as a fellow I spent the summer of 1946 writing part of the rough draft of this volume; and the staffs of several archives of France, who have treated me as co-operatively by mail in late years as once they treated me in person. Other libraries and historical societies have been equally co-operative in spirit, though I have called less upon them, and I have mentioned them in the footnotes whenever I have had occasion to use their resources. Private collectors such as Stuart W. Jackson and Walter P. Gardner have continued to be most generous to me, and Theodore E. Norton, the curator of the Gardner-Ball collection when it was deposited in the Lafayette College Library (it is now at Indiana University), has never failed to give me the benefit of his knowledge and patience.

Some of the material in this volume first became familiar to me through the work of students. Among those to whom I am indebted in that way are Professor Helmut Hirsch for a report on Lafayette's associations with Mesmer, Miss Augusta Lansing for one on Lafayette in Germany in 1785, Mrs. Charlotte Watkins Smith for another on Lafayette's relations with Jefferson before 1789, and Mrs. Josephine Fennell Pacheco for the copy of several documents from American and Canadian archives.

My research assistants during the preparation of this manuscript have been Miss Margaret Maddox, Mr. Howard A. Vernon, Dr. Jane L. Cates, Mrs. Barbara H. Reed, Dr. Henry Folmer, Mr. Richard Herr, and Mr. Niel B. Dunlap. I have, I fear, often tried their patience, but they seem to feel with me that it has been in a good cause. For that feeling, as well as for their devotion to their work, I am grateful.

My friends Hill Shine, W. T. Hutchinson, and Margaret Maddox read and corrected the manuscript. Fruma Gottschalk, Ezio Cappadocia, and Niel Dunlap read the proofs and helped to prepare the Index. The staff of the University of Chicago Press has been, as always, most co-operative.

The funds for this study continue to be furnished by the Social Science Research Committee of the University of Chicago, and I am still using materials that I gathered when I was a fellow of the John Simon Guggenheim Memorial Foundation. Needless to say, my research project would have had to be much more modest than it has become if such funds had not been available to me, and I am glad again to have an occasion to express my gratitude for them.

LOUIS GOTTSCHALK

CHICAGO, 1949

Note to the second printing: Since the first printing of this volume, the collection of Mr. Stuart W. Jackson has passed into the possession of the Yale University Library, and the Fabius collection has been divided between the Bibliothèque Nationale (Paris) and the Cornell University Library, each receiving the whole either in the originals or in microfilms. The references below to these collections (as also to the Gardner-Ball Collection; see p. viii above) have been allowed to stand as of 1949.

L. G.

CHICAGO, 1964

TABLE OF CONTENTS

CHAPTER I

The Grammar of Liberty

[The French Revolution] has apparently burst forth like a creation from a chaos, but it is no more than the consequence of a mental revolution priorly existing in France. The mind of the nation had changed beforehand, and the new order of things has naturally followed the new order of thoughts. . . . The American constitutions were to liberty what a grammar is to language: they define its parts of speech, and practically construct them into syntax. The peculiar situation of the then Marquis de la Fayette is another link in the great chain.

THOMAS PAINE[1]

T HE War of the American Revolution formally ended with the signing of a preliminary peace early in 1783. By January, 1789, the French Revolution was unmistakably on its way.

Thus almost six years elapsed between the time when the Marquis de Lafayette, major-general in the Continental Army of the United States of America, found himself no longer at the head of American soldiers and the time when he stood forth as a daring leader of the French revolutionary cause. They were six years of rapid growth for the young general. In 1783 he was *"the* Marquis" for Americans and *"the* friend of Washington" for Frenchmen. A figure of world renown at the age of twenty-six, celebrated by poet and artist for his part in humbling Britain and freeing America, he had as yet formulated only a vague understanding of what America might mean in the history of his own country. But he realized with pious clarity his own devotion to Washington. "In everything I do I first consider what your opinion would be had I an opportunity to con-

1. *The rights of man*, ed. M. D. Conway (New York, 1895), pp. 336 and 338.

I

sult it," he wrote to his former commander-in-chief.[2] Not having known a father's love or guidance even in infancy, he had placed his "adoptive father" and general on a pedestal so high that it soon became a source of amazement to some and of irony to others. America, for one thing, meant *Washington* to him.

For another it meant *Liberty*. A few years after the peace Lafayette wrote to Washington, "The ideas of liberty have been since the American Revolution spreading very fast," and he rejoiced that French minds were "getting enlightened by the works of the philosophers and the example of other nations."[3] Foremost among the nations that furnished examples was the United States.

But what was the *Liberty* that the United States illustrated? If we were to believe the autobiographies of Lafayette's contemporaries (and the unreliability of autobiographies is notorious), *Liberty*, even as early as 1783, meant to him a republican form of government. Lafayette's own memoirs, written piecemeal at scattered intervals after 1783 and carefully revised and idealized by filiopietistic editors, give the distinct impression that he was a full-fledged republican even before he first escaped from frustration in France to seek a glorious career in America. And it is true that, when once he began to be interested in becoming an American soldier, he started to talk the jargon that Silas Deane, William Carmichael, and other Americans in Paris used. As time went on, he talked it with greater fluency and conviction. When at last he returned from the war, the most conspicuous of the French aristocrats who had fought the victorious fight for American independence against British tyranny, he had become popularly identified with "republicanism."

But what was a "republic" to the sophisticates who used that word in the 1780's? Not a kingless state, since the elective kingdom of Poland was generally called a republic. Not a democracy, since the aristocratic states of Venice and Genoa and the

2. June 29, 1782, Louis Gottschalk (ed.), *The letters of Lafayette to Washington 1777-1799* (New York, 1944), pp. 252-53.

3. Oct. 9, 1787, *ibid.*, p. 327.

middle-class federations of Switzerland and the Netherlands were also called republics. Writers like Montesquieu and Rousseau were careful to distinguish between republics and democracies. Democracy, they said, was possible only in small, easily defended states, where men were patriotic and unselfish. Only "if men were gods," Rousseau had said, could he believe in democracy; and he repeated Montesquieu's dictum that democracies could exist only if their citizens were virtuous—meaning, thereby, patriotic to the point that they put service to their countrymen above self, and equality above honor. Until the death of Rousseau and Voltaire in 1778, liberal political writers believed that a big and complicated state like France should be an enlightened monarchy or, as some of them said, a "legal despotism." By that they meant a strong royal state in which the king would feel himself bound by the laws of Nature and of Reason. The example of the American republic was the first to give them pause.

Before 1783 Lafayette knew little or nothing about Montesquieu, Rousseau, and Voltaire. There is no sure sign that he had ever read a page of any contemporary *philosophe* (with the possible exception of Raynal) or that he had any systematized theory of politics beyond a sentimental attachment for America and an inbred conviction that France was greater than England or any other country in the world. It was no insurmountable contradiction for him that France was a powerful monarchy and the United States a weak confederation of republics. The badness of some features of French government, he felt, could easily be exaggerated. He had challenged the English diplomatic agent Lord Carlisle to a duel because that worthy had dared to call his country "an enemy to all civil and religious liberty" and to question its motives in aiding America.[4] And, in what seems to have been his only discourse on French politics before 1783, he had contended that fundamentally France's government was better than England's. The highest French law courts or parlements, he thought, were a more effective check on royal authority than was the British Parliament, French law and judges superior to English justice (except for

4. Louis Gottschalk, *Lafayette joins the American army* (Chicago, 1937), p. 278.

the English jury system), and France more tolerant of minority religions than England. Nor was he merely an apologist for French monarchy; on several occasions he had lost patience with the inefficiency of American democracy, going so far at one time as to wish that Washington would make himself a dictator. If he was still sentimental about America in 1783, it was not yet because he believed in the "people" or disbelieved in kings.[5]

When, however, he came to write the several pieces that make up his *Mémoires*, he was more of a democrat than he had been in his younger days (though still not an unqualified one), and he had come to believe that he always had been a republican. So he told several stories about himself that, if taken at their face value, would show that he was indeed a politically daring man even in his twenties. At no time was he surer of his early republicanism than in 1799, when, from a place of exile outside France, he hoped to take a leading part in the improvement of the French Republic of the Directory. "The heart of Lafayette," he then wrote, "was naturally republican," and he told several anecdotes to show how republican that heart had been from the beginning. For example, he remembered having written home when he had first come to America at nineteen years of age, "I have always thought that a king was a useless being at best; from here he cuts a much sadder figure still." On his first voyage back to France, when asked by the king's ministers about the relative prosperity of each colony, he had answered (at least, so he recalled about twenty years later): "It is in inverse ratio to the influence of royal authority." When he next returned, he recollected saying to Queen Marie Antoinette, who wished to address Washington as she might have addressed any of the contemporary European rulers: "Those people, Madame, are only kings; Washington is the general of a free people." Still later, when at a review of French royal troops he wore his American uniform, of which the sword belt bore a device that interested Louis XVI, Lafayette remembered

5. *Ibid.*, pp. 267 and 330; Louis Gottschalk, *Lafayette and the close of the American Revolution* (Chicago, 1942), pp. 4, 10, 27, 128, 146, 177, 181, 183–85, 202–3, 228, and 286–87.

explaining that it was a tree of liberty growing out of a broken crown and scepter.[6]

Lafayette was not a liar. He did not deliberately deceive others. Like other frail human beings, however, he was not above deceiving himself by romanticizing his youth and exaggerating his own cleverness and foresight. Moreover, it would have been only too easy around 1799 to give to the half-truths of 1779 or 1782 an earnestness that at that time, being half-jests, they were not intended to convey. At any rate no contemporary evidence supports these recollections twenty years removed from the events they recalled. On the contrary, what evidence there is seems to indicate that Lafayette (perhaps unconsciously) reserved his republican sentiments for Americans and still spoke a monarchical language to Frenchmen.[7] He was not above thinking (and, as it proved, with justification) that the compliments of kings would be pleasing even to republican ears like those of John Adams.[8] Good manners rather than political conviction still determined the tenor of his remarks before 1783. It is hard to believe that he would have spoken as bluntly as his later recollections would imply to the kings, queens, and ministers of the 1780's.

Lafayette was not a republican in 1783 if by "republican" is meant a believer in popular, kingless government. Nor is that to his discredit. There were few believers in popular government in those days, whether in France, England, or America. What Lafayette himself usually meant when he used the word "republicanism" before 1783 was the elective principle by which even in a monarchy representatives of at least some of the people might share in the government of the realm. As late as 1799, in the very essay in which he tried to show how "republican" he had always been, he declared, "While acknowledging the indications of republicanism that I have just cited with perfect good faith, while admitting that all these recollec-

6. *Mémoires, correspondance et manuscrits du général Lafayette publiés par sa famille* (Paris, 1837–48) (hereafter called *Mémoires*), III, 196–97; Harvard College Library, Sparks MSS XXXII, fols. 127–28 and 130–31.

7. Louis Gottschalk, *Lafayette comes to America* (Chicago, 1935), pp. 171–73; *Lafayette and the close of the American Revolution*, pp. 293 and 367.

8. Gottschalk, *Lafayette and the close of the American Revolution*, pp. 360–61.

tions might have given ground to the suspicions of zealous royalists, I can with the same sincerity assert that Lafayette [he
frequently talked of himself in the third person] has all his life
frankly and wholeheartedly supported constitutional monarchy."[9]

In 1799, when Lafayette defined republicanism to include
wholehearted support of constitutional monarchy, republics
were no longer the rare class-controlled things they once
had been. By that time the old republics of Holland,
Switzerland, and Genoa had undergone democratic changes
and Venice had disappeared into the larger Cisalpine
Republic—all of them, along with several other recently repub-
licanized states, under the aegis of a republican France. Republicanism, which in the eighteenth century had been regarded
as a form of government fit only for small cantons, provinces,
or city-states capable of defending themselves only by creating
federal unions, had come to be regarded as a vigorous, aggressive form of government which might, it was hoped or feared,
sweep all other forms aside. It was no longer necessary in those
days for a Frenchman to be apologetic for being a republican.
On the contrary, the temptation was great to claim to have
been more republican before the Revolution than one in fact
had been. It is not surprising, therefore, to find that Lafayette's
memory induced him to believe that before 1789 he had been
a more pronounced republican than the documents of the 1780's
indicate. But for that very reason his statement that he had
"all his life frankly and wholeheartedly supported constitutional monarchy" gains in credibility.

Lafayette, then, on the eve of the French Revolution was
"republican" only in the sense that he believed that France,
while remaining a monarchy, should have a constitution that
would restrict the power of the monarch. For a member of the
court nobility, that was not a unique attitude. The highest
tribunals—the parlements—had maintained in recurrent political crises throughout the eighteenth century that France
was actually a constitutional monarchy and that the aristocracy, usually speaking through the parlements and the now-de-

9. *Mémoires*, II, 200.

funct Estates General, had a traditional right to share with the king in the government of the nation. As Lafayette's one discourse on French politics before 1783 showed, he was aware of and approved that aristocratic interpretation of the French constitution.[10] Although he does not seem to have read Montesquieu, he knew of Montesquieu—had in fact traveled through part of America with Montesquieu's grandson—and was therefore probably aware that Montesquieu had made a historical and philosophical presentation of that point of view. And if Montesquieu's grandson had not enlightened him, his own relative, the Chevalier de Chastellux, one of the rare noblemen of the court who had acquired a reputation as a *philosophe*, could have done so—perhaps on the same journey. If history were not limited by rules of documentation, it would be easy to present the conversation of the three French gentlemen—one a young American major-general whose recent political experiences were rapidly deranging his stock of traditional prejudices, another the grandson of that French writer to whom enlightened conservatives most often resorted, and the third a French general who had himself acquired a leading reputation as a social philosopher—as they jogged along a Pennsylvania road talking about the differences in French, English, and American institutions. It was shortly after that journey that Lafayette's lone disquisition on the parlements was written.[11] In it he defended them against implied criticisms.

If Lafayette's political education had ended there, he would perhaps never have become distinguishable from the great number of court nobles who supported the theory of the French constitution put forward by Montesquieu and the parlements. But the young soldier's learning was not book learning. No evidence exists that before 1783 he had digested any literature beyond the classics he had been required to study in the Collège Du Plessis, where he had gone to school. Except for comments about Chastellux as a friend and a casual reference to the publicist Raynal, not a single one of the great contemporary writers was mentioned by name or citation in his numerous ex-

10. Gottschalk, *Lafayette and the close of the American Revolution*, pp. 183–85.
11. *Ibid.*, p. 184.

tant letters before that date. His devotion to "liberty" and "republicanism" was limited, as a French military aristocrat's ought to have been, usually encompassing only the victims of English "tyranny"—America and Ireland[12]—but rarely and moderately expressed on behalf of the victims of French or American tyranny.

In fact, against France's and America's outstanding social evils, Lafayette had as yet broken no lance. Though he apparently wished to follow King Louis's example in 1779 in setting his serfs free, he was not familiar enough with his own estates to know whether they had any serfs or not. Though he was kind and paternalistic to his hungry and needy tenants, especially when he visited his hereditary Chavaniac during the famine of 1783, he was nonetheless an absentee landlord. He had seen his lands only once in a decade, leaving them meanwhile to an intendant to run at a profit by squeezing debtors, soliciting reduction of taxes, and making new investments. In America a social problem prevailed that was eventually to help cause one of the world's most bloody civil wars—Negro slavery. But only recently had Lafayette indicated that he thought of Negroes as anything but property to be bought and sold (except in the case of a slave who had rendered outstanding service in the Virginia campaign of 1781).[13]

The young marquis's silence on social ills was not attributable to a lack of opportunities for protest. One of the most recent pieces of literature to create a furor in France had been the *Compte rendu* by Jacques Necker, director of the royal finances (1781). Here Necker had revealed, among other extravagances, how large a part of the royal revenue went into paying unearned pensions. Nevertheless, Lafayette's intendant had recently (1779) renewed a claim for an annual pension paid to Lafayette because he had been orphaned in the Battle of Minden. It amounted to only 600 livres, which was certainly a negligible

12. *Ibid.*, pp. 19, 31, and 52–54.
13. Gottschalk, *Lafayette comes to America*, pp. 64 and 141; *Lafayette joins the American army*, p. 69; *Lafayette and the close of the American Revolution*, pp. 9, 50–51, 280, 330, 373–75, 401–2, and 417–18; Louis Gottschalk and J. L. MacDonald, "Letters on the management of an estate during the Old Regime," *Journal of modern history*, VIII (1936), 64–81; Louis Gottschalk and M. H. Sheldon, "More letters on the management of an estate during the Old Regime," *ibid.*, XVII (1945), 147–52.

sum in an income of around 120,000 livres. But Lafayette continued to collect it yearly until he developed a new conscientiousness regarding social injustices of that kind—which was not yet. Among the agencies of liberal protest that were springing up in France were the Masonic lodges. They were still genteel clubs, where the members, largely noblemen and noblewomen, clergy, and wealthy *roturiers*, mildly hoped for a better world. Lafayette apparently had become a Freemason before he first left for America, but he was inactive as such before 1783.[14]

Lafayette's postdated boasts of "republicanism" during and immediately after the American War must therefore be reappraised. He had volunteered to go to America to serve "the American cause," to be sure, but the American cause was, when he first heard of it, an effort to break up the British Empire. "Freedom" and "liberty" meant freedom for part of that empire from the British tyrant. Without using slogans like these, other French soldiers, some of whom never developed into revolutionaries, also threw their swords into the American side of the balance merely for the sake of fighting a traditional enemy. The difference between them and Lafayette was that he adopted the American cause earnestly from the moment he contracted at age nineteen to be an American major-general. He did so for a variety of reasons. Chief among them were a characteristic resentment against oppression, a sense of frustration in his own normal career, and an ability and willingness to exploit wealth, friends, and influence to gain prestige. Being younger and more susceptible, living closer to George Washington, and receiving more deference from other American leaders, he learned to talk the language of republicanism both grammatically and politically with increasing correctness. By the time he had made two visits to America and fought four campaigns, he was almost an expert. When the American War was over, he was nearly as ready to speak the American language as his native tongue, and he was prepared in proper season to voice American ideas even before Frenchmen.

14. Gottschalk, *Lafayette comes to America*, p. 22; *Lafayette and the close of the American Revolution*, pp. 51, 367–69, and 433–34.

As yet, those ideas did not include republicanism for France. There constitutional monarchy seemed quite enough. But upon his return in 1781 from his second stay in America, Lafayette's philosophy began to include such things as open affiliation with the Masons, visiting and befriending tenants, financing an experiment in Negro emancipation, and attacking French mercantile and financial privilege through special tariff arrangements for American traders. He once even used the phrase "natural right against tyranny" in a letter to a Frenchman, though an obscure Frenchman.[15]

It would be a mistake, however, to believe that by 1783 Lafayette had become a revolutionary. The few reform proposals that he entertained were moderate, and he intended that they should be achieved through lawful channels. Many other Frenchmen had ideas like them, and some had even more radical ones. Yet very few of those Frenchmen were of the court nobility, and of those few, some, like Charles and Alexandre de Lameth, had also been turned in the liberal direction largely by American influences. The French court nobles who, like Chastellux, had learned to talk the eighteenth-century idiom of Reason were rare exceptions before the American Revolution. But now there was an American vogue. Either by direct contact or vicariously, America had helped to make liberals even in the milieu of traditional conservatism.

In 1783 Lafayette did not foresee that France would have a revolution. If he had foreseen it, he would not have been happy about it. But he was ready for change for reasons both of political principle and of personal ambition. And change, as his astute contemporary Chateaubriand understood, was the idea of the century.[16] One who could call every important American figure a friend and Washington a father would not hesitate to sweep away a few anachronisms that stood in the path of human happiness, especially if that path also led to new fields of personal glory. And the less he hesitated, the more he encouraged others. Thus he became a leader of a force that even with-

15. Gottschalk, *Lafayette and the close of the American Revolution*, p. 361. Cf. pp. 401–2 and 415–17.

16. Quoted in Gottschalk, *Lafayette and the close of the American Revolution*, p. 422.

out him would have gone resistlessly forward. He was eventually to discover that he could do nothing to stop it, once it had begun. But before that sad discovery came, he was one of the people's leaders and so he had to follow them. Both conviction and honor pointed down the same road, and it led toward revolution—and personal disaster.

BIBLIOGRAPHICAL NOTES[17]

The above interpretation of Lafayette's gradual development as a liberal is based on my previous biographical studies. For my reply to the scholars who have questioned this thesis see "The attitude of European officers in the Revolutionary armies toward General George Washington," *Journal of the Illinois State Historical Society*, XXXII (1939), 20–50.

17. These Bibliographical Notes are intended only to supplement the footnotes, which should also be consulted. Full bibliographical data are given only the first time a work is cited. The Index is so arranged as to make it easy to find these first citations.

CHAPTER II

From Youth to Manhood

THE passage from youth to manhood is never abrupt, and yet a day comes when the man is easily distinguishable from the boy. For the Marquis de Lafayette that day was somewhere in the spring of 1783. The American War had ended. That meant that his career was to become European rather than American, and political rather than military. His youthful passion for the Comtesse de Hunolstein had likewise ended.[1] That meant a greater interest in his home and in a more sedate type of woman. Moreover, as was duly testified in documents deposited with his intendant, "Monseigneur Marie-Joseph-Paul-Yves-Roch-Gilbert du Motier, Marquis de la Fayette, major-general in the armies of the United States of North America, Baron of Reignac, Vissac, St. Romain, Seigneur de Kaufrait, St. Quihoet, Le Plessix, La Touche, and in part of the County of Ploeuc, L'Isle Aval, and Veau Couronné," had recently (September 6, 1782) turned twenty-five years of age and was therefore no longer a minor in the eyes of the French legal authorities.[2] He could now manage his own property, spend his own money, and make his own plans without consulting guardians and older male relatives. He could even buy a home of his own.

There were five in the Lafayette family now. The devoted Marquise Adrienne de Noailles-Lafayette had presented him with four children, three of whom were still alive in the spring of 1783. Anastasie was not quite six, her brother George Wash-

1. Gottschalk, *Lafayette and the close of the American Revolution*, pp. 417-19, and *Lady-in-waiting, the romance of Lafayette and Aglaé de Hunolstein* (Baltimore, 1939), pp. 99-102.
2. Gottschalk, *Lafayette and the close of the American Revolution*, pp. 374-75.

ington de Lafayette was nearly four, and Virginie was only a few months old. There were to be no more children for the Lafayettes. Hitherto they had all been obliged to live under the roof of his father-in-law, the Duc d'Ayen, heir of the illustrious Noailles. Lafayette respected his worldly and witty father-in-law and loved the motherly Duchesse d'Ayen. Yet one of the first things he had done on reaching his majority was to order his intendant, Jacques-Philippe Grattepain-Morizot, to look for a separate home for his family. The Lafayettes were thenceforth to be Lafayettes rather than Noailles.

The spring of 1783 found Lafayette visiting his native village of Chavaniac in Auvergne. It was there that he definitely determined to give up Aglaé de Hunolstein. In April, when he left Chavaniac to return to Paris, both the American War and Aglaé were things of the past. When, accompanied by his old aunt, Mme de Chavaniac, who had tended him in his childhood, he once more turned his horses' heads toward Paris, a new career lay before him.

The route to the metropolis ran through the town of Riom, the ancient capital of Auvergne's dukes. There, on April 5, the city fathers, the town police, and a brass band turned out to honor their illustrious compatriot. The people shouted "Vive Lafayette!" in admiration of the hero who had brought new luster to one of Auvergne's most famous families, and the city notables offered him the *vin d'honneur* in traditional token of their esteem for their celebrated young guest. He listened graciously to the speeches of three red-robed city dignitaries before he and his aunt were allowed to proceed.[3]

The effervescence of Lafayette's fellow-Auvergnats was no display of mere provincial patriotism. Equal enthusiasm was to be found in high places, in the big cities, and among sophisticates. The poet Cerutti was one of those who sang the praises of the "noble and modest Lafayette"[4] who "at twenty was the world's support," and a reviewer of Cerutti's poems believed the lines devoted to Lafayette to be among his best. Other poets

3. [Louis Bachaumont and continuators], *Mémoires secrets pour servir à l'histoire de la république des lettres en France depuis MDCCLXII jusqu'à nos jours* (London, 1783-89), XXII, 276-77 (May 14, 1783).

4. "L'aigle et le hibou," *Œuvres diverses de M. Cerutti* (Paris, 1792), II, 11.

joined in the paean.[5] Even quite sober, scholarly souls beheld in the young hero a modern exemplar of the classical virtues. A new fragment of Xenophon having been recently unearthed, a French reporter of the episode found that Xenophon's Alcibiades was only a prototype of his countryman: "All that Xenophon says of his young Athenian would pass for fabulous in our day if la Fayette had not achieved it."[6] When a new French edition of *Plutarch's lives* was under contemplation, the publisher proposed to dedicate it to Lafayette—"a young hero whose modesty equals his courage and wisdom" and whose career would recall to readers that of the brilliant young Scipio Africanus.[7]

When poet and scholar alike marveled that one so young should be so great, mere rulers could not be less impressed. Shortly after Lafayette arrived in Paris, Louis XVI felt called upon to present him, despite his youth, with the coveted Cross of the Order of St. Louis, reserved for the most distinguished soldiers of the realm.[8] The recommendation of the Maréchal de Ségur, minister of war, cited the new Chevalier of St. Louis (with only slight exaggeration) for "twelve years of service, of which nearly six were in America, where he was present at all engagements and where he was very usefully employed also for purposes of negotiations."

Now, too, Morizot succeeded in finding for Lafayette a home of his own. It was at No. 183 Rue de Bourbon (now roughly 81 Rue de Lille) close to the Palais-Bourbon. It cost around $200,000 without furniture. Remodeling and furnishings, for which the best talent in France was employed, made the total cost about 100,000 livres higher (and a livre then would easily buy what a dollar would buy today). The furniture alone cost 50,000 livres. To meet the expense, Lafayette had to sell one of his best properties—the Hôtel de La Marck in Paris. Morizot, years afterward, insisted that Lafayette's real estate deals in

5. *Journal de Paris*, Apr. 2 and May 18, 1783.

6. *L'année littéraire* (1783), IV, 278.

7. *Ibid.*, II, 66–68. Cf. Jean Cussac to Franklin, [1783?], American Philosophical Society (Philadelphia) (hereafter abbreviated APS), Franklin papers, Vol. XL, No. 36.

8. Étienne Charavay, *Le général La Fayette, 1757–1834* (Paris, 1898), pp. 563–64; cf. p. 98.

the period from 1777 to 1783 (of which this was one of the most important) reduced his annual income by 28,000 livres. But it was still 118,000 a year,[9] and the young paterfamilias did not begrudge the loss. For years he had dreamed of the time when he and Adrienne would be "big enough to have our own house, live there happily, entertain our friends, establish an atmosphere of ease, and read the papers of foreign countries without caring to go ourselves to see what is happening."[10] Now at last his dream had come true.

When the Lafayettes moved to their magnificent new quarters, it became one of the social centers of Paris. There the Noailles and the Chastelluxes could be found busily engaged in conversation with the Jays, the Adamses, and other visiting celebrities. Franklin frequently attended the regular Monday dinners. Mrs. Jay and Mrs. Adams often came to chat with Mme de Lafayette about the joys of home, their friends, and their children. The house became a sort of rendezvous for Americans in Europe.[11]

Adrienne de Lafayette, who directed the new ménage, was a domestic soul. She shone at her best as wife, parent, and hostess. She took after her mother, who was descended from the *noblesse de la robe* (magisterial nobility) and was noted for simple piety, rather than after her father, who was a proud, soldierly Noailles and one of the wits of Paris. Lafayette, however, was not a stay-at-home. His active temperament, his penchant for political intrigue, his anxiety to be respected by important people, and his devotion to his circle of friends led him to others' homes.

Several fashionable salons frequently saw the young general, He sometimes visited "the Circle" of the Prince de Conti, where

9. André Girodie, *Exposition du centenaire de La Fayette 1757–1834, catalogue* (Paris, 1934), pp. 130–32, No. 200; Charavay, p. 99; François Boucher, *American footprints in Paris; a guidebook of historical data pertaining to Americans in the French capital from the earliest days to the present times,* trans. and ed. F. W. Huard (New York, 1921), p. 70; Virginie de Lasteyrie, *La vie de Madame de Lafayette précédée d'une notice sur la vie de sa mère Mme la Duchesse d'Ayen* (Paris, 1869), pp. 82–83; Gilbert Chinard, *The letters of Lafayette and Jefferson* (Baltimore, 1929), pp. 304–7; Henry Mosnier, *Le château de Chavaniac-Lafayette* (Le Puy, 1883), pp. 56–57.

10. Gottschalk, *Lafayette joins the American army,* p. 103.

11. There are at least fourteen invitations to dinner in the Franklin papers, APS. Cf. Frank Monaghan, *John Jay* (New York, 1935), pp. 217 and 227.

the sprightly Comtesse de Boufflers reigned. There he was likely to find boon companions like the Prince de Poix, Adrienne's cousin, and the Comte de Ségur, her uncle. The Comtesse de Hunolstein had once been a member of "the Circle," too, but vicious gossip was now coupled with her name and she was no longer to be found in high society.[12] Another salon which Lafayette occasionally visited was that of the financier Jacques Necker and his benevolent wife at St. Ouen. Here the *princesses combinées*—the Princesse de Poix, the Princesse d'Hénin, and the Duchesse de Lauzun—also came. Adrienne's aunt, the Comtesse de Tessé, was one of the intimate group around the princesses. She was a Noailles, too, the sister of the Duc d'Ayen, and somewhat of a wit and *philosophe* in her own right. She lent a genteel note of learning and dilettantism to the circles in which she moved. She was one of the marquis's most trusted friends and confidantes, and her house at Chaville was a sort of second home to him.

It was at the Neckers' salon that Lafayette first met the Comtesse de Simiane. She was the sister of his friend and fellow-"American," the Comte de Damas. She was twenty-two years of age and reputed to be one of the most beautiful women in France. Soon there were those who believed that only one so brave as Lafayette deserved one so fair as Simiane.[13] Théodore de Lameth, whose mother was a Broglie and who knew the high society of his day, never believed that Mme de Simiane's reputation should have suffered, since Lafayette was "more ardent in politics than with women."[14] There were others who knew the doings of society and thought it was the Princesse d'Hénin rather than the Comtesse de Simiane who explained

12. Louis Dutens, *Mémoires d'un voyageur qui se repose* (London, 1806), II, 127–28; Gottschalk, *Lady-in-waiting*, pp. 102–4; Bachaumont, XXIII, 35–37 (June 30, 1783).
13. Eugène Welvert (ed.), *Mémoires de Théodore de Lameth* (Paris, 1913), pp. 109–10 and 127–28; Charles Nicoullaud (ed.), *Mémoires of the Comtesse de Boigne 1820–1830* (New York, 1908), I, 21, and III, 4–5; [F. G. de La Rochefoucauld-Liancourt (ed.)], *Mémoires de Condorcet sur la Révolution française, extraits de sa correspondance et de celles de ses amis* (Paris, 1824), II, 157; Arthur Chuquet (ed.), *Souvenirs du Baron de Frénilly, pair de France (1768–1828)* (Paris, 1909), pp. 277–78; *Lettres autographes composant la collection de M. Alfred Bovet décrites par Étienne Charavay* (Paris, 1887), I, 286, No. 793; C. A. Sainte-Beuve, *Portraits littéraires* (Paris, 1862–64), II, 157.
14. MS memoirs of Théodore de Lameth, Bibiliothèque Nationale (Paris), nouvelles acquisitions françaises 1387, fols. 231–32.

Lafayette's interest in the Neckers' salon.[15] At any rate, Aglaé
de Hunolstein, having entered a convent, shortly became only
a memory. Lafayette's friendship for Mme de Simiane, on the
other hand, was to last for decades. She was not only more
beautiful, she was also more discreet than poor Aglaé had been.
Still, when in 1783 Mme Vigée-LeBrun did two portraits of her,
it was already commonly believed that the young marquis
(whose face the artist found "pleasant" and whose tone and
manner "gave no sign whatever of his revolutionary inclinations") was "looking after" the "pretty" countess.[16] The aristocratic world of eighteenth-century France was more disposed
than most worlds to love a lover, and even those little inclined
to be tolerant toward Lafayette were ready to forgive him for
his devotion to Mme de Simiane.

Adrienne meanwhile busied herself with her household, her
babies, and her charities. One of her favorite philanthropies at
this time was a school to teach the farmers of Auvergne how to
spin and weave. Her husband had first interested the government in such a school, arguing that it not only would increase
the earning capacity of the peasantry but would keep them
from migrating in the winter. Meanwhile, he had turned the
matter over to her.[17]

A report from the inspector of manufacture in the province
approved of the proposal and suggested the village of St.
Georges d'Aurac as the proper place for the school. Aurac was
in the center of the lands belonging to Lafayette and had an intelligent curé, who could be counted on to co-operate. The curé
thought such a school would cost 6,000 livres. In a society as

15. Henriette La Tour du Pin de Gouvernet, *Journal d'une femme de cinquante ans,
1778–1815,* ed. Comte Aymar de Liederkerke-Beaufort (Paris, 1913), I, 288. I have
found only one indication of unusual friendliness about this time between Lafayette
and the Princesse d'Hénin. That was when he tried to rent Franklin's house at Passy
for her and her mother upon Franklin's departure (see Lafayette to W. T. Franklin,
[*ca.* July 9, 1785], APS, Franklin papers, Vol. CVIII, No. 39).

16. *Souvenirs de Madame Vigée le Brun* (Paris, [1882]), II, 305–6 and 361. Cf. Gottschalk, *Lafayette comes to America,* p. 156 and *Lady-in-waiting,* pp. 56 and 105–6;
Ernest d'Hauterive (ed.), *Journal of the Comte d'Espinchal during the Emigration,* trans.
Mrs. Rodolph Stawell (London, 1912), pp. 222–23 and 409; Gouverneur Morris, *A diary
of the French Revolution 1789–1793,* ed. B. C. Davenport (Boston, 1939), I, 15.

17. Lafayette to Montaran, March 30, 1783, Archives Nationales (Paris) (hereafter
abbreviated AN), F¹²1376, folder dated 1782. Cf. Gottschalk, *Lafayette and the close of
the American Revolution,* p. 374.

closely intermarried as the aristocracy of eighteenth-century France, Lafayette could expect support in high places. Ormesson, the minister of finance, was a cousin. He agreed that the abundance of wool in Auvergne had never been well exploited and that migration had become a serious problem. Believing, besides, that Lafayette might be disposed to contribute his own funds, the minister set aside 6,000 livres, and so a project was begun whereby both landlord and tenants might hope to benefit from the good will of the government.[18]

In the eighteenth century those who were convinced that constitutions rested upon immutable Laws of Nature and the imprescriptible Rights of Man were likely to be equally convinced of the natural brotherhood of man. Many of them derived that concept from an early religious training, now discarded or disregarded, but the irreverent *philosophes* also taught a similar doctrine. For most of them the fundamental nature of mankind was the same in high or low, rich or poor, white or colored, civilized or savage. They merely translated the biblical virtues of charity and brotherly love into the secular virtue of lay and private humanitarianism. In that regard Lafayette was to be no less a child of his century than in his quest for justice based upon Nature and Reason. He had already engaged casually in some of the lay philanthropies of his day—sympathy for the slave, vocational training for the unskilled, and alms for the poor. Now he was to do so more conscientiously, more boldly, more frequently, and in wider fields. His philanthropic bounty, whether in Europe or America, was not to be altogether free from the desire to win popular approval. Such approval was the secular substitute for the rewards that came from the church's treasury of good works, and the benefactions that he showered upon Americans were to earn a greater sum in that coinage than those which fell upon Europeans.

For the time being, however, Lafayette's philanthropies were limited to obtaining favors for relatives and comrades. He asked

18. Lafayette to Ormesson, July 17, 1783, Archives du Ministère des Affaires Étrangères (Paris), correspondance politique, États-Unis (hereafter abbreviated AAE, corr. pol., É.-U.), Vol. XXV, fol. 47; Compte (curé) to Mme de Lafayette, June 10, 1783, AN, F¹²1376, folder dated 1782; Mme de Lafayette to Montaran, Apr. 7 and July 15, 1783, *ibid.*, and report dated July 22, 1783, *ibid.* Germain Martin (*Buffon, maître de forges; La Fayette et l'école pratique de tissage de Chavaignac* [Le Puy, 1898]) has told this story but places it incorrectly in 1785.

the minister of war for promotions and money grants for former aides who had served him in Spain[19] or America.[20] For a devoted officer who had followed him in all his campaigns he begged a pension as a wedding gift,[21] and for a young relative a post in the ministry of war.[22] He likewise wrote letters to influential Americans on behalf of friends or friends' friends expecting to cross the Atlantic[23] in the wave of emigration that rolled from Europe to America. This habit of pulling wires was an old one. It was a sign at once of his good nature and of his political intuition, helping to cement old friendships and to make new ones.

Lafayette needed to make friends, for it was obvious that he had already made enemies. He had become too conspicuous by the many unusual distinctions he had won in a monarchical society, where, as Montesquieu's good judgment had discerned, the desire for honor was the fundamental principle. He had been made *maréchal-de-camp* and Chevalier of St. Louis over the heads of several men senior both in years and service, and some of them never forgot it. He was often surrounded by the most beautiful women of the court, and some found it hard to forgive him that, too. He was regarded as the outstanding hero of the American War, and some of the lesser lights were frankly jealous of his fame.[24] One day the aging Duc de Choiseul, one of the

19. Lafayette to the Maréchal de Ségur, [1783], AN, Marine B⁴210, fol. 163, and to [the Comte d'Estaing], June 30, *ibid.*, fol. 166 (on behalf of the Vicomte de Barral and the Comte de Roux).

20. Lafayette to La Colombe, Apr. 26, 1783, AN, C258, dossier 1901, p. 8 (erroneously dated 1785 in Ulysse Rouchon, *Le Chevalier de La Colombe, un ami de La Fayette* [Paris, 1924], pp. 22–23); and to the Comte d'Estaing, May 4, 1783, AN, Marine G 171 (on behalf of Michel Capitaine du Chesnoy).

21. Lafayette to the Maréchal de Ségur, *ca.* May 10, 1783, collection of S. W. Jackson, Gloucester, Va. (on behalf of the Chevalier de Gimat).

22. Lafayette to "Monsieur," [1783], *ibid.* (on behalf of a nephew of his former guardian, the Abbé de Murat).

23. Cf. Lafayette to John Dickenson, May 12, 1783, Historical Society of Pennsylvania; to Washington, May 18, June 10, and June 12, Gottschalk, *Letters*, pp. 263–64; to Franklin, [May] 21, [1783], APS, Franklin papers, Vol. XLII, Part 2, No. 147; to R. R. Livingston, June 10, New York Public Library (hereafter abbreviated NYPL), Bancroft transcripts; to Nathanael Greene, June 10, Clements Library (Ann Arbor, Mich.). These letters introduced M. Pean, Dr. Edward Bancroft, M. de Beaune, Count Wengiersky, M. de Fontenille, and M. de Sailly.

24. Cf. "Lafayette jugé par le Comte d'Espinchal," *Revue rétrospective*, XX (1894), 293; *Mémoires de Lameth*, pp. 108–9; Rivarol quoted in A. F. Bertrand de Moleville, *Histoire de la Révolution de France* (Paris, 1801–3), IX, 333; Prince de Ligne quoted in Gottschalk, *Lady-in-waiting*, pp. 55–56; A. F. Allonville, *Mémoires secrets de 1770 à 1830* (Paris, 1838–45), I, 97–102.

most illustrious of the late Louis XV's ministers, apparently annoyed by the fuss over the young conqueror, called him *Gilles Caesar*. Gilles was the clownish knave of contemporary drama, immortalized by Watteau. Choiseul's bad pun quickly passed from ear to ear among those who had reason to find it amusing.[25]

One enemy of Lafayette, however, was not malicious—perhaps because he did not have to envy the young man's popularity among his own countrymen. That was the British general Sir Henry Clinton. Clinton's correspondence had recently been published in England, and when Lafayette read it, he found that it contained a passage that might easily lead to embarrassment for him. One of Clinton's communications during the Virginia campaign of 1781 had indicated that Lord Cornwallis might be opposed by about two thousand Continental soldiers and "(as Lafayette observes) a small body of ill-armed peasantry." Right after the words "ill-armed peasantry," which contained a thought that Lafayette had indeed had, Clinton had himself added "full as spiritless as the militia of the Southern provinces, and without any service."[26] While Lafayette had never had a high regard for militia, he had not in fact made so invidious a comparison. The context of Clinton's remark, however, seemed to imply that it was taken from one of Lafayette's intercepted letters. Fearing that he might become the innocent object of American resentment, the marquis wrote to Clinton asking him to acknowledge that it was he and not Lafayette who was the author of that passage. The British general replied with the "candour and politeness" that his erstwhile enemy had expected, graciously admitting that the remark was not taken from an intercepted letter.[27] Lafayette asked an old American friend,

25. Espinchal in *Revue rétrospective*, XX (1894), 293; Allonville, I, 100; Boigne, I, 21; *Mémoires du général B°ⁿ [P. C. F.] Thiébault, publiés sous les auspices de sa fille Mlle Claire Thiébault* (Paris, 1893–95), V, 362 n.; Frénilly, p. 42; Maximilien Robespierre, *Le défenseur de la constitution*, in *Œuvres complètes*, ed. Gustave Laurent, IV (Nancy, 1939), 242–43, n. 26.

26. Cf. Clinton to Cornwallis, Aug. 2, 1781, B. F. Stevens (ed.), *The campaign in Virginia 1781: an exact reprint of six rare pamphlets on the Clinton-Cornwallis controversy*, etc. (London, 1888), II, 112.

27. Lafayette to Clinton, Apr. 30, 1783, Clinton papers, Clements Library (this letter has often been cited incorrectly as of Apr. 29); Clinton to Lafayette, May 12, *ibid*.

Henry Laurens (whose health had obliged him to seek a cure in England), to see that this explanation was published abroad.[28] Printed in the French and English newspapers,[29] the exchange of letters between Lafayette and Clinton did both men credit.

Lafayette was to find, however, that he had embarked upon an arduous labor. The path of the lover of historical truth is not smooth. The ease with which one can deceive is surpassed only by the ease with which one can deceive one's self. The flood of literature on the American Revolution (and subsequently on other revolutions with which Lafayette was to be connected) grew larger. He continued unrelenting, however, in his self-imposed task of keeping the record straight. Few would dare to go to press with accounts of events in which he had played a part without first consulting him, and those who dared had to run the risk of having their work minutely examined and meticulously criticized by him. Thus, little was written and still less went unchallenged that was unfriendly. The "cult" of Lafayette, the story of the unsullied hero of purest motives and rarest wisdom, defying evil men and cruel times in the cause of truth and reason, was to emerge—because it was true in part, but also because, in the effort to correct the patent errors of others, Lafayette himself sometimes committed the more subtle one of being himself deceived.

While finding animosity in high places, Lafayette remained an idol of the people. When his brother-in-law, the Vicomte de Noailles, returned from America to Paris, a crowd gathered around his house—because, explained one chronicler, "this young officer is placed by his exploits and his good sense at the level of M. de la Fayette."[30] This was the Noailles whom Lafayette had once envied and taken as a model. In America, meanwhile, not only was the correspondence of high officials in state and army concerned with his merits and doings, but he was mentioned on

28. Lafayette to Laurens, July 6, 1783, A. S. Sally, Jr. (ed.), "Letters from the Marquis de Lafayette to Hon. Henry Laurens," *South Carolina historical and genealogical magazine*, IX (1908), 178.

29. Cf. *Courrier de l'Europe*, July 25, 1783; *The remembrancer, or impartial repository of public events . . . 1775–1784* (London, [1775]–84), XVI (1783), Part II, 292.

30. François Métra *et al.*, *Correspondance secrète, politique et littéraire; ou mémoires pour servir à l'histoire des cours, des sociétés et de la littérature en France, depuis la mort de Louis XV* (London, 1787–90), XIV, 296.

solemn occasions such as divine services and on convivial ones such as toasts at banquets.[31] It was not surprising that the common people of France should share America's enthusiasm for "the Marquis," who had identified himself so fully with America. His actions were calculated (frequently with cool deliberation) to produce that result. He had not intended to rouse dislike among his fellow-aristocrats, but popularity had its price and he was prepared to pay it. It was clear that he could either court popular favor and win resentment in high places or disdain popular favor and win aristocratic approval.[32] The choice for him was easy. Both inclination and principle, both the ideal of Washington and the desire for glory, would lead him to cultivate his popularity.

BIBLIOGRAPHICAL NOTES

The *Mémoires secrets*, usually designated as by Louis Petit de Bachaumont were, after his death (1771), carried on by a series of continuators, including M. F. Pidansat de Mairobert and Mouffle d'Angerville. In the 1780's the comments on Lafayette were generally unfriendly.

The scholarly museum and exhibition catalogues by André Girodie, particularly that entitled *Exposition du centenaire de La Fayette*, frequently contain information about manuscript and iconographical materials not otherwise available.

The number of memoirs that give eye-witness testimony about Lafayette naturally increases as he becomes increasingly famous. They are, however, not correspondingly reliable. Not only do they speak frequently of events known merely at second hand, but also they are often quite biased. Lafayette was a controversial figure, and it was difficult for partisans and opponents alike to comment upon him impartially. Espinchal's *Journal*, which is available in several partial versions but has never been entirely published, is probably the most hostile for the pre-Revolutionary period. Lafayette's own *Mémoires* are, of course, the most friendly, not only because Lafayette seldom ascribed to himself any but the most noble motives but also because the editors, members of his own family, often revised his text. Such revision seldom did violence to the essential meaning of the original, but it often gave to both Lafayette's style and behavior a polish that the original did not have.

31. President Ezra Stiles (Yale), cited in H. Niles (ed.), *Principles and acts of the Revolution in America* (Baltimore, 1822), p. 474; *Maryland Gazette*, May 1, 1783 (dinner of the governor of Maryland).

32. *Mémoires*, IV, 4-5; and Gottschalk, *Lafayette and the close of the American Revolution*, pp. 350-51.

CHAPTER III

"Essential Servant of the United States"

THE Marquis de Lafayette had been brought up to be a soldier and, for a young man of twenty-five, he had done very well at his trade. But now peace had come, and it did not seem likely that he would win many more laurels in that calling. As he looked around among the other worlds that might be conquered, diplomacy seemed to be the most pregnable. He had never hesitated to pull wires and to use his own influence or that of his friends when there were personal advantages to be gained.[1] He now maneuvered Washington into asking a further favor for him. It would be gratifying if he could be the American representative at the ratification in London of the final terms of peace.[2]

Robert R. Livingston, the American secretary for foreign affairs, hesitated, however, when Washington suggested that appointment. To send a foreigner on such a mission, he feared, might be beneath the dignity of the new republic. Washington quickly acknowledged that it might have been a mistake to have made the suggestion. "There is no man upon Earth I have a greater inclination to serve than the Marquis La Fayette," he admitted, "but I have not a wish to do it in matters that interfere with, or are repugnant to, our national policy, dignity, or interest."[3] So Lafayette did not receive the honor he coveted.

1. Cf. Lafayette to Washington, Sept. 30, 1781, Gottschalk, *Letters*, pp. 234–35, where he asked the commander-in-chief as his "best friend" to remove General Benjamin Lincoln to a less active area than Yorktown so that he might himself have charge of the Franco-American right wing commanded by Lincoln.

2. Gottschalk, *Lafayette and the close of the American Revolution*, pp. 402–3.

3. Livingston to Washington, Apr. 9, 1783, Library of Congress (hereafter abbreviated LC), Washington papers; Washington to Livingston, Apr. 16, J. C. Fitzpatrick (ed.), *The writings of George Washington from the original manuscript sources*

If the marquis was disappointed at this quiet rebuke, he gave no sign of it. "Glory," he once said, "was always dearer to me than ambition. . . . My ambition has always been to be above ambition."[4] There were some, however, who doubted that he made a sufficient distinction between his glory and his ambition. John Adams, who frequently dined with the Lafayettes and had occasion to observe him closely, was one of them. He thought he saw in Lafayette an "unbounded ambition which it concerns us to watch."[5] And Lafayette recognized that some Americans had "strong prejudices" against his interference in American diplomatic affairs. He confessed to Washington (from whom he found it "impossible," he said, "to conceal any thought") that "it often happens people do not understand each other," even though "they hardly could be able to find out a cause of complaint."[6]

Adams' suspicion was misleading if it was based upon any doubt of Lafayette's loyalty. The young general was incapable of promoting his ambition by doing anything he thought dishonest or contrary to the interest of his country or the United States. He sought honors, and he used his money, prestige, and influence to remain in the public eye; but he was incapable of betraying his principles, and he seldom took a mean advantage of persons or situations. On the contrary, a natural kindness and a compelling desire to be liked often led him to make sacrifices and to victimize himself for others. Some years later, when he was under fire, he exclaimed in all sincerity (although not with complete truth), "If in my letters, speeches, deeds, or thoughts throughout my life there is to be found a single one which liberty and philanthropy might disclaim, rest entirely assured that it is not mine."[7]

1745–1799 (Washington, 1931–44), XXVI, 327. Cf. Washington to Lafayette, May 10 and Oct. 12, ibid., XXVI, 421, and XXVII, 185–88; and Livingston to Lafayette, May 1, Francis Wharton (ed.), The Revolutionary diplomatic correspondence of the United States (Washington, 1889), VI, 404–5.

4. Mémoires, IV, 405–6.

5. Gottschalk, Lafayette and the close of the American Revolution, p. 423.

6. Lafayette to Washington, July 22, 1783, Gottschalk, Letters, p. 266.

7. Lafayette to Johann Wilhelm von Archenholtz, Mar. 27, 1793, Jules Thomas (ed.), Correspondance inédite de La Fayette: lettres de prison, lettres d'exil (1793–1801) (Paris, [1903]), p. 190.

Lafayette had expected to go to America in June, 1783, after witnessing the ratification of peace in London. When June came, he was still in France, acting whenever he could as an unofficial liaison between the French minister of foreign affairs and the American delegates. By that time he had learned that Livingston might eventually decide not to send him to represent the United States at London.[8]

While awaiting Livingston's final decision, Lafayette found it easy to be useful to America (and thereby conspicuous in high places) in other ways. He had already assumed the role of public advocate of cordial trade relations with America. The French foreign office needed little to be persuaded that the best way to win the advantages England had once enjoyed in American commerce was deliberately to embark upon a policy of special concessions to American merchants. The treaty of alliance between France and the United States had called for one or more duty-free ports in France for American goods. Even before the war was over, acting on the behest of some French merchants, Lafayette had asked that Bayonne, Marseille, Dunkirk, and Lorient be designated as places where American merchants might expect especially favorable privileges. Those cities were already partly free ports, where foreign merchants might deposit certain kinds of goods without paying specified import taxes. Lafayette hoped to make them completely free for Americans.[9] During the war, while he was away in Spain upon his last military assignment, Lorient had in fact been made a free port. Upon his return to France he learned about this concession before it was officially announced and undertook to urge American merchants to take advantage of this concrete demonstration of French good will.[10]

8. Lafayette to [Livingston] (not Hamilton), Feb. 5, 1783, Wharton, VI, 241; to Greene, June 10, Greene papers, Clements Library; to the American commissioners, May 12, Jared Sparks (ed.), *The diplomatic correspondence of the American Revolution* (Boston, 1830), X, 141; to Vergennes, June 17, AAE, corr. pol., É.-U., Vol. XXIV, fol. 354–55; John Adams, "Diary," C. F. Adams (ed.), *The works of John Adams* (Boston, 1856), III, 366 and 376.

9. Gottschalk, *Lafayette and the close of the American Revolution*, pp. 415–17.

10. Lafayette to Washington, June 10, 1783, Gottschalk, *Letters*, pp. 264–65; to Greene, June 10, Greene papers, Clements Library; to Vergennes, June 12 and 17, AAE, corr. pol., É.-U., Vol. XXIV, fols. 332 and 354–55; to Congress, July 20, Wharton, VI, 578–79; Barclay to Livingston, Sept. 14, [W. A. Weaver (ed.)], *The diplomatic corre-*

As a result, Lafayette soon found himself being consulted as an expert in business affairs—he who until then had paid no attention to how his own money was invested or properties were managed. American merchants coming to France in the expectation of preferential treatment found it easy and natural to address themselves to him, if indeed he did not himself seek them out. Others indicated from America their intention to avail themselves of his generosity. His influence in court circles stood them in good stead. When an American merchant found himself in dispute with the French tobacco monopoly (the farmers-general) over the price of his cargo, the American consulate appealed to the marquis; and shortly the ministers of foreign affairs and of finance were engaged in a controversy over the French system of monopolies.[11] When asked by American merchants what were the privileges extended to them in the newly designated "free port" of Lorient, he brought the question directly to the Comte de Vergennes, minister of foreign affairs.[12] He soon elicited an answer that was as favorable as anyone had a right to expect: a free port was defined as "a place to which all merchandises, foreign as well as domestic, may be imported and from which they may be exported freely."[13] The marquis saw to it that this generous definition became known to the Congress of the United States and to the world at large.[14]

The early summer months of 1783 were thus largely taken up with business affairs. Although more prosaic than war, this sort of activity brought its own kind of satisfaction. August, however, found Lafayette once more riding in his coach along the rough highways of France, escorting his aunt back to the ancestral château. His wife Adrienne and her sister, Mme de

spondence of the United States of America from the signing of the definitive treaty of peace, September 10, 1783 to the adoption of the constitution, March 4, 1789 (Washington, 1837), I, 490; Lafayette to Robert Morris, Dec. 26, LC, papers of the Continental Congress (hereafter abbreviated PCC) 156, fols. 369–71.

11. Ormesson to Vergennes, June 24, 1783, AAE, corr. pol., É.-U., Vol. XXIV, fols. 390–91; Vergennes to [Captain?] Ridley, July 29, *ibid.*, Vol. XXV, fol. 104.

12. Lafayette to Vergennes, June 12, 1783, *loc. cit.*

13. Vergennes to Lafayette, June 29, 1783, AAE, corr. pol., É.-U., Vol. XXIV, fol. 411. Wharton (VI, 509) gives a misleading translation of this letter.

14. W. C. Ford *et al.* (eds.), *Journals of the Continental Congress, 1774–1787* (Washington, 1904–37), XXVI, 333; *Gazette de Leyde,* Oct. 1, 1784.

Roure, were with them. It was Adrienne's first trip to Chavaniac, and it remained forever in her sentimental memory as a
noteworthy event in her life.[15]

On the way to Chavaniac, Lafayette's party stopped at Fontainebleau. There he met Colonel Matthias Ogden, who had
served under him in the Continental Army and who, being a
merchant as well as a soldier, had come to France on business.
Lafayette learned that his old comrade represented a number of
New Jersey officers who planned to establish a mercantile house
and counted on him to help them. Lafayette sent him to interview his cousin Ormesson, minister of finance, who was urged
to remember that Ogden's purpose was to "ruin English competition."[16] Similar letters went to Vergennes and to the Duc de
Castries, minister of the navy and the colonies.[17]

Ogden had brought letters from America.[18] They revealed
that Congress, much impressed with Lafayette's success on his
brief, unofficial diplomatic mission in Spain just before the close
of the war, now wished him to take on a new unofficial responsibility. Fearful that the final treaty would not grant American
merchants sufficient time to pay off their debts to Englishmen,
President Elias Boudinot urged him not only to take up the
matter of debt settlement with the American commissioners in
Paris but also to point out its importance to the French ministry.

Lafayette again seized upon the opportunity to play a small
part in international diplomacy. Arrived in Chavaniac, he wrote
to the French minister of foreign affairs and to the American
commissioners in Paris about Congress' forebodings. He also informed both Boudinot and Washington (who had expressed no
interest in the matter) of what he had done and how happy he
was to do it. Lafayette's efforts on this occasion, however,
proved less effective than usual. Vergennes's good offices elicited
from the English representatives merely the answer that they

15. Mme de Lafayette, "Duchesse d'Ayen," Lasteyrie, p. 85.
16. July 17, 1783, AAE, corr. pol., É-.U., Vol. XXV, fol. 47.
17. Lafayette to Vergennes, July 17, 1783, ibid., fol. 46.
18. Boudinot to Lafayette, Apr. 12, 1783, E. C. Burnett (ed.), *Letters of members of
the Continental Congress* (Washington, 1921-36), VII, 135-36; Washington to Lafayette, May 10, Fitzpatrick, XXVI, 297-301.

had no authority to negotiate with regard to the debts of individuals.[19]

Congress had formally granted Lafayette permission to stay in France.[20] He did not yet know that, however, and felt apologetic about not returning, since war was still nominally going on and he was a major-general in the American army. Hostilities, however, were over in all but name. Washington had already determined to retire to private life soon and had imparted that decision to Lafayette.[21] The French Africanus wrote to the American Cincinnatus from Chavaniac to indicate his approval. His words left no room for doubt of his sincerity. Washington's conduct, he reported, had been highly praised throughout Europe. "Your returning to a private station is called the finishing stroke to an unparalleled character. Never did a man exist who so honourably stood in the opinions of mankind, and your name, if possible, will become still greater in posterity." Washington, in Lafayette's opinion, was the first man to unite everything that was great with everything that was good. "Never did one man live whom the soldier, State's man, patriot and philosopher could equally admire, and never was a Revolution brought about that in its motives, its conduct, and its consequences could so well immortalize its glorious Chief. I am proud of you, my dear General. Your glory makes me feel as if it was my own."[22]

Lafayette stayed in Chavaniac about two weeks. On his return to Paris he passed through the Auvergne town of Langeac. There the townsfolk showed the same pride in him that other Auvergnats had exhibited on earlier occasions. This time, in fact, a still higher note of confidence was struck. The feudal rights of the lord of Langeac happened at the moment to be for sale, and Lafayette was one of the potential buyers whom the citizens of the town hoped to get. As they solemnly presented him the *vin d'honneur*, they hinted that they would like him to

19. Lafayette to Vergennes, July 21, 1783, AAE, corr. pol., É.-U., Vol. XXV, fol. 75; to Boudinot, July 20, Wharton, VI, 578–79; to Washington, July 22, Gottschalk, *Letters*, pp. 265–67; Vergennes to Lafayette, Aug. 5, AAE, corr. pol., É-.U., Vol. XXV, fol. 130; Lafayette to Congress, Sept. 7, Wharton, VI, 679–81.
20. *Journals of the Continental Congress*, XXIV, 234 (April 10, 1783).
21. Washington to Lafayette, Apr. 5, 1783, Fitzpatrick, XXVI, 297–301.
22. Lafayette to Washington, July 22, 1783, Gottschalk, *Letters*, pp. 265–66.

become their new lord. Their spokesman read to him an address which, after declaring that his glory already surpassed that of his most illustrious ancestors, concluded, "If circumstances permit, we shall be infinitely pleased to belong to you by possession just as we are already yours in spirit." The hint was not lost on Langeac's guest of honor, but in managing his own affairs he moved more slowly than where American business was concerned. Several years were to pass before he actually purchased the seignorial survivals in Langeac.[23]

Arrived in Paris, Lafayette found himself once more immersed in the affairs of American businessmen. When Franklin presented Colonel Ogden at court, the marquis went to Versailles to be present at the ceremony. When the American house of Grubbs and Company found itself embarrassed with commodities which, now that peace had come, were a glut on the American market, Lafayette made its plight a matter for ministerial attention. Something of the contemporary relation of commerce to politics can be gathered from the fact that he did not hesitate to point out that Robert Morris, the American minister of finance, was interested in Grubbs and Company. He also helped Thomas Barclay, the American consul-general in Paris, to make appointments with French officials in order to talk business.[24]

Early in September, 1783, Lafayette abruptly left Paris for Nancy in Lorraine. That departure interfered temporarily with his intercession in high places on behalf of American merchants. An old military associate, Colonel Jeremiah Wadsworth, of Connecticut, recently had joined the number of American businessmen whom peace and the quest for profits had brought to France. The marquis felt called upon to explain to Wadsworth that he was "nailed to this place [Nancy] by the illness of an intimate friend, who has been at the point of death, and to whom,

23. Address of citizens of Langeac to Lafayette, Aug. 4, 1783, J.-B. Belmont, "La belle journée ou relation fidèle de la fête donnée à M. le Marquis de Lafayette par les habitants de Langeac, le 13 août 1786," in Paul Le Blanc, *Tablettes historiques du Velay*, II (1872), 315; Mosnier, pp. 24–26.

24. Ogden to Franklin, Aug. 25, 1783, APS, Franklin papers, Vol. XXIX, No. 103; Lafayette to Vergennes, Aug. 26, AAE, corr. pol., É.-U., Vol. XXV, fol. 227; to Congress, Sept. 7, Wharton, VI, 679–81; Barclay to Livingston, Sept. 14, [Weaver], *Diplomatic correspondence*, I, 489–90.

at the present period, my absence would do infinite harm."[25] The "intimate friend" was apparently his wife's aged grandfather, the son of Louis XV's illustrious Chancellor d'Aguesseau.[26]

Lafayette was still at Nancy when at last the definitive terms of peace between the allies and England were ready to go off to America, and he had proposed that his recently appointed aide-de-camp, Lewis Littlepage, should be their bearer. Littlepage was a young Virginia adventurer who had once been under John Jay's tutelage but had recently become involved in a bitter quarrel with Jay over money matters. Despite that unpleasant fact (perhaps unknown at the time to Lafayette), the marquis had introduced his aide to the French ministers and had attached him to Colonel Ogden as an interpreter. Though Franklin was easily won over to the appointment of Littlepage as the bearer of the treaty, Jay and Adams selected Adams' secretary. When Littlepage found he was not to receive the honor, he challenged Jay to a duel, which, however, never took place. The episode did little to diminish the "strong prejudices" that Lafayette had already detected regarding his interference in American diplomatic affairs.[27]

The definitive treaty of peace put an end to Lafayette's active service with the United States army. Knowing the commander-in-chief's intention to retire to private life, he might have offered his own resignation. Since he did not resign, he ought to have returned to his post. But it was not in his nature to surrender a sphere of influence and honor, and excuses for not returning to America were readily found. He was aware that the American consul Barclay felt that he should remain in France. While still in Nancy, he asked Barclay to express that opinion to Congress; and Barclay, who in fact needed Lafayette's support in his negotiations, did so—explaining a little

25. Sept. 28, 1783, Gov. Joseph Trumbull collection, Connecticut Historical Society.

26. Lasteyrie, p. 86.

27. See above, p. 24; Lafayette to Vergennes, July 17, 1783, AAE, corr. pol., É.-U., Vol. XXV, fol. 46; to Ormesson, July 17, *ibid.*, fol. 47; Littlepage to Franklin, Sept. 1, APS, Franklin papers, Vol. XXIX, No. 118; Monaghan, pp. 159–61 and 223–24.

awkwardly, however, that he troubled Congress only at the marquis's request.[28]

Lafayette reinforced Barclay's statement of his case with his own protestations. He made a special effort to impress upon the president of Congress his interest in all questions affecting the United States. "In every American concern, Sir, my motives are so pure, my sentiments so candid, my attachement so warm, so long experienced, that from such a heart as mine, nothing, I hope, will appear intruding or improper." He thereupon proceeded to give advice as a loyal American officer. He felt called upon to express his consternation at reports that Congress planned to disband the United States army without adequately providing for the back pay or future welfare of either officers or men. And he was emphatic that co-operation among the states must be preserved and strengthened: "I, above all, earnestly hope, and most fervently pray, the ennemies of liberty, or such as are jealous of America, may not have the pleasure to see us deviate from the principles of the Foederal Union." He concluded his lengthy letter with a repetition of his desire to be considered a servant of the United States. "When it is thought my presence here can be dispensed with, or in case the situation of affairs did persuade me it is more useful in America, I will not wait for any thing else to join a wished for and beloved shore. Any orders, either to come or to stay, to do such or such thing, in a word any commands whatever Congress are pleased to give me, I shall most cheerfully gratify both duty and inclination in obeying them, and as every moment in my life is devoted to love and respect, so will the happiest among them be employed to serve the United States."[29]

By the same packet Lafayette wrote also to General Washington and General Greene.[30] To both he likewise expressed his

28. Barclay to Livingston, Sept. 14, 1783, [Weaver], *Diplomatic correspondence*, I, 489–90.

29. Sept. 7, 1783, LC, PCC 156, fols. 361–62. Sparks (*Diplomatic correspondence*, V, 417) gives this letter in an incorrect and revised version, which is borrowed by Wharton (VI, 679–81).

30. Lafayette to Washington, Sept. 8, 1783, Gottschalk, *Letters*, pp. 267–70; to Greene, Sept. 8, Parke-Bernet Galleries Catalogue 251, John Gribbel Collection, Part II, p. 88, No. 376.

anxiety to do all he could for Americans. His more confidential
letter to Washington, however, created an impression quite different from that he had given to Congress. There he had stated
explicitly that the American commissioners in Paris had found
his services useful. In writing to Washington, whose good will he
counted upon, he implied the opposite, admitting that since his
return from Spain he "was not much consulted upon politics"
by them. He insisted, however, that he was still needed in France
to promote American trade. To be sure, he lamented his absence
from Washington's headquarters. Never, he said, had he felt
more at home anywhere in the world. "Every mention, every
rememberance of America," he wrote, "makes me sigh for the
moment when I may enjoy the sight of our free and independant
shores. . . . Should I receive the least hint, or see myself that,
by the situation of affairs, every good man's influence is wanting
upon the spot, then, my dear General, no public affairs (for my
own are out of the question), no season of the year, no impedi-
ment in the world can prevent my flying to a beloved country
whose happiness, glory, and liberty are dearer to me than my
own life." Nevertheless, he wished to serve Congress as a diplomatic agent in Europe "in the way of information and advice."
He therefore sought to enlist Washington's aid in getting direct
orders to stay. "Never shall I more glory and better enjoy myself than in the title of an essential servant of the United
States."

Thus it happened that the end of the American War did not
bring to a close Lafayette's career as a liege man of the United
States. The loyalty was mutual. The Americans gladly continued to accept the young Frenchman's services both out of remembrance of past favors and out of a lively sense of favors yet
to come, and he clung to his American connections with an ardor
that was molded of both the desire to serve and the desire to
win deference. Above all, he wanted the admiration of Washington. "I hope, "he wrote, "my dear General will approuve my
conduct, which approbation, I confess, in every instance will
ever prove necessary to my happiness and self satisfaction."

BIBLIOGRAPHICAL NOTES

In a number of instances above, quotations have been taken from the manuscript document though reference has been made to the best available printed version. The fact that editors have frequently corrected the style, orthography, and punctuation of Lafayette's originals explains occasional differences in our versions from those given in the printed texts cited. Where the differences are marked, however, the footnotes will indicate the manuscript source as well as the best available printed source.

The well-known caution with regard to the editorial work of Jared Sparks needs to be repeated here. He frequently omitted important passages from his collections and regularly "Englished" Lafayette's Gallicisms. This is noticeably less true, however, of the letters in his *Correspondence of the American Revolution; being letters of eminent men to George Washington, from the time of his taking command of the army to the end of his presidency* (Boston, 1853) than of his earlier editorial works. Wharton sometimes borrowed Sparks's versions without emendation.

CHAPTER IV

Concessions for Americans

OON after Lafayette returned to Paris from Nancy, he was immersed in court functions once more. Among the distinguished visitors to the French court that fall was William Pitt, son of England's "Great Commoner." Pitt was only twenty-four years old, almost two years younger than Lafayette. He had already been a member of the British cabinet and was now a conspicuous figure in the opposition. With Pitt were two friends and colleagues, Edward J. Eliot, who was soon to become his brother-in-law, and William Wilberforce, who was to win great renown as a philanthropist. All three had opposed the policy of repression that the British government had followed in America and, now that peace had returned, had joined the parade of Englishmen across the Channel in order to improve their knowledge of France, the French, and the French language. At Fontainebleau, where Louis XVI's court had withdrawn for a short season of festivity, admiring courtiers crowded around Pitt "in shoals."[1]

Lafayette first met Pitt when the young Englishman had dinner at the Duc de Castries's home with a few French celebrities. It was arranged that, when Pitt's party returned to Paris, they were to dine at Lafayette's home on the Rue de Bourbon. Four days later a brilliant company sat down to one of the most unusual of Lafayette's Monday dinners. The marquis had invited Franklin to meet "the famous William Pitt . . . whose abilities and circumstances are so uncommon." Franklin, despite his gravel, yielded to Lafayette's persuasion that he would

1. Wilberforce to Henry Bankes, Oct. 28, 1783, R. I. and Samuel Wilberforce, *The life of William Wilberforce* (London, 1838), I, 44.

be "the center upon which moves the whole party"[2] and attended, accompanied by his grandson, William Temple Franklin. In addition to Pitt, England was represented by Wilberforce, Eliot, and three other young English gentlemen of illustrious families, all friends of Pitt. France and her American ally were represented by the host and hostess, the Franklins, Lewis Littlepage, the Vicomte de Noailles, Madame de Boufflers, and five other "rebels." Thus there met at a friendly table eighteen conspicuous figures from three countries until recently engaged in a bitter struggle. The conversation turned upon the Spanish Empire; and, since there were no representatives of Spain present, they were able to agree that the Spanish colonies ought to be free.[3]

For some of the guests, Franklin did not turn out to be the center of the party. Though responding to Franklin's friendliness, Wilberforce was more interested in Lafayette. Already inclined to think approvingly of his French contemporary as a bold champion of liberty, he was now also favorably impressed with Lafayette's simplicity. He noted that the Lafayette establishment was run on the plain "English model," that the marquis avoided card playing and the other amusements fashionable at court, and that he obviously received deference from those whose example he refused to follow—"above all from the ladies."[4] Lafayette, for his part, thought Pitt the center of the party. He was pleased with his English contemporary because of "his wit, modesty, nobility and character," which he found "as interesting as the role for which his position marks him."[5]

Pitt himself left no direct record of his recollections of that dinner. Lafayette, however, recorded a revealing comment that he attributed to his distinguished guest. It made clear that the young English statesman shared Wilberforce's impression (though perhaps with less approbation) of Lafayette's boldness as a champion of liberty. "As long as England remains a monarchy," Pitt was reported to have told his host, "we can

2. Lafayette to Franklin, Oct. 13 [20], APS, Franklin papers, Vol. XLII, No. 140.
3. *Ibid.*; Lafayette to unknown, [Oct. 21, 1783], *Mémoires*, II, 160; and Wilberforce's diary quoted in Wilberforce, I, 41 (which says "Page," but Littlepage is meant).
4. Wilberforce, I, 42.
5. Lafayette to unknown, [Oct. 21, 1783], *Mémoires*, II, 160.

hardly hope to see you in London."⁶ It was not made clear whether that remark was intended as a threat or a regret. In either case, its edge was soon dulled by other comments; for some of the "eminent characters" among the English gentlemen who came flocking to Paris informed Lafayette that he was reputed in England to be the American representative to ratify the treaty. He relayed this report to Washington, stating, with a mock modesty that could hardly have escaped attention, that it was "a rumour for which I cannot account."⁷

When Lafayette sat down early on the morning following his dinner to describe his impressions of his illustrious guests, he could not help gloating over the recent blow to British pride. Despite Pitt's ambiguous remark, he wrote, he would like to visit England, not in order to pay court to the king but to become acquainted with the opposition. "Since we won the war, I admit that I find great pleasure in seeing Englishmen. The humiliation of the previous war and their insolence during the peace had given me a feeling of hatred for them that only increased with the horrors they wreaked upon America, and the association of their name with that of tryanny has habitually prejudiced me against them. But now I meet them with pleasure, and whether I go as a Frenchman, an American soldier, or merely a simple individual, I shall be unembarrassed in the heart of that proud nation." Yet, he confessed, he had not entirely forgiven them. "Without being foolish enough to regard them as personal enemies, I cannot forget that they are the enemies of the glory and prosperity of France, for when it comes to patriotism, I can astonish the world as much as I am supposed to have done by my *sensibilité*."⁸

The struggle of motives in Lafayette's mind was thus betrayed. *Sensibilité*, the eighteenth-centruy's unabashed tenderness for humanity, was commendable but must not drive out *patriotisme*. America's sufferings from English tyranny were unbearable, but so were Britain's past victories over France and her future threat to France. Monarchy in England was an

6. *Ibid.*; cf. P. W. Clayden, *The early life of Samuel Rogers* (London, 1887), p. 134.
7. Nov. 11, 1783, Gottschalk, *Letters*, p. 271.
8. Lafayette to unknown, [Oct. 21, 1783], *Mémoires*, II, 160–61.

unfortunate survival, but if Lafayette saw in the French monarch, as did Wilberforce, "so strange a being (of the hog kind) that it is worth going miles for a sight of him,"[9] he had not yet indicated it.

This dinner in October, 1783, should have helped make legend. Here important personages in the affairs of three nations broke bread together—England's great-minded young Pitt and great-hearted Wilberforce, the "pleasing enthusiastical" French-American Lafayette and the "sweet woman" his wife,[10] and their illustrious American guest Franklin. Furthermore, the time was critical for their countries: it was the morrow of a great revolution in the British Empire and the eve of a great revolution in France. Yet the meetings led to no lasting results. In future days, when Wilberforce and Lafayette were to become champions of the Negro, they would renew their acquaintance. Otherwise this meeting of great men, from which something dramatic might have been expected, bore no fruit. They impressed each cther only casually. Some years later, when revolution lent a more vivid significance to Pitt's earlier sentiment, Lafayette was to claim that Pitt had even then found in his principles "too much democracy,"[11] and it does appear to be true that both Pitt and Wilberforce considered their host's attitudes somewhat strange for a French aristocrat. But if he entertained a republican program for any European country at this time, he had so far given voice to it only on that occasion, for it is not to be found as yet in his numerous letters or elsewhere. His written words still displayed hatred of England and devotion to France and America—emotional reactions to easily identified symbols—rather than intellectual affinity for abstractions like Mankind and the Rights of Man.

In keeping with his Anglophobia but more out of a desire to promote the good will of France for her American ally, Lafayette resumed his patronage of Franco-American merchants immediately on his return to Paris. The instructions sought from Congress that should give him some sort of official status

9. Wilberforce to Henry Bankes, Oct. 28, 1783, Wilberforce, I, 44.
10. Wilberforce's diary, quoted *ibid.*, p. 41.
11. Rogers' diary, quoted in Clayden, p. 134.

had not yet come. But his old comrade, Colonel Jean-Baptiste Gouvion, who had recently returned from the United States, assured him that Congress counted on him to act as a friend at court for American merchants.[12] Believing his own knowledge in these affairs "very imperfect,"[13] he consulted Franklin, Barclay, Wadsworth, and others, "collecting the opinions of every American merchant within . . . reach and . . . bent upon representing what may be most advantageous in mercantile regulations."[14] Fortified with the information these gentlemen furnished, he tried to influence French officials concerned with the regulation of commerce. Franklin noted his new activity with approval. "The Marquis de la F.," he reported, ". . . loves to be employed in our affairs, and is often very useful."[15]

In the midst of these endeavors Ormesson fell from office. He had rashly engaged in a struggle with the formidable farmers-general. These gentlemen were the officially designated financiers who had the exclusive right to bid for certain royal monopolies like salt and tobacco. "The Farm" (as the cartel of the farmers-general came to be called) was a recognized power in both commercial and political circles. Wiser ministers than Ormesson had feared to rouse its opposition. Ormesson, however, proceeded incautiously. In October, 1783, he declared the farmers-general no longer desirable except as dependent governmental bureaucrats. Immediately the farmers appealed to the king, and Ormesson was forced to resign. He was succeeded by Charles-Alexandre de Calonne, who was pledged by the king's promise to restore the Farm.

Calonne thus became comptroller-general of finance as a friend of the farmers-general. He was, nevertheless, an enterprising and optimistic executive, unafraid of innovations and convinced that, fundamentally, France's financial structure was sound. Consequently, he was ready to give Vergennes and

12. Lafayette to Robert Morris, Jan. 10, 1784, [Weaver], Diplomatic correspondence, I, 403-4.

13. Lafayette to William Temple Franklin, Oct. 22, 1783, APS, W. T. Franklin papers, Vol. CV, No. 133.

14. Lafayette to Washington, Nov. 11, 1783, Gottschalk, Letters, p. 271; cf. Lafayette to Washington, Jan. 10, 1784, ibid., p. 276.

15. Franklin to Morris, Dec. 25, 1783, A. H. Smyth (ed.), The writings of Benjamin Franklin (New York, 1905-7), IX, 139.

Castries encouragement and support in their efforts to strength-
en the political ties that bound the United States to France.

Lafayette's readiness to serve as a liaison between the French
and the Americans in France was particularly welcome at this
juncture. The hoped-for concessions to American merchants
had been needlessly delayed. Franklin was in ill-health and
relatively inactive, and the other American envoys had gone
to England. Ormesson had been so "overburthened with the
details of his place" that he had never taken the final steps to
make Lorient in fact a free port as promised. Lafayette now
applied for a formal and public confirmation of that promise.
He appealed not only to Calonne "but to every minister that
has some thing to do with American affairs." The effect was
immediate. Calonne's good will encouraged Lafayette to believe that not only Lorient but several other ports would be declared "free" for American shipping, and the marquis exerted
himself to secure Dunkirk, Bayonne, and Marseille as well.
Bayonne seemed particularly desirable because it would permit
"a good contraband trade with the Spaniards."[16]

Lafayette began to envisage a widespread international competition for American raw materials and markets. And he believed the French would ultimately win it. He hated to think
that the English might profit by French hesitation, but he did
not feel equally disturbed by the prospect of the Spanish carrying off good prizes. On the contrary, Spanish success in such an
enterprise would cement the understanding that had existed
between Spain and the United States, both allies of France in
the common war against England. Consequently he tried to
enlist the support of William Carmichael, the United States
chargé d'affaires in Spain, to promote trade between the United
States and the Spanish West Indies. "Let liberal propositions
be immediately sent from Spain," he urged. "No time is to be
lost. The one who grants first will gain 100 per cent. Should a
free trade be established between Spain's islands and the United
States, their colonies will flourish, and it will then be so much
against the interest of Americans to interrupt such a commerce

16. Lafayette to Morris, Dec. 26, 1783, LC, PCC 156, fols. 369–71; and [Weaver],
Diplomatic correspondence, I, 388–91.

that they will join in every war against England."[17] The Spanish, however, were to prove much less receptive of free-trade proposals for their colonies than were the French.

In France, too, Lafayette found that there was a frank and powerful opposition to removing the restrictions on foreign trade in French ports. It came from the merchants and more particularly from the farmers-general. Any loosening of the tight mercantilist system of their country was regarded by them as an undue advantage granted to competitors. Merchants around Bordeaux, for example, protested that the opening to Americans of any ports in the French West Indies would quickly lead to American control of the West Indies trade. Lafayette and Franklin could thereafter expect that influential commercial interests would object to any representations that they might make on that subject.

It was events rather than theories that thus conspired once more to put Lafayette on the liberal side of a live issue. Philosophers—particularly the school of economists known as the physiocrats—had for years been advocating the removal of restrictions on trade. The ablest books to come from the pens of these economists had by this time been written. The air of Paris and Versailles was full of debate about them. Lafayette could hardly have attended as many parties and dinners as he did without encountering heated discussions between those who advocated the old mercantilism and those who championed the new physiocratic principles. He seems, however, to have met none of the physiocrats personally so far, and if he had as yet ever read a line of their writings, he had shown no sign of it either by reference or quotation. In fact, at several points in his subsequent remarks he made clear that he was quite wary of such ideas on economic theory as he had picked up from "people less ignorant than I,"[18] preferring to argue on the basis of his own personal experience. At one point, to be sure, he seemed to refer almost by name to a contemporary pamphlet entitled *Le pour et le contre* dealing with the question of American participation

17. Nov. 20, 1783, LC, House of Representatives collection, Carmichael papers, No. 102.

18. "Observations sur le commerce entre la France et les États Unis," *American historical review*, XXXVI (1931), 568.

in the French West Indies trade. He made clear, however, that he knew of its contents, if at all, only by hearsay.[19]

Furthermore, if the aristocratic young general seemed to have joined the ranks of the physiocrats more or less unwittingly, the alliance was more apparent than real. Lafayette did not favor free trade in principle, he wanted only to use trade concessions as a means of political pressure. Listening to American merchants and diplomatic agents, he acquired the conviction that there was a right and a wrong theory of economics and that the right one favored the removal of French restrictions on American trade. "The ideas upon commerce that are met with in this country," he wrote Robert Morris, the American superintendent of finance, "are far from being always right. To persuade people into their own interest is sometimes as difficult a matter as it would be to obtain a sacrifice. But the ministry and the people are wishing for intimate connections with America upon a liberal footing."[20]

Reflection upon commerce at length led to a new departure in Lafayette's career. He became a writer. He had, of course, written many letters previous to this time, and some of them were lengthy documents. But when they were not mere narratives of his experiences or expositions of his thoughts, they were likely to be on practical and immediate military problems. Now for the first time Lafayette sat down to express an extended opinion upon an economic question.

The new writer was no theoretician, however. His purpose was still immediate and practical. Moreover, it was at the request of the king's ministers that he now set forth his ideas in writing.[21] Several ministers advocated fostering American loyalty to France by a series of coolly calculated trade concessions. They did not themselves dare, however, openly to champion such a policy because of the formidable opposition it could be counted upon to excite. They therefore did not hesitate to exploit Lafayette's popularity in order to promote their scheme,

19. *Ibid.* Cf. F. L. Nussbaum, "French colonial arrêt of 1784," *South Atlantic quarterly*, XXVII (1928), 66, and "The revolutionary Vergennes and Lafayette versus the farmers general," *Journal of modern history*, III (1931), 596.

20. Dec. 26, 1783, *loc. cit.*

21. "Observations," *American historical review*, XXXVI (1931), 565 and 570.

and he proved to be on this occasion what his friend Thomas Jefferson was later to describe him—a man to whom "commerce was an unknown field" but whose good sense enabled him "to comprehend perfectly whatever is explained to him."[22] His essay on the relation of economics to politics took the form of a memorial entitled "Observations on the commerce between France and the United States."[23]

Lafayette's argument started from the major premise, axiomatic for him, that France's sacrifices in the War of American Independence entitled her to oust the English from American commerce and to get all the advantages for herself. The gratitude of Americans to France and their animosity toward England, he reasoned, would weigh heavily on the French side. Nevertheless, "business does not appear to me to be a matter of sentiment." Because "every merchant seeks a profit, . . . commercial interest guarantees impartiality."

American commerce, Lafayette went on, might some day have great international significance. France must therefore be ready to make certain concessions and changes in order to keep her recently won advantage over England. The first concession that he emphasized was a deference to American tastes. He had seen French nails outsold by English nails in Boston because the French ones had rounded heads and Bostonians preferred flat ones. He had seen Irish linen sell faster than French linen only because Americans preferred the way the Irish folded theirs. He also thought that it would be desirable to adopt "the English principle" of specialization of labor, "which uses each worker for only one thing and for each thing only the degree of effort that is absolutely necessary." He found in that principle the reason why Rouen cottons, though made of better and cheaper raw materials, sold for more than Manchester cottons. Lafayette also condemned the French system of internal tariffs as an "institution contrary to nature." It led directly to smuggling by both nationals and foreigners. He also asked that French

22. Jefferson to Madison, Jan. 30, 1787, A. A. Lipscomb and A. E. Bergh (eds.), *The writings of Thomas Jefferson* (Washington, 1903-4), VI, 69-70. See p. 108 below.
23. Quoted in full in Louis Gottschalk, "Lafayette as commercial agent," *American historical review*, XXXVI (1931), 561-70; and translated in [Weaver], *Diplomatic correspondence*, I, 391-403 (where there are some minor omissions).

manufacturers extend long-term credits to Americans as did the English. If these precepts were followed, he could foresee an excellent market in America for French goods, particularly wines and brandies.

But, "if we want Americans to buy, their opportunities to sell must be multiplied." The French mercantile system, however, had not helped Americans to find French markets for their goods. "Harshness of regulations is even more troublesome than high prices." That was due, the apparent physiocrat contended, chiefly to the farmers-general, who created delays and made arbitrary decisions on those cargoes for which their monopolistic privileges made them the only customers. Their interference was especially exasperating in the tobacco trade—one of the most important for America—with the result that American merchants had almost ceased sending that staple to France. Thus the Farm had brought France to a point where "the bait of a temporary profit or attachment to old practices might do harm to our mercantile and political interests." Lafayette saw the remedy for this unfortunate situation in a system of free ports. "Perhaps it would be best for us if all the ports of France were free," but for the present he asked for only the four already mentioned in this connection—Marseille, Dunkirk, Lorient, and Bayonne.

Yet, no matter what concessions were made, Lafayette declared, the balance of trade would still be in France's favor. Consequently, a means of compensating the Americans must be sought. It was to be found in the commerce of the United States with the French West Indies. He knew that the chambers of commerce in France opposed the promotion of trade between the Americans and the French colonies, but he felt that any disadvantage to French merchants from such a step would be counterbalanced by advantages to French workers, farmers, and colonials. Better food would also be available for the slaves in the colonies, who now were undernourished; "and since we have slaves, ought we not heed the voice both of interest and humanity?" If we do not deal with the Americans, Lafayette warned, the Spanish may do so. And the Spanish would pay for American fish, salt meats, and lumber with English manufactures, thus aiding France's rival. The importation of flour by the colonies and their exportation of sugar, he knew, were more mooted questions than those involving cruder products; but, he contended, a few simple regulations would circumvent all difficulties, making a general prohibition of trade unnecessary. "If everything is prohibited alike, the Americans and the colonists will violate everything without distinction, but the assurance of a legitimate profit would do away with smuggling, and it is that which brings about the irritations, the animosities that wipe out all the king's revenues, destroy all co-operation in favor of our commerce, and undo the bonds of politics."

It had been said, Lafayette admitted, that trade with the French colonies would build up the American merchant marine as a competitor to the French. But, he retorted (perhaps too credulously), the Americans could not construct as good or as cheap vessels as the French, nor could they sail them as cheaply. Hence France had less to fear from them than from other nations. The "Observations" ended with the request that the ministers find out the opinions of Franklin, Barclay, and other Americans in France.

When he was done, Lafayette had written his first political tract—lengthy enough to require twelve octavo pages when recently printed. It was completed around the middle of December, 1783. Lafayette first sent it to Franklin for his approbation. "If you think it may answer a good purpose," he wrote, "I will in my private capacity give it to Maréchal de Castries, M. de Vergennes, and M. de Calonne."[24] Franklin approved of the document (having probably been kept informed of its progress at every step).

The memorial had insisted that "the commerce of the kingdom and that of the colonies though divided among the [ministerial] departments, cannot, in regard to the United States, be separated."[25] Nevertheless, Lafayette was now obliged to deal separately with Calonne, Castries, and Vergennes. Vergennes should properly have been approached only after his two colleagues had

24. Catalogued "ca. 1779" [but probably of Dec. 13, 1783], APS, Franklin papers, Vol. XLII, No. 144.

25. "Observations," *American historical review*, XXXVI (1931), 566.

come to some sort of agreement, but it was apparent that he knew all about Lafayette's aspirations even before Calonne consented that he be informed.[26] The marquis appeared to be pulling the strings, but somehow they all seemed to end in Vergennes's fingers. The apparent puller of strings was in fact a sort of unofficial agent, easily repudiated if expediency should require.

The marquis first called on Calonne and submitted the memorial for his consideration. Calonne read it with "the greatest interest" but was too busy to take immediate action.[27] On Christmas Day, Lafayette again called upon Calonne. The minister promised him support and authorized him to assure Congress that something friendly would be done; meanwhile Congress was to postpone making arrangements with England as long as possible. Vergennes, of course, confirmed Calonne's promises and gave his unofficial agent permission to send the memorial to Robert Morris as the responsible finance officer of America.[28]

Lafayette sent it the next day to Morris. He took care to state that his language, being "intended to point out the inconveniences in the French trade," had presented them "in their worst point of wiew." (He almost always wrote "wiew.") He did not want Americans to believe, however, that the picture was as bad as he had painted it. The memorial had been written by a Frenchman for Frenchmen. He asked that it be regarded as confidential except for Congress and any committees that might be appointed to consider it.[29]

Whatever steps Lafayette had taken on behalf of American commerce had been taken without instructions from Congress. Anxious not to appear to have meddled without authority, he also informed Congress of his latest coup but only as if it were a trivial thing. Mentioning quite casually that he had sent Mor-

26. Lafayette to Vergennes, Dec. 25, 1783, AAE, corr. pol., É.-U., Vol. XXVI, fol. 251.

27. Calonne to Lafayette, Dec. 18 and 25, 1783, LC, PCC 137, Vol. III, fols. 529 and 533.

28. Lafayette to Vergennes, Dec. 25, 1783, loc. cit.; Calonne to Lafayette, Dec. 25, loc. cit.

29. Dec. 26, 1783, loc. cit.

ris some recent remarks on Franco-American commerce, he
went on to discuss at length the news of Europe's political complications.[30] The intelligence service that Lafayette so performed proved important to Congress. In the days when ocean
travel was slow and precarious and America's diplomatic agents
were left without resources, it was the Americanophile marquis
who sometimes first furnished Congress with important information. This time his letter gave them their earliest inkling of the
fall of the cabinet in England and of Pitt's succession as prime
minister.[31]

Despite his casualness about it, Lafayette did not really believe that his memorial paled into insignificance alongside of
cabinet crises. To make sure that Congress would not treat his
coup as a trivial incident, Lafayette wrote also to his former
aide, James McHenry, now a member of Congress from Maryland, inclosing a copy of the document.[32] He explained to
McHenry that since he had once been robbed of his proper share
of credit for obtaining French loans for America and since
nothing had come of his Spanish negotiations, he was afraid
the present matter might also be neglected. He therefore urged
McHenry to "be so kind only as to take care my commercial
efforts be known in America, and also that Congress send instructions respecting trade." A good part of his letter was devoted to impressing upon McHenry that his services in France
had been important. His boasted modesty did not keep him
from pointing to his "station in life, knowledge of courts, and
facility of accompagnying those sovereigns both in their camps
of peace and in their private parties." Congress should give him
a more precise and formal standing in order to enable him to
use these advantages better. "I do not choose to quit the American service. It is the only way I have to make a kind of official
representations in favour of America."

Thus, in more intimate communications Lafayette did not

30. Lafayette to Thomas Mifflin, Dec. 26, 1783, [Weaver], *Diplomatic correspondence*, I, 387–88.

31. Jefferson to Edmund Pendleton, [Mar. 2–4, 1784], and Samuel Hardy to Benjamin Harrison, Mar. 5, 1784, Burnett, VII, 458 and 463.

32. Lafayette to McHenry, Dec. 26, 1783, B. C. Steiner, *Life and correspondence
of James McHenry* (Cleveland, 1907), pp. 87–88.

hesitate to reveal that, while devotion to America was high among the motives that called forth his energies, the desire for recognition was not far behind. He need not have been so concerned about recognition. The Maryland newspapers soon carried an account, purporting to be an extract from a Paris letter (and conceivably furnished by McHenry), telling about the marquis's "unwearied . . . endeavors to serve us."[33] And in France a Toulouse priest published a sermon on the return of peace, implying that his chief claim to be heard was that he had known since childhood the "hero dear to America and dearer yet to France."[34]

Yet neither contemporary events nor his own personality allowed Lafayette to stop in his tireless search for new laurels. Even before he sent copies of his memorial to America, a letter had come to Franklin from Robert Morris underlining American interest in the very problems that Lafayette had made his own. "Our commerce," it stated, "is flowing very fast toward Great Britain. . . . Some articles are furnished by Britain cheaper, many as cheap, and all on a long credit. Her merchants are attentive and punctual. In her ports our vessels meet with despatch. . . . What is of no little importance is that the English having formed our taste are more in capacity to gratify that circumstance also." It might be "a disagreeable fact," but it was "not the less a fact," that American trade with French and Spanish ports would have to be carried on board English ships if at all—particularly if the Mediterranean were made unsafe by pirates. "If anything will totally ruin the commerce of England with this country," Morris inexorably continued, "it is her blind attachment to her navigation act [which closed to foreigners all trade with English colonies]. . . . If France possesses commercial wisdom, she will take care not to imitate the conduct of her rival."[35] There followed a closely reasoned argument in favor of allowing American merchants

---

33. *Maryland Gazette*, Apr. 1, 1784.

34. *Discours sur la paix, prononcé le 11 janvier 1784 par M. l'Abbé Racine, prêtre, bachelier en théologie, docteur aggrégé de la Faculté des Arts de Paris, & professeur d'éloquence au Collège Royal de Toulouse* (Toulouse, [1784]), reviewed in *L'année littéraire*, II (1784), 337–39.

35. Morris to Franklin, Sept. 30, 1783, Wharton, VI, 707–9.

easy access to the French West Indies. It was not the same as Lafayette's though it led to the same conclusions. Thus Morris officially put his government on record as asking for consideration similar to that which Lafayette, without formal knowledge of Morris' views, had unofficially recommended.

Franklin, whose ill-health had not diminished his own understanding of how to pull strings, saw to it that Lafayette received a copy of Morris' observations. "He will make a proper use of them," he explained, "and perhaps they may have more weight, as appearing to come from a Frenchman, than they would have if it were known that they were the observations of an American."[36] Lafayette, however, decided to present the ideas as coming from Morris. "Your opinion," he told Morris, "will have a great weight in the affair, because of the confidence Europeans have in your abilities, and the respect which is paid here to your character." So he had translations made of those parts of Morris' letter that he thought would interest the ministers and took them with him to Versailles.[37]

About the same time, M. de Marbois, secretary to the French legation in Philadelphia, also felt impelled to set forth his opinions on the subject of France's impending defeat in the struggle for American trade. He did so in a series of letters addressed to the Duc de Castries as minister of the colonies.[38] Marbois pointed out how annoyed American merchants were by the restrictions placed upon the colonial importation of flour and exportation of sugar. His comments reinforced the arguments of Lafayette and Morris. The opinions of all three were placed before Vergennes, who needed little persuasion. He had a summary made of Lafayette's "Observations," to which were added as marginalia brief citations from Morris and Marbois. The resulting document made an impressive brief in favor of free ports for Americans in France and in the West Indies. It preached even more succinctly than the originals on which it was based that commerce is not "a matter of sentiment but of

---

36. Franklin to Morris, Dec. 25, 1783, Smyth, IX, 139.
37. Lafayette to Morris, Dec. 26, 1783, *loc. cit.*
38. E. Wilson Lyon, *The man who sold Louisiana; the career of François Barbé-Marbois* (Norman, Okla., 1942), pp. 30–31 and 204.

calculation whose outcome should in the long run have influence even upon political power."[39]

Lafayette's persistence at length produced the desired result. The ministers of foreign affairs, the navy, and finance, as several interviews with them showed,[40] were on his side rather than on that of the interested merchants. Calonne submitted Lafayette's "Observations" to the king and supported it with arguments taken from Lafayette's oral remarks.[41] Shortly after the new year began, the ministry made the first of a series of decisions favorable to American trade. Calonne was authorized to announce it, not to Franklin, who would have been the more appropriate channel for communication between the two governments, but to Lafayette. The king, Calonne declared, had decided to grant to the United States all four of the free ports for which Lafayette had asked—Bayonne, Dunkirk, Lorient, and Marseille—with the single reservation that at Marseille tobacco would still be subject to duty. Free ports, defined as Vergennes had already defined them, were to be open both for sales and for purchases. The government intended to encourage Americans, especially at Dunkirk, by establishing stores and magazines "that shall be well supplied on terms very advantageous for their commerce." In addition, the farmers-general were instructed to give preferential treatment to North American tobacco. "And, morever, the United States will be as much favored in France in matters of commerce as any other nation . . . and Government will not suffer them to experience any kind of vexation." Any complaints against the Farm that Lafayette, Franklin, or any other American agent might transmit would receive careful attention. Precautions would be taken to keep bad French merchandise from being shipped to America. And Calonne concluded: "I am going to examine immediately how far customs and duties hurt commerce. This is an important subject and requires great attention. In fine, Sir, you may count upon me as well as the Maréchal de Castries and the

---

39. AAE, mémoires et documents, É-U., Vol. II, fol. 100.
40. Lafayette to Washington, Jan. 10, 1784, Gottschalk, *Letters*, pp. 275–76, and to Morris, Jan. 10, [Weaver], *Diplomatic correspondence*, I, 403–4.
41. Calonne to Lafayette, Jan. 9, 1784, Wharton, VI, 751.

Comte de Vergennes to be always ready to receive and listen with attention to the requests and other representations which you may think proper to make in favor of the commerce of America."[42]

The king's decision was a great personal victory for Lafayette. His satisfaction in it was all the keener because he did not fully realize the extent to which he had been used as a tool by shrewder men like Vergennes and Franklin. He immediately informed Washington, Morris, and others of his success. He went to some pains to point out that the credit for his achievement was not to be shared with the American envoys in Europe: "In all this America neither promises nor asks for anything so that she cannot be committed, and her ministers being either sick or abroad, do not, *betwen us*, so much as to mention an earnest word of the mercantile interest of America in France."[43] He suggested (though perhaps only for business reasons) that Congress consider the propriety of publishing Calonne's letter in the newspapers.[44] Yet he wished no one to think he had acted out of ulterior motives. "My attachement needs no comment, . . . my good wishes are obvious, and as to my exertions, they have been and shall be as affectionate as my heart, as constant as my love to the public and the individuals in the United States."[45]

Congress was duly appreciative of the wisdom of Lafayette's suggestions. It voted not only to publish but also to transmit to the executives of the several states the contents of Vergennes's and Calonne's letters on the subject of free ports. The president was also instructed to write a letter to the marquis "expressing the high sense which Congress entertain of his important services relative to the commerce of France and these United States, and particularly to free ports." The letter was to state

42. This translation is based on the French text quoted in Charavay, p. 102 and n.; it differs somewhat from the translation in Wharton, VI, 751–52.

43. Lafayette to Washington, Jan. 10, 1784, Gottschalk, *Letters*, p. 276.

44. Lafayette to Morris, Jan. 10, 1784, [Weaver], *Diplomatic correspondence*, I, 403–4; and LC, PCC 156, fols. 392–93.

45. Lafayette to Knox, Jan. 8[10?], 1784, Massachusetts Historical Society. Lafayette seems to have dated this letter January 8, but from internal evidence that date would appear to be an error for January 10. Another hand has dated it January 12, which is also possible.

further "that there is every reason to expect mutual and permanent advantages from these liberal measures adopted by His Most Christian Majesty, and that an extension thereof to his West India colonies, will, in the opinion of Congress, increase these advantages and produce the most salutary effects."[46]

Thus a splendid victory was won for good will and freedom of trade between the French monarchy and its republican ally. Though it was won against the opposition of merchants and bankers, it could hardly be said to have been a victory of economic principles over vested interests. To be sure, the well-known physiocrats Dupont and Morellet were in frequent communication with Vergennes, and, moreover, Dupont had long been employed in the ministry of finance. Yet their share in this decision was small. In fact, Dupont was in principle opposed to special grants for a favored nation. This was not an instance of the direct influence of intellectuals upon the course of political events. What had really happened was something much less subtle. The ministry of foreign affairs and the American plenipotentiary, working toward the same political end— a strong Franco-American alliance—had found an excellent public champion in a popular hero. A triumvirate thus was formed of Vergennes, Franklin, and Lafayette. Advocating a scheme that already had many supporters, they easily won friends and baffled foes. Though they were in some regards in sympathy with the physiocrats, it was politics and not principle that fashioned their philosophy and determined their success.

BIBLIOGRAPHICAL NOTES

It will be noted that quotations from Lafayette's writings above are sometimes in idiomatic English. That is because they are translations from his idiomatic French. He did not always write idiomatic English.

46. *Journals of the Continental Congress,* XXVI, 332–33 (May 3, 1784); cf. Morris to Congress, Apr. 16, 1784, Wharton, VI, 793–94, and May 19, [Paris M. Davis], *A complete history of the Marquis de Lafayette, major general in the army of the United States of America, in the War of the Revolution: embracing an account of his late tour through the United States to the time of his departure, September, 1825: by an officer in the late army* (New York, 1826), pp. 150–51; and *Journals of the Continental Congress,* XXVII, 471 (May 28, 1784). If the president ever sent such a letter, Burnett does not seem to have found it. But Morris did send one; see Morris to Lafayette, May 19, Wharton, VI, 809–10, and below chap. vi, p. 74.

The editors of Lafayette's *Mémoires* have placed his letter describing his dinner with William Pitt in 1786 (II, 160–61), and subsequent biographers have followed them. Wilberforce's papers, however, as published in part by his sons, Robert Isaac and Samuel, make it possible to date this letter exactly —October 21, 1783. On the other hand, Wilberforce's editors have added to his writings their own post-Revolutionary impressions of Lafayette (I, 41–42), making it appear that Wilberforce found in Lafayette a republicanism that was certainly premature.

Good discussions of Lafayette's relation to Vergennes's and Calonne's commercial policies are to be found in the articles by F. L. Nussbaum, "The French colonial arrêt of 1784" and "Vergennes and Lafayette versus the farmers general" (see n. 19 above). My article "Lafayette as a commercial agent," *loc. cit.*, is more fully elaborated above. Pierre Clément and Alfred Lemoine (*M. de Silhouette, Bouret, les derniers fermiers généraux: études sur les finances du XVIIIe siècle* [Paris, 1872], pp. 231–33) tell the story of how Calonne succeeded Ormesson; Gustave Schelle (*Du Pont de Nemours et l'école physiocratique* [Paris, 1888], pp. 216–17 and 221, n. 2) gives the background for the above presentation of Dupont's inactive role in connection with the four free ports.

CHAPTER V

Against an American Aristocracy

J UST as conditions rather than theories made Lafayette appear to be a pupil of the physiocrats, so conditions were
also to make him a champion of the Rights of Man. In
that connection, however, intellectual influences were to play
a somewhat more discernible part, though they were to be
expressed with an American rather than with a French accent.
The new home on the Rue de Bourbon became a sort of
American shrine. Its presiding divinity was George Washington,
whose portrait was its "chief ornament." Admiral d'Estaing's
house held another such ornament, and Estaing once genially
described how the two *sensible* Frenchmen, in their frequent conversations, would turn their eyes toward their former commander's picture. "We many times repeat to each other," he imparted to Washington, "that among the celebrated men whom
antiquity boasts, none has performed actions of such difficulty
and importance as those which you have just so gloriously ter-
minated. They reflect the greater honor on humanity, since it
was to defend its cause that you became a conqueror and since
you had no other purpose while you were fighting than to
assert its rights. You are, Sir, the only such hero we know of."[1]
If Washington was the prophet of the new dispensation, its
bible was the Declaration of Independence. One day Lafayette
asked Franklin's grandson to find for him a copy of the Declaration. He wanted, he said, "to have it engraved in golden letters at the most conspicuous part of my cabinet, and when I
wish to put myself in spirits, I will look at it, and most volup-

1. Dec. 25, 1783, E. E. Hume (ed.), *General Washington's correspondence concerning
the Society of the Cincinnati* (Baltimore, 1941), p. 39. The translation has been somewhat modified here.

tously read it over."[2] When the document arrived and was duly engraved, Lafayette placed it in one side of a double frame, leaving the other empty, and hung it in his study. The reason for this curious behavior, he announced, was that he was "waiting for the declaration of the rights of France."[3] It was not the words of Montesquieu, Voltaire, or Rousseau that he put upon his wall; it was the words of Jefferson. It was not a philosophical creed that he meant to study to put himself "in spirits"; it was a political pronunciamento.

A chance to implement this American creed arose shortly afterward. In the spring of 1783, when it was clear that the fighting was over and that the army of the United States would soon be disbanded, several of its ranking members planned "a society to be formed by the American officers and to be called the Cincinnati." In May an assembly of representatives from the army met at Fishkill, New York, and accepted an "institution" of the society. This institution bound the officers of the American army into "one society of friends" to keep alive the associations formed "under the pressure of common danger, and, in many instances, cemented by the blood of the parties." Some of the society's principles were liberal. The members pledged themselves "to preserve inviolate those exalted rights, and liberties of human nature, for which they have fought and bled, and without which the high rank of a rational being is a curse instead of a blessing." They swore "to promote and cherish, between the respective states, that union and national honor so essentially necessary to their happiness and the future dignity of the American empire." They promised always to show to each other the spirit "of brotherly kindness in all things."

Yet the society was not a democratic one. Membership was to be hereditary and the society "to endure as long as they [the members] shall endure, or any of their eldest male posterity, and, in failure thereof, the collateral branches who may be

2. Nov. 19, 1783, APS, Franklin papers, Vol. CV, No. 152.
3. *Mémoires*, III, 197. Cf. *Mémoires de Weber, frère de lait de Marie-Antoinette, reine de France* ("Bibliothèque des mémoires relatifs à l'histoire de France pendant le 18ᵉ et le 19ᵉ siècles," ed. M. Fs. Barrière, Vol. VIII) (Paris, 1885), p. 79, and *Memoirs of the Margravine of Anspach* (London, 1826), II, 195-96.

judged worthy of becoming its supporters and members."
Furthermore, only those were made eligible for membership who
were officers at the end of the war or previously had served honorably as officers for three years and were willing to contribute
the equivalent of one month's pay to the society. Since they
also had to buy the badge of the society, poor men would have
found it difficult to be Cincinnati. Frenchmen who had served in
the Continental Army were eligible on the same terms as American officers, as well as members of the French forces who had
been admirals or commanders in the navy or generals or colonels
in the French expeditionary army under the Comte de Rochambeau during the war.[4]

Lafayette was the senior officer among the Frenchmen who
had served in the Continental Army. Consequently, Washington,
as president of the society, decided to vest him with authority
"to take the signatures" of such French officers of the American
army as "are entitled and wish to become members," to receive
their month's pay, and to give them the society's badge "on
their paying for them." Rochambeau was to do the same for
the eligible officers of his command.[5] Major Pierre-Charles
L'Enfant, a French engineer in the American service, who was
going to France on his own affairs, was directed to find an artist
to make the badges and to deliver them to Rochambeau and Lafayette. When L'Enfant left the United States, he was the bearer of instructions making Lafayette an influential figure among
the French Cincinnati. The marquis was empowered to help
select and initiate the members of the Cincinnati from among
the "foreign officers who are qualified."[6]

L'Enfant incidentally also bore another letter requesting
Lafayette to buy for Washington a silver tea set and other articles of French plate. "I do not incline," said Washington, "to
send to England (from whence formerly I had all my goods)
for any thing I can get upon tolerable terms elsewhere."[7] Wash-

4. E. E. Hume, *La Fayette and the Society of the Cincinnati* (Baltimore, 1934), p. 2,
and *Washington's correspondence concerning the Cincinnati*, pp. 1–8.

5. Washington to Knox, Oct. 16, 1783, Fitzpatrick, XXVII, 195.

6. Washington to Lafayette, Oct. 20, 1783, *ibid.*, p. 202. (The same letter is also given
as of October 30, pp. 214–15.)

7. Oct. 30, *ibid.*, p. 216.

ington soon changed his mind, however. Within a month the English finally evacuated New York, and the American army moved in. There Washington found the plated ware that he wanted (presumably of English manufacture) and wrote Lafayette to disregard his earlier request.[8] If this order and its subsequent cancellation had been known when Lafayette composed his "Observations on the commerce between France and the United States," it might have furnished him with a telling example of the difficulties that French manufactures encountered in American markets. The cancellation, as a matter of fact, came too late. Lafayette's zeal to serve Washington had already led him to send off the desired service.[9]

L'Enfant delivered his messages in the middle of December, 1783. Lafayette, who was far from eager to retire modestly to private life, thus found himself a power among the Cincinnati. Educated Frenchmen were familiar with the story of the legendary Roman patrician, Cincinnatus, who, having been made dictator by his fellow-citizens when his country faced defeat, surrendered his authority after the crisis had passed and quietly returned to his farm. The badge of the Society of the Cincinnati recalled that story. Hanging from a two-inch ribbon of blue (for the United States) and white (for France), it portrayed an American bald eagle with outstretched wings (fortunately looking like a turkey, thought Franklin, since he considered the bald eagle "a bird of bad moral character"[10]). Engraved on the eagle's breast was a medallion showing (on the obverse) Cincinnatus receiving the sword of office from the senators of Rome and (on the reverse) Fame crowning Cincinnatus with a wreath. The principal motto on the reverse read (in rather awkward Latin, which was later improved): *"Omnia reliquit servare rem publicam"* (He left everything to serve the republic). No matter how inappropriate that picture of republican sacrifice might have been for several unbending aristocrats in France who were soon to sport it, there was a certain justice in it for Lafayette.

8. Dec. 4, 1783, *ibid.*, pp. 258–59.
9. Mar. 9, 1784, Gottschalk, *Letters*, p. 282; Washington to Lafayette, Apr. 4, Fitzpatrick, XXVII, 384.
10. Hume, *Washington's correspondence concerning the Cincinnati*, p. xiii.

He at least had left much (though not everything) to serve against England and therefore on behalf of the republic.

For Lafayette, too, the ideals of the society were not mere high-sounding phrases. Long before he knew of the "institution" of the Cincinnati, he had pleaded several times for a strong American union, and he had done so again in the last letter he wrote to Washington before L'Enfant brought the "institution" to France. "The more I think of it," he had declared, "[and] the more I examine European Nations, the better am I convinced that American glory, consequence, wealth, and liberty depend upon a tight, well framed Federal Union."[11] An "institution" that stressed "union and national honor" and the "exalted rights and liberties of human nature" was bound to have the young marquis's approval.

The society's greatest appeal, however, was sentimental. Lafayette saw in it chiefly an association of veterans and companions-in-arms. "The disbanding of our Army, I must confess," he wrote to Secretary of War Henry Knox,[12] "affects me with some painfull feelings—and altho' it is a proper measure not to keep a standing Army, yet I could not help sighing at the first news that the Continental Army was no more. We have so intimately, so brotherly lived together, we have had so much to fear, so much to hope, we have united ourselves through so many changes of fortune, that the parting moment cannot but be painfull." Somewhat later, in a letter to Washington, he again gave voice to this sentiment: "How pleasing it is for me to recollect our common toils, dangers, turns of fortune, our so glorious successes, and that lively attachment which united us with each other under our beloved General. Never can my heart forget the return of affection I have particularly obtained, the numberless obligations I am under my dear brother officers, and the happy hours, the happiest in my life, which I have pass in their company."[13] Probably no other man in the whole army had been more successful in it and had more right to feel sad at its dispersal than Lafayette. Without the slightest hesitation,

11. Nov. 11, 1783, Gottschalk, *Letters*, p. 271.
12. Jan. 8 [?], 1784, Massachusetts Historical Society.
13. Mar. 9, 1784, Gottschalk, *Letters*, p. 277.

he undertook to do what he could to keep its memory green. The first necessary step to achieve that end in France was obvious to a courtier. Since Frenchmen in the king's army were permitted to receive no foreign decorations except the Golden Fleece, royal authority to accept the new order would have to be obtained. Lafayette again turned to his friend Vergennes. While asking for King Louis's approval, he also sought publicity. He requested permission to describe the society and its purposes in the *Gazette de France*, which was the court's semiofficial journal, and sent copy along with his letter. The king was easily persuaded, and the council gave its formal approval on December 18, though its decision was officially reported not to Lafayette but to Rochambeau. The *Gazette de France* carried the story on December 23, and it was quickly copied in other journals.[14]

With characteristic enthusiasm but with a formality that indicated he expected his letter to be made public, Lafayette reported these successes to Washington. To be sure, there were already some people who were disturbed by "the hereditary part of the Institution," but "the general voice is in favor of our Brotherly Society, and General Washington's name as President adds a weight to the Association."[15] Writing to McHenry at about the same time, he again mentioned "the few objections" that had "been made by the public to some parts of the Institution," this time adding the hope that they might be "either mended or improved."[16] The English writer Horace Walpole, who happened to be in Paris at the time, likewise noted the great pleasure the French people derived from this new symbol of Franco-American solidarity and was amused that the French pronunciation of "Cincinnatus" led some noblemen, who "spell only by ear," to believe the society was named after an unknown St. Senatus.[17] L'Enfant reported that "here in France they are more ambitious to obtain the order of

14. Dec. 16, 1783, AAE, corr. pol., É-U., Vol. XXVI, fols. 204–8; Lafayette to Washington, Dec. 25, 1783, Gottschalk, *Letters*, pp. 272–73; *Courrier de l'Europe*, Dec. 30, 1783, and Jan. 9, 1784; *Gazette de Leyde*, Jan. 2 and 6, 1784.

15. Dec. 25, 1783, Gottschalk, *Letters*, p. 273 and n.

16. Dec. 26, 1783, Steiner, pp. 87–88.

17. To the Countess of Upper Ossory, Dec. 30, 1783, Mrs. Paget Toynbee (ed.), *The letters of Horace Walpole, fourth earl of Orford* (Oxford, 1903–5), XIII, 106; to Rev. Wm. Mason, Dec. 30, *ibid.*, p. 108.

the Cincinnati than to be decorated with the cross of St. Louis."[18]

As one of the heads of the French Cincinnati, Lafayette found sufficient reason for keeping busy and feeling important. He arranged with L'Enfant for the casting of the eagles, indorsing (to his later regret) the major's credit and authority.[19] He also had to select the members of the society from among those French soldiers who had served as officers in the Continental Army. Many applicants' titles were satisfactory, and they were quickly accepted. To help him decide doubtful cases, Lafayette appointed a board of American officers who were already members, which met at his house under his chairmanship. Some cases were referred to Franklin, either because the records were uncertain or because they did not fall clearly under the rules of eligibility,[20] but the more complicated ones had to await settlement in America.

The group who had won the honor of membership in the Cincinnati as officers in the French army completed their organization first. On January 7 twenty-five of them met at Rochambeau's house. "Old Rochambeau," complained Lafayette, who could easily behold a mote in another's eye, "wants to be as conspicuous as he can in that, as you know he does in every other affair."[21]

The French officers who had earned their badges by service in the Continental Army did not hold their initial meeting until January 19.[22] At that meeting there were fifteen Franco-American officers, all decked out in their American regimentals. Lafayette distributed the eagles of the order among them. Then,

18. To Steuben, Dec. 25, 1783, Friedrich Kapp, *Life of Frederick William von Steuben, major-general in the Revolutionary army* (New York, 1859), p. 564; cf. *Mémoires du Comte de Moré (1758–1837)* (Paris, 1898), p. 117.

19. AN, T 1640, dossier 61, No. 21; and see below, p. 262 and n. 11.

20. Lafayette to Washington, Dec. 25, 1783, Gottschalk, *Letters*, p. 273; Mar. 9, 1784, *ibid.*, pp. 276–77; Dubuysson to Franklin, Dec. 31, 1783, APS, Franklin papers, Vol. XXX, No. 164; Lafayette and Chastellux to Franklin, [1783?], *ibid.*, Vol. LVII, No. 123 (on behalf of Dr. Coste).

21. To Washington, Jan. 10, 1784, Gottschalk, *Letters*, p. 274.

22. Hume (*La Fayette and the Cincinnati*, pp. 10–11) believes that this group met also on January 7, but Lafayette's letters to Knox (Jan. 8 [?], Massachusetts Historical Society) and to Washington (Jan. 10, Gottschalk, *Letters*, pp. 274–76) do not mention any such meeting. On the other hand, they indicate that a meeting would take place soon.

as had been arranged, he conducted them in a body to Rocham-beau's house, where the French group were waiting to receive them. There L'Enfant presented Rochambeau and the French admirals with their orders, and Rochambeau in turn decorated the officers of his army.[23] Then they all sat down to a banquet which ended in toasts to Washington and the Army of the United States.

The number of applications for membership in the Cincin-nati quickly became embarrassing. "In case the badge is multi-plied," Lafayette believed, "it will loose its price in Europe."[24] And yet certain claims were entitled to careful consideration. There was, first of all, the case of French naval captains, whom Admiral d'Estaing championed as having as high rank and as much right to the distinction as army colonels. The newspapers even carried the probably exaggerated story[25] that Estaing and other French admirals had consented to receive the eagle only on the promise that naval captains would eventually be admit-ted. Lafayette supported Estaing in this matter (partly because he wanted the good will of the navy for American merchants) as well as in the admiral's plan to send to Washington an eagle generously studded with diamonds. There were likewise several deserving applicants who somehow failed to meet the require-ments. Thomas Mullens and the Marquis de Vienne, for in-stance, felt their services entitled them to the honor though there was some question whether they had served the stipulated three years. The Marquis du Bouchet had served in the Con-tinental Army less than three years and then had passed into Rochambeau's army at a rank lower than colonel. Ethis de Corny and the Chevalier de La Neuville claimed but could not prove three years' service as officers in the United States. The

23. *Gazette de Leyde*, Feb. 20, 1784; *Journal historique et politique des principaux évènemens du tems présent* (1784), I, 372–73; Bachaumont, XXV, 89 (Jan. 19, 1784). Ludovic de Contenson ("L'Ordre américain de Cincinnatus en France," *Revue d'histoire diplomatique en France*, XXVII [1913], 230, and *La Société des Cincinnati de France et la guerre d'Amérique 1778–1783* [Paris, (*ca.* 1934)], p. 33) thinks this meeting took place on January 16, but I have found no evidence to that effect.

24. To Washington, Jan. 10, 1784, Gottschalk, *Letters*, p. 274. Cf. Colonel Armand to Washington, Mar. 14, Hume, *Washington's correspondence concerning the Cincinnati*, pp. 112–13.

25. *Gazette de Leyde*, Feb. 20, 1784.

Chevalier de Mauduit-Duplessis and the Vicomte de Laumagne could not establish that they had honorably resigned from the Continental Army.[26]

The most delicate decision, however, that Lafayette had to make was with regard to General Thomas Conway. Conway's name had been inextricably associated with the maneuvers of Washington's opponents generally if somewhat erroneously labeled the "Conway Cabal." Since Conway himself was now stationed in India, Mme Conway was fearful that he would not win the coveted honor. She made no secret of her apprehension, and it was soon reported to Lafayette that Washington and he were being accused of "an implacable revenge against that man," who was represented "as having been abandonned and ruined" by him in America. Others who wished to befriend Conway (often apparently for no other reason than that they wished to deflate Lafayette) joined in, if indeed they did not instigate, her outcry. According to the perplexed marquis, secret meetings were held by Conway's advocates, and he began to suspect a new "Conway Cabal." "That whole family," he said, "is a nest of rogues."

Coyly disclaiming any merit for himself, Lafayette lamented that he nevertheless did have the consequences of merit, namely enemies, and he did not want to fall into their snare. "My popularity is great throughout the kingdom," he reported with more truth than modesty. "But among the great folks I have a large party against me because they are jealous of my reputation. In a word, the pitt [sic] to one man is for me, and in the boxes there is a division."[27] He did not want to be considered responsible for any unfriendly decisions affecting Conway. On the contrary, he supported the claims of Conway's relative, Du Bouchet, whom he privately considered "honest but a fool,"

26. Cf. Estaing to Washington, Dec. 25, 1783, Hume, *Washington's correspondence concerning the Cincinnati*, pp. 39–41; Lafayette to Vergennes, Dec. 25, AAE, corr. pol., É.-U., Vol. XXVI, fol. 251; Estaing to La Luzerne, Feb. 28, 1784, *ibid.*, Vol. XXVII, fols. 159–60; Estaing to Vergennes, Feb. 29, *ibid.*, fol. 162; Gottschalk, *Letters*, Mar. 9, 1784 (Nos. 167–70), pp. 276–82; Hume, *La Fayette and the Cincinnati*, pp. 18–19; Hume, *Washington's correspondence concerning the Cincinnati*, pp. 116–19; "Proceedings of a committee of French Continental officers held at the quarters of the Marquis de la Fayette," LC, Society of the Cincinnati papers.

27. Mar. 9, 1784, Gottschalk, *Letters*, p. 280.

and of Mullens, who had been Conway's aide.[28] Conway did not, in fact, fulfil the society's requirements, since he had resigned before having served three years in the American army. The public notoriety roused by the case, however, led Lafayette to refer the matter to Washington with a favorable recommendation. "The man is not worth troubling our heads about him," he confided, "but as he will become a pretence to a sect who have not hitherto found any against me, it may be better either to give him the badge, or if refused, to do it with that secrecy and delicacy which will not subject me to the reproach of having proposed him in order that he may be humiliated."[29]

In addition to disposing of the claims that fell properly under his own jurisdiction, Lafayette did not hesitate to give advice on matters that dealt with the officers of Rochambeau's and Estaing's forces. He advocated that the eagle be given to some who had not held the full rank of colonel at the time of their service in America and to others whose service had been in the West Indies rather than on the continent. At the same time, he repeated his warning that membership must not be too generously awarded or it would lose its value. While considering a European section of the society desirable, he preferred it to be distinct from any organization that the French officers might create[30] (and thus under his rather than Rochambeau's influence).

Meanwhile, an outburst of indignation had swept through America out of fear that the Cincinnati might eventually become a military aristocracy. Influential men like Jefferson and Samuel Adams, writers like Aedanus Burke, and the state legislatures of Massachusetts and Rhode Island attacked the order as a violation of the natural equality of mankind and a defilement of the Temple of Liberty. In France a similar outcry had arisen among Americans and French champions of America.[31] The Comte de Mirabeau first won renown as a liberal writer

28. *Ibid.*, pp. 278–80; Mullens to Washington, Feb. 13, 1784, Hume, *Washington's correspondence concerning the Cincinnati*, p. 72.

29. Gottschalk, *Letters*, p. 280.

30. *Ibid.*, pp. 276, 277, 279, and 280.

31. [Philip Mazzei], *Recherches historiques et politiques sur les États-Unis de l'Amérique septentrionale* (Paris, 1788), IV, 121–237.

and leader with a work dealing with the Cincinnati.[32] Using the society as a point of departure, the book denounced hereditary privilege in general. This attitude was shared by Franklin, who made sophisticated fun of the society's "descending honour," as well as of its "turkey" emblem.[33] He recorded, with apparent acquiescence, Mirabeau's assertion that Washington had "missed a *beau moment*" when he had accepted membership and added tersely, "The same of the Marquis de la Fayette."[34] Jay was less urbane than the Philadelphia sage. Upon returning to Paris, he found that the wisest men thought the society did no credit either "to those who formed and patronized it or to those who suffered it."[35]

Adams, now American minister at The Hague, was also displeased. Between the minister and Lafayette there had long been a polite restraint arising from Adams' general distrust of Frenchmen and Lafayette's suspicion that the American peace commissioners had not given him due credit for his accomplishments. The new Cincinnatus was sensitive about criticism of his society and had become a little impatient with Adams, who, he had heard, was "very violent against the Society of the Cincinnati and calls it a *French blessing.*" He also suspected Adams of believing that he kept postponing his return to America because of a "want of zeal." Scarcely able to hide his resentment, he wrote Adams in polite but unmistakable tones.[36] He valued the American envoy's esteem, he declared, "in point of republicanism particularly." But he must deny that the French court had done anything to create the Cincinnati (which was true) or that he had himself had anything to do with the decision to permit its establishment in France (which was not). He was not prepared to debate the merits of the society, he said. "Should it be dangerous, it must not subsist." But the purposes of the French court and his own motives, he protested, had been entirely honorable. They had been directed toward

32. *Considérations sur l'Ordre de Cincinnatus, ou imitation d'un pamphlet anglo-américain* (London, 1784). Cf. *Mémoires*, IV, 39.
33. To Sarah Bache, Jan. 26, 1784, Smyth, IX, 161–68.
34. Franklin's diary, July 13, 1784, *ibid.*, X, 354.
35. To Gouverneur Morris, Feb. 10, 1784, H. P. Johnston (ed.), *The correspondence and public papers of John Jay* (New York, 1890), III, 112.
36. Mar. 8, 1784, Adams, *Works*, VIII, 187–89.

the promotion of friendliness between France and the United States. His going to America, he further explained, had been postponed only by his efforts toward the same end. "Independent of the affectionate and dutiful regard that binds me to our gallant, patriotic army, independent of what can be said in favor of that freemasonry of liberty, it has ever been my duty and inclination to set up in the best light every thing that is done by a body of Americans."

Words like "republicanism" had flowed readily from Lafayette's pen before with more or less precision of meaning, but this was the first time he had used the phrase "freemasonry of liberty." Reflection on the significance of a hereditary order in a republic had apparently led him to associate republicanism with democracy—which was far from a necessary association in eighteenth-century parlance. With a warmth that did greater honor to his zeal than to his judgment (since he exaggerated the dangers that he once had run for democracy's sake), he reaffirmed his political faith: "As to my democratic principles, let it be remembered that, at a time when your situation was at the worst, and my disobeying this court might be ruinous, I went over a volunteer in the cause from which others could not recede unless they were deserters."

Adams' reply was courteous rather than friendly.[37] He admitted that on two or three occasions he had expressed disapproval of "the introduction into America of so great an innovation as an order of chivalry." Such a departure, he held, would be "against the spirit of our governments and the genius of our people," and he saw no reason why Americans should make a mystery of their sentiments on that subject in either Europe or America. As for Lafayette's projected return to the United States, he thought there was now "no particular motive" for it, but if the marquis went, he wished him "a pleasant voyage."

Even before Adams' minced observations reached Paris, the young Cincinnatus had decided to throw his influence against the principle of heredity. This issue, as well as the several disputed claims to membership in the society, was aired in a series of letters that were intrusted to L'Enfant in March, 1784, to

37. Mar. 28, 1784, *ibid.*, pp. 192–93.

carry to Washington. Two of those letters were personal and therefore franker than the others, which, though addressed to Washington as president of the Cincinnati, were intended for examination in the general meeting called for the next May. In the private letters Lafayette was able to speak confidentially about some of the applicants and to be less urgent in his recommendations than he wished to appear to be publicly. In the same fashion, the letters also dealt in two different ways with the issue of inherited membership. The ones meant for public consumption stated the problem merely hypothetically: "Our brotherly society has met with general applause—not a dissenting voice to be heard but in the point of heredity. That creates a debate wherein most of the Americans take the other part. Who can question but what we do not in any account wish to injure those sacred republican principles for which we have fought, bled, and conquered, and what sacrifice has not been made by us in support of these principles? Which I am sure we are ready to repeat upon every occasion."[38] But in his confidential letters Lafayette was much more outspoken. "Most of the Americans here are indecently violent against our Assossiation," he confessed. "Wadsworth [who was eligible to the society himself] must be excepted, and Doctor Franklin said little—but Jay, Adams, and all the others warmly blame the army. You easely guess I am not remiss in opposing them. And however if it is found that the heredity endangers the true principles of democraty, I am as ready as any man to renounce it." The great distance that separated him from America, he said, made it impossible for him to judge whether such apprehensions were well grounded. Therefore he asked Washington to judge and to vote for him. "I so much rely on your judgement that if you think heredity a proper scheme, I will be convinced that your patriotism has considered the matter in the best point of view. *To you alone*, I would say so much, and I abide by your opinion in the matter. I am sure your disinterested virtue will weigh all possible future consequences of hereditary distinctions."[39] Thus Lafayette furnished another striking example of his reliance

38. Mar. 9, 1784, Gottschalk, *Letters*, p. 277.
39. *Ibid.*, p. 282.

upon Washington, who, fortunately, had already decided against the hereditary principle.

Lafayette's petitions on behalf of several doubtful applicants for membership, supported as they were by Rochambeau, Estaing, and others, helped to bring about a change in the rules of the Cincinnati. All of the irregular cases that he championed (excepting only those of Vienne and Laumagne) were admitted into the society by the new rulings.[40] A gift of money raised among the French officers was politely refused, as he had suggested, with due consideration for the delicacy of their feelings.[41] Lafayette's wishes were disregarded in only one particular. The affairs of the French branch of the society were placed under the jurisdiction of a single French general assembly, and in such an assembly it could be anticipated that Rochambeau's French officers would outvote Lafayette's Continentals.

The new rules of the society also carefully avoided mention of the inheritance of membership. When the question arose at the general meeting of the society, Washington spoke in favor of discarding the hereditary principle, reading from Lafayette's more outspoken private letters to support his plea. He even threatened to resign as president if the constitution of the society were not revised to make it less "obnoxious to the people." Omission of the disputed point was agreed upon.[42]

Thereby a great victory was won for democracy, since the likelihood of a military aristocracy in the United States was reduced. Conspicuous among those who had helped to reduce it was that member of the French "nobility of the sword" who had been most prominent in the American army. The paradoxical precedent thus established was one day to be followed in France.

BIBLIOGRAPHICAL NOTES

Hume's *Lafayette and the Cincinnati* is sketchy, though it contains some useful documents. On the other hand, his *Washington's correspondence con-*

40. Hume (*La Fayette and the Cincinnati*, p. 17) says Conway was not admitted, but cf. Contenson, *La Société des Cincinnati de France*, pp. 162–63, where he is shown to have been admitted as an honorary but not as a founding member.

41. Hume, *Washington's correspondence concerning the Cincinnati*, pp. 162 and 176–77.

42. *Ibid.*, pp. 158–59.

cerning the Cincinnati, despite occasional inaccuracies and omissions, is indispensable for an understanding of the story of Lafayette's relations to the Society. Contenson's article and book perform a similar service for the French branch of the society. Contenson's biographical dictionary of French Cincinnati in his *Société des Cincinnati de France* is particularly helpful.

My *Letters of Lafayette to Washington,* having been published while war conditions prevented my consulting the papers of the Cincinnati in the Library of Congress, borrowed from Hume the incomplete text of several letters regarding the Cincinnati. The omissions fortunately prove not to be important.

The *Mémoires* of Marie Antoinette's foster-brother Weber are in large part to be ascribed to the Marquis de Lally-Tollendal, who later came to know Lafayette quite well.

CHAPTER VI

Patron of Commerce and Science

JOHN ADAMS was right. There was no good reason for Lafayette to return to America now that the war was over, especially since he could not hope to arrive in time for the general assembly of the Cincinnati. But he was so inordinately sensitive to what he thought was expected of him by Americans that he kept apologizing for staying on in France.

The excuse for delay was that American commercial problems required attention—and it was genuine. The official decision in favor of four free ports created as many problems as it settled. First of all, fees persisted even in the free ports for such things as anchorage, pilotage, and the rental of storage space. These fees, Lafayette was informed, "are always collected in a vague and troublesome manner" and "are not so useful to the King as inconvenient to the individual." Many other fees and duties continued to be payable in ports that were not free. The burden also survived of having to sell monopoly articles like tobacco either to the farmers-general or not at all. In addition, there still remained the troublesome obligation to pay internal duties and octrois on shipments, even when destined for foreign export, upon passage from one province, town, or specially privileged area of France into another.

In order to demonstrate beyond a doubt that still further concessions were necessary if American vessels were to be attracted to French ports, Wadsworth and his partner, Mr. Carter, undertook an experiment. They bought some silk and other articles to ship by way of the new free port of Lorient. The shipment, however, they knew, would have to pass through some lands belonging to the king's brother, the Comte de Provence, where it would be obliged to pay a duty high enough to eat up all the profits. They decided instead to detour, and in so doing they not only incurred an additional expense but also missed the vessel they had originally intended to catch. The experiment proved that further trade concessions were in order. They now wished to ship forty thousand bottles of champagne from Brest, and Lafayette interceded with Calonne to find out in advance what duties they would have to pay for entrance and clearance.[1]

Even before he got an answer to this request, Lafayette applied again to the minister—this time as the champion of American tobacco merchants. Because of monopoly conditions in France, American tobacco imports had yielded to imports from the Ukraine, which, Lafayette said, were poorer in quality though lower in price. To facilitate American trade, he asked again for the repeal of such fees as pilotage and anchorage and suggested in addition that Le Havre, which was commodious and near enough to England to compete successfully with English trade, be added to the list of free ports.[2]

Calonne accommodatingly inquired into the nature of the fees that still had to be paid in free ports but concluded that the sums involved were not burdensome. He submitted a statement to that effect for Lafayette's consideration. After consulting with his American friends, Lafayette rejoined that it was not the amount so much as the multiplicity of the duties that created inconvenience. He suggested, instead, a single duty, to be determined by the number of masts rather than by the tonnage of the importing vessel. Thereby the annoyances associated with customs inspection might be avoided.[3] Not content with mere letters to plead his cause, Lafayette sometimes visited Versailles, seeking out the ministers and their advisers. He took advantage of every occasion when a vessel cleared for the United States to urge speed.[4]

Thus two months passed by. Finally, Calonne, glad of "an

1. Lafayette to Calonne, Jan. 31, 1784, [Weaver], *Diplomatic correspondence*, I, 406–7.
2. Feb. 10, 1784, *ibid.*, p. 408.
3. Feb. 26, 1784, *ibid.*, pp. 409–10.
4. Lafayette to Calonne, Jan. 31, Feb. 10 and 26, and Mar. 5, 1784, *ibid.*, pp. 405–11.

opportunity of proving to the United States the favorable disposition of our Court in everything which interests them," declared his willingness to investigate what the remaining duties in the free ports were, "for whose profit they are levied, and under what title they are established." He accordingly issued orders to the authorities in the free ports to furnish an account of all duties payable by American vessels both on arrival and on departure. With this information in hand he hoped to be in a better position to urge His Majesty to adopt Lafayette's proposals. Meanwhile, he wanted Americans to realize that the duties they had to pay were the same as those imposed on all other foreign vessels and were no greater than those the English exacted. As a token of greater favors yet to come, however, he announced the immediate suppression of all export duties on French brandies.[5]

Lafayette lost no time in informing Americans at home and abroad of his latest victory.[6] Now that Calonne was committed to a friendly American policy, the marquis began to feel free to leave for the United States. He informed Washington that he would soon drop in "for a dish of tea at Mount Vernon," since he expected to depart at the end of April or the beginning of May. "Yes, my dear General, before the month of June is over, you will see a vessel coming up Pottowmack, and out of that vessel will your friend jump with a panting heart and all the feelings of perfect happiness." He had intended, he said, to leave earlier. "But a few commercial matters still keep me here —for since no body middles with them, I have undertaken in my private capacity to do what is possible for one who has neither title or instruction. It is at least a comfort that in my private capacity, I can not commit Congress, and that I never speak but of what I know."[7]

Within a few weeks, however, Lafayette once more post-

5. Mar. 8, 1784, *ibid.*, pp. 411–12.

6. Cf. Lafayette to Washington, Mar. 9, 1784, Gottschalk, *Letters*, p. 281; to [Wadsworth], Mar. 17, Connecticut Historical Society; to Morris, Mar. 9, mentioned in *Journals of the Continental Congress*, XXVII, 471 (May 28).

7. Lafayette to Washington, Mar. 9, 1784, Gottschalk, *Letters*, p. 281. Cf. Lafayette to [Wadsworth], Mar. 7 and 17, Connecticut Historical Society.

poned his departure.[8] The reason again was his championing of
Franco-American commerce. Calonne's promise to make the
ports of Bayonne, Dunkirk, Lorient, and Marseille free to
American trade had not yet been formally indorsed by the royal
council, and the marquis apparently wanted to carry to America
the formal printed declaration *de par le roi*. But bureaucratic
obstacles would not yield to his righteous impatience. Although
the step had been agreed upon in January, it was not until the
spring that Calonne formally asked Castries, in whose department fell jurisdiction over the ports, for his official approval.
"As M. Delafayette presses for the expedition of this decree
which he believes important to publish as soon as possible, I
beg you not to defer your answer," Calonne wrote.[9]

It was not until May 14 that the decree was finally issued. It
not only opened the four ports agreed upon but also held out the
promise of certain privileges elsewhere.[10] On that day Lafayette
wrote to Washington. Confident that the matter of the free
ports was settled, although the opposition of "flour merchants,
manufacturers and raisers in the country round Bordeaux" still
prevented action on the West Indies trade, the marquis announced his definite decision to set out for America. "My course
will be straight to Pottowmack."[11]

Shortly afterward, on a visit to Versailles, Lafayette felt
"obliged to stay for the Queen's concert."[12] Calonne sent Lafayette twenty-four copies of the decree while he was there. In
his covering letter the minister indicated that, although certain
steps were necessary to allow the farmers-general to adjust to
the new free areas, no vessels that had sailed from the United
States because of earlier promises of free ports would be penal-
ized. Calonne also stated that he was studying the problem of
American tobacco. While he showed a disposition to defend the
Farm against attack, he nevertheless expressed a desire to obvi-

8. Lafayette to Wadsworth, Apr. 18 and 22, 1784, Connecticut Historical Society.
9. May 10, 1784, AN, Colonies F²B8.
10. AAE, corr. pol., É.-U., Vol. XXVII, fols. 347-48.
11. May 14, 1784, Gottschalk, *Letters*, p. 283.
12. Lafayette to Franklin, [May 20, 1784], APS, Franklin papers, XLII, No. 138, 1.

ate "any uneasiness the United States may have conceived."[13] Lafayette saw to it that copies of the new decree reached America promptly. He sent one to Franklin and another to Barclay, who quickly forwarded it to the governor of Maryland.[14]

True to his word, Calonne meanwhile continued to gather information. Within a month he was able to draw up a list of all the duties payable in Marseille, Dunkirk, Bayonne, and Lorient. Bureaucratic inefficiency and the slowness of communication by post horses had resulted in the loss of three months since he had started to tabulate the data. He now sent a complete list of duties to Lafayette with the request that it be sent to the United States. If they would indicate "the demands they have to make with respect to each kind of duty," he promised to consider "the suppression, the modification, or the uniting under one head" of the items indicated.[15] To Lafayette's repeated suggestion that all such duties be transmuted to a single tax per vessel based upon the number of its masts, Calonne felt obliged to point out that the separate duties had become the feudal property of individuals and corporations other than the king. They belonged "to the Admiral, to officers of the Admiralty, and to particular cities and noblemen," who would have to be indemnified for their reduction or loss; "and you will agree," Calonne continued, "that it would not be just to reduce them, or even to suspend them, without hearing the parties concerned."[16]

Thus Lafayette's well-intentioned efforts to promote freedom of trade collided head on with feudal survivals and medieval privileges. His impatience was all the greater because he had hoped to take the news of the single mast tax to America as a token of French good will. Calonne urged patience. "The operation you desire must, whatever attention is paid to it, necessarily take up a space of three or four months. It will be doing in your absence."[17] The minister of the navy was equally disap-

13. May 17, 1784, [Weaver], *Diplomatic correspondence*, I, 413–14.
14. Lafayette to Franklin, [May 17 or 24, 1784], University of Pennsylvania Library; Barclay to William Paca, May 17, Maryland Historical Society, Vol. IX, fols. 149–50.
15. June 11, 1784, [Weaver], *Diplomatic correspondence*, I, 414–15.
16. June 16, 1784, *ibid.*, pp. 415–16.
17. *Ibid.*, p. 416.

pointing and decidedly more curt. To the suggestion that he come to some conclusion about freedom of trade in the colonies before Lafayette left, he replied: "It will be impossible for us to give that degree of liberty which you desire. All that I can foresee is that there will be a free port for the Americans in each colony, that everything which was formerly received will meet no difficulty, and that the duties will be as moderate as possible." Castries also raised the issue of vested rights. "The interest of our own commerce," he said, "demands some consideration."[18]

So Lafayette had to leave for America with less glittering prizes than he had intended to carry. It was now past the middle of June. For weeks he had been planning his trip to the United States. Several Americans and Frenchmen hoped to accompany him and made their plans accordingly—sometimes with his help. Josiah Harmar, who had come to Paris with Congress' ratification of the peace treaty and whom Lafayette had introduced to Vergennes, was among them.[19] Jay, having attended the formal exchange of ratifications, had already departed, bearing a picture of the Lafayette family for Washington, which eventually proved too large and had to be left behind for later transportation.[20] To Frenchmen who were interested, the marquis explained that he had to go to America because he had long been awaited there. "And although the Revolution is over, the thirteen states still have work to do on their federative constitution. Some persons want me to be a witness of their work in that connection; and when I yield to their friendliness by joining them, I could wish I had a fraction of the talents that could help America and further strengthen, if possible, the temple of

18. June 17, 1784, *ibid.*, p. 417.

19. Beaumont to Franklin, Mar. 28, 1784, APS, Franklin papers, Vol. XXI, Part 2, No. 126; and John Schaffer to Franklin, Apr. 8, *ibid.*, No. 143; Lafayette to Linguet [?], Apr. 20, Gardner-Ball collection, Indiana University Library; Lafayette to Vergennes, Apr. 10, AAE, corr. pol., É.-U., Vol. XXVII, fol. 275; Harmar to Mifflin, Apr. 8 and May 5, *Memoirs of the Historical Society of Pennsylvania*, VII (Philadelphia, 1860), 415.

20. Lafayette to Washington, May 14, 1784, Gottschalk, *Letters*, p. 284; Lafayette to Vergennes, [*ca.* May 14], AAE, corr. pol., É.-U., Vol. XXVIII, fol. 485; Thomas Thompson to Franklin, June 2, APS, Franklin papers, Vol. XXXII, Part 1, No. 2. Cf. Lafayette to Jay, *ca.* May 9, Jackson collection.

liberty. But at least I shall be a very benevolent spectator."[21]
If this was a case of wishful thinking—for no American had yet
asked him to take a direct part in the politics of the critical period that the United States was then passing through—it is
true that there were many who were ready to welcome him.
Among those the most cordial was Washington. Lafayette's
"beloved General" had once more "become a private citizen on
the banks of the Potomac" under the shadow of his own vine
and fig tree, where, "envious of none" and "determined to be
pleased with all," he proposed to "move gently down the stream
of life" until he slept with his fathers. To the Lafayettes' invitation to visit Paris he replied by inviting them to Mount Vernon. "I have often told you," he wrote, "and I repeat it again,
that no man could receive you . . . with more friendship and affection than I should do."[22]

Nor was Washington alone in doing Lafayette honor. Pennsylvania named one of its new western counties after him "as an
extraordinary mark of their esteem."[23] The erroneous report
quickly spread both in France and in England that this was an
estate that had been granted as a fresh mark of gratitude.[24]
Congress' recent resolution of thanks for his efforts on behalf of
Franco-American trade also reached him, accompanied by a
laudatory letter in which Financier Morris asked him to take
new steps—this time on behalf of American trade in the East
Indies.[25] America's leading naval hero, John Paul Jones, warmly
acknowledged his help in getting a satisfactory settlement for
prizes captured during the war.[26] Virginia appropriated £160
sterling to present him with a bust of himself.[27] St. John de
Crèvecœur, French consul in New York, who had just published

21. Lafayette to Linguet, Apr. 20, 1784, Gardner-Ball collection.
22. Feb. 1, 1784, Fitzpatrick, XXVII, 317–20. Cf. Washington to Estaing, May 15,
ibid., p. 403.
23. John Dickinson to Lafayette, Mar. 6, 1784, *Maryland Gazette*, Aug. 26, 1784.
24. *Gentleman's magazine*, LIII (January–June, 1783), 436, and *Courrier de l'Europe*,
XV (May 28, 1784), 339.
25. May 19, 1784, Wharton, VI, 809–10.
26. Jones to Franklin, Mar. 23, 1784, APS, Franklin papers, Vol. XXXI, Part 2,
No. 120; Jones to Castries, Mar. 26, C. H. Lincoln (ed.), *A calendar of John Paul Jones
manuscripts in the Library of Congress* (Washington, 1903), p. 190.
27. J. Ambler to the governor of Virginia, Apr. 14, 1784, W. P. Palmer *et al.* (eds.),
Calendar of Virginia state papers and other manuscripts (Richmond, 1875–93), III, 576.

a revised French edition of his popular *Letters of an American farmer*, had dedicated it to him as a liberator of America.[28] Recent verses sang his praises in France.[29] And in a foreign quarter —Ireland—he won new admirers in the family of the patriot Sir Edward Newenham.[30]

In fact, Lafayette's interest in Irish affairs and the Newenhams' interest in him were becoming notorious. The impression got around that, under cover of returning to America, he was really planning to go to Ireland in order to foment rebellion there. The Irish Volunteers had been drawing up petitions, holding conventions, and passing resolutions, asking for greater freedom and reform in Ireland. "The situation in Ireland is critical," Lafayette informed Washington; "the lord lieutenant's conduct has been foolish, and some resolutions of the people are very spirited."[31] He might have gone to their support, had he not realized that the French government would frown upon his venture and had not the British Parliament made concessions that kept Irish protests within peaceful bounds. It was actually stated in the public prints that the chivalric marquis had arrived in Ireland and had been named commandant of a national corps. He was said to be planning to enlist other French and Spanish officers, and the lord-lieutenant of Ireland had been warned that "these gentry should be watched."[32]

For a young man anxious to be talked about, Lafayette had little reason to be dissatisfied with the old worlds. And yet he

28. *Lettres d'un cultivateur américain* (Paris, 1784). Cf. J. P. Mitchell, *St. Jean de Crèvecœur* (New York, 1916), p. 143; and H. C. Rice, *Le Cultivateur Américain, étude sur l'œuvre de Saint John de Crèvecœur* (Paris, 1933), pp. 53 and 84.

29. Métra, XVI, 313 (July 9, 1784); Joseph Mandrillon, *Fragmens de politique et de littérature, suivis d'un voyage à Berlin en 1784* (Paris, 1788), p. 204; Émile Raunié (ed.), *Recueil Clairambault-Maurepas, chansonnier historique du XVIIIᵉ siècle* (Paris, 1879–84), II, 143.

30. Newenham to Franklin, Nov. 9, 1783, APS, Franklin papers, Vol. XXX, No. 78; to Lafayette, Mar. 22, 1784, *ibid.*, Vol. XXXI, Part 2, No. 118; and to Lafayette, July 5, "MSS of His Grace the Duke of Rutland, K.G., preserved at Belvoir Castle" in Historical Manuscripts Commission, *Fourteenth report*, Appen. 1, Part 1, Vol. III (London, 1894), p. 119.

31. May 14, 1784, Gottschalk, *Letters*, p. 283.

32. Lord Sydney to the Duke of Rutland, July 2, 1784, Historical Manuscripts Commission, *Fourteenth report*, Appen. 1, p. 117; Rutland to [Sydney], May 29, *ibid.*, p. 99; Arde to [Rutland], June 17, *ibid.* See also *Mémoires*, III, 222; *Journal historique et politique*, 1784, IV, 236–37; and Newenham to Franklin, [*ca.* January, 1785], APS, Franklin papers, Vol. XL, No. 142.

had found still another world to conquer—the realm of science. In June, 1783, a linen bag had been filled with heated air by the Montgolfier brothers and had risen and remained above the ground until its contents cooled. In rapid succession other balloon flights were tried, while trembling spectators gaped. Foremost among the experimenters was the scientist J.-A.-C. Charles. He had quickly inproved upon the Montgolfiers, making his balloon out of light silk and filling it with hydrogen instead of hot air. On December 1, 1783, Charles took off at the Tuileries Gardens in Paris in a lighter-than-air balloon with one passenger. They alighted twenty-seven miles away after nearly two hours in the air. Following a short rest, Charles rose again alone and traveled another nine miles.

When Charles returned to Paris, he was a hero, momentarily putting all other popular idols in the shade. Basking in reflected glory was the Duc de Chartres, who had sponsored Charles and had actually followed his flight on the ground in order to make an authentic report of it. But Lafayette also stole some of Charles's splendor. Charles went to Chartres's Palais Royal to thank his patron, and Lafayette took him there in his carriage. The crowd that gathered when Charles's presence was known and carried him back to the carriage on their shoulders was about to unharness the horses and pull him home themselves when they learned that the carriage was not their hero's but Lafayette's.[33] Thus Lafayette unintentionally got talked about once more.

A few days later Lafayette wrote a letter to the American Philosophical Society, his first scientific contribution since his election to membership in 1781. With it he inclosed a treatise entitled "An authentic narrative of experiments lately made in France with air balloons."[34] His letter did not, however, have the significance he had probably expected. Franklin had anticipated him, and the society had already ordered Franklin's letter published along with translations of the most interesting parts of the treatise. When Lafayette's communication arrived, it was merely copied by the society's secretaries. Balloon

33. Bachaumont, XXIV, 62–63 (Dec. 3, 1783).
34. Dec. 10, 1783, APS, Archives.

experiments by members of the American Philosophical Society began shortly afterward.[35]

In Paris the interest in balloons soon diminished. By March, Lafayette mentioned them only casually in his letters abroad.[36] The fad of aeronautics had by that time given way to a sweeping enthusiasm for the new science of "mesmerism." This was the "discovery" of Dr. Friedrich Anton Mesmer, lately of Vienna and now of Paris. All animal life, said Mesmer, contained a force that he called "animal magnetism." This force caused the illnesses of mankind and, if properly controlled, could cure them. And he knew how to control it, he announced. For proof, he pointed to several miraculous cures that he and his disciple, Dr. Charles Deslon, the Comte d'Artois's physician, had effected; and when the sensationalism and showmanship of Mesmer are discounted, it appears clear that he was well on the way to the discovery of hypnotism. The sick and the hypochondriac, whether rich or poor, high or low, flocked to his house for treatment, and perfectly whole and normal persons began to feel that perhaps he had found the key to the problem of disease. After all, if Nature was one, as some leading philosophers and scientists proclaimed, and the mind was only an extension of matter, why could there not be an all-pervading animal magnetism within that oneness?

Lafayette knew little about philosophic problems like monism and materialism, but he was an impressionable young man and he soon became convinced of Mesmer's merit. So did his friend Chastellux, who ought not to have been an easy mark. When, therefore, a movement began to provide Mesmer with a hospital and a school to train students, Lafayette was among those interested. He agreed to become one of Mesmer's disciples. Mesmer, however, took no chances that any of his followers would go into competition with him. So his new disciple solemnly signed a written contract (printed, in fact, except for appropriate blanks) to respect Mesmer's proprietary rights in animal

35. *Early proceedings of the American Philosophical Society for the Promotion of Useful Knowledge compiled by one of the secretaries from the manuscript minutes of its meetings from 1744 to 1838* (Philadelphia, 1884), pp. 124–26 (Mar. 19, Apr. 2 and 16, 1784).

36. Cf. Lafayette to Washington, Mar. 9, 1784, Gottschalk, *Letters*, p. 282.

magnetism, to take no pupils, to create no rival school or establishment without Mesmer's formal consent, to make no agreements with any government or municipality regarding animal
magnetism, and to treat no patients by animal magnetism except privately and singly.[37] How much the lessons were to cost
Lafayette was not indicated, but as the sum that Mesmer's
friends proposed to raise was 30,000 louis d'or from three hundred subscribers and as few among them were richer than Lafayette, his share probably was over 100 louis d'or (or from
2,000 to 2,500 livres). The original subscribers formed a new society known as the Order of Harmony.

Unharmonized skeptics had unfortunately already induced
the king to appoint a committee of physicians to investigate the
practice of animal magnetism, and Lafayette's friend Franklin
was asked to join in the inquiry. Without waiting for the committee to report, Lafayette, convinced of the truth of the new
dispensation, set out to spread its renown. He initiated William
Temple Franklin into the society.[38] He apprised Washington of
the "grand philosophical discover." Among Dr. Mesmer's
scholars, he wrote, "your humble servant is called one of the
most enthusiastic" and has learned "as much as any conjuror
ever did." Not having completely lost his sense of humor, he reminded Washington how, back in 1778, when American headquarters were located at Fishkill, they had both laughed at an
old man who had had an interview with the devil. Lafayette
promised to get permission, before he left France, to initiate
Washington "into the secret" of animal magnetism.[39]

Mesmer's precautions to protect his discovery from possible
competitors were justified. His colleague Deslon quickly claimed
to have improved upon the great secret, and Franklin's commission was called upon to decide between them. Lafayette was
not loath to try the effect of his personal friendship on Franklin.
No one would deny, he asserted, "that Mesmer is the true
preacher of Magnetism Animal, to which by the way he has
been much helped by your electric discoveries." Deslon, on the

37. Charavay, facsimile between pp. 102 and 103.
38. Lafayette to Franklin, [May 20, 1784], APS, Franklin papers, Vol. XLII,
No. 138.
39. May 14, 1784, Gottschalk, *Letters*, pp. 283–84.

other hand, was a traitor, who knew only so much of the system as Mesmer had taught him. The marquis suggested that the commission declare Mesmer the "fountain head to which you must apply" and that "in order to come to the whole truth, commissioners must plainly and oppenly go to M. Mesmer, and in the same way as other people do, be regularly let by him into his whole system."[40] The commission's report was destined, however, to be skeptical regarding the claims of all schools of animal magnetism.

But by the time the commission reported, Lafayette was to be in the United States. Preparations to embark had engaged nearly all his attention since the end of May. Despite the fact that he had recently sold some of his Britanny inheritance for over 50,000 livres (part of which had to go to his co-heir, the Marquis de Luzignem[41]), he was apparently short of cash. In days when international credit facilities were rudimentary, no gentleman dared to travel without a goodly sum in his purse. Lafayette borrowed 12,000 livres from his father-in-law and, as on previous departures, made arrangements with his wife and his intendant Morizot for the management of his estate.[42]

As usual, too, in an age when ocean voyages were seldom undertaken except by the desperate and the daring, he was called upon to carry many messages to America. He took charge of letters from friends in Paris to friends in America.[43] Adrienne sent a tender note to the Washingtons stating that her grief at again parting with her husband was somewhat assuaged by her hope that she would some day meet them in Paris or Mount Vernon.[44] The Lafayettes' seven-year-old daughter Anastasie also wrote to her "Dear Washington," telling him that her pain over her father's departure was lessened by her realization of

40. [May 20, 1784], APS, Franklin papers, Vol. XLII, No. 138.

41. Contract for sale of land to M. and Mme de Bouan, Dec. 8, 1783, Morristown National Historical Park (Morristown, N.J.).

42. Girodie, pp. 25, 35, and 36.

43. Franklin to Congress, June 16, 1784, Smyth, IX, 227; Rochambeau to Washington, June 16, Hume, *Washington's correspondence concerning the Cincinnati*, p. 199.

44. Mme de Lafayette to Washington, June 16, 1784, LC, Washington papers. Cf. Washington to Mme de Lafayette, Nov. 25, Fitzpatrick, XXVII, 496–97. For the legend that Mme de Lafayette sent Washington a Masonic apron by her husband in 1784 see Appen. I below.

the pleasure he would have in being in America.[45] Another letter came from Mesmer's pen. Lafayette had in fact persuaded the wizard to allow him to reveal at least a part of the secret of animal magnetism to Washington and to carry to the illustrious American the good wishes of the Order of Harmony. "It seems to us," Mesmer wrote, "that the man who has deserved the most from his fellowmen must be interested in the outcome of any revolution that has the welfare of humanity as its object."[46] If an anecdote that spread through Paris was true, Louis XVI asked, when the departing courtier went to take formal leave, "What will Washington think when he learns that you have become Mesmer's chief apothecary?"[47] The anecdote did not record Lafayette's reply.

Accompanied by the young Chevalier de Caraman, Lafayette left Paris around June 18. A British diplomat saw him shortly before he went, and still worried about Ireland, reported to London that Lafayette was very reserved about his plans. He was leaving "for no apparent reason, and therefore in the circumstances of this case, suspiciously."[48] The two young men were in Lorient on June 23, waiting for a favorable wind to take them out of the harbor. Lafayette bustled around among local officials and merchants, polling their attitude on the complete freedom of the port, and sent an account of their views to the ministry, generously discounting those that disagreed with him.[49] He kept Adrienne informed of his delays by unfavorable winds, and she in turn informed Franklin.[50] He also wrote to

45. Girodie, p. 54. Cf. Washington to Mlle de Lafayette, Nov. 25, 1784, Fitzpatrick, XVII, 497-98.

46. Mesmer to Washington, June 16, 1784, LC, Washington papers. Cf. Washington to Mesmer, Nov. 25, Fitzpatrick, XXVII, 498.

47. Maurice Tourneux (ed.), *Correspondance littéraire, philosophique et critique par Grimm, Diderot, Raynal, Meister,* etc. (Paris, 1877-82), XIV, 25 n.; and Allonville, I, 101.

48. David Hartley to the Marquis of Carmarthen, Jan. 9, 1785, Clements Library.

49. To [Calonne], Feb. [error for June] 25, 1784, collection of H. E. Gillingham, Germantown, Pa. Cf. Lafayette to Vergennes, June 28, AAE, corr. pol., É.-U., Vol. XXVII, fol. 475.

50. Mme de Lafayette to Franklin, June 28, 1784, APS, Franklin papers, Vol. XXXII, Part 1, No. 33.

Littlepage, promising to do what he could, when he reached Virginia, to unravel that young man's tangled affairs.[51]

While Lafayette was still in Lorient, he learned that the Society of the Cincinnati had eliminated the inheritance of membership in their order. With an ill-concealed sense of personal satisfaction, he sent John Adams a copy of the new regulations. "My principles have ever been against heredity," he declared quite truthfully, even if he had been careful not to make public declarations in Europe to that effect. "In every circumstance, my dear Sir, depend upon it, you will find me what I have ever been, and perhaps with some *éclat*, a warm friend to the army, a still warmer advocate for the cause of liberty; but those two things, when the army is put to the proof you will ever acknowledge to agree with each other."[52]

On June 28, 1784, the "Courrier de l'Europe," one of a line of packets recently created by the French government, lifted anchor and spread her sails. Lafayette's last message went to Vergennes. "The ship that carries us is very pretty, but," he lamented, "I shall be well shaken up in it and quite sick." He was consoled by the thought that during his stay in America, he could serve his country. As, for a third time, he left the shores of France behind to brave the Atlantic in a wooden sailing vessel, he gave vent to his nostalgia in a burst of patriotic fervor: "I shall make haste to come back to my country and my friends. That is a feeling that becomes stronger the more one travels, but it can grow no greater in my heart. Although the desire to be useful or to prepare myself to become so often makes me run around, I shall always be unhappy to leave, always overwhelmed with joy on again beholding my country."[53]

BIBLIOGRAPHICAL NOTES

The story of Lafayette's relations with Mesmer is given in Helmut Hirsch, "Mesmerism and Revolutionary America" *American-German review*, X (October, 1943), 11–14, though with some exaggeration perhaps of the

51. Cf. Littlepage to Benjamin Lewis, July 10, 1784, H. E. Hayden, *Virginia genealogies: a genealogy of the Glassell family of Scotland and Virginia* (Wilkes-Barre, Pa., 1891), pp. 406–7.
52. Adams, *Works*, VIII, 205–6.
53. Lafayette to Vergennes, June 28, 1784, *loc. cit.*

political implications of mesmerism. There are helpful details in Dr. Augustin Cabanès, *La Princesse de Lamballe intime d'après les confidences de son médecin, etc.* (Paris, [1922]). Franklin's part in the controversy is told in Carl Van Doren's *Benjamin Franklin* (New York, 1938), pp. 713–17.

That some of the Mesmerists under the leadership of Nicolas Bergasse eventually assumed a political role is not incredible. The supposition that Lafayette was associated with Bergasse's liberal society, however, rests on no better testimony than the *Mémoires (1754–1793)* of J.-P. Brissot (ed. Claude Perroud [Paris, 1911], II, 54). It is highly doubtful. Brissot did not know Lafayette at this time, and he does not claim to have been a member of the Bergasse group himself. His memoirs give, only at second hand and at a time when he was unfriendly to Lafayette, a summary of a conversation (or conversations) with Bergasse. Although Lafayette was a Mesmerist and knew Bergasse, no other evidence is available to confirm Brissot (or Bergasse, as the case may be). Brissot's testimony on the same page about "another society" is, however, more reliable because his testimony there is first hand. See below, pp. 380–81.

CHAPTER VII

Ambassador of Good Will

O N THE surface the third voyage of the Marquis de Lafayette to America seemed nothing more than a private affair—a sentimental journey of a young veteran
to the scenes of his triumphs and the firesides of his companions-in-arms. But Lafayette was no ordinary tourist. He was a
general in both the French and the American armies. He was an
intimate of the French ministers and the leading American
statesmen. He was the outstanding unofficial champion of closer
Franco-American ties at a time when it was doubtful whether
the new American nation would choose to guide its destiny by
the English or by the French star. Vergennes and Castries were
too wise in the ways of international politics not to recognize
that, though without credentials of any kind, the marquis was
the best ambassador of good will that France could send to
America. Even if they had failed to perceive the full advantage
to be derived from his popularity, others would have reminded
them of it. When the English government, hoping to reinforce
its spiritual hold upon its former colonies, permitted the Church
of England to continue to ordain American Anglicans, Admiral
d'Estaing counted upon the romantic appeal of France's young
missionary to America to counterbalance that shrewd maneuver. "The Marquis de La Fayette is certainly as good an apostle
as the bishop of London," he wrote to Castries.[1] Vergennes's and
Castries's subordinates in America were to show that they were
no less astute than Estaing.

The "Courrier de l'Europe" was one of the finest vessels of
her day engaged in transatlantic commerce. But even the larg-

1. Aug. 19, 1784, Contenson, *Société des Cincinnati*, p. 68.

est vessels were but frail craft before steel and steam took the horror out of ocean travel. For thirty-five days the "Courrier" was buffeted by wind and wave. Lafayette, always a poor sailor, suffered as only landlubbers can until he got his sea legs. For his companion Harmar, however, the trip was "a fine passage."[2]

When nausea had passed, monotony, unrelieved even by storm, set in. A single untoward event made the voyage memorable and turned out to be to the greater glory of animal magnetism. One of the cabin boys of the "Courrier" fell off a rope and, as Lafayette reported the incident, "was killed." But Mesmer's devout disciple, applying the methods of the master, "cured him." When the marquis wrote his friend the Prince de Poix about it, he was as concise and matter of fact as if he were relating something less than a miracle.[3]

The "Courrier" reached New York on the evening of August 4, but Lafayette waited until morning to announce his arrival. His friends were surprised to see him, since no one in New York knew that he was coming. The closest he had ever been to New York City before was on wishful reconnaissance from the other side of the Hudson, for the British had held it firm against all his schemes on his earlier visits to America. Many of his old companions had now returned there to live, and as the word spread that "the Marquis" had returned, soldiers and citizens alike came to his lodgings to greet him. That evening a banquet was given in his honor attended by St. John de Crèvecœur, the French consul, and veteran officers in full uniform. It was something like a meeting of the New York Cincinnati. Lafayette sat at the head of a table of one hundred covers, Crèvecœur reported, while "the flag of America, unfurled on the roof of the house, heralded, as it waved in the breeze, the joy in our hearts as well as the solemnity of the occasion that was being celebrated."[4]

2. Charles Thomson to Franklin, Aug. 13, 1784, Burnett, VIII, 856. Cf. Lafayette to Poix, Aug. 13, privately communicated; Lafayette to Vergennes, Aug. 13, AAE, corr. pol., É.-U., Vol. XXVIII, fol. 135; D. E. C. Branchi (translator), "Memoirs of Philip Mazzei," *William and Mary College quarterly historical magazine*, 2d ser., X (1929), 259 n.

3. Lafayette to Poix, Aug. 13, 1784, privately communicated.

4. St. John de Crèvecœur, *Lettres d'un cultivateur américain adressées à Wm. S...on esqr depuis l'année 1770 jusqu'en 1786* (Paris, 1787), III, 317-18. Cf. Baron de Beelen-

Thus Lafayette at last captured New York. General Horatio Gates, whom he had once suspected of being an enemy of Washington (and therefore his own enemy), was much impressed with him. Gates recognized the political implications of Lafayette's visit. "The Marquis has an old head upon young shoulders," he wrote Franklin, "and if he steers clear of our paltry parties, may do us, and France, much good."[5] The welcome visitor spent a day or two examining the city's defenses, which had so long defied the American besiegers. Then he moved on to Philadelphia. Caraman, who had struck at least one American lady as being "a beautiful chevalier,"[6] was still with him.

On August 7 the two travelers were in New Jersey. They stopped at Jones's Tavern, from which Lafayette sent his old acquaintance Samuel Adams his apology for not having gone first to Boston. He expressed his joy at being on the "heartly beloved shores" of America in a time of peace. "Those houses I saw burning I now see to have been rebuilt and the poole of liberty [i.e., liberty pole] now stands in every spot upon a firm, and I hope ever lasting foundation."[7]

Two days later Lafayette and Caraman were in Philadelphia. The news of their arrival had preceded them, and ten miles out of town they were met by a number of old officers of the American army and the Pennsylvania militia, the City Troop of Horse, and some civilians—Robert Morris among them. From the moment of Lafayette's entry until the unheard-of hour of ten o'clock, the church bells rang. The streets and neighboring doors and windows filled with people who strained to see him and cheered as he passed by. Still accompanied by fellow-officers, he went to call on President John Dickinson of Pennsylvania, who delivered a formal address to commemorate the occasion. The procession then moved to the city's finest hostelry, the City Tavern, where Lafayette had first met Washington in

Bertholff to Comte Barbiano de Belgiojoso, Aug. 12, 1784, *American historical review*, XVI (1911), 569. Lafayette's letter to the Cincinnati, [Aug. 5, 1784?] (Hume, *Lafayette and the Society of the Cincinnati*, pp. 32–33), probably is to the guests on this occasion.

5. Aug. 16, 1784, APS, Franklin papers, Vol. XXXII, Part 1, No. 83.

6. Eliza Livingston to Francisco de Miranda, Aug. 8, 1784, *Archivo del General Miranda*, XIII, *Revolución francesa* (Caracas, 1931), 202.

7. Aug. 7, 1784, NYPL, Bancroft collection.

1777. There they dined and, as veterans will, exchanged recollections of the war. When it grew dark, lights appeared in all the windows to keep the city gay.[8]

In his anxiety to be on his way to Mount Vernon, Lafayette had planned to spend only two days in Philadelphia,[9] but the hospitality of the city would allow no such unseemly haste. On the day after his arrival the officers of the Pennsylvania Line, which had served with him in the Virginia campaign, paid their respects. A committee consisting of Generals Arthur St. Clair, Anthony Wayne, and William Irvine waited on him with an address—ponderous for all its brevity—honoring one who, when freedom was "destitute of foreign friends," had generously stepped forth as the advocate of America's rights. Lafayette answered with a lighter touch, recalling the glorious part of the Pennsylvania Line in the Yorktown campaign. The next day he had a "long conversation" with Robert Morris on the situation of American affairs.[10] He must have learned from the superintendent of finance much that confirmed his worst fears about the precarious state of the Union.

The next afternoon the Pennsylvania legislature sent a committee to bid him welcome on behalf of the state. Again Lafayette listened to his praises—this time as "chief" among the "distinguished characters whose zeal in our cause drew them from their native country and connections to partake with us the toils and hazards of the arduous conflict."[11] In his reply Lafayette did not content himself merely with clichés about the blessings of peace. He openly pleaded for "the federal union" which, "as it supports the national consequence and, of course, the commercial wealth of America, as it cherishes that sacred friendship between the states which is so necessary, will show to the greatest advantage the blessings of a free government."[12]

8. *The Pennsylvania Packet or the General Advertiser*, Aug. 16, 1784; Thomson to Franklin, Aug. 13, Burnett, VIII, 857; J. Thomas Scharf and Thompson Westcott, *History of Philadelphia* (Philadelphia, 1884), I, 437; *Minutes of the Supreme Executive Council of Pennsylvania, Pennsylvania colonial records*, XIV (Harrisburg, 1853), 176; Robert Morris' diary, Aug. 9, LC, Morris papers.

9. Lafayette to Washington, Aug. [10], 1784, Gottschalk, *Letters*, pp. 284-85.

10. Morris' diary, Aug. 11, 1784, *loc. cit.*

11. *Pennsylvania Gazette*, Aug. 18, 1784. Cf. *Mémoires*, II, 98.

12. *Maryland Gazette*, Aug. 26, 1784.

That day, too, Lafayette visited Barbé-Marbois, who was acting as French chargé d'affaires in America.[13] A few months earlier Marbois had quarreled with an erratic Frenchman named Longchamps and had been caned. The episode had by this time assumed international proportions because the French legation wished to have Longchamps extradited for trial, while the culprit, claiming Pennsylvania citizenship, refused to recognize the authority of the French government. Thus arose a dispute over extradition and the privileges of foreign diplomatic agents in the United States. To Lafayette this strain in Franco-American relations, having developed only after he had left France on his self-appointed mission of good will, was doubly embarrassing. For the time being he preferred not to mention it. He wrote the governor of Pennsylvania that day, to be sure, but only to thank the state for having given one of its western counties the name "Fayette" (of which he had learned only as he was leaving France). It made him proud and happy, he said, to know that thenceforth his name would be united with "this commonwealth, her civil as well as political liberties," which were dear to his heart and "whose spirit is so favorable to the rights of mankind."[14]

To complete the day's activities, a special meeting of the American Philosophical Society was called on Lafayette's request. Twenty-two members—an extraordinarily large attendance—listened while Lafayette set forth "the wonderful effects of a certain invisible power in nature called *animal magnetism.*" He told them of the miraculous cure he had effected on board the "Courrier de l'Europe." "Persons may be so impregnated with this power," Lafayette explained, "as to exhibit many phenomena similar to those of metallic magnetism." He did not, however, think himself at liberty to describe the process more fully (though he did not explicitly mention his contract with Dr. Mesmer).[15]

13. Hugues Montbas, *Avec Lafayette chez les Iroquois* (Paris, 1929), p. 28.
14. *Maryland Gazette*, Aug. 26, 1784.
15. *Early proceedings of the American Philosophical Society*, pp. 126–27. Cf. Thomson to Jefferson, Mar. 6, 1785, E. A. Duyckinck (ed.), "The Thomson papers, 1765–1816," *New York Historical Society collections for the year 1878*, XI (New York, 1879), 198–99.

The next day the well-pleased traveler wrote to his friends in France to tell of his warm reception by a grateful republic. He was delighted to discover how quickly the country had risen from its ruins and how enterprising were citizens who had once been soldiers.[16] Then, after submitting the latest letters of Calonne and Castries for Morris' examination,[17] he started off for Mount Vernon. Marbois reported home that the marquis's reception had surpassed anything of the kind that had ever occurred during the war. "Not even for General Washington was more done."[18]

Urged on by his eagerness to see Washington, Lafayette arrived in Baltimore late on August 14. Two days of festivity there, and he was on his way once more, promising to return by September.[19] He reached Mount Vernon on August 17. This was his first meeting with his "adoptive father" after a separation of three years. No witness has left a description of their reunion, but the younger man's frequent and unabashed protestations of affection and his "beloved General's" more reticent but gratified acceptance of them suggest a picture of talkative effervescence on Lafayette's side and of quiet pleasure on Washington's.

The next ten days were spent in receiving visitors, chatting with and about mutual friends, writing to absent companions-in-arms, and drinking to their health at friendly dinners.[20] "Never was General Washington so great," Lafayette wrote to Poix, "as in the simplicity of his retirement." He and the general spent "very sweet hours" together "speaking of the past and the present, and talking a bit of politics about the future."[21]

16. Lafayette to Vergennes, Aug. 13, 1784, *loc. cit.*; to Poix, Aug. 3, privately communicated.

17. Lafayette to Morris, Aug. 14, 1784, [Weaver], *Diplomatic correspondence*, I, 405. This letter is dated from Philadelphia. If it is not misdated, it shows that Lafayette left Philadelphia on August 14, though other sources reported that he had done so on the 13th; cf. Thomson to Franklin, Aug. 13, Burnett, VIII, 857; and *Maryland Gazette*, Aug. 26.

18. To Vergennes, Aug. 15, 1784, AAE, corr. pol., É.-U., Vol. XXVIII, fols. 142–43.

19. *Maryland Gazette*, Aug. 26, 1784; McHenry to Franklin, Aug. 24, APS, Franklin papers, Vol. XXXII, No. 89.

20. Washington to Rochambeau, to Chastellux, and to Duportail, Aug. 20, 1784, Fitzpatrick, XXVII, 458–61; Lafayette to Greene, Aug. 25, American Art Association, catalogue 4217, sale of Jan. 8–9, 1936, No. 242. Lafayette to the Chevalier d'Anterroches, Mount Vernon, Aug. 15 (*sic*), Harvard College Library, is apparently dated in error; Aug. 19 was probably meant.

21. Lafayette to Poix, Aug. 20, 1784, privately communicated.

They discussed the problem of settling the west against the opposition of the Indians. Washington favored purchasing the Indians' land and treating them kindly, but there were some who preferred a more ruthless policy.[22] The "beloved General," contemplating a visit to his western lands, wanted Lafayette and Caraman to go with him. But the marquis, remembering his promises to return to the east and to visit New England, resisted the temptation. Once at least, Washington and his two French guests went to Alexandria to be entertained by the gentlemen of the town at Lomax's Tavern. "Maurice [Caraman] claims that the general and I got a little tipsy at Alexandria, but," Lafayette jested, "that's an abominable slander."[23]

Washington's proposed trip to his western lands cut short the Frenchmen's visit. On August 28 they began their journey back to Baltimore. The leave-taking was not solemn since it was agreed that they would all meet again at Mount Vernon in the fall. On August 31 Lafayette was at Annapolis and the next day reached Baltimore.[24]

In Baltimore he was again feted. An address from the leading citizens of the city stressed his services to Baltimore during the war and his recent efforts to promote freedom of trade between the United States and France. Lafayette's reply was a modest disclaimer of all merit on his part, a graceful reference to the courage of Baltimoreans in the face of the enemy, and a promise to continue his championing of commerce. The recent Irish immigrants to the city also sent him a declaration of their gratitude for his defense of "an injured people." Lafayette's response indicated that he had not forgotten Ireland's special interest in American success: "In the cause of oppressed humanity, all good men sympathize, and happy are they when they can unite their efforts. . . . But in the approbation of the sons of Ireland, every admirer of true honor, liberal patriotism, and national virtue must find a peculiar delight." Afterward, upon sending a

22. Cf. Lafayette to Washington, Oct. 8, 1784, Gottschalk, Letters, p. 286. Cf. Washington to James Duane, Sept. 7, 1783, Fitzpatrick, XXVII, 133-40, and to Jacob Read, Nov. 23, 1784, ibid., pp. 485-90.

23. To Poix, Sept. 15, 1784, privately communicated. Cf. Pennsylvania Gazette, Sept. 8, 1784.

24. Madison to Jefferson, Sept. 7, 1784, Gaillard Hunt (ed.), Writings of James Madison (New York, 1900-1908), II, 77; Maryland Gazette, Sept. 2, 1784.

copy of his address to the French foreign office, he indicated—probably with tongue in cheek—that he had raised no international issue since he had spoken to the Irishmen of Baltimore only as citizens of America.[25] That evening he graced a banquet at Grant's Tavern, which was followed by a ball at the City Hall. Three hundred notables of Baltimore and its environs crowded into the ballroom to honor the illustrious guest.[26]

The next day Lafayette "fell in with" James Madison, formerly a member of Congress and a leading citizen of Virginia. Having just embarked upon a tour of the northern states, Madison also happened to be in Baltimore on his way to Philadelphia.[27] He was so much exercised at the time over the dispute concerning the Mississippi River that it is hard to believe his meeting with Lafayette was entirely accidental. The marquis was a prominent figure in that dispute. When he had visited Madrid in 1782, he had elicited certain promises to the United States from Floridablanca, the Spanish minister. Despite those promises the Spanish had recently taken advantage of their position on the Mississippi to make difficulties for American shippers.

Madison exploited the time that he and the marquis traveled together to present the American side of the controversy. Both France and Spain, he argued, had advantages to derive from a friendly American trade down the Mississippi. But if Spain continued to be intractable, a rupture was certain. France must therefore use "every engine" to divert Spain. Otherwise, France as Spain's ally would likewise incur American displeasure, for the Americans would throw themselves into the arms of the English. Lafayette did not need to be persuaded. He promised to write to Vergennes on the subject and to let Madison see what he wrote. He felt, however, that Spain would prove stubborn about opening the Mississippi.[28]

Madison and Lafayette, still accompanied by Caraman,

25. Oct. 12, 1784, AAE, corr. pol., É.-U., Vol. XXVIII, fol. 318.
26. Crèvecœur, III, 326–30; *Pennsylvania Gazette*, Sept. 8, 1784; J. Thomas Scharf, *The chronicles of Baltimore* (Baltimore, 1874), pp. 236–38.
27. Madison to James Madison, Sr., Sept. 6, 1784, Hunt, II, 76; to Jefferson, Sept. 7, *ibid.*, p. 77.
28. Madison to Jefferson, Sept. 7, 1784, *ibid.*, p. 78.

reached Philadelphia on September 4. Congress was not in session, and the Committee of States which replaced it in the interval could not even boast a quorum. The marquis let it be known that, in his opinion, the ineffectiveness of the central government would harm America's prestige in Europe.[29] Still he did not lack attention. "Wherever he passes," Madison noted, "he receives the most flattering tokens of sincere affection from all ranks."[30] If Madison had stopped to reflect, he would perhaps have discerned that the very weakness of the American confederation accounted in part for the warmth shown to Lafayette at every hand. The marquis was the most prominent figure of the American Revolution who belonged to no state and had no regional loyalty within the Union. By his very foreignness, he belonged equally to the whole nation—a symbol of the co-operation that had once meant strength and victory and was now so sadly lacking.

Lafayette visited Madison again while they were in Philadelphia. He found him writing to Thomas Jefferson about their conversations during their journey from Baltimore. Although Madison was secretive enough to write in cipher concerning the Mississippi question, Lafayette asked pointed questions. Madison admitted that he was writing to Jefferson and let his visitor guess, without being explicit, what he was writing about.[31]

In Philadelphia, Lafayette stopped at Barbé-Marbois's quarters,[32] and the French chargé d'affaires probably had something to do with his decision to include in his tour a visit to the Indians of New York.[33] A powwow was to take place at Fort

29. Jacob Read to Benjamin Guerard, Sept. 9, 1784, Burnett, VII, 589.
30. Madison to Jefferson, Sept. 7, 1784, Hunt, II, 77. Lafayette probably sat on September 7 for a portrait by Charles Willson Peale (see Peale to Paca, Sept. 7, 1784, C. C. Sellers, *The artist of the Revolution, the early life of Charles Willson Peale* [Hebron, Conn., 1939], p. 235). See also p. 108 below.
31. Madison to Jefferson, Sept. 7, 1784, Hunt, II, 79.
32. Beelen to Belgiojoso, Nov. 14, 1784, Hanns Schlitter (ed.), *Die Berichte des ersten Agenten Österreichs in den Vereinigten Staaten von Amerika Baron de Beelen-Bertholff an die Regierung des österreichischen Niederlande in Brüssel, 1784–1789* ("Fontes rerum austriacarum," Vol. XLV [Vienna, 1891]), p. 339.
33. Madison to Madison, Sr., and to Jefferson, Sept. 6 and 7, 1784, Hunt, II, 76–86; Lafayette to the Indian commissioners, Sept. 30, Harvard College Library, Lee papers, Vol. VIII. Lafayette wrote Jay (Nov. 25, PCC 156, Vol. II, fol. 396) that the idea came to him only on passing through New York, but the decision was obviously made earlier.

Schuyler (until recently called Fort Stanwix), where a treaty of peace was to be made between the United States and the Indian allies of England. Since this was to be the first formal understanding between the new republic and its Indian neighbors, it was a great event. Much of the future development of the two American peoples was to hinge upon it, and England's imperial policy would have to be adjusted accordingly. Lafayette, remembering his conversations on the Indian problem with Washington, wished to attend. His presence was likely to prove useful, he believed, and so he undertook to meet the American commissioners there. He urged Madison to go with him. Although Madison had not intended to journey so far west, he promised to go to New York City anyway and there decide on his further course.

The three companions arrived in Trenton on September 10 and in New York on the 11th. For over a week New York had been preparing for Lafayette's return. The gentlemen of the city had planned parties and dinners so earnestly as to make the ladies resentful that they were "not *permitted* to join and discover *their joy* on the occation of his again returning."[34] The ladies were not to be entirely disappointed, however. Lafayette stayed in New York four crowded days, and again Madison was impressed by the "cordial esteem and affection" of gentlemen and ladies, old and young alike, that everywhere greeted the marquis.[35]

On the day after his arrival the Common Council of the city ordered that a "respectful address" be presented to Lafayette (along with Washington, Jay, Governor George Clinton, and General Friedrich von Steuben) with the "freedom of the city" in a golden box.[36] Lafayette's old friend Alexander Hamilton undertook to find out how the presentation should be addressed and reported that the salutation that would best answer the purpose was "The Right Honorable the Marquis De la Fayette

34. Susan Livingston to Miranda, Sept. 3, 1784, *Archivo del General Miranda*, XIII, 204.
35. To Jefferson, Sept. 15, 1784, *Letters and other writings of James Madison, fourth president of the United States* (Philadelphia, 1867), I, 101.
36. A. E. Peterson (ed.), *Minutes of the Common Council of the City of New York 1784–1831* (New York, 1917), I, 73.

Maréchal de camp of the armies of His Most Christian Majesty and Major General in the service of the United States."[37] If that seemed rather an ornate title for one who was to be honored "by the affections of a free people," it might easily have been made more ornate and under similar circumstances in France probably would have been.[38]

While waiting for the formal presentation to take place, other personages kept the city's guest occupied. On September 13 the Revolutionary officers, with General Alexander McDougall at their head, regaled their noble comrade at Cape's Tavern, where the noise of clinking glasses was drowned out by the roar of cannon. On the 14th he was called upon to befriend a worthy countryman who had arrived in New York shipwrecked and almost penniless.[39] The certificate designating Lafayette "a freeman and citizen of the City of New York" was presented that evening at a big banquet, which was attended by the most respectable of the city's twenty-three thousand inhabitants. Mayor James Duane read an elegant address, which the council had previously approved, praising the marquis's sacrifices for the cause of liberty. The marquis replied with equal elegance. The dinner lasted until nine o'clock. On the next day Lafayette's acceptance of the "new tie that connects me with this city" was duly entered in the minutes of the Common Council.[40]

Thus New York City set the example, which other American municipalities were soon to follow, of making Lafayette a citizen by a special act of naturalization. He enjoyed it all immensely—particularly because, as he wrote to his crony Poix, "The English here make long faces at our gatherings, and the racket with

37. Hamilton to Richard Varick, Sept. 12, 1784, Mercantile Library (New York).

38. *Minutes of the Common Council*, I, 74. Cf. M. A. Prudhomme (ed.), *Collection des inventaires sommaires des archives communales antérieures à 1790: Isère, Villa de Grenoble*, Part 4 (Grenoble, 1924), G G 113, where Lafayette's title is given on a baptismal record as godfather (by proxy). It includes "Chevalier de Saint Louis et de l'Ordre de Cincinnatus."

39. Lafayette to Washington, Sept. 14, 1784, Gottschalk, *Letters*, p. 285 (on behalf of D.-J.-A. Duché [or Ducher], later employed in the French consular service in the United States).

40. *Minutes of the Common Council*, I, 73–77. Cf. Crèvecœur, III, 332. E. Y. Smith ("Lafayette was given the freedom of the city of New York in 1784," *Gazette of the American Friends of Lafayette*, No. 4 [August, 1944]) thinks Lafayette called personally on the Common Council on September 15; *Minutes of the Common Council*, I, 76–77, imply that he did not.

which the city resounded yesterday and the day before yesterday must have been a scarcely agreeable celebration for them."[41] Altogether Lafayette did not take these ceremonies too seriously, much though he enjoyed the acclaim they won for him and useful though he believed them to be for the friendly relations of France and the United States. "As far as a private person can," he explained to Vergennes, "I try to discover and serve my country's interests here. The City of New York has presented me with *the freedom of the city*—a compliment *à l'anglaise* which I first assured myself was of no consequence."[42]

Madison, like Lafayette, looked upon all these demonstrations of cordiality as improving the bonds that tied the United States to France. He hoped that they might become as widely known in France as in America[43] and was pleased when at last the marquis found time to keep his promise to write to Vergennes on the Mississippi question. That letter proved a somewhat delicate one for an ambassador of good will to compose. The United States was at the moment in no position to ask favors of the French government since it was standing on its dignity in the Longchamps affair. No word had yet been received in America indicating how the French foreign office would react in the matter, but it could safely be assumed that they would support the position taken by the French legation in Philadelphia. Lafayette was particularly embarrassed because Longchamps claimed to be a protégé of the Noailles family. "I wish the devil had carried him off six months ago," he protested privately.[44] But to Vergennes he contented himself with assurances of the "indignation and good will" of the Pennsylvania authorities. The incident was to drag on until Marbois himself interceded to win a pardon for his assailant, who meanwhile remained in jail.

Lafayette needed no better reminder than the Longchamps fiasco of the confederation's inadequacy in dealing with even the most trivial international problems. Briefly apologizing for the insult to France's representative, his letter to Vergennes hastened on to deal with commerce. He rejoiced that the falling-off

41. Sept. 15, 1784, privately communicated.
42. Sept. 15, 1784, AE, corr. pol., É.-U., Vol. XXVIII, fol. 201.
43. To Jefferson, Sept. 15, 1784, *Letters and other writings of Madison*, I, 101–2.
44. Lafayette to Poix, Sept. 15, 1784, privately communicated.

of English credits to American merchants would lead to more trade with France. But, he pointed out, French trade could reach inland America only along the rivers, the most important of which was the Mississippi. Interference with that trade by Spain would lead to disputes. "The Americans love us," he warned, "but they hate Spain very heartily."[45] He showed Madison this part of his letter and promised to write at greater length on the subject in his next one.[46]

Madison had meanwhile decided to go to the Indian powwow with Lafayette and Caraman. A warm friendship had grown up among them.

BIBLIOGRAPHICAL NOTES

Mitchell's biography of Crèvecœur gives many significant details not otherwise easily available about the relations of Lafayette and Crèvecœur. Crèvecœur's own account of Lafayette's American tour in 1784 is highly inaccurate, especially as to chronology. J. A. Stevens ("Visit of Lafayette to the United States in 1784," *Magazine of American history*, II [1878], 724-33) and J. B. Nolan (*Lafayette in America day by day* [Baltimore, 1934]) have sometimes been led astray by his inaccuracies but are usually helpful guides in determining Lafayette's itinerary. Crèvecœur must be corrected by the numerous newspaper accounts (which, however, generally copied from each other) and by contemporary correspondence.

Local histories, like that of Baltimore by Scharf, are too prone to accept local tradition as fact but can be helpful if used critically. J. B. Nolan in "Lafayette in Pennsylvania" (*Pennsylvania history*, I [1934], 135-46) and in "Lafayette and the American Philosophical Society" (*Proceedings of the American Philosophical Society*, XXIII [1934], 117-26) has told the relevant parts of this story well, though he is mistaken about the alleged coolness of Lafayette's reception in New York.

45. Sept. 15, 1784, AAE, corr. pol., É.-U., Vol. XXVIII, fol. 201. The references to the Longchamps affair are omitted in the version given in *Mémoires*, II, 107-8 .

46. Madison to Jefferson, Sept. 15, 1784, *Letters and other writings of Madison*, I, 101-2.

CHAPTER VIII

Indian Powwow

THE commissioners appointed by Congress to make peace with the Indians were Arthur Lee, Richard Butler, and General Oliver Wolcott. When they were named, a new interest in Indian affairs was precipitated. The state of New York announced its intention of forcing the issue of the frontier posts that England had not yet evacuated, since two of them (Forts Oswego and Niagara) were located in the Indian territories of New York. Thus the meeting at Fort Schuyler could be expected to become something more than an ordinary powwow. Besides the Indian problem, the relations of the American confederation with its member-states and with the British Empire would be called into question. In fact, the commissioners of New York, disregarding the claims of the confederation, reached a separate understanding with the Indians at Fort Schuyler even before the federal commissioners arrived.

The English also showed a lively concern with what was happening. The possible presence of Lafayette at the meeting disturbed them for the very reasons that it pleased the Americans. "I know the character of the Marquis to be enterprising," the governor of Canada wrote,[1] apprehensive of an attack upon the frontier forts. The British were right to fear Lafayette, and not merely because he was enterprising. He was bound to have more influence than the American commissioners. France was universally respected by the Indians, who still called the French their "fathers," and Lafayette was living testimony that the alliance

[1]. Sir Frederick Haldimand to Lord Sidney, Oct. 24, 1784, Public Record Office (London), Colonial Office 42/46, fol. 523; cf. fol. 472 (Oct. 2, 1784) and Madison to Jefferson, Oct. 17, Hunt, II, 83-84.

of his country with the United States was sincere and lasting. Furthermore, his own personal prestige among them was great. He had been adopted into the Iroquois tribe in 1778 and had been given the name of Kayewla after one of their great warriors. As Kayewla he was a symbol of the continued friendliness of the French king to his "children." No one else was French, American, and Indian at the same time.

Lafayette, Madison, and Caraman had intended to leave New York for Fort Schuyler on September 15, 1784, but were delayed. Two days behind schedule, they began tediously to move up the Hudson in a barge. Contrary winds kept them from reaching Albany before September 23,[2] but Lafayette's fears that they might be too late proved unfounded, for only one of the commissioners of Congress had arrived in Albany. Just as they reached that town, however, Marbois overtook them[3] and was soon prompted by curiosity and official interest to accompany them to the conference.

The commissioner whom Lafayette found in Albany was General Wolcott. It was his opinion that Kayewla's influence with the Indians was important to the success of the negotiations, and Lafayette decided to go on to Fort Schuyler ahead of the commissioners.[4] On the way his party stopped to visit the Shaker mother-community at Niskayuna near Watervliet. They reached Niskayuna on Sunday (September 26) and attended church services. The French chargé saw in the Shakers only a curious sect who expressed their religious fervor through physical agitation resembling convulsions and who believed that they could cure illness and pain by faith. But to Lafayette they furnished a possible example of the workings of animal magnetism, particularly since they healed disease by laying-on of hands. He tried to "mesmerize" one of the community but was interrupted by an elder who asked whether he acted in the name of a good or a bad spirit. "Certainly in the name of a good spirit," Lafayette

2. Madison to Jefferson, Sept. 15, 1784, *Letters and other writings of Madison*, I, 101; *Connecticut Courant*, Sept. 28, 1784; Lafayette to unknown, Sept. 24, Historical Society of Pennsylvania.

3. Montbas, p. 33; "Extrait du journal d'un voyage chez les sauvages oneidas, tuscororas, etc.," AAE, corr. pol., .É-U., Vol. XXVIII, fols. 204–38.

4. Lafayette to the commissioners, Sept. 30, 1784. Harvard College Library, Lee papers, Vol. VII; Madison to Jefferson, Oct. 17, Hunt, II, 83. See also p. 108 below.

replied. Marbois did not think Lafayette had much success, however. Except that the Shakers were as favorably impressed as Marbois was amused that so fine a gentleman should take them so seriously, nothing came from these new observations of Mesmer's disciple.[5]

The day after the visit to the Shakers, a party consisting of Lafayette, Madison, Marbois, Caraman, and some Indian servants began the trek up the Mohawk Valley. Though the scenery was "superb," the journey proved to be a trying one. The country was spotted with ruined houses and other unmistakable signs of savage warfare. As they advanced farther into the wilderness, houses became fewer and more like fortresses. The standard of living among the white settlers with whom they stopped fell off perceptibly, and sometimes they had to feed their hosts out of their own provisions. The weather grew colder and they had to wear their warmest clothing. They had started out in a huge and unsteady phaeton, but after eighty miles of rough road they abandoned it and went ahead on horseback. Despite five barrels of brandy carried by five tireless Indians (one of whom turned out to be a captive Frenchman and became their interpreter), everyone began to feel miserable except Lafayette, "who," Marbois reported, "appears to be proof against heat, cold, drought, moisture, and the intemperance of the weather." He had made this journey before in a colder season (the winter of 1778) and knew what to expect. He had come prepared with a cloak of gummed taffeta, which had been wrapped in newspapers that stuck to the gumming—with the result, Marbois jested, that one was able to read the latest European journals whenever Lafayette put on his cloak.[6] The party spent two nights in the wilderness, encountering "some bad places, which in the dark might be dangerous," and reached Fort Schuyler on the afternoon of September 29, 1784.[7]

Only a small band of Iroquois and other Indians had remained in the vicinity of the fort after the negotiations with the

5. "Extrait du journal," loc. cit.; Lafayette to Poix, Oct. 12, 1784, privately communicated.
6. "Extrait du journal," loc. cit. Cf. E. P. Chase (ed.), Our Revolutionary forefathers: the letters of François, marquis de Barbé-Marbois (New York, 1929), pp. 185–93.
7. Lafayette to the commissioners, Sept. 30, 1784, loc. cit.

state of New York. They had built themselves bark huts and were waiting patiently for the commissioners of Congress. But Lafayette, packed with his companions into a single hut, was less patient. The visitors soon learned that the Indians were still bitterly divided in their attitude toward the United States. Some called themselves "Whigs" and were friendly, others called themselves "Tories" and were unfriendly. Fights sometimes broke out between the two factions, and the first night's rest of the guests at Fort Schuyler was broken by the noise of battle, the wounded seeking aid at the fortress. Even families were torn asunder, as Marbois discovered from a violent quarrel between two brothers that occurred in his own quarters. Only after the young Indians' father and their wives had interceded would they consent to smoke the pipe of peace.[8]

The commissioners seemed in no hurry to reach Fort Schuyler, although Lafayette was already ten days behind schedule and proposed to leave by October 3, even if the conference were not over by that time. With so small a representation of Indians, Marbois doubted whether a new understanding could be reached in any event before the end of the year. To Lafayette this situation presented a challenge. Dr. Samuel Kirkland, the missionary at the fort, shared Wolcott's opinion that the marquis's presence was indispensable to the success of the negotiations. He tried to induce Lafayette to speak to the Indians who were within reach even though the commissioners had not yet come. These Indians were particularly attached to France and had a strong affection for Kayewla. The English, it appeared, had been spreading the word among them that the alliance between the United States and France, while only temporary, included secret understandings that boded ill for them. Kayewla should use his influence, Kirkland thought, to reassure them. Yet recognizing that he was present only in a private capacity and had no authority to speak either for France or for the United States, Lafayette demurred. He did, however, write a letter to the commissioners, suggesting that probably he should

8. Marbois to Vergennes, Sept. 30, 1784, [J. F. Jameson?], "Marbois on the fur trade, 1784," *American historical review*, XXIX (1924), 729 and 731.

accede to Kirkland's suggestion and requesting instructions as to what he should say.[9]

This letter reached the commissioners when they were only a day or two's travel away from the fort. Wolcott having been detained by illness, only Lee and Butler received it. Lee, who had never been one of the marquis's admirers and had always been suspicious of France, replied. He explained that even after they reached the fort, they would be unable to begin their business until Wolcott arrived, but they would then be happy to furnish Lafayette with an opportunity to address the Indians as he might think proper.[10] This was a patent though polite rejection of Kayewla's good offices.

While this exchange of letters was in progress, however, an awkward predicament had arisen at Fort Schuyler. Discretion demanded that the distinguished Frenchmen should visit the friendly Oneida Indians without delay. Lafayette was thus brought face to face with a problem in etiquette that might easily prove embarrassing. He would be royally entertained by the Oneidas and would be expected to invite their chiefs to Fort Schuyler in return. But if they came to Fort Schuyler, they would probably expect some sort of ceremonial oration from him, and he did not yet know whether the commissioners would approve of his making any kind of speech. In the dilemma he consulted Madison. Madison proposed skirting the issue by a casual, noncommittal invitation that would leave Lafayette free either to make a formal address or to engage in mere courtesies when the chiefs returned his visit. That was what the marquis decided to do.[11]

Late on September 30 Lafayette, accompanied by Marbois and Caraman, arrived at Oneida Castle, about eighteen miles away from Fort Schuyler. One of the Oneida chiefs, named Great Grasshopper, had visited Philadelphia in 1781 and still wore the Bavarian hunting costume that the French minister had given him on that occasion. Another of the company proved to be an Indian who had formerly served Lafayette. They sat

9. *Ibid.*, pp. 728–30; Lafayette to the commissioners, Sept. 30, 1784, *loc. cit.*; Madison to Jefferson, Oct. 17, Hunt, II, 83–84. See also p. 108 below.

10. Commissioners to Lafayette, Oct. 1, 1784, Harvard College Library.

11. Madison to Jefferson, Oct. 17, 1784, Hunt, II, 84.

down to supper, all drinking from wooden goblets except Lafayette, who as guest of honor had a broken glass that had been
mended with gum. Everyone prepared his own food and the
palefaces provided their own table utensils. After dinner, upon
their guests' request the Indians danced, at the same time sing-
ing a monotonous song built upon one word and two notes, accompanied by only a tom-tom. They danced for two hours,
constantly increasing the speed of their movements. Finally the
white visitors became fatigued and asked them to stop. But they
wanted to go on, and the tired guests could go to bed only after
Lafayette's former servant persuaded them to desist.[12] Perceiving in this exhibition a form of animal magnetism, Mesmer's
disciple afterward semijokingly proposed to write an "Essay on
savage dances," to be read to the Union of Harmony.[13]

The next day the marquis's party was ready to return to Fort
Schuyler. They learned, however, that their horses had
"strayed." When they offered a reward, the horses were
"found" within half an hour. They got back to the fort without
further mishap.

Since the commissioners did not all arrive until October 2,
Marbois had a chance to make some interesting anthropological
observations. Despite the suspicious "straying" of horses at the
Oneida Castle, he discovered that animals were generally allowed to roam untethered and that the standard of honesty
among these Indians was admirable. Brawls, too, he gathered,
were quickly mediated, and drunkenness, though frequent,
was easily forgiven. He and his European companions found
living in huts and bathing in cold streams a dismaying though
invigorating experience, but the Indian servants of his party
apparently were less dismayed. Marbois suspected that they
took advantage of the easy marriage and divorce that prevailed
among the Indians to find themselves temporary wives and
domestic comforts. "In general, these children of nature," Marbois concluded, "are not at all what the writers of Europe say
who have never seen them."[14]

12. Chase, pp. 194–98.
13. Lafayette to Poix, Oct. 12, 1784, privately communicated.
14. Chase, pp. 197 and 201–4.

A few "savages" were in fact white men who had gone native. They, as well as some genuine Indians, spoke French, and all, white and red, seemed to have a great regard for France. Lafayette tried to get Peter Otsiquette, the young son of a Frenchman and an Indian squaw, to go to France with him. Although tribal formalities made it difficult to get the consent of all the people whose permission was necessary, he was eventually to succeed; for, as Marbois testified: "Mr. de la Fayette has their confidence and their devotion to an extraordinary degree. Those who have seen him before have a great urge to see him again. They have communicated their enthusiasms to their friends, and they seem proud to wear around their necks some trinket that he once gave them."[15]

Before the commissioners arrived, Lafayette and his party witnessed the reconciliation of the friendly Oneidas with the Senecas, who had supported the English. The Oneida chief, Great Grasshopper, accompanied by five of his braves and still wearing the Bavarian hunting costume that the French minister had once given him, solemnly approached the huts of the Senecas. The chief of the Senecas came out to meet them. They sat down together on the grass, exchanged compliments, smoked a pipe of peace, and then separated. The next day the Senecas visited the Oneidas, and the same ceremony was repeated. "I thought myself at the Diet of Ratisbon," said Marbois.[16]

It is not clear whether Lafayette's presence had anything to do with this first step toward peace. The Indians embarrassed him, however, by attributing to him an importance that far exceeded his actual capacity, since he was only a private person and a foreigner. When Lee's letter arrived clearly implying that he ought to make no oration until the negotiations began, it further embarrassed him. After Lee and Butler themselves arrived, his predicament became still worse. He was now placed definitely in a position where the Indians expected him to take a leading part in the negotiations and the commissioners expected him not to. When he expressed his quandary to the com-

15. "Extrait du journal," *loc. cit.* Cf. John Lincklaen, *Travels in the years 1791 and 1792 in Pennsylvania, New York, and Vermont; journal of John Lincklaen, agent of the Holland Land Company* (New York, 1897), p. 69, and see below, p. 141 and Appendix II.
16. Chase, p. 205.

missioners, they were guarded, appearing to believe it premature to begin any kind of negotiations when neither side was
fully represented. Since Butler was one of his old officers, Lafayette attributed this reluctance to Lee alone, but that explanation did not diminish his embarrassment. Finally, however,
when Wolcott arrived, it was decided that the marquis should
make a formal declaration to the Indians. He wrote it out and
showed it to Marbois in order to make sure that there would be
nothing in it at which the English might take offense. Then it
was submitted to the commissioners, who agreed that he should
pronounce it after first being formally introduced by them.[17]

The next day (October 3) the commissioners called the warriors together in a council. As the weather was cold, they sat
around an open bonfire.[18] Some of the chiefs from Canada and
the Six Nations were there. Four of the Nations (Mohawks,
Cayugas, Onondagas, and Senecas) had been hostile to the
Americans, and two (Oneidas and Tuscaroras) had been friendly. Lafayette suspected some Tory chieftains of still being unwilling to bury the hatchet.[19] France was officially represented
by Marbois and unofficially by Lafayette and Caraman. There
were about forty warriors present, some armed as if for battle,
others dressed in grotesque masquerade.[20]

The meeting began with General Wolcott's request for attention to the remarks of Lafayette. "He is," said the general, "a
great man among the French, one of the head warriors of the
great Onondio [Louis XVI], and as you all know, a general in the
American army and a headman among us, who comes with his
friends to pay you a visit and give you the advice of a father."[21]

17. Lafayette to Vergennes, Oct. 12, 1784, AAE, corr. pol., É.-U., Vol. XXVIII,
fol. 317; Madison to Jefferson, Oct. 17, Hunt, II, 84–85. See also p. 108 below.
18. Chase, pp. 214–15; "Diary of Griffith Evans," Henry E. Huntington Library
and Art Gallery, San Marino, Calif., MSS, under date of Oct. 3.
19. Lafayette to Washington, Oct. 8, 1784, Gottschalk, *Letters*, p. 286; Auguste
Levasseur, *Lafayette in America in 1824 and 1825; or, journal of a voyage to the United
States*, trans. J. D. Godman (Philadelphia, 1829), II, 187.
20. Montbas, p. 96.
21. N. B. Craig (ed.), *The olden time; a monthly publication devoted to the preservation of documents and other authentic information in relation to the early explorations and
the settlement and improvement of the country around the head of the Ohio* (Pittsburgh,
1846–48), II, 407; cf. Marbois to Vergennes, Oct. [4?], 1784, AAE, corr. pol., É.-U.,
Vol. XXVIII, fols. 322–26.

Then Lafayette "with grace and nobility"[22] addressed the Indians in French as they sat around the fire and smoked their pipes. His words were interpreted by Dr. Kirkland. The marquis reminded them of his previous appearance among them. He had at that time warned them to remain at least neutral in the conflicts of the white men. The Americans would defend their liberty, he had told them, and "the great Onondio like the sun would clear away the clouds." Those who had advised them otherwise had been greviously mistaken. Now they must listen to him again. They must stay out of the quarrels of Europeans. "Be wiser than the white men, keep peace among you." The alliance of the Americans and the French would certainly last, and the Indians ought to join it, giving their lands not to the first comer for a barrel of rum but to the Americans on reasonable terms.[23]

Thereupon a chief of the Mohawks arose and, addressing the twenty-seven-year-old Kayewla, chief of the great Onondio, as "my father," admitted that Lafayette had been right. The Indians hoped to play a better role in the future than they had played in the past. Kayewla's word would therefore be spread throughout the Six Nations, and they would meet on the morrow to give him their answer.

Accordingly the assembly dispersed to meet again the next day. Great Grasshopper, speaking for the friendly tribes, opened the meeting on October 4 with an expression of gratitude for Lafayette's good advice. They remembered, he said, that Kayewla had warned them against the British seven years earlier. His words had all come true, and they would heed his new message with pleasure. He gave Lafayette as a token of friendship a wampum belt that he had long ago received from the great French soldier Montcalm. Politely returning the belt, Lafayette replied that he was glad that it had been preserved. France, he said, would always be ready to hold one end of it while the Americans held the other, thus binding together "the

22. Montbas, p. 96.
23. A translation of this speech certified by Lafayette is given in *Olden time*, II, 428–29, and *Pennsylvania magazine of history*, XIV (1890), 319–20, but the above version is based upon "Relation de ce qui s'est passé à l'ouverture du traité entre les États-Unis et les nations sauvages au Fort Stanwix, le 3 et 4 octobre 1784," AAE, corr. pol., É.-U., Vol. XXVIII, fols. 290–93. See also "Diary of Griffith Evans," *loc. cit.*

French and their children." They must all close their ears hence-forth to mutual enemies.

A Huron chief next arose to speak for the unfriendly tribes. They had received word from the governor of Canada, he said, that the war was over and they must make peace. Following him came a Seneca chief. Also addressing Lafayette as "my father," he likewise recalled Kayewla's predictions of seven years before: "The great Onondio would form a chain with America that would shine forever." But the English, he protested, had misled them. If the Americans would now be kind, "peace will spread among all the nations." And he too gave Lafayette a wampum belt.

Replying, Lafayette first expressed gratitude to the governor of Canada for urging peace. Now that the Indians had seen the error of their ways, they must forget their animosities. He could then go away rejoicing "in the return of his paternal affection" and fully confident that a satisfactory treaty would be made with the United States.[24] Thus Kayewla, usurping the right to speak for the great Onondio, solemnly sought to make peace with the Indians. Madison thought that the answers of the sachems and the behavior of the audience "denoted the greatest reverence for the orator."[25] Marbois was struck by the lack of eloquence and order in the Indians' harangues. "They heap up all sorts of incoherent ideas and facts, without paying attention to their natural relationship."[26] It was perhaps with the same impression in mind that Lafayette proposed to one of the most eloquent Indians that he learn English, only to have the Indian reply that he would be afraid of corrupting his native pronunci-ation and idiom.[27]

Almost three weeks of further parley proved necessary before peace was agreed upon. Lafayette did not, however, wait for the end of negotiations. The easy sale of brandy, which the commis-sioners were able to stop only by calling in the militia, made it appear that he would have had to wait a long time. Having al-

24. "Relation de ce qui s'est passé au Fort Stanwix," *loc. cit.*
25. Madison to Jefferson, Oct. 17, 1784, Hunt, II, 85.
26. Chase, p. 199.
27. *Nouveaux mélanges extraits des manuscrits de Mme Necker* (Paris, 1801), I, 134–35 (Princeton University Library).

ready postponed his New England journey longer than he had intended, he left Fort Schuyler on the very day of his last meeting with the Indians.[28]

If Kayewla's participation in the treaty negotiations had had the effect anticipated, it was not immediately apparent. The commissioners, delayed by slothful Indians and unruly whiskey dealers, finished their work only on October 22—which was, however, much earlier than Marbois at one point had thought possible.[29] The final treaty guaranteed to the Indians all their lands within New York, except the posts of Oswego and Niagara, in return for all claims westward between Lake Erie and the Ohio River.

The presence of a French nobleman and general at the powwow had emphasized its international character. Marbois had busied himself so thoroughly with copying Lafayette's speeches and the Indians' replies for an official account that Madison, who wanted to send copies to Jefferson, could not get at the originals.[30] All agreed that the marquis had been the most conspicuous figure at the conference. "My influence with the Indians was found greater than I myself could expect," Lafayette informed Washington,[31] and, in Madison's opinion, "the commissioners were eclipsed."[32] Madison in fact suspected that Lee, jealous of the marquis's influence, had hastened his departure. Lafayette allowed his companion to guess, however, that, though he, too, was suspicious of Lee's attitude, he was not offended by it. He was free to go on with his plans in other quarters and yet to state truthfully that he had stayed at Fort Schuyler as long as the commissioners had thought he could be useful.[33]

Lafayette had told Madison that he had "three hobbyhorses"—the Franco-American alliance, the American union,

28. "Diary of Griffith Evans," *loc. cit.*, under date of Oct. 4, 1784; Montbas, p. 97.
29. *American historical review*, XXIX (1924), 730.
30. Madison to Jefferson, Oct. 11, 1784, Hunt, II, 80. Cf. B. Langan to Sir John Johnson, Nov. 15, Newberry Library (Chicago), American history MSS.
31. Oct. 8, 1784, Gottschalk, *Letters*, pp. 285–86.
32. Madison to Jefferson. Oct. 17, 1784, Hunt. II, 85.
33. Lafayette to Washington, Oct. 8, 1784. Gottschalk, *Letters*, p. 286; and Lafayette to Hamilton, Oct. 8, 1784, J. C. Hamilton (ed.), *The works of Alexander Hamilton* (New York, 1850–51), I, 421.

and Negro emancipation. "The two former are the dearer to him," Madison surmised, "as they are connected with his personal glory. The last does him real honor, as it is a proof of his humanity. In a word, I take him to be as amiable a man as his vanity will admit, and as sincere an American as any Frenchman can be; one whose past services gratitude obliges us to acknowledge and whose future friendship prudence requires us to cultivate." Madison perceived, however, that Lafayette's motives were not altogether quixotic. The young Frenchman sought publicity from his ventures. He expected his speeches to be printed in the United States and eventually to become known abroad. Thus his service to the alliance would "form a bright column in the gazettes of Europe."[34] In that expectation the marquis was not to be disappointed. He had a sort of Midas touch, it appeared. Everything he did seemed to turn into a golden opportunity, although sometimes only as a result of careful burnishing on his part.

BIBLIOGRAPHICAL NOTES

Anna White and Leila S. Taylor (*Shakerism, its meaning and message* [Columbus, Ohio, 1905], pp. 239–41) tell a story on the testimony of an unnamed witness of a visit of Lafayette to Niskayuna and his interest in a Shaker named Abijah Wooster. They date the episode 1781. That date, however, is impossible. They also give other details that are not easily credited. They undoubtedly have the same event in mind that Marbois describes.

The accounts of Lafayette's speeches to the Indians were published prematurely by St. John de Crèvecœur (see below, p. 128). Crèvecœur apparently got his version of the speeches from Marbois. From his version the *Pennsylvania Packet*, November 17 and 19, 1784, the *Massachusetts Centinel*, November 29 and December 1, and other newspapers took their copies. It later became the basis of the account in Crèvecœur's *Lettres d'un cultivateur américain* (1787), III, 334–42, and was borrowed from there by the editors of Lafayette's *Mémoires* (II, 98–104). Lafayette, embarrassed or pretending to be embarrassed by the publication of this account before an official report had been made by the commissioners, apologized to Congress (see below, p. 129). In his letter of apology he called the published account "inaccurate." It nevertheless differs only in minor details from the version sent by Marbois to Vergennes and that certified by Lafayette (see above, p. 104, n. 23). I have relied on the latter versions. It is somewhat interesting that where the English versions speak of "belts of wampum," the French speak of *colliers*.

Historians of the Indians disagree regarding who were the most prominent chiefs at Fort Schuyler. It seems probable that they were Joseph Brant, Red Jacket, and Cornplanter. See above, n. 19, and cf. Anonymous, "Principal

34. Madison to Jefferson, Oct. 17, 1784. See p. 108 below.

events in the life of the Indian chief Brant" (*New England historical and genealogical register*, III [1849], 64). Esther V. Hill ("The Iroquois Indians and their lands since 1783," *Proceedings of the New York State Historical Association*, XXVIII [1930], 339, n. 14) thinks Red Jacket was not there. The articles in *Olden time* (II, 406–72) are still very helpful.

Marbois's associations with Lafayette's tour of 1784 are contained in his own accounts, which are partly published in Montbas's *Avec Lafayette chez les Iroquois* and are more fully given in translation in Chase's version of Marbois's letters. There are additional descriptions by Marbois in the letters and reports, cited above, to the ministry of foreign affairs.

Madison's share in these events is well narrated in Irving Brant, *James Madison, the nationalist (1780–1787)* (Indianapolis, 1948), pp. 325–35.

Griffith Evans, an American soldier who witnessed Lafayette's activities at Fort Schuyler on October 3 and 4, 1784, left an unpublished diary that is now in the Huntington Library.

Since the first printing of this work, a new edition of the papers of Jefferson, edited by Julian P. Boyd (Princeton, 1950———), has become available for the period under consideration in this volume. I have, however, deemed it unfeasible within the technological limitations of this reprinting to change the references from other editions to the Boyd edition; fortunately, Boyd's versions rarely differ significantly from the passages here quoted. One important exception, however, relates to p. 107 above, where "as amiable a man as his vanity will admit" read in the first printing (following Hunt, II, 85–86) "as amiable a man as can be imagined." Boyd explains (*The papers of Thomas Jefferson*, VII [1953], 444–52, esp. 451–52, n. 5) the reason for his amelioration of the Hunt version, and he carefully re-examines Lafayette's activity at Fort Schuyler.

CHAPTER IX

Republican Gratitude in New England

THE journey back to Albany proved easier than the weary jogging through the forests toward Fort Schuyler. Lafayette, Madison, Marbois, Caraman, and their party (eleven in all) boarded a boat rowed by five men on October 4, 1784, and dropped down the Mohawk River toward Schenectady. This time they had more leisure to note that Indian atrocities still kept the remote countryside denuded, that farming improved as they got closer to civilization, and that the shallowness of the river and the danger of the cataracts interfered with navigation. They had to port for half a mile around Little Falls. Going overland from Schenectady, they spied the Dutch gables of Albany on October 7.[1]

Arrived in Albany, Lafayette communicated his safe arrival to his friends, referring with studied modesty to his unexpectedly great prestige with the Indians.[2] He also felt called upon to try his influence with Americans. Jay had just been proposed for the office of secretary of foreign affairs and was hesitating to accept. In the past Lafayette had not always felt confident of Jay's loyalty to France. Still, the probable alternate, if Jay refused to serve, would have been the consistently Francophobe "A[rthur] L[ee]"; and Lafayette, remembering his most recent encounter with Lee, confided to Hamilton that Lee "does not

1. Marbois's journal quoted in Montbas, pp. 97–98; [J. F. Jameson?], *American historical review*, XXIX (1924), 732–34. Marbois (and hence others) gives the dates of the return trip to Albany as October 6–8, but see Lafayette to Jay, Oct. 7, 1784, Johnston, III, 132. Chase, p. 215, gives an altogether erroneous date.
2. Lafayette to Washington, Oct. 8, 1784, Gottschalk, *Letters*, pp. 285–87; and Lafayette to Hamilton, Oct. 8, 1784, *Works of Hamilton*, I, 421.

hit my fancy."[3] So he felt called upon again to pull some wires. "Your refusal could not but be attended with very bad circumstances," he wrote Jay. He offered to change his itinerary and meet Jay anywhere, if it would help to reach a decision.[4] In the end that did not prove necessary, since Jay accepted without it.

Lafayette rested at Albany only long enough to visit the booming seventy-foot waterfalls at Cohoes and the battlefield of Saratoga.[5] On October 8 he set out on his long delayed eastern tour. He had learned that some French naval vessels had anchored at Newport and accordingly revised his schedule so as to return to Virginia on board one of them. In fact, he was led to assume that a forty-gun frigate was officially placed at his disposal by the French government.[6] Leaving Marbois and Madison behind, he and Caraman left for Connecticut on October 8, arriving at Hartford after a three-day jog.

Here the townspeople turned out to honor the marquis in a way that had not been equaled since he had left New York City a month before. A burst of artillery announced his arrival, and a gathering crowd escorted him into town. The next day a public banquet took place at Hartford's best hostelry, Bull's Tavern, with the city's officials and leading celebrities as hosts. Before dinner Mayor Thomas Seymour delivered an address in honor of "a nobleman who forsook the pleasures of his native country, risqued his life and fortune in the cause of liberty, and by his exertions both in the council and in the field so gloriously shared our toils and contributed to our successes." The mayor's eloquent story of why Lafayette had left France and what he had sought in America was nothing but the truth, though not the whole truth, and bore abundant witness to the credence that had already been attained by the Lafayette legend. Hartford's gratitude, Mayor Seymour admitted with disarming candor, was based upon the expectation of his "continuing to us the favour of that nation to whose assistance we are so greatly in-

3. Oct. 8, 1784, LC, Hamilton papers. The initials are omitted from the printed version in *Works of Hamilton*, I, 421.
4. Oct. 7, 1784, Johnston, III, 132.
5. Montbas, p. 98; Crèvecœur, III, 342.
6. Lafayette to Washington, Oct. 8, 1784, Gottschalk, *Letters*, p. 286; *Mémoires*, II, 8.

debted for our liberty and independence." The marquis's reply
was a skilful mixture of modesty, courtesy, and exhortation for
continued Franco-American solidarity.[7]

Taking advantage of a brief stopover in Hartford, Lafayette
turned his hand to diplomacy once more. Thomas Jefferson had
gone to France as a member of a commission to negotiate treaties of commerce with European nations and was generally expected to replace Franklin at the court of Versailles. Lafayette
took advantage of their slight acquaintance to give Jefferson
some words of encouragement and advice. He offered his house
to Jefferson as "a second home," urging him to look upon Mme
de Lafayette as a "brother's wife." Pointing to his own success
at Fort Schuyler, he advised Jefferson to create the impression
abroad that America's Indians presented no great problem despite a recent "trifling" frontier disturbance. He took occasion
again to pray for a strong federation of "all the states" to "insure their eternal union and, of course, their interior happiness,
commercial wealth, and national consequence."[8] Jefferson did
not hesitate long to avail himself of the marquis's hospitality.

From Hartford, Lafayette also wrote home. A report to
Vergennes apologized for the semiofficial liberties he had taken,
explaining that he had regularly consulted with Marbois. He
also renewed his plea that France profit from England's diplomatic folly to increase its own following in America.[9] In a less
formal letter to Poix, he indicated that he was beginning to feel
sorry for himself. He and Caraman, he said, spoke of France all
day long, repeating with renewed pleasure at night what they
had said in the morning. "Seven months' absence, and volun-
tary absence at that, are a pretty long penance, and if Heaven
takes them into account, it ought to counterbalance the sins of
my whole life." He spoke facetiously of his experiences with the

7. *Connecticut Courant*, Oct. 19, 1784.

8. Oct. 11, 1784, Chinard, *Lafayette and Jefferson*, p. 51. It is generally assumed
that Jefferson and Lafayette had met personally in April or May, 1781, in Richmond,
when Lafayette was campaigning in Virginia and Jefferson was governor (see *ibid.*,
p. 9). There is no conclusive evidence to that effect, however. Although Lafayette's
letter to Jefferson of April 27, 1781, and Jefferson's to Lafayette of May 14, 1781 (*ibid.*,
pp. 39 and 42) speak of an intention to meet, the fact that such a meeting is
nowhere explicitly mentioned would, in the case of two such conspicuous figures, make
it uncertain that it actually took place.

9. Oct. 12, 1784, AAE, corr. pol., É.-U., Vol. XXVIII, fol. 317.

Indians. "I could not lose my scalp," he wrote, referring to his premature baldness, "because you cannot lose, the proverb says, what you don't have." He could hardly wait until December to be in Paris again. "I could be there now if the devil had not transported me to the other side of the Ocean. If he offered me the whole New World, he would not make me renounce that part of the old one where I had the good fortune to be born and where I have that of living. There is nothing in my opinion so charming as to be an Auvergnat, and, be it said without vanity, even from Haute-Auvergne, and to live on the Rue de Bourbon in a house which, if it is not the most beautiful, is at least infinitely pleasant." Even in this more intimate letter, however, he implied that Americans were not mistaken in considering him useful to their purposes.[10]

On October 13 Lafayette and Caraman left Hartford. Passing hastily through Worcester, Massachusetts, they reached Watertown, a few miles west of Boston, on the morning of October 15. Couriers stationed along the road had spread word that Lafayette was coming, and he was met at Watertown by Revolutionary officers from Boston and its environs. Together they ate "an elegant dinner" in the town's little inn, as a band played martial airs. "Joy, friendship and unity agitated every breast and was visible on every countenance." At the end they drank "a number of well adapted toasts."

When dinner was over, the whole party set out for Boston. They passed through Cambridge, ferried across the Charles River, and entered Roxbury, where a company of Roxbury Artillery joined the procession. Crossing the Boston Neck, they entered the city as the Boston Artillery fired a salute and the town bells clanged out. The French naval frigate "Nymphe" was anchored in Boston Harbor, and its captain proved to be the Comte de Grandchain, who had helped to negotiate Cornwallis' capitulation at Yorktown. Grandchain placed his vessels at the marquis's disposal. The captain, as well as the French consul Létombe, also took part in the welcoming celebration, giving it an official French flavor. Preceded by a band and a military escort carrying the American and French flags, accompanied by

10. Oct. 12, 1784, privately communicated.

his old comrade-in-arms General Henry Knox, flanked by Caraman and Grandchain, and followed by the French consul, the
Continental officers, and the town's celebrities in carriages, Lafayette rode his horse down the main avenues of Boston between
rows of enthusiastic spectators peering from street and windows.
At the Liberty Pole the crowd broke into cheers. At State Street
his military escort saluted and left him, but the veterans and the
crowd followed him to his lodgings at the Whig Hall Tavern.
They did not disperse until he had made them a little speech of
thanks from the balcony and they had cheered him once again.
The bells kept ringing until night, and Whig Hall Tavern and
the American Coffee House were illuminated in the evening.[11]
"I really felt emotions which were peculiarly animating," wrote
a young man who had been one of the Boston crowd.[12]

A single voice of protest is on record against the day's warm
demonstration of republican gratitude. It came from Major
William North, formerly aide of General von Steuben. Neither
North nor Steuben ever fully understood America's enthusiasm
for their French comrade. "What with a villainous wind,"
North wrote to Steuben from Boston, "and the foolish parade
which has been made with the Don Quixote Lafayette, I have
not had a moment's peace. He arrived here on Friday, amidst
the acclamations of foolish disbanded officers and the town
rabble. Seated on a little horse (for the sake of Christ I am sorry
it was not an ass) he made his public entry."[13]

The next day General Knox and the veteran officers of the
Massachusetts Line waited on the marquis at his lodgings.
Knox, acting as their spokesman, delivered an address extolling
French aid in winning American independence, calling upon
patriotic and enlightened historians "to enumerate the marquis's actions in the field and his efforts to promote the happiness of the United States," and placing him "on the same list
with Condé, Turenne and so many other immortal heroes of
France." Lafayette's response again disowned much of the

11. *Massachusetts Centinel,* Oct. 16, 1784; cf. Crèvecœur, III, 345. *Boston magazine,* I
(October, 1784), 537, says Lafayette lodged at the Bunch of Grapes.
12. S. E. Baldwin, *Life and letters of Simeon Baldwin* (New Haven, [1918?]), p. 228.
13. Oct. 19, Friedrich Kapp, *The life of Frederick William von Steuben, major
general in the Revolutionary Army* (New York, 1859), p. 629.

praise, generously distributing it among his gallant troops, the French king, and the French people.[14]

The next day was Sunday. Puritanical Boston, whose leading newspaper, the *Massachusetts Centinel*, had sermonized the day before and was to sermonize again the next Saturday "on the prevailing custom of visiting on the Sabbath," stayed quietly at home or in church. On Monday the state of Massachusetts took official cognizance of its distinguished visitor. The legislature, remembering that Tuesday would be the third anniversary of Cornwallis' surrender at Yorktown, passed a resolution inviting him to visit them that day and requesting the governor, the lieutenant-governor, and the state council also to attend. They proposed to congratulate the marquis "on his safe arrival in America after the final establishment of a peace to which his friendly influence in Europe and his distinguished exertions in a military character in America have largely contributed."[15] Accordingly, at noon on October 19, the governor, his staff, and the two houses of the legislature met in the Senate chamber. Governor John Hancock, an old acquaintance, delivered a speech appropriate to the occasion, and Lafayette made "a polite and elegant reply."[16] He complimented Massachusetts as "the spot where the flame of the American Revolution first began to kindle" and promised always to look after its interests.[17]

When the state ceremony ended, the marquis became the center of less august functions. At one o'clock the artillery companies of Roxbury and Boston paraded down State Street and then fired a "national" (thirteen-gun) salute. It was answered by the cannon of the Castle and Captain de Grandchain's "Nymphe" in the harbor. At two o'clock Lafayette and some of the most distinguished citizens, soldiers, and foreigners in Boston marched to Faneuil Hall, again escorted by the artillery. There, as well-spaced salutes boomed forth, they regaled themselves at a banquet given by the merchants of the city. The marquis's seat was placed under a fleur-de-lis, the symbol of the

14. Crèvecœur, III, 349–52.

15. J. P. Baxter *et al.* (eds.), *Documentary history of the state of Maine*, 2d ser. (Portland, 1869–1916), XX, 405; *Massachusetts Centinel*, Oct. 20, 1784.

16. *Massachusetts Centinel*, Oct. 20, 1784.

17. *Boston magazine*, I (October, 1784), 540.

French monarchy, in a huge arch of flowers. After dinner there were thirteen toasts, honoring the United States, Louis XVI, Washington, Massachusetts, France, Saratoga, Yorktown, justice, the rights of man, the arts and sciences, and other worthy subjects. Each toast was followed by a thirteen-gun salute from the willing artillery outside and a clapping of hands inside the hall. The third toast, the one to Washington, was the high point of the banquet. At a prearranged signal a curtain behind Lafayette was pulled, revealing "a most capital picture of His Excellency General Washington, crowned with a wreath of laurels." Lafayette led the applause, "with a countenance mingled with pleasure and surprise, and a tear of friendship starting in his eye,"[18] and "many were the friendly tears that involuntarily started from the company."[19]

When the festivities were over and the guests had departed, "all the wine and fragments of provision of every kind which were left at the hall were carefully collected and sent to the almshouse and goal [sic] that the hearts, even of the miserable in confinement and distress, might expand upon this joyous occasion."[20] That evening, for the first time since the outbreak of war nine years earlier, the street lamps of Boston were lighted. Fireworks brightened a reception at the home of Mary Hayley, the sister of the famous British politician, John Wilkes. There Lafayette told the envious Major North confidentially that he was especially pleased at this honor because it came from an Englishwoman.[21]

Boston's newspapers gloried in the exceptional events of the Yorktown anniversary. The *Centinel* had to leave out several items prepared for the next day's issue in order to make room for its account of the celebration and for two poems in honor of Lafayette. The shorter poem had one merit at least. It indicated by a bad pun that in Boston the hero's name was pronounced

18. *Ibid.*, p. 539; cf. Lafayette to Washington, Oct. 22, 1784, Gottschalk, *Letters*, p. 287.

19. Joseph Barrell to S. B. Webb, Oct. 21, 1784, W. C. Ford (ed.), *Correspondence and journals of Samuel Blachley Webb* (New York, 1893–94), III, 40.

20. *Boston magazine*, I (October, 1784), 539.

21. North to Steuben, Oct. 19, 1784, Kapp, p. 629; cf. *Massachusetts Centinel*, Oct. 20, 1784.

more nearly like its French original than some English approximations:

> From whence, Columbia, do thy blessings flow?
> And whence does war inexorably cease?
> Does not the western hemisphere yet know
> 'Twas Heav'n's great FYAT lull'd the world in peace?[22]

The longer poem breathed hatred of England and gratitude to France. The mere accident that Lafayette's visit corresponded with the Yorktown anniversary thus served the cause of Franco-American solidarity better than he could have planned.

Soon Lafayette was called upon to put to good use his youthful application to the study of Latin. The Corporation of Harvard College voted on October 20 to admit him into the "rights, privileges, dignities and honors" of a doctor of laws. The next day he journeyed to Cambridge to receive his degree. Governor Hancock went with him. There, at a dinner in College Hall, he was presented with a diploma—in a Latin no less flowery than the English addresses to which he had recently been obliged to listen. It eulogized the young doctor not only as "a conspicuous friend to our republics in peace as well as in war" but also as a successful advocate of America's commerce. It stated that from Lafayette's friendship might arise "beneficia haud pauca"—a hint which, in those academic precincts, somehow seemed appropriate in Latin whereas the English words "not a few advantages" might have seemed out of place. It bestowed barely deserved praise on Lafayette's accomplishments in "many and varied sciences" and in "natural, international and civil law," and eulogized his more genuine philanthropic and military achievements.[23]

The prospect of "beneficia haud pauca" definitely improved for some Bostonians while Lafayette was among them. General Knox, James Warren, and Samuel Breck spoke to him about the disaster that had befallen the whaling industry of Marblehead, Nantucket, and other fishing towns of New England. Not only had the war played havoc with boats and men, but now the

22. A. B., "Epigram to the Marquis de la Fayette," Oct. 7, 1784, *Massachusetts Centinel*, Oct. 20, 1784. The longer poem was entitled "Verses on the arrival of the Honorable the Marquis de la Fayette" by A Youth, Oct. 19, 1784.

23. *Publications of the Colonial Society of Massachusetts*, X (1907), 326.

English, once the best customers for whale oil, were excluding American merchants from their markets. If France would only give American oil shippers favorable terms, all might yet go well for the American fishing industry. Lafayette listened to "proper sentiments on that subject," and Boston merchants were soon to learn that they had had "a good effect."[24] He also conversed with a businessman named James Swan on the obstacles in Franco-American commerce and made the suggestion that Swan should write a memorial on the subject—a suggestion which Swan eventually followed.[25]

Jealousy of the marquis's triumphs nestled in other breasts than North's. Governor Hancock, for a time, thought the ceremony at Harvard College had been somewhat unbecoming, because he fancied he had been slighted by being seated opposite President Joseph Willard and the marquis at what appeared to be the foot of the table. But he was discreet enough to express his displeasure only privately, and eventually it was explained to him that his place had been intended to be the next highest to the president's.[26] Perhaps, too, Baron von Steuben did not relish the picture of a general's stooping so low as to pick up an honorary degree. At any rate a story got around that on a subsequent occasion the baron halted his troops outside a university town and said to them, "You shall spur de horse vel and ride troo the town like de debbil, for if dey catch you, dey make one doctor of you."[27] The story is probably apocryphal, however, for Steuben commanded no troops after Lafayette began collecting degrees, and he was not himself above accepting a regency in the University of the State of New York. Nor was Lafayette aware of any animosity on Steuben's part, if it existed,

24. Warren to John Adams, Apr. 30, 1786, *Warren-Adams letters* ("Massachusetts Historical Society collections," Vols. LXXII–LXXIII [Boston, 1917–25]), II, 272. Cf. Lafayette to Knox, May 11, 1785, Massachusetts Historical Society, Knox papers, and to Breck, May 13, [Davis], *Complete history*, p. 153.

25. James Swan, *Causes qui se sont opposées aux progrès du commerce entre la France et les États-Unis de l'Amérique, etc.* (Paris, 1790), pp. 16 and 267. This pamphlet was based upon a manuscript completed around 1787, translated by M. Létombe and sent to the French foreign office. Cf. Howard Rice, "James Swan, agent of the French Republic, 1794–96," *New England quarterly*, X (1937), 467, n. 6.

26. Willard to Hancock, Feb. 19, 1785, *Publications of the Colonial Society of Massachusetts*, X (1907), 320–22.

27. H. E. Scudder (ed.), *Recollections of Samuel Breck with passages from his notebooks (1771–1862)* (Philadelphia, 1877), p. 260.

for he made it his business to speak to his friends on behalf of the baron's claim for back pay.[28]

More serious than these episodes was the reaction of a revolutionary from another continent, the Venezuelan Colonel Francisco de Miranda. Miranda now met Lafayette for the first time at Boston and saw in his movements something quite sinister. To the Hispanic colonel the Gallic marquis seemed a "mediocre character . . . endowed with . . . activity and perpetual motion," and his tour appeared to be "one of those sleight of hand performances by which France tried to delude mankind," although any discerning person could see that they were "ridiculous political farces." The "excessive and absurd demonstrations" of New England's towns, Miranda thought, were possible only because Americans were a "guileless people, as yet inexpert in politics."[29]

On the evening after he became a doctor of laws the marquis attended a children's ball in his honor. Here several hundred girls and women surrounded and ogled him and vied for his attention. He was reminded of one of Poix's favorite songs about King Solomon, "though God has not given me the great charms of that wise prince."[30] It is perhaps just as well that the words of that song were unknown to the several good ladies who on this occasion initiated a proud family tradition that they had danced with Lafayette.

The persistence of Boston's hospitality meant another upset in Lafayette's schedule. He felt obliged to send word to Washington and others explaining that he would not be able to reach Virginia until November. Captain de Grandchain would then take him on the "Nymphe" to Yorktown. If Washington was as disappointed as Lafayette thought he might be, the edge was probably taken off his disappointment by the marquis's graceful way of putting part of the blame on him. "I am sorry our meeting again is differed [i.e., deferred]—but when you are absent, I endeavour to guess what you would have advised me to do—

---

28. Lafayette to Hamilton, Oct. 22, 1784, *Works of Hamilton*, I, 423.

29. W. S. Robertson (ed.), *The diary of Francisco Miranda, tour of the United States, 1783-84* (New York, 1928), p. 121. Cf. W. S. Robertson, *The life of Miranda* (Chapel Hill, 1929), I, 53.

30. Lafayette to Poix, Oct. 22, 1784, privately communicated.

and then to do it. I am sure you would advise my staying here some time longer."[31]

A message that was sent off to Hamilton had a double purpose in mind. It not only carried an apology for Lafayette's delay but it also contained a not very subtle request that Hamilton use his influence with the New York delegates to Congress in order to acquire new honors for Lafayette. "Upon reflecting to my situation, my love for America, and yet the motives that might render it improper for her to employ me in a public capacity," he wrote, "I have confined myself to a plan which, at the same time it gratifies my attachement and serves the United States, cannot have any shadow of inconvenience. After having told me they know my zeal, I wish Congress to add that they want me to continue those friendly and I might say patriotic exertions—that in consequence of it, their ministers at home and their ministers abroad will have a standing order to look to me as one whose information and exertions will ever be employed to the service of the United States, and when they think it is wanted to communicate with me upon the affairs of America, that Congress will, whenever I think it proper, be glad of my correspondance." The suggestion, though it robs the subsequent resolutions of Congress of all spontaneity, was not ill-intentioned. By such an arrangement, Lafayette explained, "every minister may conceal from me what he pleases, may write to me only when he pleases, and should he ever think my assistance is wanting, he has a title to ask, I have one to give it —and my connection with America is for ever kept, without giving jealousy, upon such a footing as will remain at the disposition of each public servant of Congress."[32]

Lafayette and Grandchain decided to sail the "Nymphe" to Virginia around November 1.[33] That gave the marquis about ten days in which to continue his sentimental journey. Taking advantage of the interval to visit Rhode Island and New Hamp-

31. Lafayette to Washington, Oct. 22, 1784, Gottschalk, *Letters*, p. 287. Cf. Lafayette to [Madison?], Oct. 22, Historical Society of Pennsylvania; to Hamilton, Oct. 22, *Works of Hamilton*, I, 422; and to Poix, Oct. 22, privately communicated.

32. Lafayette to Hamilton, Oct. 22, 1784, LC, Hamilton papers. The printed version (*Works of Hamilton*, I, 422-23) varies in slight details.

33. Lafayette to [Madison?], Oct. 22, 1784, *loc. cit.*

shire, he left Boston for Providence on October 22. Again the now familiar thirteen-gun roar of the "national" salute rang out to greet his party as he entered the city, and bells and cheers rent the customary silence around Beacon Hill. The next day was Sunday. Since celebrations would be unseemly, Lafayette devoted the Sabbath to a visit with his old commander, General Nathanael Greene. His boat reached Newport that evening. He was met at the landing by the mayor and the town's dignitaries, who escorted him to Greene's house.[34] The serious conversation of the two veteran generals gave rise to a family tradition that Lafayette talked "hopefully of the future of his France." But subsequent developments indicate that they talked of Greene's future too.[35]

On Monday the marquis returned to Providence in time for a dinner given in his honor by the Cincinnati of Rhode Island at Henry Rice's Tavern. Governor William Greene and Lieutenant-Governor Jabez Bowen as well as Caraman, Grandchain, and Major L'Enfant, who had recently returned from France, also attended and joined in drinking the usual thirteen toasts. General James Varnum, who had served with Lafayette in the Rhode Island campaign of 1778, presented the address of welcome, to which Lafayette replied with congratulations on "the blessings of peace and the firmly established principles of liberty." His reply was addressed "to the late officers of the army, now citizens of the State of Rhode Island"—a neat touch for a member of a hereditary military aristocracy.[36]

The next day (October 26) the General Assembly of Rhode Island gave him a dinner, also at Rice's Tavern. Here the governor delivered an oration commemorating the honored guest's "military ardor," which "resulted from a regard to the rights of mankind." In his response Lafayette took occasion again to urge a strong federation. "May these rising states unite in every measure, as they have united in their struggles; and may their wealth and consequence, so much founded in federal union, baffle the calculations of jealousy and fulfill the enthusiastic

34. *Newport Mercury*, Oct. 30, 1784.
35. G. W. Greene, *The life of Nathanael Greene, major-general in the army of the Revolution* (New York, 1871), III, 522. See below, pp. 161, 209-10, and 404-5.
36. *Newport Mercury*, Oct. 30, 1784.

hopes of patriotism."[37] The state of Rhode Island paid Henry Rice £38 7s. for sixty-two dinners, fifty-one bottles of madeira, thirty-two bottles of claret, nine bottles of porter, thirty-two bowls of punch, and some bitters. That meant about a bottle and a half of wine and somewhat more than half a bowl of punch for each diner.[38] Lafayette did not drink enough of it, however, to keep him out of his carriage. Pressed by his schedule, he left for Boston immediately after dinner, as thirteen cannon boomed out behind him.[39]

Boston was this time only the starting-point for a journey to New Hampshire. The people of Lynn caught a fleeting glimpse of Lafayette, Caraman, and Grandchain on October 28.[40] On the next day the travelers were in Salem, which had spent the previous two days in feverish preparations for their arrival. Here the familiar round, of which Lafayette never seemed to tire, began again. A reunion of Revolutionary veterans in the newly remodeled Concert Hall filled the day—to the accompaniment of pealing bells, rousing cheers of joyous, bareheaded crowds, florid addresses of notables, elegant replies by Lafayette, and the customary thirteen toasts. One of the toasts echoed Lafayette's federal sentiments: "May we never withhold from Government the essential powers of doing good from a jealous apprehension of doing evil!" He himself gave the concluding toast: "The town of Salem—may the elements conspire to her prosperity!"[41] Well might he have thought the town a prosperous one, since one of the local pastors noted that "the poor had no part" in the dinner.[42] The ball that followed that evening lasted until after midnight. Lafayette, having a stiff knee, "walked" only one minuet.

37. J. R. Bartlett (ed.), *Records of the state of Rhode Island and Providence Plantations*, X (1865), 67–68.

38. Oct. 26, 1784, state papers of Rhode Island (courtesy of the late Mrs. F. P. Gleeson); cf. Bartlett, X, 78.

39. *Massachusetts Centinel*, Oct. 30, 1784.

40. Alonzo Lewis and J. R. Newhall, *History of Lynn, Essex County, Massachusetts, etc.* (Lynn, Mass., 1864), p. 351.

41. *Massachusetts Centinel*, Nov. 3, 1784; *Independent Chronicle and the Universal Advertiser* (Boston), Nov. 4, 1784; F. E. Oliver (ed.), *The diary of William Pynchon of Salem: a picture of Salem life, social and political, a century ago* (Boston, 1890), p. 198; G. F. Dow (ed.), *The Holyoke diaries, 1709–1856* (Salem, Mass., 1911), p. 112.

42. William Bentley, *The diary of William Bentley, D.D., pastor of the East Church, Salem, Massachusetts* (Salem, Mass., 1905–14), II, 3.

Before daybreak the French gentlemen were once more on their way. They soon became the cause of a series of wrangles in "each circle, club, and tea-table in Salem" over "neglects and affronts respecting the entertainments and ball for the Marquis."[43] But, innocently and unaware, they continued their progress. Late on October 30 they reached Portsmouth, New Hampshire. The town had not expected them, and so no bands blared forth and no artillery fired salutes when the three distinguished Frenchmen entered. Only the church bells clanged out the town's welcome as the people cheered. The next day being the Sabbath, there were no dinners, speeches, or toasts. But at dawn on Monday the Portsmouth Artillery began to make up for lost time with thirteen-gun salutes. Flags were broken out in all the streets, and the church bells once more rang forth. The "national" salutes were repeated until the visitors—at ten o'clock—began their journey back to Boston, amid the cheers of a self-appointed escort that took them as far as Greenland. The good Portsmouthians, under the impression that he would return, promised themselves "a better opportunity of testifying" how hospitable they could be toward "so exalted a character."[44]

Lafayette and his party moved even more rapidly southward than they had come northward. The next stop, reached that very day, was Newburyport, where (if family tradition is to be believed) Lafayette, by sitting down for a cup of tea, conferred immortality on a table belonging to Nathaniel Carter's family.[45] After a night's rest they pushed on, leaving the Boston highway to visit Marblehead (November 2). Samuel Breck of Boston had by this time joined their party. They were escorted into the town in the early afternoon by a number of gentlemen who met them on the road. Guns, bands, church bells, and cheers again mingled in tumultuous welcome. Cries of "Long life to the Marquis de Lafayette!" rang out as he passed through the crowd in the Training Field, "where provision was made to elevate the

43. *Diary of William Pynchon*, p. 199.
44. *Massachusetts Centinel*, Nov. 10, 1784.
45. Cecil Howard, "Thomas and Esther (Marlowe) Carter and their descendants," *Essex Institute historical collections*, LXV (1929), 504.

soul."[46] They were re-echoed by spectators cramming the doors and windows of neighboring houses. The parade ended at Elbridge Gerry's house.[47] Here the guest of honor received a formal address of welcome, in which the town's heavy suffering during the war was delicately assigned as the reason for "not fully manifesting the principles of hospitality we feel on this joyful occasion." Lafayette answered "in the dignified stile of a nobleman,"[48] referring again to Marblehead's numerous casualties during the war. Only light refreshment was served here because they soon moved on to "a genteel house"[49] where "joy and festivity prevailed." After dinner came the usual number of toasts—including one "to the memory of the heroes who have fought, bled and died in the glorious cause of their country," accompanied by a dirge that "produced ideas of solemnity and reverence." At the close Lafayette offered a fourteenth toast— "The town of Marblehead and unbounded success to their fisheries!" At six o'clock, though the community had prepared a ball in his honor and were disappointed that he could not attend, the marquis hastened on "with the speed of a Roland."[50] His party was escorted out of the town by its most distinguished citizens, amid more bursts of cannon, music, and cheers.

Without stopping for further ceremony (for the "Nymphe" was already behind schedule), the marquis and his friends rode on to Boston. On or about November 3 the frigate set sail for Virginia. Despite promises and hopes, New England was not to see Lafayette again for forty years.

BIBLIOGRAPHICAL NOTES

The best study of the relations of Lafayette and Jefferson is contained in Chinard's prefatory remarks to the separate chapters of his *Lafayette and Jefferson*.

The tendency of local newspapers to write up flowery reports of con-

46. *Massachusetts Centinel*, Nov. 20, 1784.
47. J. T. Austin, *The life of Elbridge Gerry, with contemporary letters* (Boston, 1828–29), I, 467–68.
48. *Massachusetts Centinel*, Nov. 20, 1784. Crèvecœur (III, 356–58) inserts a passage about the paucity of men at the gathering that is not contained in the contemporary accounts.
49. Probably the Lee House (see Samuel Roads, *The history and traditions of Marblehead* [Boston, 1880], p. 351), but it may be Gerry's house—in which case the house mentioned above was some other.
50. Robertson, *Diary of Miranda*, p. 121.

temporary social events and of later local history to repeat uncritically local lore and family traditions makes it necessary to be especially on one's guard against unconfirmed testimony. Local archeologists and museums often increase the historian's difficulties by including in their collections mementos and remains that are not well authenticated.

I have found it necessary to differ in several details from the itinerary of Lafayette given by both Crèvecœur and Nolan.

CHAPTER X

Farewell to Washington and Congress

THE "Nymphe" took about twelve days to make the trip from Boston. On the evening of November 15 Lafayette walked once more along Yorktown's single thoroughfare, which he had last trod as a victorious general three years before.[1] Accompanied by Caraman and Grandchain, he went on to Williamsburg, where the town authorities presented him with a fitting address, which the marquis fittingly answered.[2]

The next day Thomas Nelson, who had once been a general under Lafayette's command, brought together the town's celebrities to meet the marquis at dinner. Philip Mazzei, well-known Italo-American patriot, and James Madison, president of William and Mary College and cousin of Lafayette's recent companion among the Iroquois, were also guests. Nelson's house in Yorktown had been destroyed in the siege of 1781, and he now lived in a smaller one in Williamsburg. A bon mot, entirely appropriate to the occasion, was soon attributed to Nelson: if his visitors felt too crowded, they must put the blame on the skill of the French artillery.[3]

To each of the guests the marquis had something of interest to say. He roused in President Madison "the highest anxiety to know the real discoveries made in animal magnetism."[4] To

1. Mazzei to Madison, Nov. 15–16, 1784, R. C. Garlick, Jr., *Philip Mazzei, friend of Jefferson, his life and letters* ("Johns Hopkins studies in Romance literatures and languages," extra Vol. VII [Baltimore, 1933]), p. 92.
2. *Maryland Journal and Baltimore Advertiser*, Dec. 7, 1784 (courtesy of James W. Foster, director of the Maryland Historical Society).
3. Mazzei, *Recherches*, II, 201, n. 1.
4. Rev. James Madison to Jefferson, Apr. 10, 1785, Anon., "Letters of Rev. James Madison, president of the College of William and Mary, to Thomas Jefferson," *William and Mary College quarterly historical magazine*, 2d ser., V (1925), 80.

Mazzei he spoke of the financial troubles of their mutual friend, Lewis Littlepage. Nelson, for his part, made plain to his guests that he was pleased to have served under "his young and brave commander."[5]

Having proposed to meet Washington and Madison in Richmond by the middle of November, Lafayette hastened on. Washington was already waiting in the Virginia capital. He had been lionized for several days when Lafayette and his two companions joined him on November 18. They went together to Trower's Tavern that afternoon to an "elegant dinner" that the Richmond merchants arranged in their honor. Patrick Henry, just elected governor of the state, and other dignitaries were among those present.[6]

The Virginia House of Delegates, the same day, unanimously resolved to present Lafayette their "affectionate respects." Their resolution made appropriate references to his "cool intrepidity and wise conduct" in the Virginia campaign of 1781.[7] Patrick Henry and Lafayette's recent traveling companion James Madison were on the committee that brought him these greetings. The marquis had already begun to consider Madison a friend "as my heart reckons but few men"[8] and was now to add Patrick Henry to his host of admirers. When a son was born to the governor soon afterward, he was named Fayette.[9]

The next day Lafayette acknowledged the Delegates' resolution with equally appropriate remarks. He extolled the patriotism of Virginia in her time of trial. He carefully uttered the words "federal union" as he praised the state for shedding the blood of her sons "in defense of her sister states." With the problem of Negro emancipation in mind, he prayed that Virginia would "continue to give to the world unquestionable

5. Mazzei, *Recherches*, II, 201 n.; Mazzei to King Stanislaus Poniatowski, Jan. 30, 1789, H. R. Marraro, "Mazzei and his Polish friends," *Quarterly bulletin of the Polish Institute of Arts and Sciences in America*, II (1944), 788.

6. *Virginia Journal*, Dec. 2, 1784 (American Antiquarian Society); *Pennsylvania Packet*, Nov. 30.

7. *Journal of the House of Delegates of the Commonwealth of Virginia for the session beginning October 18, 1784*, p. 28 (meeting of Nov. 18).

8. Lafayette to Madison, Dec. 15, 1784, collection of Oliver R. Barrett (Chicago, Ill.).

9. W. W. Henry, *Patrick Henry: life, correspondence and speeches* (New York, 1891), I, 615.

proofs of her philanthropy and her regard to the liberties of all mankind."[10] Further comment on that subject might have been indiscreet.

On the next day Lafayette revealed himself again as a benefactor of the oppressed. A Richmond Negro named James had been employed as a spy when Lafayette in 1781 was shuttling back and forth in Virginia, alternately eluding and following Cornwallis. James now hoped for some suitable recognition of his "essential services," and Lafayette wrote out for him a testimonial bearing witness that he had "industriously collected and most faithfully delivered" intelligence of the enemy's dispositions and had "perfectly acquitted himself with some important commissions." James eventually (1786) won his freedom by act of the Virginia legislature.[11] Nor did the marquis's philanthropy stop with the humble. He also undertook to petition the governor of Virginia on behalf of some French merchants to whom the state owed money. On this petition, however, he got no action.[12]

For a week after Washington's arrival in Richmond the city was kept alive with "feasting, balls, illumination & firing of cannon."[13] On Monday, November 22, Washington and Lafayette, still accompanied by Caraman and Grandchain, started for Mount Vernon,[14] where they arrived the following Wednes-

10. *Journal of Delegates beginning October 18, 1784,* p. 30. Cf. Mazzei, *Recherches,* IV, 133-34; and *Mémoires,* II, 8.

11. Facsimile in *Virginia magazine of history and biography,* XXXIX (1931), 106; L. P. Jackson, *Virginia Negro soldiers and seamen in the Revolutionary War* (Norfolk, Va., 1944), pp. 9-12.

12. Lafayette to Governor Benjamin Harrison, Nov. 21, 1784, New York Public Library, Em. 9287; *Journal of Delegates beginning October 18, 1784,* p. 33 (Nov. 23).

13. William Anderson to Thomas Massie, Nov. 20, 1784, *Virginia magazine of history,* XXIII (1915), 183.

14. It is possible that they passed through Fredericksburg and visited Washington's mother. The family tradition, however, seems to have been that Lafayette made a special trip to Fredericksburg for that purpose (see G. W. P. Custis, "General Washington," *New England historical and genealogical register,* XI [1857], 4, and *Recollections and private memories of Washington* [New York, 1860], pp. 144-45). Custis, who was three years old at the time, is not a reliable witness, even if, as is unlikely, he were present at the supposed visit of Lafayette to Mary Washington. Armand Carrel, "La mère de Washington," *Revue américaine* (1827), reprinted in M. Littré and M. Paulin, *Œuvres politiques et littéraires d'Armand Carrel* (Paris, 1857), V, 48-55, is a nearly verbatim translation (with omissions) of Custis, *Recollections,* pp. 134-47; Custis' early chapters were first printed in the *United States Gazette* and the *National Intelligencer* (Washington), *ca.* 1826 (see Custis, *Recollections,* pp. 9, 68, and 120).

day. Washington immediately made preparations for meetings with old comrades.[15]

The next day was devoted in good part to penning gracious acknowledgments of the several letters that Lafayette had brought from France—acknowledgments that the same willing messenger was now to carry back. With Mme de Lafayette, Washington unbent enough to feign a tone of gallantry. "The pleasure I received in once more embracing my friend," he wrote, "could only have been encreased by your presence, and that opportunity I should thereby have had of paying, in my own house, the homage of my respectful attachment to his better half. . . . The Marquis returns to you with all the warmth and ardour of a newly inspired lover. We restore him to you in good health, crowned with wreaths of love and respect from every part of the Union."[16] To little Anastasie de Lafayette he sent "a kiss to her from me (which might be more agreeable from a pretty boy)."[17] A gracious reply was also written to Dr. Mesmer, which, however, betrayed a lingering skepticism regarding the powers of animal magnetism.[18] Several other messages that the marquis had brought to Mount Vernon were acknowledged.[19]

Lafayette himself wrote a letter that day which probably caused him no little embarrassment. Consul St. John de Crèvecœur had somehow got hold of copies of the speeches made at Fort Schuyler—perhaps from Marbois, conceivably from Lafayette himself. Not taking the trouble to verify them carefully and probably recognizing in them some good Franco-American propaganda, he had translated and published them in the American newspapers. When Lafayette learned of this indiscretion with regard to presumably secret diplomatic documents, he hastened to make amends. He wrote not only a protest to Crèvecœur but also an apology to John Jay as prospective secretary of state. "Such deviation . . . from the manner in which we servants of the United States ever did business," he felt, called for an explanation. It would be provided satisfac-

---

15. Washington to Henry Lee, Nov. 24, 1784, Fitzpatrick, XXVII, 496.
16. Nov. 25, 1784, *ibid.*, p. 497.   18. *Ibid.*
17. *Ibid.*, p. 498.   19. *Ibid.*, pp. 498–500.

torily, he hoped, by his letter of protest to Crèvecœur, which Jay was to read and correct or approve. He sent both letters by special messenger, requesting Jay to convey his apologies also to Congress. But neither Congress nor Jay, it developed, felt the matter was so shocking as the marquis had feared they might. When Crèvecœur sent a notice to the papers explaining that he had published the speeches without Lafayette's knowledge, everyone seemed satisfied.[20]

One of the subjects of conversation, as Washington and Lafayette strolled along the walks or sat on the veranda of Mount Vernon, was the problem of the Mississippi. Lafayette was somewhat surprised to find that Washington was not so indignant as Madison about Spain's closing the river. In fact, Washington felt that Spain had made a tactical error from which the United States might even derive some benefit. If the western pioneers were furnished with outlets for their goods by canals connecting the transappalachian rivers with the James and the Potomac, they would develop renewed interest in their eastward associations while their resentment against Spain would mount. If, on the other hand, Spain were to open the Mississippi, it "would weaken America and transform the back country people into Spaniards."[21] Lafayette recognized the wisdom of this attitude but still felt committed to Madison's position. American antipathy to Spain did not fit into his picture of Franco-American solidarity.

During this visit to Mount Vernon, Lafayette adopted Washington's household as his own. His "beloved General's" wife was an old friend, since she had spent the war winters at headquarters. He now came to feel closely attached also to other members of Washington's family, who were at Mount Vernon in force. Martha Washington was assisted as hostess by her daughter-in-law, Eleanor Calvert Custis, who had been widowed a few years before and had recently remarried. Her new husband, Dr. David Stuart, and her four children, the only grandchildren of

20. Lafayette to Jay, Nov. 25, 1784, LC, PCC 156, fol. 396 (with slight variations in [Weaver], *Diplomatic correspondence*, I, 417–18); *Journals of Congress*, XXVII, 672 n. (Dec. 8); *Pennsylvania Packet*, Dec. 11, 1784; Mitchell, p. 142, and n.

21. Lafayette to Carmichael, Mar. 10, 1785, LC, House of Representatives collection, Carmichael papers, No. 104. Cf. Lafayette to Madison, Dec. 15, 1784, *loc. cit.*

Mrs. Washington, were also guests at Mount Vernon. Lafayette became attached to them, and especially to George Washington Parke Custis, Eleanor's only son. Since the young gentleman was only three years old and apparently quite rolypoly, Lafayette learned to call him "Squire Tub." George Augustine Washington, the general's nephew and once Lafayette's aide-de-camp, was there, too, as well as Frances Bassett, whom young George was soon to marry. A few years afterward, when the young Washingtons had a son, they named him George Fayette Washington. Dr. David Griffith, the Washingtons' pastor, also became one of the marquis's new friends, and, indifferent Catholic that Lafayette was, he would engage the devout Episcopalian in friendly discussions "on Mrs. Washington's Bible."[22] And at Mount Vernon, Lafayette came to know more affectionately the mother, the sister, the brothers, and other relatives and friends of his "beloved General," either because he visited with them or because he heard them talked about frequently and intimately. Washington's house thus became for him a symbol of home that intensified his filial devotion to his "adoptive father."

The stay at Mount Vernon was all too short. The "Nymphe" had already sailed back to New York and was scheduled to cross the Atlantic before the dead of winter. On Sunday, November 28, Washington, Lafayette, Grandchain, and Caraman left the home on the Potomac. The marquis and his friends were on their way home, and Washington, who had come to love his young companion dearly—among other reasons, because the young man candidly and insistently claimed that love—was going part of the way with them. They reached Annapolis the next day, and Lafayette found himself again involved in the familiar round—greetings by the governor and the General Assembly, his own responses, and a ball attended by gaping dignitaries.[23] The address of the Maryland executive complimented the young general on his "devotion to the rights and liberties of

22. Lafayette to Griffith, Dec. 25, 1786, G. M. Brydon, "David Griffith, 1742–1789, first bishop-elect of Virginia," *Historical magazine of the Protestant Episcopal church*, IX (1940), 230, and Lafayette to Washington, Mar. 19, 1785, Gottschalk, *Letters*, p. 294. Also consult Index, *ibid.*, pp. 395, 416–17, and *passim*.

23. *Maryland Gazette*, Dec. 2 and 9, 1784.

mankind." That of the legislature not only mentioned his glorious military services but also attributed to him in part the commercial concessions recently made by the French king. Lafayette blandly admitted, in his reply, that "affection conspired with interest to cherish a mutual intercourse" between the two allies. He also took occasion once more to advocate "the federal union so necessary to all."

But time pressed and Lafayette had to move on to New York. He begged Washington to go with him. "But the season was too much opposed to it," and Washington would not consent.[24] And so, on December 1, 1784, Lafayette and Washington parted. In separate carriages they rode along the highway that would soon branch off, leading the one onward to Baltimore, Philadelphia, and New York and the other back to Mount Vernon. Washington quietly nursed the premonition that he would never again meet his devoted disciple. "In the moment of our separation upon the road as I travelled," he wrote to Lafayette after he reached home, "and every hour since, I felt all that love, respect and attachment for you with which the length of years, close connection and your merits have inspired me. I often asked myself, as our carriages distended, whether that was the last sight I ever should have of you? And though I wished to say no, my fears answered yes. I called to mind the days of my youth, and found they had long since fled to return no more; that I was now descending the hill I had been 52 years climbing, and that though I was blessed with a good constitution, I was of a short lived family and might soon expect to be entombed in the dreary mansions of my fathers. These things darkened the shades and gave a gloom to the picture, consequently to my prospects of seeing you again; but I will not repine, I have had my day."[25]

Lafayette was only a little more than half Washington's age. He was troubled by no thoughts of mortality as lengthening distance shut his revered commander from view. With the buoyancy of his twenty-seven years he was certain that he would return

24. Washington to James Duane, Apr. 10, 1785, Fitzpatrick, XXVIII, 125.
25. Dec. 8, 1784, *ibid.*, p. 7. Washington did not go to Baltimore and Philadelphia as stated in *Mémoires*, II, 7; cf. Washington to Knox, Dec. 5, Fitzpatrick, XXVIII, 5.

again and again to Mount Vernon, even if there was no chance of persuading Washington to visit France.[26] And so, much less saddened by the parting than his older friend, he went blithely on his way with Caraman and Grandchain.

The three travelers reached Philadelphia probably on December 5, and the next day Lafayette visited Trenton. There he found a "numerous and well choosen Congress"[27] but one that had small prestige. The Articles of Confederation gave it little coercive power; the states jealously limited that little; and its members were seldom ready or willing to exert such authority as they had. They even failed to attend meetings regularly. Congress, in fact, was not much more than an outward symbol of the Confederation's inner weakness. One of its members, an old friend of Lafayette, had recently demanded "if it is not a prostitution of the name of government to apply it to such a vagabond, strolling, contemptible crew as Congress."[28]

Lafayette had long feared that the Confederation was in danger of becoming impotent. The unwillingness of the states to surrender their sovereignty and the lackluster of the delegates to Congress had become notorious. He knew, as his friends Washington and Hamilton knew, that this was a critical period in American affairs. It might lead the United States either to greatness among the world's powers or to the feebleness that eighteenth-century political thinkers regarded as inevitable in republican federations. He had written often and spoken much of late on behalf of the federal union as he passed from town to town. He did not hesitate now to avail himself of the opportunity to speak directly to Congress about it. Having long planned to be received by Congress, he now asked for the opportunity to present his "tribute of respect and gratitude."[29]

Probably no one, not even Washington, would have been more cordially heeded by Congress, now approaching its nadir, than Lafayette. He represented none of the states and had the confidence of all. He had visited ten of them in a journey of over

26. Lafayette to Washington, Dec. 21, 1784, Gottschalk, *Letters*, pp. 288–89.
27. *Ibid.*, p. 289.
28. John Francis Mercer, quoted in Burnett, VII, xlvii.
29. Lafayette to R. H. Lee, Dec. 6, 1784, C. E. Godfrey, *The Mechanics Bank, 1834–1919, Trenton in New Jersey; a history* ([Trenton?], 1919), pp. 26–27.

eighteen hundred miles during the last four months. North Carolina, South Carolina, and Georgia were the only ones he had not touched—which had not, however, kept the Charleston Library Society from electing him to honorary membership.[30] He symbolized the common cause of the disunited Confederation better than any other person, having no regional interest of his own, calling to mind the bountiful ally of all thirteen members, and holding forth the prospect of favors yet to come. Nothing about him suggested the centrifugal tendencies of the states. On the contrary, he had gone out of his way to identify himself with the idea of federal union.

Given several days' warning by Lafayette, Congress made a special effort to prepare for his reception. Richard Henry Lee, who was one of his oldest acquaintances in America, was president of Congress, and John Jay, who had frequently been his guest at the Rue de Bourbon, and John Francis Mercer, who had served under him in Virginia, were among its most influential members. Moreover, Jay had probably learned from their mutual friend Hamilton what Lafayette wanted Congress to say to him.[31] A committee, of which John Jay was one, was formally appointed to consider the departing visitor's request to call upon Congress. "The merit and services of the Marquis render it proper," this committee concluded, "that such an opportunity of taking leave of Congress be afforded him as may strongly manifest their esteem and regard for him."

Accordingly, a special committee consisting of twelve members, one from each state except Maryland (for which no representative was present), was designated to bid the young general farewell. John Jay represented New York and was chairman. The committee was instructed by Congress to assure Lafayette how highly appreciated were his efforts to promote the welfare of the United States both in America and in Europe. This appreciation had been "perfectly confirmed" by "the recent marks of his attention to their commercial and other interests." Furthermore, "the United States regard him with particular affection,

30. Lafayette to the president of the society, Dec. 19, 1784, *Newport Mercury*, May 21, 1785.
31. See above, p. 119.

and will not cease to feel an interest in whatever may concern his honour and prosperity." Congress also resolved to send a letter to Louis XVl setting forth "the high sense which the United States in Congress assembled entertain of the zeal, talents and meritorious services of the Marquis of Fayette" and recommending him "to the favour and patronage of his Majesty." The next day another resolution authorized the secretary of war to present Lafayette with one of the standards surrendered by Cornwallis as a token of Congress' admiration for his bravery at Yorktown.[32]

The marquis had meantime returned to Philadelphia. There he had occasion to serve once more as a friend of liberty and literature. While at Mount Vernon he had learned of a young Irish patriot named Mathew Carey, who had emigrated to America because of trouble with the British authorities. Carey had come to Philadelphia and was having a hard time making a living. Lafayette summoned him, promised help, got several Philadelphia friends interested, and sent him $400. With this sum Carey was able to start the *Pennsylvania Herald* and eventually to become one of the prominent figures of American journalism. Later Lafayette wrote to Washington and Madison to enlist their aid for Carey. When the grateful young man called to thank his benefactor, Lafayette was already well on his way back to Trenton.[33] Among others whom the marquis tried to see while still in Philadelphia was Franklin's daughter, Sarah Bache, but she was not at home when he called.[34]

During the Philadelphia visit Lafayette had probably again stayed at the French legation and spoken with Marbois.[35] The French chargé remained preoccupied by the annoying complications created by the erratic Longchamps. Although this affair was several months old by this time, it had dragged on. Anxiety

32. *Journals of Congress*, XXVII, 673–74 and 680 and n. (Dec. 9 and 10, 1784).

33. Not Princeton, as Carey thought, and not, as he also thought, merely "to avoid the expression of the gratitude of the beneficiary" (see Mathew Carey, "Autobiography," *New England magazine*, V [1833], 490). Cf. Lafayette to Carey, [December, 1784], Parke-Bernet Galleries, catalogue No. 731, sale of Jan. 28, 1946, item 154; Lafayette to Washington, Dec. 21, Gottschalk, *Letters*, pp. 289–90; to Madison, Dec. 17, Barrett collection.

34. Sarah Bache to B. F. Bache, [December, 1784], Parke-Bernet Galleries, catalogue No. 731, sale of Jan. 28, 1946, item 8.

35. Beelen-Bertholff to Belgiojoso, Nov. 14, 1784, Schlitter, p. 339.

to maintain the dignity of Pennsylvania citizenship might have pushed public opinion over to Longchamps's side if he were extradited, and a powerless Congress was inclined to leave the whole matter in the hands of the Pennsylvania authorities. The awkward situation did nothing to increase respect for the government of the United States. On the other hand, it did increase Lafayette's apprehension that the French court might be displeased.[36]

Lafayette had informed President Lee that he would again be in Trenton on the evening of December 10.[37] The leave-taking of Congress was therefore arranged for December 11. When not occupied with those arrangements, Lafayette busied himself with promoting French interests with members of Congress. He asked for a promotion for a compatriot in the American navy and compensation for French-Canadians who had fought on the American side. He openly expressed to Jay and other members of Congress his concern regarding the probable dissatisfaction of the French court in the Longchamps case and promised to use his influence to avert unpleasant consequences when he returned.[38]

The formal leave-taking took place at Congress' usual meeting hall, the Long Room at the French Arms in Trenton. Jay opened the meeting by communicating the resolution of Congress. Lafayette replied with a longer than usual address. After first expressing his gratitude for Congress' favors, he recalled his early devotion to the United States and praised the Franco-American alliance. That alliance, he declared, was "well rivetted by mutual affection, by interest, and even local situation." He next spoke earnestly of the need for unity in the United States. "In unbounded wishes to America, Sir, I am happy to observe the prevailing disposition of the people to strengthen the Confederation, preserve public faith, regulate trade, and in a proper guard over continental magazines and frontier posts, in a gener-

36. Cf. Rufus King to Gerry, May 1, 1785, Burnett, VIII, 108.
37. Lafayette to Lee, Dec. 6, 1784, Godfrey, pp. 26-27.
38. King to Gerry, May 1, 1785, Burnett, VIII, 108; Lafayette to Jay, Dec. 12, 1784, Jackson collection (on behalf of André Barré or La Barre); to Congress, Dec. 12, 1784, LC, PCC 35, fols. 93-94; and to Jay, Feb. 8, 1785, PCC 156, fols. 401-2 ([Weaver], *Diplomatic correspondence*, I, 419-20, omits the passage on the Longchamps affair).

al system of militia, in foreseeing attention to the navy, to insure every kind of safety." Then came words more outspoken for liberty and more prophetic of the near future than probably he himself realized: "May this immense temple of freedom ever stand a lesson to oppressors, an example to the oppressed, a sanctuary for the rights of mankind! And may these happy United States attain that complete splendor and prosperity which will illustrate the blessings of their government, and for ages to come rejoice the departed souls of its founders!"[39] Never before had he so clearly expressed the hope entertained by lovers of liberty all over the world that the United States would not only be successful as an experiment in free government but might also become "a lesson to oppressors" abroad.

But Congress' guest had no suspicion as yet that his own king, Louis XVI, would ever be numbered among the oppressors. Though in later years he was to think that even at this early date he had begun to hope for a republican constitution in his own country,[40] every word of his and of his hosts on this occasion breathed respect for and gratitude to the French monarchy. In fact, when he later revised his speech for the press, he even added the words "with a beloved king" to a passage describing the part France had acted "in the cause of mankind." He explained to John Jay, to whom he sent the revised version for the official record, "I have clapped in a little bit of French sugar plumb, because I thought it fair to bend a little on that gentleman's side."[41]

And Congress was no less saccharine. A letter to Louis XVI had been prepared by Jay's committee and signed by "the unanimous order of Congress." While recommending Lafayette for his talents and "his disposition to perpetuate the amity and good understanding which we pray God may ever subsist between France and America," it implored "the Author of all good" to "continue to bless Your Majesty, your family, and people, and keep you and them under his holy protection."[42]

39. *Journals of Congress*, XXVII, 684 (Dec. 13, 1784) (corrected in accordance with the original in LC, PCC 19, Vol. II, fol. 263).

40. *Mémoires*, II, 8, and III, 198.

41. Lafayette to Jay, Dec. 12, 1784, Jackson collection.

42. *Journals of Congress*, XXVII, 682–83 (Dec. 11, 1784).

Lafayette was himself designated to bring this letter to Franklin in order that it might be properly delivered to "our great and good Ally." Along with it went a letter from Lee to Franklin, also speaking warmly of Lafayette's "former and recent services to America."[43]

Although not a word explicitly assigned to the marquis the semiofficial diplomatic post that his letter to Hamilton had suggested,[44] he had good reason to feel pleased with his reception. He afterward boasted that Washington was the only other person ever to be so honored by Congress.[45] On the same day that Lafayette took leave of Congress, he was likewise received by New Jersey's governor and legislature, then also meeting in Trenton. Again he listened to a complimentary address, and again he made a gracious response. Here, too, he referred to the need to secure "the blessings of the revolution, so nobly purchased" by "the united strength and wisdom of this federated republic."[46] He spent the next day, a Sunday, in relative quiet. On December 13 he set off for Elizabethtown and New York, which he reached on the 14th.[47]

If Lafayette was not yet the full-fledged revolutionary that he was later to become, his leave-taking of Congress had nevertheless not been without its effect on revolutionary events. Carefully prepared for publication and printed in full in many newspapers throughout the land,[48] his farewell address once more spread the gospel that he had been preaching on his tour through the principal cities of ten of the United States. Preserve the French alliance, it said, and unite into a strong confederation if you wish to prosper and to have weight in the world. That Congressmen were impressed by this message Jay himself testified. And in reporting the episode, Jay too seemed cheered.

43. Lee to Lafayette and to Franklin, Dec. 11, 1784, J. C. Ballagh(ed.), *The letters of Richard Henry Lee* (New York, 1914), II, 308-9. Cf. Lee to Lafayette and to the postmaster of New York, Dec. 14, *ibid.*, pp. 310-11.

44. See above, p. 119.   45. *Mémoires*, II, 8.

46. J. O. Raum, *History of the city of Trenton, New Jersey* (Trenton, 1871), pp. 294-95.

47. Lafayette to Jay, Dec. 12, 1784, *loc. cit.*; Trenton Historical Society, *A history of Trenton, 1679-1929, etc.* (Princeton, 1929), p. 212; *Pennsylvania Packet*, Dec. 23, 1784.

48. E.g., *Pennsylvania Packet*, Dec. 18, 1784; *Connecticut Courant*, Dec. 28; *Boston magazine*, I (December, 1784), 628; *Newport Mercury*, Dec. 25.

In a letter to Franklin that Lafayette was to carry to France, Jay revealed not only his own optimism about continued friendship with France but also his own good opinion of Congress. "There are many respectable members here," he asserted. "Federal ideas seem to prevail greatly among them, and, I may add, a strong disposition to conciliation and unanimity." And James Monroe, delegate from Virginia, in imparting to Jefferson how well Lafayette had been received, praised Congress for its "perfect good temper and propriety." Since the delegates seemed to understand "the interests of the Union" and to be inclined toward "the most general and liberal principles to promote it," he foresaw "great good to the Union from this Congress."[49] Lafayette himself thought that it was "a numerous" and "a very respectable" body and that it would "do a great deal of good."[50]

BIBLIOGRAPHICAL NOTES

Different parts of Mazzei's papers have been made available by Garlick, Marraro, and Ciampini (see below, p. 224, n. 10). He proves to have been an admiring but generally reliable witness of Lafayette's activities in 1784 and after. Crèvecœur (III, 360–76) gives an inexact account of the events in this chapter.

The account of Lafayette's 1784 trip contained in *Mémoires*, II, 7–9, is inaccurate. It is made up of parts of both manuscripts used by the editors of the *Mémoires* (see I, 3). "Manuscrit no. 1" is now in the Sparks MSS (Harvard College Library) under the title of "Observations sur la guerre de la Révolution américaine et particulièrement sur le Général Lafayette." "Manuscrit no. 2" is now in the Manuscripts Division of the Library of Congress under the title of "Observations sur quelques parties de l'histoire américaine par un ami du Gal Lafayette." The latter has been carefully translated and annotated by Mrs. Jane L. Cates (unpublished doctoral dissertation, University of Chicago, 1946). Both sets of "Observations" contain details that have been omitted from the *Mémoires*, but the omissions for this episode are not significant.

49. Jay to Franklin, Dec. 13, and Monroe to Jefferson, Dec. 14, 1784, Burnett, VII, 624 and 627.

50. Lafayette to Madison, Dec. 15, 1784, *loc. cit.* Cf. Lafayette to Knox, Dec. 16, 1784, Knox papers, Massachusetts Historical Society.

CHAPTER XI

Symbol of American Unity

THE "Nymphe" had had an accident. She had run aground in New York Harbor on her way back from Yorktown. Captain Grandchain decided, when he had estimated the damage, that she must for safety's sake sail with the monthly packet, whose schedule required it to leave on December 20.[1]

That gave Lafayette about a week in New York. He spent a good part of it with General Greene, who had come to visit him.[2] He also engaged in business conversations with several merchants and exchanged ideas with Crèvecœur about establishing a bureau of commercial information in France. Crèvecœur advocated such an establishment with Lafayette as president and even gave the marquis samples of American products to take home with him.[3] Furthermore, the two men requested Washington, as a gesture of friendliness, to send a number of Kentucky seeds to the royal botanical garden in Paris.[4]

Lafayette also spent some of his week in New York writing farewell notes. To his friends in New England he apologized for not returning as he had promised.[5] An especially lengthy and affectionate letter went to Madison, indicating satisfaction with Congress and undying interest in the problems of the United

1. Washington to Lafayette, Dec. 23, 1784, Fitzpatrick, XXVIII, 17–18; *Pennsylvania Packet*, Dec. 23.
2. Lafayette to Washington, Dec. 21, 1784, Gottschalk, *Letters*, p. 289.
3. Lafayette to unknown, Dec. 17, 1784, LC, James McHenry papers; to Monroe, Dec. 19, NYPL, Monroe collection; Mitchell, pp. 143 and 257.
4. Lafayette to Washington, Dec. 17, 1784, Gottschalk, *Letters*, p. 288.
5. To Knox, Dec. 16, 1784, Massachusetts Historical Society, Knox papers; to Samuel Adams, Dec. 19, NYPL, Samuel Adams collection; to Elbridge Gerry, Dec. 19, Austin, I, 468; and to Governor Trumbull, Dec. 19, Connecticut Historical Society.

States. Lafayette assured Madison of his continued concern over the closing of the Mississippi. He hoped, however, that "Congress will act cooly and prudently by Spain who is such a fool that allowances must be made."[6]

A young Englishman who happened to be traveling in New York at this time noted the marquis's appearance. He was irresistibly reminded of Washington by the similarity of the expression in the eyes. But Lafayette suffered from the comparison. Although the traveler found no indication of great genius in the face of either man, Washington seemed to him "a finer and taller figure."[7]

When, finally, the time came to board the "Nymphe," the ceremony at parting was elaborate enough to satisfy Lafayette's innermost craving for adulation. He was accompanied to the Whitehall stairs by Governor George Clinton of New York, Consul St. John de Crèvecœur, General Nathanael Greene, General Samuel B. Webb, General John Lamb, Colonel Nicholas Fish, many other officers, and a considerable number of citizens. As the barge that carried the party to the frigate passed the Battery, he was honored with the "federal salute" of thirteen guns. When they reached the "Nymphe," he was handed on board by the governor on one side and the French consul on the other. The frigate then saluted the American flag, and the Battery replied. The New York papers, reporting the incident, praised the recipient of these honors not only as "brave in the field and generous to our army" but as "a warm, steady, disinterested and influential friend at the court of France." In the fashion of the day, the newspapers of other cities copied this eulogy.[8]

Before the "Nymphe" sailed, Governor Clinton delivered to Lafayette a letter from Washington bidding him a sad farewell. The older general was unabashed both in his resignation to the idea that they might never meet again and in his sentimental affection for his young comrade. "It is unnecessary, I persuade

6. Lafayette to Madison, Dec. 15, 1784, Barrett collection.
7. D. S. Robertson (ed.), *An Englishman in America 1785, being the diary of Joseph Hadfield* (Toronto, 1933), p. 14.
8. *Pennsylvania Packet*, Dec. 29, 1784; *Connecticut Courant*, Dec. 28; *Massachusetts Centinel*, Jan. 8, 1785; *Pennsylvania Journal and Weekly Advertiser*, Dec. 29, 1784.

myself, to repeat to you, my dr. Marqs., the sincerity of my regard and friendship, nor have I words which could express my affection for you, were I to attempt it."⁹

The idea that he might never see his venerated chief again drew from Lafayette a feeling protest: "My whole soul revolts at the idea, and could I harbour it an instant, indeed, my dear General, it would make [me] miserable." But, he was persuaded, they would meet again—certainly at Mount Vernon, if not in Europe. And then, as he realized that they were going to be separated by a wide ocean, he added: "Every thing that admiration, respect, gratitude, friendship, and filial love can inspire, is combined in my affectionate heart to devote me most tenderly to you. In your friendship I find a delight which words cannot express. Adieu, my dear General; it is not without emotion that I write this word, altho' I know I shall soon visit you again. Be attentive to your health. Let me hear from you every month. Adieu, adieu."¹⁰

His Most Christian Majesty's frigate "Nymphe" sailed out of New York Harbor on December 21, 1784. She carried several passengers who must have appeared quite strange to the seagoing worthies in her crew. Noblemen like Lafayette and Caraman who traveled deadhead on His Majesty's vessels were not unknown, but white boys of good family and Indians were rare. In keeping with the promise made at Fort Schuyler, the Oneidas had agreed that one of their young half-breeds named Peter Otsiquette should go with Kayewla to France as a favorite servant. But Otsiquette had gone off to Quebec, and Lafayette had to rest content with his family's promise to send him to France the next year. Meanwhile he had chosen an Onondaga boy of twelve named Kayenlaha to take with him.¹¹ The young savage

9. Washington to Lafayette, Dec. 8, 1784, *Fitzpatrick*, XXVIII, 7; cf. Washington to Clinton, Dec. 8, *ibid.*, p. 6.

10. Dec. 21, 1784, Gottschalk, *Letters*, pp. 288–90.

11. *Gentleman's magazine*, LV (1785), 148; *Courrier de l'Europe*, Feb. 11, 1785; Lafayette to Wadsworth, Apr. 16, Connecticut State Library, Gov. Joseph Trumbull collection; to William Constable, May 13, 1785, *Magazine of American history*, XI (1884), 546; Mme de Lafayette [*sic*] to Jefferson, *ca.* August, 1786, Chinard, *Lafayette and Jefferson*, p. 104; Jared Sparks, *The life of John Ledyard, the American traveller; comprising selections from his journal and correspondence* (Cambridge, Mass., 1828), p. 200. For the confusion of Kayenlaha with Otsiquette see Appen. II below. Lafayette

could speak no French, and the "Nymphe" must have appeared bewildering to him. He probably little suspected the curiosity that he on his side excited in the minds of the Frenchmen who beheld him. Lafayette's party also included a fourteen-year-old white boy named John Edwards Caldwell, orphan of a chaplain in the American army. Lafayette was taking him to France at the behest of some of his father's friends to complete his education.[12] Lafayette, Caraman, Caldwell, and Kayenlaha shared the misery of a mid-winter voyage, punctuated by nothing more interesting than seasickness. They were pushed rapidly ahead by strong winds and landed at Brest after a crossing of only thirty days.

The significance of Lafayette's pilgrimage of six hundred leagues through ten American states had not yet been fully appreciated in France. Adrienne had spent most of the period of his absence in Chavaniac with her mother and children and had returned to Paris only in November.[13] The European journals, having to depend for distant news chiefly on copying from each other, had not yet had a chance to reprint from the American press the numerous encomiums of her wandering husband. The Anglo-American revolutionary, Thomas Paine, perhaps because he was all too willing to believe the worst of royal ministers, afterward received the impression (probably from Lafayette himself) that Vergennes deliberately kept at least one of the marquis's speeches out of the press. That one was the farewell address to Congress. According to Paine, Vergennes considered the reference to America as a standing lesson to oppressors and

is himself called "Kayenlaa" in Olden times (II, 407 and 428–29), but that is an error for "Kayewla."

12. Nicholas Murray, "A memoir of the Rev. James Caldwell of Elizabeth-town," Proceedings of the New Jersey Historical Society, III (1848), 88–89. [Davis], Complete history, pp. 170–71, and, hence, others say that George Washington Greene was aboard the "Nymphe," but see below, p. 404. Lafayette had hoped also to take Bushrod Washington, the nephew of the general, along with him, but he decided not to go (see Gottschalk, Letters, p. 289). C. H. Hunt (Life of Edward Livingston [New York, 1864], pp. 44–45) states that Lafayette had also, at one time, considered taking Edward Livingston to France. He does not make clear whether that was in 1781 or 1784. I can find no supporting evidence for either supposition.

13. Lasteyrie, pp. 85–88; C. F. Adams (ed.), Letters of Mrs. Adams, the wife of John Adams (Boston, 1848), pp. 215–16; [Caroline A. de Windt (ed.)], Journal and correspondence of Miss Adams, daughter of John Adams . . . written in France and England in 1785 (New York, 1841–42), I, 33.

an example to the oppressed too provocative for Frenchmen to read.[14]

Nevertheless, while Lafayette was overseas, his name had won new luster in France. It was kept in the papers by the accounts of Congress' appreciative reception of his earlier efforts to promote Franco-American commerce.[15] Shortly after he left, Adrienne attended a session of the Grand Chamber of the Paris parlement, and the advocate-general, upon spying her, converted his speech into a eulogy of her husband. That episode was likewise reported in the papers.[16] Nor were the ministers given a respite from his importunities while he was gone, for Adrienne proved to be a better beggar than he for his school at St. Georges d'Aurac.[17] Neither his fame nor his causes suffered the slightest oblivion during his seven months' absence.

Yet (as we have seen)[18] it was not to build up or to cast down Lafayette's personal reputation that certain French officials had smoothed his way in America. Their motives were more definitely political. The French foreign office could not be indifferent to the gaping cracks in the edifice of American union. They not only revealed weakness in an ally, they also made it hard for France to derive full advantage from a friendly commercial policy; for if there were no centralized authority in the United States, thirteen separate states would have to be dealt with.

And the event proved that no French messenger could have been more successful than Lafayette in carrying to America the good word of union and alliance. More than any other man who had a claim to the gratitude of Americans, he belonged equally to all Americans. Washington was a Virginian. Franklin, still abroad, was a Pennsylvanian. Adams was a New Englander. Every American seemed to belong to a state first, to a region next, and to the United States only afterward. But Lafayette belonged to no state or region. During the war he had campaigned in New England, the middle states, the South. Since

14. M. D. Conway (ed.), *Rights of man; being an answer to Mr. Burke's attack on the French Revolution* (reprinted from *The writings of Thomas Paine*, Vol. II [New York, 1895]), pp. 282–83.

15. Cf. *Gazette de Leyde*, Oct. 1, 1784 (suppl.).

16. *Ibid.*, July 6, 1784; *Courrier de l'Europe*, July 9.

17. Memorandum dated Dec. 4, 1784, AN, F^{12}1376, folder dated 1782.

18. See above, p. 83.

1777 he had visited every state in the Union but Georgia. He was the only surviving major-general of the Revolution to have no residence in any of the states and yet to be known throughout them all. His strength as a cementing force for both the American union and the Franco-American alliance, self-evident when his journey began, had grown as it progressed.

When Lafayette left America, it was undeniable that his mission had helped the forces that were producing the hoped-for results. Typical of the outpourings that had regularly dotted the sparse columns of American newspapers as he moved from city to city and state to state was a dispatch from Baltimore after he first passed through Maryland.[19] It eulogized him in glowing sentences for his aid to America: he had fought in the war, he had secured loans, he had won free ports in France for American commerce, he had secured a favorable change in tariff duties; and all this had been done only out of disinterested friendliness with no expectation of recompense for his sacrifices. Other papers had printed equally ardent tributes. The versifiers of the country had used much printer's ink to extol the marquis.[20] His name had become more than ever a household word. Babies and places had been christened after him. College degrees, freedom of cities, honorary membership in societies, and statues had been awarded him.[21] He had become a kind of national patron saint.

At least one American leader, lamenting the lack of cohesion among the states even more than did the French, revealed that "the Marquis's" mission had tended to foster unity. Shortly after Washington returned to Mount Vernon on leaving Lafayette in Maryland, he had reflected upon "the fatality attending all our public measures." He waxed wroth at "particular states counteracting the plans of the United States when submitted to them, opposing each other upon all occasions, torn by internal disputes, or supinely negligent and inattentive to everything which is not local and selfinteresting, and very often short sighted in these." With Lafayette in mind he wrote:

19. *Maryland Gazette*, Aug. 26, 1784.
20. See above, p. 116, and L. M. Miner, *Our rude forefathers: American political verse, 1783–1788* (Cedar Rapids, Iowa, 1937), p. 34, n. 12.
21. See above, pp. 87, 93, 115, 126, 130, and 133, and below, pp. 145–47 and 150, and Miner, pp. 225, n. 55, and 226.

"Would to God our own countrymen, who are entrusted with
the management of the political machine, could view things by
that large and extensive scale upon which it is measured by foreigners, and by the statesmen of Europe, who see what we
might be, and predict what we shall come to."[22] His most recent
source of information regarding what foreigners and European
statesmen thought had been none other than his guest the marquis. And Washington, to whom the theme was already familiar,
was probably not the only American to be induced by Lafayette's mission to ponder further upon the effect of American
disunion abroad. The young Frenchman's speeches had harped
upon that subject. He had given equal emphasis only to the idea
of Franco-American solidarity. Liberty, prosperity, and peace
had been subordinate motifs implicit in those major themes.
When his mission was over, he had talked about the necessity
of national unity more often, before more people, and in more
places than any other champion of the good cause; and nearly
everyone was ready to believe that he had no personal or regional purpose to serve, that he had acted only as the patron of
American well-being.

But a patron saint must not remain a foreigner. Following the
example that New York City had set in September, 1784, other
places in the United States now made Lafayette a citizen. He
had hardly ceased to be buffeted by the Atlantic winds that returned him to France when the state of Maryland decreed a
special act of naturalization in his honor. It provided that "the
Marquis de la Fayette and his heirs male for ever, shall be, and
they and each of them are hereby deemed, adjudged, and taken
to be, natural born citizens of this state, and shall henceforth be
entitled to all the immunities, rights and privileges, of natural
born citizens thereof." The proposal, introduced in the Maryland Senate shortly after Lafayette's visit in Annapolis and
passed while he was still in the United States, became law on
January 22, 1785. Maryland's announced intention was to "perpetuate a name dear to the State," because it was that of a hero
who had "disinterestedly refused the usual rewards of command
and sought only to deserve what he attained, the character of

22. Washington to Knox, Dec. 5, 1784, Fitzpatrick, XXVIII, 5.

patriot and soldier."²³ Washington happened to be in Annapolis
at the time, concerned with the problem of inland navigation
that eventually helped to precipitate a demand for a "more perfect Union." He soon learned of Lafayette's new citizenship and
thus, quite accidentally but nonetheless fittingly, became the
first to inform him of it.²⁴

New England, not to be outdone by New York City and
Maryland, also adopted the French "patriot and soldier." On
February 22 the city of Hartford made Lafayette and his son
(as well as Crèvecœur and his sons) citizens.²⁵ During the same
week Massachusetts conferred citizenship upon him and his
heirs in order to commemorate his "virtuous exertions."²⁶

Virginia finally added its name to the list of places claiming
American's Marquis and did so with an additional flourish. The
Richmond government had decided, back in 1781, to present to
Lafayette a bust of himself. That decision had struck Washington and others as "odd,"²⁷ and so while Lafayette was traveling
in the United States in 1784, it was resolved to make the bust
a gift to the city of Paris instead and to place another copy of
it in the Virginia capital alongside a statue of Washington.²⁸ In
January, 1785, Patrick Henry found a "double pleasure" as governor and as friend in informing Lafayette of the state's new
decision. It was Virginia's intention, he declared, "that the
gratitude of those who claim you as their fellow-citizen may be

23. Maryland Historical Society, "Votes and proceedings of the Senate of the
state of Maryland," November session, 1784, pp. 7, 14, 17, and 18; "Votes and proceedings of the House of Delegates of the state of Maryland," November session, 1784,
pp. 43, 47, and 48; "Laws of Maryland, made and passed at a session of Assembly,
begun and held at the city of Annapolis, on Monday the first of November in the year
of Our Lord one thousand and seven hundred and eighty-four," chap. xii. Whether this
and the similar laws discussed below are valid today has been a subject of much speculation (see Appen. III, below).
    24. Dec. 23, 1784, Fitzpatrick, XXVIII, 18.
    25. Connecticut Courant, Mar. 1, 1785; Crèvecœur, III, 344. This Hartford citizen-
ship apparently was responsible for a belief in some quarters that the state of Connecticut had granted Lafayette citizenship (cf. Crèvecœur, III, 342–44; Gazette de
France, May 6; Gazette de Leyde, May 10 [suppl.]), but no official record of such an act
has been found.
    26. Baxter (ed.), Documentary history of the state of Maine, 2d ser., XX, 248–49.
    27. Gottschalk, Lafayette and the close of the American Revolution, p. 341; cf. Madi-
son to Monroe, Dec. 4, 1784, Hunt, II, 97.
    28. Journal of Delegates beginning October 18, 1784, p. 49 (meeting of Dec. 1);
W. W. Hening (ed.), The statutes at large; being a collection of all the laws of Virginia
from the first session of the legislature in the year 1619 (Richmond, 1810–23), X, 553.

as conspicuous as the merit it wishes to perpetuate."[29] The honor came as no surprise to the recipient, since he had learned about it from his friend Madison before he had embarked at New York.[30] Nearly a year was to pass, however, before Virginia formally followed the example already set by Maryland and Massachusetts. In November, 1785, the Virginia legislature, "being solicitous to bestow the most decisive mark of regard which a republic can give," voted him citizenship in that state (without mentioning his heirs or descendants).[31]

Thus Lafayette became the only man who was a citizen of several of the United States at the same time—two cities (New York and Hartford) and three states (Maryland, Massachusetts, and Virginia) having granted him that title. The honor, of course, was not entirely free. It was expected to be paid for in new favors. John Jay, writing to Lafayette on American diplomatic complications with a candor that would have been unbecoming in a secretary of foreign affairs addressing a foreigner, apologized for his frankness: "I write to you freely, but you are my fellow-citizen, and therefore it does not appear to me necessary to attempt to dress my ideas à la mode de Paris."[32] Jay apparently counted upon him to be not only American but more American than French and predicted that he would "probably be distinguished by the appelation of Americanus."[33]

Thus along with the flag, the Articles of Confederation, and Congress, the young French aristocrat had become a symbol of American unity. Nor was it only in the United States that that was true. Thomas Jefferson, on arriving in Europe, had found a general impression that "everything in America was anarchy, tumult, and civil war" and attributed this suspicious attitude to deliberate British propaganda. But the enthusiastic welcome that had greeted the young hero in every quarter of the Confederation "gave a check to those ideas."[34] America had shown

29. Jan. 29, 1785, Henry, II, 262.
30. Lafayette to Madison, Dec. 17, 1784, Barrett collection.
31. Hening, XII, 30; *Journal of the House of Delegates of the commonwealth of Virginia for the session beginning October 17, 1785*, pp. 15 (meeting of Oct. 31, 1785) and 16 (meeting of Nov. 1).
32. Jan. 19, 1785, Johnston, III, 139.
33. Jay to Mme de Lafayette, Aug. 13, 1785, *ibid.*, p. 163.
34. Jefferson to Madison, Sept. 1, 1785, Lipscomb and Bergh, V, 108.

its ability to unite at least in gratitude and love for its leaders. And when the returning hero went out of his way to speak of the "peace, plenty and happiness" he had witnessed "where the horrors of a most cruel war had been so long raging," when he insisted that "every part of America is thriving very fast," when he expressed his pleasure "with the general disposition of the people, the good intentions of the states, [and] the excellent collection of the present Congress," he induced many to share with him the hope that "the United States will attain that degree of splendor and energy which a free and generous nation has a right to expect."[35]

The reassurance that Lafayette brought back from America must have been highly gratifying to the shrewd men like Vergennes, Calonne, and Castries who had exploited his popularity in America for their own ends. If they could have recognized the subtle changes that had taken place in their young friend, they might have been less pleased. He had certainly been a willing puppet of these wire-pullers, as in the past, but this time he had been less unsuspecting. The collaboration he had got from every French official in America might once have appeared as merely a polite tribute to one who fell in the category of "very important persons," but it had been so general and uniform that it now stood revealed as the product of a recognized policy, if not of a single directing hand. The French legation had been his home at Philadelphia. He had regularly consulted with the French chargé d'affaires and the French consuls. They had stood beside him in the parades, negotiations, and banquets in which he took part. They had reported back to the foreign office what he and they did, and he had himself frequently written to the minister of foreign affairs. The agents of other countries had informed their governments of his movements. He had traveled in America and returned to France in a royal warship, and its captain had been his constant companion for a large part of his tour. Thus Vergennes's and Castries's agents had been his agents. True, he had enjoyed some of these privileges on earlier occasions in America. But he was no longer so callow as he once

35. Lafayette to Carmichael, Mar. 10, 1785, LC, House of Representatives collection, Carmichael papers, No. 104.

had been. He must have understood, no less than Miranda with less information at his disposal,[36] that all this official kowtowing could not have been without design. He had never before hesitated to exploit his personal position, and he had frequently allowed himself to be exploited too, but now he seemed to understand more fully that exploitation was a two-way process—that people did things for him because he was useful to them and not merely because he was what he was.

Nor was greater sophistication the only change wrought in Lafayette's personality by his transatlantic sojourn. He returned to France more than ever the champion of American aspirations. Liberty, federal union, a freer trade, a strong alliance, abolition of slavery, international peace—these were ideals that had regularly entered his speeches and addresses in America. They were no longer merely the private opinions of a soldier, as nearly all his earlier pronouncements on such subjects had been. They had been proclaimed before large assemblages and public bodies and had been spread broadcast in the newspapers. He was now publicly committed to them both in America and in France. He was "typed" more unmistakably than other "Americans" in France, who had not rededicated themselves to the American cause by a recent pilgrimage. He was to find it harder hereafter to speak with a rising or falling accent on liberty according to the preferences of his audience.

Washington perceived that the outcome of the admiring Frenchman's visit would be something more than mere personal satisfaction. "Our amiable young friend, the Marquis de la Fayette," he wrote to Knox, "could not be otherwise than well pleased with his reception in America. Every testimony of respect, affection and gratitude has been shewn him, wherever he went; if his heart therefore had not been impressed with these expressions (which I am far from supposing) the political consequence which he will derive from them must bear them in his remembrance, and point to the advantages wch. must flow."[37]

Washington spoke with his wonted foresight. Lafayette's trip to America was destined to make him a more important figure

36. See above, p. 118.
37. Jan. 5, 1785, Fitzpatrick, XXVIII, 26.

in France as well as in America. When Louis XVI received Congress' letter praising his well-deserving subject, he replied, "The justice which you do to the Marquis de la Fayette confirms more and more the opinion we have also of his zeal and talents, and cannot but add to the desire we have of giving him further marks of our satisfaction."[38] Royal satisfaction, however, was to prove more fleeting than republican gratitude.

BIBLIOGRAPHICAL NOTES

It has been found necessary to correct some of the legends regarding the 1784 journey as they were encountered above. Others have been treated separately in Appendix I below. Special emphasis has been given to [Davis], *Complete history*, because, being one of the best of the early biographies, it has been relied upon too uncritically by subsequent biographers. In addition to the misstatements already indicated, this work is responsible for the belief that Lafayette received an honorary degree from Princeton University in 1784. The records of the trustees of Princeton show that he was awarded this degree in 1790, though the diploma was not presented until 1824 (courtesy of Malcolm Young, reference librarian, Princeton University). Lafayette also received an honorary LL.D. from the University of the State of Pennsylvania on November 23, 1787 (see the letter of E. W. Mumford, secretary of the University of Pennsylvania, to S. W. Jackson, May 20, 1932, in Jackson's compilation entitled "Honorary degrees conferred on Lafayette 1784–1824," Lafayette College Library, Easton, Pennsylvania).

Paine's *Rights of man* contains a long passage on the radicalism of Lafayette. It is altogether unreliable, not only because Paine got much of his information at second hand, probably from Lafayette himself several years after the events concerned, but also because Paine, idealizing Lafayette, was making an odious comparison between his hero's enlightenment and Edmund Burke's traditionalism.

38. May 10, 1785, [Weaver], *Diplomatic correspondence*, I, 133; cf. R. H. Lee to Washington, July 23, 1785, Ballagh, II, 377.

CHAPTER XII

Trade as a Tool of Diplomacy

THE "Nymphe" sailed into Brest Harbor on January 20, 1785. It had spent a tedious and uneventful month on the Atlantic, despite the rumor in America that its crossing had been boisterous and marred by accident.[1]

For once Lafayette seemed to be in no hurry. Four days later he was no nearer Paris than Rennes, the capital of the province of Brittany. It happened that the provincial estates of Brittany were then in session. Lafayette, still a large property-holder in that province, felt it appropriate to attend the session. As the famous young general entered the meeting room, he was greeted with a round of applause, interrupting a report by the committee on canals. A seat was made for him on the barons' bench close to the president, and the interrupted report was resumed. When the worthy abbé who was reading it came to a passage dealing with the advantages derived from the Breton canals during the recent war and expected during the forthcoming peace, he interjected a remark on "how pleasant it was to be in the presence of one who had contributed to achieving that desired peace." Lafayette, having to proceed on his journey, soon withdrew but not without first making a little speech of thanks for his cordial reception and expressing the hope that he might soon become a member of the assembly. "He would always preserve a Breton heart," he promised.[2] His Breton heart came along with his Breton lands from his maternal grandfather. The heart at least had not notably affected his life in the past, but

1. Lee to Washington, Apr. 18, 1785, Ballagh, II, 349; Lee to Lafayette, June 11, *ibid.*, p. 369.
2. *Gazette de Leyde*, Feb. 15, 1785; Bachaumont, XXVIII, 141–42 (Feb. 15).

this chance identification with Breton politics was to have significant consequences in the near future.

Lafayette reached Paris around January 27. His wife Adrienne once more breathed easily after her "long separation and lively fears." She gratefully reveled in his account of the honors showered upon him in America and unashamedly admitted to their mutual friends her joy upon his return to the blessings of home.[3] Thomas Jefferson was among the first to learn of his arrival, for at the earliest opportunity he sent word of the death the preceding fall of Jefferson's youngest daughter.[4]

Within a few days the marquis was once more busily engaged in society and politics. John Adams had been in Paris for some time with his family, co-operating with Franklin and Jefferson in the negotiation of commercial treaties. The Adamses had called on Mme de Lafayette during her husband's absence, and she had gone to their house for dinner. Young Miss Abigail Adams thought Adrienne was a fine woman, friendly and easy of manner, "sprightly and very pleasing." "I had always heard," Abigail confided in her journal, "she was handsome; I do not think her so; she was not painted, and very little dressed." They spoke English, of which Adrienne knew a little.[5] Lafayette now returned the courtesy that the Adamses had shown his wife. On January 30 he called on them—to the confusion of young Abigail, who was not "properly dressed"—and gave them a heartening account of the prosperity of Massachusetts and the growing union of America.[6]

Until recently Adams had been stationed in The Hague, and conversation soon got round to the current threat of war between Austria and Holland. The ground of dispute was the navigation of the Scheldt River in the Austrian Netherlands (Belgium). The Austrians were anxious to develop the commercial potentialities of the Scheldt, but it was closed by earlier treaties, to which France was a party. The Austrian ruler, Em-

3. Mme de Lafayette to Carmichael, [February, 1785], LC, House of Representatives collection, Carmichael papers, No. 109. Cf. Jay to Mme de Lafayette, Aug. 13, Johnston, III, 162–63.

4. *Journal of Miss Adams*, I, 45 (Jan. 27, 1785).

5. *Ibid.*, pp. 30–33 (Oct. 28, Nov. 7–18, 1784).

6. *Ibid.*, p. 46 (Jan. 30, 1785); "Diary," *Works of John Adams*, III, 389–90 (Jan. 31).

peror Joseph II, would have much preferred to exchange these
Belgian Netherlands for some territories in Bavaria, to which
he had a tenuous claim, but Frederick the Great of Prussia,
seeking to preserve the balance of power in Germany, objected.
The French court, torn between Queen Marie Antoinette's
Austrian loyalties and its interest in defending Holland and the
German princes against Austrian aggression, hoped to maintain
peace. Yet guns had already been fired and armies were everywhere on the alert by the time Lafayette returned home. Among
the Dutch provinces the old animosity between Republicans
and Royalists seemed ready once more to burst into open conflict. John Adams, suspicious of Frenchmen in general and of
Lafayette in particular, noted his visitor's extraordinary interest in the prospects of an Austro-Dutch war. Both men recalled
that Vergennes had hoped to place a French generalissimo in
command of the Continental Army after the War of American
Independence began. Lafayette thereby gave the first intimation that he now knew (if he did not know before) that his
friend the Comte de Broglie had once had ambitions along that
line. As Lafayette left, he confided to Adams that he himself
entertained a similar ambition with regard to the Dutch Republic, even at the risk of offending the queen. "Although he
would not serve a foreign prince," he indicated, "he would
serve a republic," and he "would be easy" about compensation.[7]
Somehow Lafayette seemed to think that Adams could be helpful in realizing his latest fancy, but the matter apparently never
came up between them again.

Two weeks later the Lafayettes and the Adamses found themselves together in a numerous company at Benjamin Franklin's
house in Passy and, a week after that, at the Lafayette mansion
on the Rue de Bourbon. Miss Abigail was impressed with the
great modesty, reserve, and good manners of the young general,
the amiability of his wife, and their obvious affection for their
three children ("the more remarkable in a country where the
least trait of such a disposition is scarce known"). The two older
children—Anastasie, now nearly eight, and George, past five—
had been taught to speak English and to sing some English

7. *Works of John Adams*, III, 389–90.

songs.[8] Subsequently Abigail was to learn that the Lafayettes also avoided the late parties and heavy gambling that were so common in aristocratic Parisian society, and her esteem for them mounted still higher. Apparently nothing more serious than the marquise's preference for American to French women was discussed at either dinner.[9]

The Lafayettes now renewed their regular Monday night dinners. In fact, they had had invitations printed with only blanks to fill in for the date and the guest's name. Any American in Paris was likely to be found at these "American dinners," as they came to be called. And so Abigail and her parents were at the Rue de Bourbon again two weeks later with much the same company, mostly Americans. The next week the Lafayettes once more returned the Adamses' call. If the Dutch crisis entered the conversation on any of these occasions, it was kept confidential by all who took part in it.[10]

To his friends in America the marquis confessed that the prospect of war in Europe was some slight compensation for having had to leave "favorite plans" in America.[11] "Where I would serve," he informed Washington, "I had not yet time to arrange—but it will not be with my dear General, and every thing is so short of that happiness, that nothing, when compared to it, can possibly please me."[12] American newspapers soon printed a curious anonymous letter from Versailles in which Lafayette, impelled by his love for republican principles, was depicted as urging Washington to give the Dutch the benefit of his wisdom.[13] The writer, whoever he was, understood Lafayette somewhat but Washington not at all.

Shortly after his return to France, Lafayette resumed his unofficial status of America's friend at court. His first responsibili-

8. *Journal of Miss Adams*, I, 47 and 49 (Feb. 14 and 21, 1785); cf. Mrs. Adams to Mrs. Mary Cranch, Mar. 13, *Letters of Mrs. Adams*, pp. 235–36.

9. *Journal of Miss Adams*, I, 49–50 and 59 (Feb. 21 and Mar. 20, 1785).

10. *Ibid.*, pp. 52 and 56 (Mar. 7 and 14, 1785). Cf. I. M. Hays (ed.), *Calendar of the papers of Benjamin Franklin in the library of the American Philosophical Society* (Philadelphia, 1908), III, 249.

11. To Jay, Feb. 8, 1785, [Weaver], *Diplomatic correspondence*, I, 419–20.

12. Feb. 9, 1785, Gottschalk, *Letters*, p. 291.

13. *Newport Mercury*, Mar. 6, 1785.

ty was to smooth out the Longchamps affair.[14] The French government, as had been feared, had already demanded that Longchamps be extradited. Lafayette's explanations, however, along with the intercession of other suppliants, finally induced Vergennes to consent to leave the matter to the Pennsylvania courts.[15]

The business of being a self-appointed representative of the United States also involved Lafayette once more in Spanish diplomacy. The Mississippi problem was another issue that he made his own. He now furnished Jefferson with copies of his *aide-mémoire* regarding the concessions elicited from the Spanish minister of foreign affairs when he had visited Madrid in 1783. These concessions had included a promise, implicit and conditional but nonetheless reassuring, concerning the Mississippi: "The fear of raising an object of dissention is the only objection the [Spanish] king has to the free navigation of the Mississippi River."[16] By reminding both sides of this promise, Lafayette obviously intended to do his bit toward resolving the Mississippi conflict by diplomacy.

Washington, however, soon confirmed his own preference for a purely American solution of the issue by the creation of an eastern outlet for frontier products. "The inland navigation of our rivers," he wrote, would open "free and easy communications with the Western Territory (thereby binding them to us by interest, the only knot which will hold)."[17] To that end, he had helped to form the Potomac Navigation Company and the James River Navigation Company, authorized to improve the two river systems and build canals between them and the west-

14. Lafayette to Jay, Feb. 8, 1785, LC, PCC 156, fols. 401–2. The printed versions leave out the references to Longchamps. See Louis Gottschalk, "Notes on an unpublished letter from Lafayette to Jay," *Gazette of the American Friends of Lafayette*, No. 6 (March, 1946).

15. Lafayette to Washington, May 11, 1785, Gottschalk, *Letters*, p. 297; Lafayette to Jay, May 11, LC, PCC 156, fol. 418 (the printed versions of this letter also omit the references to Longchamps). Cf. Lyons, pp. 41–43.

16. Lafayette to Floridablanca, Feb. 19, 1783, LC, PCC 156, fol. 329; Lafayette to Jefferson, Feb. 14, 1785, Chinard, *Lafayette and Jefferson*, p. 89. Cf. Gottschalk, *Lafayette and the close of the American Revolution*, p. 409.

17. Feb. 15, 1785, Fitzpatrick, XXVIII, 72. Lafayette received this letter *ca.* March 6; see Lafayette to W. T. Franklin, Mar. 6, 1785, APS, Franklin papers, Vol. 106, No. 147.

ern waters. Washington even enlisted the marquis's help in finding qualified French engineers for the enterprise.

Lafayette still hoped for a magnificent gesture from Madrid
that would strengthen the Franco-Spanish-American understanding. Accordingly he spoke to the French ministers about
suggesting to the Spanish that New Orleans be made a free
port. He also addressed himself to the newly appointed French
ambassador, the Duc de La Vauguyon. They all proved to be
quite cynical, however, regarding Spanish generosity.[18] Another
possible solution would have been the sale of New Orleans to
America, but the marquis felt certain that the Spanish would
likewise be deaf to any such proposal.[19]

Hoping to rouse the Spanish government to unwonted
heights, Lafayette resorted to an old ruse. It was common in the
eighteenth century for government agents to open and read letters suspected of having political significance. Counting upon
the custom to be observed in this instance, Lafayette wrote to
William Carmichael, the American minister at Madrid, about
his conversations with Washington on the Mississippi question.
He took care to state emphatically the Spanish case in favor of
free navigation. Washington's interest in opening the James and
Potomac rivers, he explained, was due to fear that the settlers
of the western country might otherwise be alienated from their
American loyalties and won to Spain. "When America gets the
[free] navigation [of the Mississippi], all the back country
people, as they are severed from the States by chains of mountains seventy miles wide, will break off their connection with
you [i.e., the United States], put themselves under Spanish influence, and as they are composed of emigrants from every nation and of course attached to none, they will become a check
upon you. . . . Should it on the contrary be possible for the
Spaniards to shut up the Mississipy, the back country settle-

18. Lafayette to Madison, Mar. 16, 1785, Historical Society of Pennsylvania; to
Henry, Mar. 16, Gilbert Chinard (ed.), *Lafayette in Virginia; unpublished letters from the
original manuscripts in the Virginia State Library and the Library of Congress* (Baltimore,
1928), pp. 63–64; to Washington, Mar. 19 and Apr. 16, Gottschalk, *Letters*, pp. 293
and 295; to Jay, Mar. 19, LC, PCC 156, fols. 408–10 (with omissions in [Weaver],
Diplomatic correspondence, I, 421–22, and in other printed versions).

19. Lafayette to Washington, Mar. 19, 1785, Gottschalk, *Letters*, p. 293, and to
Jay, March 19, *loc. cit.*

ments will be forced into an union with this side of the mountains—and as these settlements are growing much faster than
you have any idea of, they will influence the United States into
unfriendly measures." He had secret information, he claimed,
that England, scheming to keep Spain and the United States
embroiled, was using her influence with "leading men" to prevent a peaceful solution of Spanish-American affairs.[20] Despite
such maneuvers, the controversy did not appear to him to be
difficult to solve. The wise course, he stated for prying Spanish
eyes to read, would be for the Spanish government to open the
Mississippi and make New Orleans a free port, "though General
Washington thinks it would weaken America and transform the
back country people into Spaniards." He pretended to be revealing these confidences only because Carmichael was a good
friend of the Franco-American alliance[21] (which implied friendliness toward Spain).

This equivocal letter, though studiously phrased so as to take
in overinquisitive Spaniards, did not misrepresent Washington's
point of view. Lafayette, however, did not expect his little ruse
to have great consequences. He was certain that the Spanish
would remain obdurate. Engineering projects on the James and
the Potomac therefore soon became for him "the first political,
mercantile and national plan which can now employ the United
States," and he undertook to look for French engineers.[22]

Thus Lafayette found himself actively involved in the events
that were eventually to lead to the "more perfect Union" of the
United States. He wore out many a quill in the good cause. On
March 16 alone he penned eight letters to America. To General
Greene, for instance, he wrote: "You have asked my opinion
upon the effect that would result in Europe in case Congress
have powers to regulate trade and measures are taken to restore
public credit. The effect, my dear Sir, would be greater than can
be imagined. I wish those who oppose these measures could
come to this side of the Atlantic, hear what is said of the prob-

20. Lafayette to Carmichael, Mar. 10, 1785, LC, House of Representatives collection, Carmichael papers, No. 104.

21. *Ibid.*

22. Lafayette to Washington, Apr. 16, 1785, Gottschalk, *Letters*, p. 295.

able division among the States, of the neglect that is likely to take place in every concerns of public faith, public energy, public safety—and altho' those bad omens are, thank God, ill founded, altho' American patriotism, virtue and wisdom cannot but being roused to every thing that is good and great, provided you give the people time to consider and judge their own faults, yet I cannot hear those ideas spocken without heartly wishing no time may be lost in ensuring the consequence and prosperity of the American Confederation."[23] To Elbridge Gerry he expressed a similar opinion: "The more I consider the situation of affairs, the more impressed I am with the necessity to strengthen the foederal union, to make commercial regulations, to do every thing that can ensure union and energy."[24] The president of Congress was exhorted: "Above all, my dear Sir, do attend to the confederation, to union and harmony, to every regulation that can give security to the commerce, energy to the government, faith to the public creditors. . . . The fate of future ages does probably depend upon what will be done this year."[25] And a few days later the American secretary of foreign affairs was informed: "I . . . am happy to hear that foederal ideas are thriving in America. The more I see, I hear, and I think in Europe, the more I wish for every measures that can ensure to the United States dignity, power and public confidence."[26] Few advocates of American union were more importunate than the young Franco-American patriot.

Meanwhile, Lafayette also busied himself with promoting American commercial interests. When he returned from the States, he learned that the French ministers, no less anxious than he to win American good will, had continued their friendly policy in his absence. By a decree of August 5, 1784, they had kept their earlier promises to him and had gone a great way toward meeting the demands of American merchants for special privileges in the French West Indies. The decree permitted free

23. Clements Library, Greene papers.

24. LC, Gerry papers.

25. APS, R. H. Lee correspondence, Vol. II, fols. 282–83. The version in R. H. Lee, *Memoir of the life of Richard Henry Lee and his correspondence* (Philadelphia, 1825), II, 109–10, is inaccurate in some details.

26. Lafayette to Jay, Mar. 19, 1785, *loc. cit.*

importation of certain enumerated articles—specifically excepting flour and sugar, however—into certain ports of the French
West Indies, which thereby became free ports. In some quarters
this decree was regarded as a triumph of political considerations
over economic interests.

By the time Lafayette returned from America, this decree had
been in force long enough for the protest of French merchants
to have become crystallized. In his letters to America he turned
this protest to political uses. He pointed out that French traders
and planters were being required to make a great sacrifice and
were becoming quite vocal about it.[27] Yet French sacrifices
seemed to have been in vain, since American traders still preferred to do business with England. England, on the other hand,
was obviously disinclined to make any concessions to the Americans, who were at that very moment vainly soliciting a friendly
trade agreement and the evacuation of the forts on the Canadian frontier. Despite this discouraging situation, the marquis
spread broadcast his promise to continue to solicit further cod-
dling of American trade.[28]

While striving to build up French confidence in America, Lafayette sought also to bolster American confidence in France.
To some of his American correspondents, he sent copies of a recent work on the administration of French finances. It was by
Lafayette's friend Jacques Necker, formerly director-general of
French finance, who was generally believed to be an economic
wizard. Even while in office, Necker had taken the attitude that
the public was entitled to know and to discuss questions of public finance. His new book pointedly criticized the French fiscal
system. Yet Necker, probably because he believed it true, gave
the impression that government revenue was fairly close to government expenditure, and he therefore did not describe the royal
treasury's condition as discouragingly as the facts might have

27. *Ibid.*

28. To Jay, Feb. 8, 1785, *loc. cit.*; to Elias Boudinot (New Jersey Historical Society),
Breck (Yale University Library), Gerry (LC, Gerry papers), Greene (Clements Li-
brary), Henry (Chinard, *Lafayette in Virginia*, pp. 63–64), Knox (Knox Memorial
Association, Thomaston, Me.), R. H. Lee (APS, Lee correspondence), and Madison
(Historical Society of Pennsylvania)—all of Mar. 16; to Jay (*loc. cit.*) and to Wash-
ington, Mar. 19 (Gottschalk, *Letters*, p. 293); to Wadsworth, Apr. 16 (Connecticut
State Library, Trumbull collection).

warranted. Lafayette considered the work interesting because it had raised bitter controversy between Necker's partisans and critics. He copied for several American correspondents an optimistic passage concerning the resources of France, with comments of his own indicating that he was on the side of Necker's partisans. He apparently thought that the publication of this statement would increase American confidence in the French government.[29] It was obvious that he himself had no conception as yet of how feeble the French fiscal structure was.

At the same time, France's international situation also began to appear less precarious. Vergennes, making clear that he would support the Dutch in their effort to keep the Scheldt River closed, nevertheless hoped to preserve peace with Austria. Prussia indicated her readiness to join France if Joseph II made an effort to upset the balance of power among the German states. Under the circumstances, Joseph preferred negotiation to force. By the middle of March, Lafayette was fairly certain that there would be no war. He began to contemplate a long-cherished trip to Prussia to see the armies of the great Frederick.[30]

The birth of the unfortunate child who was destined never to rule as Louis XVII of France provided an exciting interlude to the affairs of state. Lafayette went off to Versailles upon hearing of the queen's delivery. A few days later Mme de Lafayette invited Jefferson and the Adamses to attend a *Te Deum* at the Cathedral of Notre Dame, where the king was to be present. Since even puritanical Abigail thought such ceremony necessary in a monarchy and her younger brother John Quincy thought the *Te Deum* a charming rite, Lafayette is to be forgiven if he temporarily forgot his republicanism to act as a courtier. The Chevalier de Gouvion, who was now his constant companion and who was a little more cynical than the young Adamses,

---

29. Probably taken from "Tableau des dépenses de la France, et vues générales d'économie," which is chap. xii of Necker's *De l'administration des finances de la France* ([Paris?], 1784), II, 385-532.

30. Lafayette to Boudinot, Breck, Greene, Henry, Knox, and Madison, Mar. 16, 1785, and to Jay and Washington, Mar. 19, all cited in n. 28 above.

doubted whether all the ceremony at Notre Dame was acceptable to God Almighty—but very few persons, Gouvion remarked, had come there for the sake of God.[31]

The next few weeks passed uneventfully. The Monday dinners continued to thrill Abigail Adams and to impress upon her the excellence of the marquis and his wife. Adrienne seemed more interested than her husband in showing off their children and appeared less fearful of the possible annoyance to their distinguished guests.[32] The Lafayettes, still in their twenties, apparently enjoyed the responsibility of educating the young. Though they already had assumed custody of Kayenlaha and John Caldwell, they looked forward to adding General Greene's son, George Washington Greene, to the number of their charges. The marquis also urged Alexander Hamilton and General Knox to send their sons to be educated in Paris. He believed that American boys should be educated in France and French boys in America and intended to send his own son to Harvard College when he grew up.[33]

Kayenlaha's position in the Lafayette household was that of a privileged servant. He occasionally went with his master to social functions. Once he accompanied the marquis to a ball at Chaville near Versailles, in the home of Adrienne's aunt, the Comtesse de Tessé. Rigged out in all his savage finery, which nevertheless left him almost naked, he did a tomahawk dance to his own accompaniment while another of the guests (probably Caraman) imitated him. A little French boy at the party was quite frightened by the spectacle, and when Lafayette left the group of admiring guests and tried to coax the child to join the dance, he encountered only mild success. The boy acquired

---

31. *Journal of Miss Adams*, I, 65–69 (Mar. 29–30, 1785); C. F. Adams (ed.), *Memoirs of John Quincy Adams, comprising portions of his diary from 1795 to 1848* (Philadelphia, 1874–77), I, 16–19 (March 28–April 1). The dates given by J. Q. Adams are the correct ones.

32. *Journal of Miss Adams*, I, 66–71 (Mar. 29, Apr. 4 and 8, 1785).

33. Lafayette to Hamilton, Apr. 13, 1785, Hamilton, *Works*, I, 423–24; to Greene, Apr. 16, Clements Library, Greene papers; to Knox, May 11, Massachusetts Historical Society; *Journal of Miss Adams*, I, 71 (Apr. 8, 1785).

a dislike of Lafayette on that occasion which lasted the rest of his life.[34]

The education of John Caldwell meanwhile progressed. Lafayette had found a good boarding school for him, where he could learn French and Latin in preparation for his medical studies. The lad's religion had at first caused some trouble, since Protestants were still deprived of legal standing in France. Lafayette was assured, however, that John would not be required to attend Catholic services and that every precaution would be taken "to ensure his perseverance in the relligion of his fathers."[35] Young Caldwell's education was thus the cause of Lafayette's first personal contact with religious intolerance in France. Shortly afterward he informed Washington that "Protestants in this kingdom are my present object."[36]

The Lafayettes also practically adopted the Washingtons. The correspondence between the two families continued and the ties between them grew stronger. Packages of gifts, including a French doll with its dressing table, went from the children of the Rue de Bourbon to those on the Potomac. Lafayette himself sent good breeding animals for which Washington had expressed a desire.[37] Whenever a regular packet arrived from America without bringing a letter from Mount Vernon, Lafayette fretted. "The distance is already so great in itself," he remarked on one such occasion, "and so much greater for the feelings of the tenderest friendship that the only means ought to be scrupulously observed that tend to alleviate the cruel separation. . . . Think often of your bosom friend, your adoptive son, who loves you so tenderly, and who is with every sentiment of respect, gratitude and affection your devoted friend."[38]

34. Maurice de Barberey (ed.), *Correspondance et souvenirs du Comte de Neuilly* (Paris, 1865), pp. 10–11. The Indian whom Neuilly speaks of might have been Otsiquette, in which case the episode would have occurred somewhat later (see below, Appendix II).

35. Lafayette to Boudinot, Mar. 16, 1785, *loc. cit.*

36. Mar. 19, 1785, Gottschalk, *Letters*, p. 294.

37. Girodie, pp. 53–54, No. 78a; Lafayette to Washington, Apr. 6 and May 13, 1785, Gottschalk, *Letters*, pp. 295 and 299; Washington to Lafayette, Feb. 15, 1785, and to Mme de Lafayette, May 10, 1786, Fitzpatrick, XXVIII, 74 and 418.

38. Apr. 16, 1785, Gottschalk, *Letters*, pp. 294 and 296.

On his side, Washington, though equally cordial, was somewhat less demonstrative. When he wrote to the marquis or to members of the Lafayette family, his thought was cloaked in a kind of pompous banter such as a reserved man might use to cover up his embarrassment at his own tenderness.[39] An unfriendly observer might have mistaken his manner for affectation. Friends, however, easily discovered the warmth of Washington's feelings for his "adoptive son." When, for example, Mazzei visited Mount Vernon on the eve of his departure for Paris, Washington spoke a great deal about Lafayette and made no secret of his affection for his young admirer.[40] Nevertheless, he did not exert himself as much as his protégé to show his devotion. To Lafayette's request for Kentucky seed for the royal botanical gardens, for example, he replied simply that distance made the task difficult though he would do his best. If the seeds ever were sent, it was not until nearly a year after they were quite formally requested.[41] Lafayette would have fussed more over Washington's slightest intimation.

While waiting for warmer weather to permit his trip to Prussia, Lafayette continued to act as the champion of American traders in France. The stubborn American preference for the English had led the French ministry to consider reducing the number of packets in transatlantic trade. Lafayette, hoping to avoid such an admission of defeat, valiantly strove to increase the number of American commodites sold in France. He urged the virtues of American hemp and timber upon the French navy and shipbuilders. He tried to interest the street-lighting companies of several French cities in New England whale oil despite Calonne's desire to revive the French whaling industry.

Some of the ministers' unwillingness to grant further favors, Lafayette recognized, was due to the pressure brought by French merchants resentful of the concessions already made to

39. Cf. Washington to Lafayette, May 12, 1785, and to Mme de Lafayette, May 10, 1786, Fitzpatrick, XXVIII, 140 and 417–19.

40. H. R. Marraro (trans.), *Memoirs of the life and peregrinations of the Florentine Philip Mazzei 1730–1816* (New York, 1942), p. 286.

41. Washington to Lafayette, Feb. 15 and July 25, 1785, Fitzpatrick, XXVIII, 74–75 and 209.

American traders, who persisted in preferring English markets.[42] But he could not hide from himself that part of the difficulty lay in the absence of unity in the United States. "Every thing in Europe more and more convinces me of the necessity there is for the States to give Congress powers to regulate trade," he wrote Washington.[43] He made the same plea to Greene: "The more I see, the more I reflect, the more I am impressed with the necessity to give Congress powers to regulate trade."[44] To a former aide-de-camp, William Constable, now engaged in commerce, he was even more explicit: "The more I live on this side of the Atlantic, the more I see the necessity to invest Congress with powers to regulate trade. . . . Let the Confederation be strengthened, a proper guard be appointed for the frontiers, a good plan of militia adopted, political and mercantile views to be federal and the five per 100 impost be generally fully adopted, and then I don't care for the snarls or attacks of any power in Europe."[45]

The struggle to uphold American prestige in Europe was further complicated by the inadequacy of diplomatic intelligence. To the hazards of the eighteenth-century postal and courier system were added for Americans the delays and dangers resulting from ocean voyages and the decentralization of government at home. Upon the departure of the Adams family for London, where John Adams was to be the American minister, Mrs. Adams remarked that she did not expect, on quitting France, to know as much of American affairs as before. "For no person is so well informed from all the States as the Marquis de la Fayette. He has established a correspondence in all the States and has the newspapers from every quarter."[46] In fact, the marquis knew before Adams, and Adams had to learn from him, who his secretary in London was to be.[47] And Jefferson com-

42. Lafayette to Wadsworth, Apr. 16, 1785, Connecticut State Library, Trumbull collection; to Constable, May 13, *Magazine of American history*, XI (1884), 545–46; to Greene, June 12, Clements Library.

43. Apr. 16, 1785, Gottschalk, *Letters*, p. 295.

44. Apr. 16, 1785, *loc. cit.*

45. May 13, 1785, *Magazine of American history*, XI (1884), 545.

46. To Mrs. Cranch, May 10, 1785, *Letters of Mrs. Adams*, p. 249.

47. Adams to Lee, Apr. 29, 1785, Lee, *Memoir of Lee*, II, 141.

plained that if it were not for Lafayette and the Duc de La Rochefoucauld he would be entirely without intelligence from America.[48] Lafayette, on the other hand, afraid that his correspondence was "under inspection," prodded the Franklin household for their information.[49]

Despite these difficulties, Lafayette tirelessly filled his role of America's patron. Remembering the pleas of the Boston merchants for the unfortunate American whalers, he tried to win duty-free importation of whale oil into France. Calonne, however, proved adamant. He preferred to encourage French rather than American fisheries. Lafayette therefore appealed to private concerns interested in buying oil. He approached M. Tourtille Sangrain, who held the contract for lighting the streets of Paris. Sangrain undertook, if a company were formed in Boston capable of meeting his stipulations, to buy about a thousand tons of oil in three different qualities at market prices. The most profitable part of the oil, the spermaceti used in making candles, would not need to be included—thus increasing the profit to the American merchants. Apparently Sangrain knew little about spermaceti and Lafayette did not enlighten him. On the other hand, American commissioners and merchants in Paris were regularly informed at every step of the negotiations and were naturally pleased. Still they thought that the contract would be even more profitable if the shipments to Sangrain could be exempted from duty. Lafayette was able to wring this limited concession from the ministers, on condition that Sangrain's oil be delivered to specified ports on a single invoice and be paid for in French goods.[50]

Lafayette had kept his horses ready during three days of hectic negotiations, hoping to dash off to Franklin's house with the

48. Jefferson to Monroe, Apr. 15, 1785, P. L. Ford (ed.), *Writings of Thomas Jefferson* (New York, 1892–99), III, 45.

49. Lafayette to W. T. Franklin, [*ca.* Apr. 29, 1785], APS, Franklin papers, Vol. 108, No. 43.

50. Lafayette to [John Adams], May 8, 1785, Chinard, *Lafayette and Jefferson*, pp. 89–90; to Wadsworth, May 11, Connecticut State Library, Trumbull collection; to Breck, May 13, [Davis], *Complete history*, pp. 153–54; Higginson to John Adams, Aug. 8, J. F. Jameson, "The letters of Stephen Higginson," *Annual report of the American Historical Association*, I (1896), 724; Lafayette to [Breck?], [Dec. 3, 1785?], *Pennsylvania Packet*, June 24, 1786.

welcome news. The old Duc de Choiseul was dying, however, and the usual social amenities kept him from bringing the contract immediately. Hardly had the ancient statesman breathed his last when the triumphant marquis announced his success to Franklin, Adams, and Jefferson.[51] If they approved, he proposed to send Sangrain's contract, government passports, and samples of oil to Jeremiah Wadsworth of Hartford and Samuel Breck of Boston by young John Quincy Adams, who was returning to America. He hoped also that his friends William Constable and James McHenry, though they were not New Englanders, might be included in the deal, if only to handle the French goods to be received in return for the whale oil.[52] This was a deal that might come to 800,000 livres, and the marquis was "happy at having, at last, obtained a point which may be agreeable to New England and the people of Boston."[53]

The American agents in Paris, of course, had no objections to so favorable a contract, and final terms were fixed at a meeting at Jefferson's house.[54] And so when John Quincy Adams left France, he carried with him not only Sangrain's contract, passports, and samples but also a sheaf of letters from Lafayette to interested persons in America (not to mention a brace of English hounds for Washington). Without appearing to boast, these letters showed that the proud French aristocrat and soldier was quite pleased with his commercial and diplomatic skill. The Longchamps affair had been satisfactorily settled, the Mississippi question was still open, and now he had concluded a transaction that bade fair to make several Americans richer than they had been before and to bring relief to the depressed whaling enterprises of New England.

On the other hand, Lafayette had treated French merchants in a cavalier fashion. Being no middle-class money-grubber himself, he had won favors for Americans at the expense, or at least

51. To W. T. Franklin, [May 8, 1785], APS, Franklin papers, Vol. 107, No. 96; to [Adams], May 8, Chinard, *Lafayette and Jefferson*, pp. 89–90. The presence of the letter to Adams in Jefferson's papers shows that Jefferson was likewise informed.

52. Lafayette to [Adams], May 8, Chinard, *Lafayette and Jefferson*, pp. 89–90; tc Wadsworth, May 11, *loc. cit.*; to Constable, May 13, *loc. cit.*

53. To Breck, May 13, 1785, [Davis], *Complete history*, p. 154.

54. Lafayette to [Breck?], [Dec. 3, 1785?], *Pennsylvania Packet*, June 24, 1786.

contrary to the express wishes, of French businessmen. His purpose was political—to wean American commerce from England in order to strengthen the Franco-American alliance. He scoffed at his countrymen for being shortsighted. "When trade will be better known betwen the two nations, the French merchants will be made sensible of advantages to themselves that are worth purchasing by some sacrifices."[55] He had small patience with French "mercantile prejudices"[56] such as the desire for exclusive markets in the West Indies or for the promotion of the French whaling industry. Not that he loved French economic interests less but that he loved Franco-American solidarity more.

If French merchants were displeased, Lafayette's opinions struck a responsive chord in American hearts. When the businessmen of New England learned that Lafayette had handsomely fulfilled his promises to watch over American fishing interests, they were gratified, though they saw shortcomings in the terms proposed and hoped for still better ones.[57] President Lee, endeavoring to explain British control of American trade as the result of the greater enterprise of British shipping interests, joined Lafayette in lamenting European restrictions upon American commerce;[58] for Lee, like Lafayette, was a landlord and not a merchant. The fisher folk of Nantucket were to express their gratitude to their patron in their own simple way.[59]

BIBLIOGRAPHICAL NOTES

The detailed diaries and correspondence of the Adamses furnish domestic details not otherwise available about the Lafayette household. Young Abigail's dates are sometimes confused. Edith H. Sichel, *The household of the Lafayettes* (Westminster, 1897), and M. MacDermot Crawford, *Madame de Lafayette and her family* (New York, 1907), which is the same as *The wife of Lafayette* (London, 1908), both give absorbing details. Sichel is still more absorbing but less reliable than Crawford. Neither author is thorough.

Jared Sparks, *Diplomatic correspondence of the American Revolution*, etc. (Boston, 1829–30), contains several of the letters of Lafayette to John Jay

55. Lafayette to Boudinot, Mar. 16, 1785, *loc. cit.*
56. Lafayette to Jay, Feb. 8, 1785, [Weaver], *Diplomatic correspondence*, I, 420.
57. Higginson to Adams, Aug. 8, 1785, *loc. cit.*
58. June 11, 1785, Ballagh, II, 369.
59. See below, p. 254.

during this period. For some reason Sparks omitted from them references to the Longchamps's affair and, as usual in his earlier work, made other omissions and revisions. [Weaver] *Diplomatic correspondence*, in some of these instances, duplicated Sparks's versions without going to the originals. The same is true of the letter of March 19, 1785, in Lafayette's *Mémoires* (II, 119–20). It has been found most convenient usually to give references to [Weaver], *Diplomatic correspondence*, if the text is to be found there. Occasionally, however, when the omissions or revisions are significant, reference is made to the originals.

CHAPTER XIII

Toleration for Frenchmen?

B^Y THE spring of 1785 the channels most likely to lead to glory and adventure seemed dammed. Ireland, in whose troubled waters Lafayette had hoped to fish, was undergoing a period of political doldrums. His wish that "Holland would a little Un State Holder herself"[1] [i.e., would weaken her stadholder's power] was now frustrated by the peaceful settlement that Vergennes was about to achieve. A request from Governor Patrick Henry to help Virginia spend £10,000 on war material led the marquis momentarily to expect that fighting might break out in America, and in that expectation he urged his American friends not to forget how useful he would be if an attack were made on the English in Canada or on the Spanish in Mexico.[2] Still, such a war, however possible, did not seem imminent. The contemplated tour of Prussia and Austria, though it held engaging possibilities, had to be postponed for several months, since maneuvers were not to take place until late in the summer. Lafayette therefore had to find a more immediate outlet for his energies. For the first time in his life he turned his crusading zeal upon religious abuses at home.

Lafayette had been baptized a Catholic and named after half-a-dozen Catholic saints. He had been married in a Catholic church to a Catholic girl, whose mother and paternal grandmother were notedly devout. His children were being brought up by their mother as Catholics, even if the last two (George and Virginie) had been given names reminiscent of America as

1. Lafayette to Wadsworth, May 11, 1785, Connecticut Historical Society, Trumbull papers.
2. Henry to Lafayette, Mar. 30, 1785, Henry, III, 289–90; Lafayette to Henry, June 7, *ibid.*, pp. 298–99.

well as of Catholic hagiolatry. He himself, as became an eighteenth-century court aristocrat, did not take his Catholicism
very seriously. He had, to be sure, described himself as *ancien
catholique* the first time he had left France for America; and to
receive the Order of St. Louis, he had had to take an oath to
live and die in the Catholic faith. But those were mere formalities.

In America he had encountered people of many sects, and
some of his best friends there were Protestants. Only two occasions are recorded on which he discussed religion with them. On
the first one he defended his own country's church policy, claiming that tolerance was practiced more genuinely in Catholic
France than in Protestant England. If he was not altogether
right, his error was due rather to his zeal as a Frenchman than
as a Catholic. He had no compunction, for example, about proposing that Irish Protestants be stirred up to take part in the
struggle for Ireland's independence of England.[3] The second occasion was his recent discussion of the Bible with Dr. Griffith
at Mount Vernon, where he had taken so un-Catholic a point of
view as to describe himself jestingly later as "one who is himself
suspected of a very strong tincture of Presbyterianism."[4] Still
more recently, when there was some reason to believe that there
might be a war between Protestant America and Catholic Spain,
he had slyly reminded influential friends in America that, since
his father and mother had been "very good Catholicks"[5] and he
was himself Roman Catholic "or supposed to be so at least if any
thing,"[6] he could be helpful in a struggle against a Catholic country. To be sure, he had hoped that such a war could be averted,
but only because Spain was an ally of France.

Of late, however, Lafayette had become greatly distressed by
the humiliations to which he had found the Protestants of
France subjected. Since he had learned his history lessons quite
well as a boy, he undoubtedly had long been familiar with the

3. Gottschalk, *Lafayette comes to America*, pp. 132 and 163; *Lafayette and the close of
the American Revolution*, pp. 10, 53, and 184–85.

4. Lafayette to Griffith, Dec. 26, 1786, Brydon, p. 230. See below, p. 273 and n. 46.

5. To Knox, May 11, 1785, Massachusetts Historical Society.

6. Lafayette to Washington, May 11, 1785, Gottschalk, *Letters*, p. 297.

story of the French Huguenots. By the Edict of Nantes, the gallant King Henry IV had granted special privileges to the Huguenots, but the edict had been revoked by Louis XIV less than a century later. In the century that had passed since then, they had been obliged to live under certain restrictions. Still, Lafayette had not realized until recently how hard those restrictions were. In helping Franklin to present the claims of an American widow to the estate of her husband, who had been a French volunteer in the Maryland Artillery, he had learned that marriages performed by Protestant ministers were not valid in France.[7] When he had tried to find a boarding school for John Caldwell, he had found that it was necessary to get special permission "to ensure his perseverance in the relligion of his fathers, and to dispense him even with attending the Roman Catholic ceremonies." It was shortly thereafter (as we have seen) that he wrote Washington that he had made the Protestants of France his "present object."[8]

Lafayette soon joined forces with Chrétien-Guillaume Lamoignon de Malesherbes, friend of Rousseau and protector of the *philosophes*. Malesherbes had once been minister of Louis XVI's household and, having in that capacity had jurisdiction over religious affairs, had consistently championed toleration. In 1776, however, pressure from the queen, the clergy, and the parlements had defeated a reforming ministry's proposals for social, economic, and religious change, and Malesherbes had been the first of that ministry to resign. During his subsequent retirement, he had maintained his interest in the Protestants. Now, in 1785, he was active once more in their behalf, proposing that the Revocation of the Edict of Nantes should in its turn be revoked. He furnished Lafayette with a number of books on the legal aspects of the question.[9]

The Duc de Castries likewise was interested in the plight of the Protestants. Several other ministers whose departments

7. Lafayette to McHenry, Dec. 26, 1783, Huntington Library, HM 157; Franklin to Samuel Chase, Jan. 6, 1784, Smyth, IX, 153 and n. (on behalf of Mme Levache nee Ann Howard).

8. See above, p. 162 and nn. 35 and 36.

9. Eug[ène] L[iebert], *Le château de La Grange* (Coulommiers, 1866), pp. 215–16. Cf. *Mémoires*, II, 180–82.

were more directly concerned with religious affairs than Castries's were not indifferent although they apparently wished to keep their official skirts clear in so delicate an issue.[10] Lafayette himself thought that Vergennes and Keeper of the Seals Miroménil were among that group, but it was particularly true of the Baron de Breteuil, Malesherbes's successor as minister of the king's household. When, therefore, the young reformer became involved in the new cause, he found tacit support in some high places.

Huguenot toleration now became one of Lafayette's great crusades. More realistic than the quest for Irish independence or Dutch republicanism, more moving than the freedom of Franco-American trade, and less remote than American unification, it helped temporarily to fill his need for adventure and approbation. It was a cause that he knew would have the approval of Washington and his other American friends as well as of those French circles whose esteem he most sought. He had no illusion that his new enterprise would be simple. The clergy could be expected to oppose it, and they would find vigorous support right in his own family from his wife's grandmother, the Maréchale de Noailles, although Adrienne herself, despite her devotion to the church, would stand by him staunchly.[11] It would be necessary to proceed with great caution. A misstep might not only make all that was done look silly but might even create legal complications for those involved. When Lafayette, whose virtues did not usually include discretion, announced his new purpose to his correspondents overseas, he sent his messages by John Quincy Adams, whom he could trust to guard their secrecy. Each message impressed upon its recipient the need to be cautious in discussing the project. They were to use code words or to avoid mention of it altogether in their replies.[12]

By mid-May, Lafayette's plans regarding the Protestants had

10. Lafayette to Washington, May 11, 1785, Gottschalk, *Letters*, p. 296.

11. Cf. Charles Read, "Le mémoire du Duc de Bourgogne," *Bulletin de la Société de l'Histoire du Protestantisme français*, 4th ser., XLI (1892), 452 n.; Joseph Dedieu, *Histoire politique des Protestants français (1715–1794)* (Paris, 1925), II, 266; Lasteyrie, pp. 209–11.

12. Cf. Lafayette to Washington, Mar. 19 and May 11, 1785, Gottschalk, *Letters*, pp. 294 and 296.

crystallized. Except for Malesherbes and Castries, who were in the conspiracy, Washington was the first to learn of it. The marquis wrote to his mentor in a cipher they had agreed upon: "102 [Protestants] in 12 [France] are under intolerable 80 [despotism]. Altho' oppen persecution does not now exist, yet it depends upon the whim of 25 [king], 28 [queen], 29 [parlement] or any of 32 [ministry]. Marriages are not legal among them. Their wills have no force of law, their children are to be bastards, their parsons to be hanged. I have put it into my head to be a 1400 [leader] in that affair, and to have the situation changed. With that wiew I am going, under other pretences to visit their chief place of abode with a consent of 42 [Castries] and an other."[13] He would later, he said, endeavor to interest Vergennes and other officials of the king. "It is a work of time, and of some danger to me, because none of them would give me a scrap of paper, or countenance whatsoever. But I run my chance. 42 [Castries] could only receive the secret from me because it is not in his departement. Don't answer me about it, only that you have my ciphered letter by M. Adams. But when in the course of the fall or winter you will hear of some thing that way, I wanted you to know I had an hand in it." This letter was "particularly recommended" to young Adams' care.[14]

Since the days when the Protestants had flourished under Henry IV's benign regime, they had persisted in the Midi. They now lived beyond the pale, formally outlawed, obliged to carry on their religious rites clandestinely, and never knowing when some act of bigotry might bring on a new repression. Large Protestant groups were to be found at La Rochelle and Montpellier, and at Nîmes they were particularly numerous. There, even after Louis XIV revoked the Edict of Nantes, they led a generally peaceful existence, though one that might be upset at any time by a *cause célèbre* stirred up by some officious police officer or zealous cleric. The aged Paul Rabaut and his son, Jean-Paul Rabaut-St. Étienne, had accepted the risk of serving as their pastors.

13. The "other" was Malesherbes (see *Mémoires*, II, 121 n.). Lafayette apparently had no code number for Malesherbes and did not dare to identify him more explicitly.

14. May 11, 1785, Gottschalk, *Letters*, pp. 296–97; the version in *Mémoires*, II, 121–22, does not indicate that the original was partly in cipher.

Mystery and intrigue were a tonic to Lafayette, and again he acted with the circumspection of a grand conspirator. Possibly, in view of the friendliness of some ministers and his own secure position at court, studied precautions were unnecessary. In fact, he had recently (May 29) been accorded the trust and honor of entry into the royal chamber.[15] Yet it was probable that such confidence might not have been lightly granted to a recognized Huguenot-lover. In any event, he was resolved to be careful. Under pretext of taking his old aunt, Mme de Chavaniac, home, he would visit his birthplace in Auvergne. From there, he would go on to Nîmes, ostensibly to see some of the towns that might be interested in American commerce but in reality to call upon the leaders of the Protestant communities.

Lafayette's self-imposed obligations as protector of all Americans almost upset these plans. Just as he was getting into his carriage to begin his journey to the Midi, a letter from an old acquaintance in London, Dr. Edward Bancroft, was delivered to him. It brought him news of Billy, General Knox's youngest brother, about whose whereabouts there had been much concern during Lafayette's visit to Boston. Billy "was disordered in his head" and had been confined to "an house" in London but was much better and would soon be released. Although he lived in an age when the mentally ill were little understood and often mistreated, Lafayette reacted with characteristic kindliness and good sense. His first inclination—at least he so reported to General Knox—was to rush off to London. But, recollecting that his movements could not be kept secret (and probably, though he did not say so to General Knox, not wanting to postpone his mission to the Protestants), he determined to send a trustworthy servant in his stead. The servant was to bring Billy to Paris, with Dr. Bancroft if possible. There the unfortunate man would be placed in the charge of Mme de Lafayette, who would take him for a rest to Chavaniac. If necessary, the marquis promised, he would return to Paris rapidly and go to London under a fictitious name to help Billy. "Now, my dear friend, that I have found him out," he assured Knox, "you may be as easy as if you were yourself in Europe."[16]

There is no record that Billy Knox ever became Lafayette's guest either in Paris or in Chavaniac. He died in America in 1797 totally insane. But the good intentions of the benefactor are all the more striking because they remained a secret—unlike many of Lafayette's other good intentions. The marquis had also recently—and less reticently—tried to befriend an American in Spain who had fallen afoul of the law, but his intercession with Floridablanca and Carmichael came too late. The gentleman had meanwhile died.[17]

Deterred only momentarily on his new errand of mercy by the hardships of stranded Americans, Lafayette arrived in Chavaniac around June 12. From there he wrote to Knox reassuring him regarding his brother.[18] He also wrote for General Greene's consumption his maiden essay on education. It was in the form of an outline of his proposals for the schooling of their sons if young Greene were sent to France to study. "Leaving them in my house has an inconvenience, wiz being spoiled by the complasancy of servants, besides the want of emulation. A school education, while it unites the advantages of equality and concurrence, is not without a great danger of corrupting the morals. In these great capitals boys are very forward, and their company, particularly for the younger ones, may be too instructive." He therefore proposed to put the two lads in the establishment of a carefully selected tutor. They would attend classes at a good school, returning to their tutor's to play and to do their homework. On holidays they might go for walks or visit with the Lafayettes. They would be independent, yet supervised, and close enough to be brought home in case of illness.[19]

16. Lafayette to Knox, June 12, 1785, Massachusetts Historical Society.

17. Lafayette to Breck, [June 2, 1785], S[amuel] B[reck], "Interesting notices of the life of the Marquis de La Fayette," *Portfolio*, 3d ser., V (1815), 504. The date of this letter is given in [Davis], *Complete history*, pp. 138–39. The "hellish tribunal" was perhaps the Inquisition, as is generally thought, but that is not altogether clear.

18. June 12, 1785, *loc. cit.*

19. Lafayette to Greene, June 12, 1785, Clements Library.

The rest of Lafayette's brief stay in the Midi (about ten days) was devoted to the Protestant cause. He went to Nîmes under pretext of seeing some leading merchants. In the course of this business, however, he found occasion to interview the harassed old Pastor Rabaut. One of the small group in Paris conspiring for the cause of tolerance had been in touch with Rabaut since the previous winter,[20] and so Lafayette's visit was not unexpected. When the patriarch of "the churches of the desert" learned that the young champion of American liberty was now going to bring the good fight nearer home, he repeated the Nunc Dimittis of Simeon upon at last beholding the young Jesus.

Before Lafayette left Nîmes he also saw Rabaut-St. Étienne. After cross-examining the younger Rabaut thoroughly, he decided to work through him rather than his aged father. Making Rabaut-St. Étienne promise to keep what he heard a secret even from his father, Lafayette revealed what Malesherbes and others were doing in Paris in the good cause. It was agreed that the marquis should quietly prepare the way at Versailles for the younger Rabaut personally to present to the king a plea for toleration.[21]

On the way back to Paris, Lafayette stopped at Lyon, which, with its 135,000 inhabitants, was the second largest city of France. He reached it on the morning of June 22 and took the precaution to visit the Archbishop of Lyon first. After dining with the archbishop, he began an inspection of the local factories under the guidance of a leading Lyon merchant. He impressed his eager hosts by his interest in mechanical details and his desire to promote the commerce of Lyon with the United

20. Rabaut to Pastor Gobinaud, Mar. 2, 1785, Charles Dardier (ed.), *Paul Rabaut, ses lettres à divers (1744–1794)* (Paris, 1892), II, 353–54. Dardier thinks this was Lafayette himself, but it seems more likely to have been Malesherbes. Cf. Rabaut-St. Étienne to the Committee of Bordeaux, Feb. 12, 1788, *ibid.*, p. 394. The impression that Lafayette had begun to correspond with the Rabauts in January, 1785, rests upon a misdated letter (see below, p. 215, n. 208).

21. *Mémoires*, II, 182; F. A. Boissy-d'Anglas, "Notice sur Rabaut-Saint-Étienne," in Rabaut-St. Étienne, *Précis de l'histoire de la Révolution française* (new ed.; [Versailles], 1822), pp. ix–x; Rabaut-St. Étienne to the Committee of Bordeaux, Feb. 12, 1788, Dardier, II, 394; Charles Dardier, "Le centenaire de l'Édit de Tolérance de 1787," *Bulletin de la Société de l'Histoire du Protestantisme français*, 3d ser., XXXVI (1887), 520–21. Dedieu (II, 254) thinks that this conversation took place with the older Rabaut, but between Lafayette's and Rabaut's testimony he sees a contradiction that is not necessarily there.

States. From the factories he went to the City Hall, then ate some ices with some of the city's admiring businessmen at one of their favorite cafés, then examined the library of the local college, and then climbed one of the Lyon hills to get a better view of the city.

On their return, Lafayette's party passed the meeting place of the Société du Patriotisme, a local Masonic lodge made up principally of officers of the Lyon citizen militia. A delegation from the society met him and besought him to honor them with his presence, and he consented "with as much modesty as grace." This visit of the "adored of Frenchmen" was one of his still rare associations with Freemasons. It was a gala event for the Lyon lodge. "This," said the orator of the day, "is the way the demi-gods once appeared unexpectedly in the midst of those whom they wished to honor with their favors." The lodge made their illustrious brother an honorary member.[22]

From the Société du Patriotisme, Lafayette went to call on the royal commandant of the province. He intended to go that evening to the theater, but the crowd that jammed the theater entrance to greet him discouraged him. "His modesty," the *Journal de Lyon* reported, "induced him to steal away from the cheers and acknowledgments that seemed to await him."

The next day proved equally glorious and strenuous. After breakfast he was initiated into the technique of silk manufacture and later inspected the local hospital. The Lyon *Journal* proudly recorded his statement that he had never seen a larger or more interesting one. He then visited a gold refinery, again called on the archbishop, and afterward inspected the Lyon stock exchange, where he inquired about the technicalities of bookkeeping. As he left the stock exchange, the local militia took charge of him, intent upon showing him the honors due a visiting general. He went to their quarters, talked to their officers, read the honorific inscriptions on their walls, accepted some

22. "Passage à Lyon de M. le Marquis de la Fayette," *Journal de Lyon*, II (1785), 190–99 (Bibliothèque Municipale et Universitaire de Clermont-Ferrand, MS 987). Cf. Charavay, p. 118 n., and Paul Olivier, *Iconographie métallique du Général Lafayette*, etc. (Paris, 1933), p. 24, No. 40. The *Journal de Lyon* says that Lafayette was accompanied by "a distinguished officer who had followed him in his campaigns and was, like him, a member of the Order of Cincinnatus." This might have been Gouvion.

flowers and refreshments, and reviewed the changing of the guard.

Before Lafayette left Lyon, he also made several calls upon the dean of the Lyon cathedral, where some of his ancestors had been canons. The crowning event of his visit, however, was the farewell dinner given by the commandant of the province. The officers of the bourgeois militia had been invited and felt particularly impressed. After dinner the commandant himself toasted "the young hero's" health, whereupon fanfares and cheers broke forth. Then a song especially written in Lafayette's honor was sung, while the marquis's "most engaging and most rare modesty" excited everyone's praise. The song was later reprinted in the august columns of the metropolitan *Mercure de France.* It greeted "the hero of two worlds" in five stanzas and choruses, ending:

> Ah! How pleasant is our lot,
> And how glorious is our soldier!
> He can battle, win and drink,
> And he deigns to sing among us.[23]

The commandant's guest departed to the accompaniment of a military band, but it was not before he had seen some public works, made some more visits, and witnessed some fireworks that he was permitted to leave Lyon. That was not until 10:30 P.M. on June 23. The Lyon visit had been as grueling a test of endurance as any he had had to pass in the United States. And when the marquis at last left the second city of France behind, the conquered Lyonnais were as ready as Americans had always been to acknowledge their "admiration and gratitude." One of Lyon's poets in fact depicted him as endowed not only by Mars with courage but also by Love with beauty, and no American poet had yet permitted himself that much license.[24]

Lafayette was back in the capital before the end of June, where his presence was soon characteristically testified by the

---

23. Dec. 10, 1785, pp. 52–53:
> "Ah! Combien notre sort est doux,
> Et que ce guerrier a de gloire!
> Il sait combattre, vaincre et boire,
> Il daigne chanter avec nous."

24. "Passage à Lyon de M. le Marquis de la Fayette," *loc. cit.*

renewal of his demands upon the government for favors to Americans.[25] He immediately got ready to leave for Berlin and the Prussian army's summer maneuvers. A few days, however, had to be sacrificed to the great Houdon, whom Jefferson had selected to do the statues of Washington and Lafayette decreed by the Virginia legislature. There was barely leisure enough for a plaster cast to be made of the marquis before he started on his journeys again. He also provided Houdon with letters of introduction to use in America.[26] "Only the love of glory and respect for you," he wrote Washington, could have induced the illustrious sculptor to cross the seas. More time was also consumed in helping Barclay shop for war materials for Virginia, in greeting Mazzei, who had just come to Paris, and in meeting the American explorer, John Ledyard.[27]

In the midst of his busy preparations for the German tour, Lafayette had to give attention also to importunate Protestants. Shortly after he had left Nîmes, Rabaut-St. Étienne instructed one of France's most famous Huguenots, the astronomer Jacques Poitevin, to see him and the "celebrated magistrate whose enlightenment and reputation may be helpful to my friends." (Such roundabout phrases were necessary to avoid mentioning names.) "The hero of America," wrote the middle-aged pastor, "has become my hero. I hope he will permit me to place my respects at his feet and to assure him of the deep appreciation and high regard that I shall feel for him as long as I live."[28]

Poitevin called upon Lafayette shortly. Although he was left to wonder what means "the warrior" (as he called Lafayette) had at his disposal to achieve his noble purpose, he was im-

25. Lafayette to Vergennes [?], June 30, 1785, AAE, corr. pol., É.-U., Vol. XXX, fol. 85; John Paul Jones to Castries, [July 3?], 1785, *Jones calendar*, p. 192.

26. Lafayette to Washington, July 9, 1785, Gottschalk, *Letters*, p. 300, and to Dickinson, July 9, Historical Society of Pennsylvania. Cf. Jefferson to Henry, Aug. 22, H. A. Washington (ed.), *The writings of Thomas Jefferson*, etc. (New York, 1861), I, 403.

27. Barclay to Henry, Aug. 23, 1785, *Calendar of Virginia state papers*, IV, 49–50; Mazzei to Jefferson, July 9, Garlick, p. 97; Sparks, *Ledyard*, p. 161.

28. Rabaut-St. Étienne to Lafayette, June 22, 1785, Anon., "Les promoteurs de l'édit de 1787 qui a restitué l'état civil aux Protestants de France: correspondance de Lafayette, Paul Rabaut, Rabaut-Saint-Étienne, de Poitevin (1785–1788)," *Bulletin de la Société de l'Histoire du Protestantisme français*, III (1855), 333.

pressed with the marquis's zeal and activity.[29] Within a few days Lafayette put Poitevin in touch with Malesherbes. The two men were greatly pleased with each other. They agreed that Rabaut-St. Étienne should come to Paris in the fall, when, there was reason to believe, conditions would be ripe for their "lawsuit" (as they called their cause). "The warrior" soon learned from "the celebrated magistrate" how matters stood. He therefore had every right to believe, when on July 9 he finally set out for his long-delayed visit to Prussia, that the cause of toleration was in good hands and well under way.[30]

Before Lafayette left French soil, he felt called upon to render an account of his mission in the Midi to the one whose approval he most sought. "I have been lately visiting some French towns where I spoke great deal about American trade," he reported to Washington, "and fully answered the wiews I had the honour to communicate in a former letter."[31] This was necessarily a brief and cryptic report, but the writer was certain that Washington would understand and approve.

BIBLIOGRAPHICAL NOTES

Michael de La Bedoyere ("Lafayette and the church," *Catholic world*, CXXXIX [1934], 166–70) overdraws the loyalty of Lafayette to Catholicism.

Henri Doniol (*Le Comte de Vergennes et P. M. Hennin, directeur au département des affaires étrangères ... 1749–1787* [Paris, 1898]) maintains (pp. 86–87) that Vergennes led the cause of Protestant toleration from behind the scenes. That is not improbable, but the available evidence does not show it.

Charles Read's *Lafayette, Washington et les Protestants de France 1785–1787* (Paris, 1893) is an exhortatory rather than a scholarly work. Read has, however, made available through his articles in the *Bulletin de la Société de l'Histoire du Protestantisme français* a number of significant documents.

29. Poitevin to Rabaut-St. Étienne, Aug. 1, 1785, *ibid.*, p. 335.

30. Lafayette to Poitevin, [July 6, 1785], Poitevin to Malesherbes, July 11, and Rabaut-St. Étienne to Poitevin, Aug. 17, *ibid.*, pp. 334 and 337.

31. July 14, 1785, Gottschalk, *Letters*, pp. 300–301.

CHAPTER XIV

Enlightened Despots

LAFAYETTE evidently intended to spare no expense on his
tour of Germany. He left Paris with a generous letter of
credit from the firm of Messrs. Jean Cottin fils and
Jauge, Paris bankers, after settling a bill with his liveryman
Lebrun for over 1,100 livres.[1] At last he was embarked on an
excursion that he had dreamed of making ever since he had been
a fledgling in Washington's army.[2] He was accompanied by the
Chevalier de Gouvion, who was now a lieutenant colonel on the
French general staff and who practically lived at Lafayette's
house.[3] His itinerary included Deux Ponts, Cassel, Berlin
("where I am told Lord Cornwallis is also going"), Silesia,
Saxony, Bohemia, Vienna, the German battlefields, and Holland. He expected to be in Paris again by the middle of October,
after having paid his respects to King Frederick II of Prussia
and Emperor Joseph II at their capitals. It was to be a crowded
three months' excursion. "I will have the pleasure to speack
much of you," Lafayette informed Washington, "but had rather
speack with you."[4]

Before leaving France, Lafayette and Gouvion stopped at
Sarreguemines on the French border. There the marquis wrote
to Washington, bringing him up to date on his latest activities.[5]
He also sent his adieus to the Franklins, who at last were going
home. He wished, he said, that "he could accompagny them to

1. Receipt dated Aug. 5, 1785, Essex County Country Club (West Orange, N.J.);
AN, T 333, inventaire Lafayette émigré.
2. Lafayette to Ayen, Sept. 11, 1778, *Mémoires*, I, 210–11.
3. *Journal of Miss Adams*, p. 69 (Apr. 4, 1785).
4. Apr. 16 and July 14, 1785, Gottschalk, *Letters*, pp. 295 and 300.
5. July 14, 1785, *ibid.*, pp. 300–301.

the happy shores of freedom"[6] and inclosed letters of introduction for William Franklin to General Knox and other Americans. He had earlier bespoken Washington's interest for the
"very deserving young man" whom "the doctor loves . . . better than any thing in the world."[7] It was not presumptuous,
even if ironic, for the Marquis de Lafayette to think that the
grandson of Benjamin Franklin would find his letters of recommendation useful in America.

Lafayette created a mild furor as he passed through Germany. People of all stations went great distances to see the
young hero of the American Revolution.[8] His first important
stop was at Cassel, the capital of Hesse-Cassel. There, in the
land that had hired out the hated mercenaries employed by
England in the war against America, he had occasion to show
that eighteenth-century officers and gentlemen harbored no
grudges against former enemies, no matter how embittered later
generations might become. He saw Baron Wilhelm von Knyp-
hausen, the commanding general of the Hessians, whom he had
faced in several sharp encounters during the war, and several
others of "our Hessian friends." "I told them they were very
fine fellows," he reported to Washington. "They returned
thanks and compliments. Ancient foes ever meet with pleasure,
which, however, I should think must be greater on the side that
fought a successfull cause."[9]

On the way to Berlin the travelers visited Brunswick, where
a nephew of the famous lieutenant of Frederick the Great was
now duke. Lafayette found that the Duke of Brunswick, though
a sovereign in his own right, was still a general in the Prussian
army and enjoyed its confidence. The Frenchmen were well received by the duke. Nevertheless, on this, or some subsequent
occasion during this tour, began the distrust that was to lead
Lafayette some time later to call Brunswick "the most insincere
of men," devoid of frankness and love of liberty. Brunswick

6. July 14, 1785, APS, Franklin papers, Vol. XXXIII, No. 161.

7. July 14, 1785, Gottschalk, *Letters*, p. 301.

8. H. L. V. Ducoudray-Holstein, *Memoirs of Gilbert M. Lafayette* (Geneva, N.Y.,
1835), pp. 89-90. Holstein is imaginative, but in this instance the letters of Lafayette
bear him out.

9. Feb. 6, 1786, Gottschalk, *Letters*, p. 303.

thought that the marquis had been secretly instructed to negotiate with Prussia, and Lafayette came to believe that Brunswick wished him to carry away the impression (which eventually proved false) that the Prussians had no purpose in the Netherlands but to retain the stadholder without increase of power.[10]
In the tense atmosphere of German politics of the day that was
enough to make each man suspicious of the other.

Lafayette and Gouvion reached Berlin about three weeks before the summer maneuvers were to begin. That gave the marquis time for an interlude of social activity. He was formally
presented to King Frederick on the day of his arrival. As the
aged monarch advanced cordially to receive him, Lafayette
caught his first glimpse of the warrior who had already passed
into German lore as the crafty but admirable "Old Fritz." It
gave him somewhat of a shock. "Notwisdanding what I had
heard of him," he subsequently wrote to America's foremost
soldier, "[I] could not help being struck by that dress and appearance of an old, broken, dirty corporal, covered all over with
Spanish snuff, with his head almost leaning on one shoulder,
and fingers quite distorted by the gout. But [and this gracious
admission came after he had seen Frederick on maneuvers]
what surprised me much more is the fire and some times the
softeness of the most beautifull eyes I ever saw, which give as
charming an expression to his phisiognomy as he can take a
rough and threatening one at the head of his troops."[11] This
portrait of Old Fritz (aged seventy-three) by young Lafayette
(aged twenty-eight) for middle-aged Washington (aged fifty-
three), for all its gallicism, was one of the most eloquent passages that Lafayette ever penned. When a middle-aged Lafayette was to be presented to a young Napoleon Bonaparte for
the first time, he was to be forcefully reminded of this first encounter with Old Fritz. Apparently, in the course of time, the
impression made by the worn-out appearance of the Prussian

10. Lafayette to Maubourg, Jan. 22, 1792, collection of Louis Gottschalk (Chicago,
Ill.). Cf. Comte de Mirabeau to the Abbé de Périgord (Talleyrand), June 12, 1786,
Henri Welschinger (ed.), *La mission sécrète de Mirabeau à Berlin (1786-1787)* (Paris,
1900), pp. 104-5; *Mémoires*, II, 214 n.; Comte de Ségur, *Décade historique [ou tableau
politique de l'Europe]* in *Œuvres complètes*, ed. P. Tardieu (Paris, 1824-30), IV, 112-13.

11. Feb. 6, 1786, Gottschalk, *Letters*, p. 304.

conqueror gave way to the recollection of his cordiality and brilliance.[12]

Lafayette was "received with distinction by the Prussian court."[13] At their first meeting, Frederick and he talked freely about the United States. That afternoon the Marquis de Lucchesini, brilliant young Italian who was Frederick's personal companion, called on the distinguished Frenchman. In the course of their conversation Lafayette again introduced the subject of the United States, promoting the commercial treaty then under negotiation between Prussia and the new American nation. Lucchesini remembered until long afterward—and none too pleasantly—the French aristocrat's enthusiasm for the land of liberty.[14] Lafayette was received also by Frederick's nephew, the Crown Prince Frederick William, and his wife, and on August 3 he went to the little castle at Schönhausen to pay his respects to Frederick's neglected queen.[15] What these ceremonious calls upon foreign royalty cost in money (and presumably in effort) is revealed by the fact that the marquis now borrowed 2,400 livres in specie from the firm of C. C. Engel of Berlin against his Paris letter of credit.[16]

Lafayette next visited Prince Henry, Frederick's younger brother, at his country palace in Rheinsberg, about fifty miles northwest of Berlin. Henry was almost as famous a soldier and lover of French culture as the king but was less caustic of tongue and more liberal of thought. Rheinsberg was practically a French town, largely settled by Huguenot refugees from France. Built in the days when Frederick was crown prince and a devotee of Watteau and Voltaire, it was reminiscent of the Trianon palace at Versailles. Frederick had given it to Henry as a wedding present, and here Henry usually lived because he did not get on well with his royal brother.

Lafayette found Prince Henry, his entourage, and Rheinsberg

12. *Mémoires*, III, 199, and V, 164.

13. Comte d'Esterno to Vergennes, Aug. 2, 1785, AAE, corr. pol., Prusse, Vol. CCIV, fols. 311v–312.

14. Lafayette to Jefferson, Sept. 4, 1785, [Weaver], *Diplomatic correspondence*, I, 435; *Mémoires*, III, 199.

15. Esterno to Vergennes, Aug. 2, 1785, *loc. cit.*

16. Receipt of Aug. 5, 1785, *loc. cit.*

very congenial. He arrived during dinner on August 5 and stayed several days. Henry would call on him immediately after breakfast, and they would go walking until dinner. Then they would play lotto and talk of France, for which Henry had an affection that Lafayette found "truly touching." They went together to see a performance of Marmontel's *Huron*, which interested Lafayette "both as Frenchman and as savage." It was perhaps on this occasion that Henry enlisted Lafayette's help in his effort to get some French actors for the Rheinsberg theater. The marquis returned to Berlin on the evening of August 8, "exceedingly pleased" with his trip and convinced that it would be useful to him in the future.[17]

In Berlin he found his old companion-in-arms, the Chevalier Duportail, who had been the commanding general of the American engineers during the War of Independence and who was now a brigadier in the French service. Duportail had also come to Prussia to witness the grand maneuvers. From Berlin, Lafayette, Gouvion, and Duportail[18] went to Potsdam, where a preliminary review of troops took place. Then the king and his guests set out for Silesia. They were in Breslau on August 17, and grand maneuvers began a few days later. At Breslau they found other officers from France, as well as from England and elsewhere.[19]

For eight days Lafayette was one of the distinguished guests who regularly sat down at the king's table for dinners that lasted three hours. Among them, in addition to Lord Cornwallis, whom Lafayette had expected to find, was also the Duke of York, second son of the English king. Crown Prince Frederick William was likewise part of the company.[20] The cynical Old

17. Lafayette to [Mme de Tessé], Aug. 7, 1785, *Mémoires*, II, 128–29. See also Dieudonné Thiébault, *Souvenirs de vingt ans de séjour à Berlin* ("Bibliothèque des mémoires relatifs à l'histoire de France pendant le 18ᵉ siècle," ed. J. F. Barrière, Vol. XXIII [Paris, 1860]), p. 248.

18. Probably on August 12 (see Esterno to Vergennes, Aug. 16, 1785, quoted in Charavay, p. 121, n. 4), but the *Gazette de Leyde*, August 16 (suppl.), says that Duportail had already gone on.

19. Lafayette to [Mme de Tessé], Aug. 7, 1785, *Mémoires*, II, 129; to Knox, Feb. 11, 1786, Jackson collection; *Gazette de Leyde*, Aug. 30, 1785 (suppl.); *Courrier de l'Europe*, Sept. 6, 1785, quoted in Charavay, p. 122 n.

20. Lafayette to [Frederick William?], Sept. 29, 1785, Jackson collection. See below, n. 58.

Fritz deliberately placed Lafayette between the Duke of York and Lord Cornwallis. Conversation at first was confined to the king, the duke, and the marquis, but eventually two or three others would join in. Frederick, confirmed skeptic that he was, plied the young French optimist with searching questions about the resources of the American union and its future prospects. Lafayette loyally replied in defense of the Americans and their form of government. Sometimes he feared that the Duke of York might feel embarrassed.[21]

The king apparently enjoyed his guests' discomfiture at his sallies. Was it true that Washington was going to take a house in London? he asked the Duke of York. And (after Lafayette had somewhat heatedly insisted that America would never have either king or aristocracy) had M. le Marquis ever heard what happened to a certain young man who had tried to import ideas of liberty into a certain country? No? Well, he was hanged. A few years later, when Crown Prince Frederick William had become king, Lafayette was to be a prisoner in a Prussian jail and was to recall, probably without relish, what Frederick had said. Nevertheless, he now lost none of the king's table talk. He admired "the vivacity of his wit, the endearing charms of his adress and politeness," so far as to understand how "people could forget what a tyrannic, hard hearted and selfish man he is."[22]

Cornwallis did not enjoy himself so thoroughly as Lafayette did. "My reception in Silesia," he recorded, "was not flattering; there was a most marked preference for La Fayette; whether it proceeded from the King's knowing more of France, and liking better to talk about it, I know not."[23] But he did not take his discomfiture out on Lafayette. On the contrary, "La Fayette and I were the best friends possible in Silesia," he declared.[24]

21. Lafayette to Jefferson, Sept. 4, 1785, [Weaver], *Diplomatic correspondence*, I, 435; to Jay, Feb. 11, 1786, *ibid.*, p. 441; Harvard College Library, Sparks MSS XXXII, pp. 145–47.

22. Lafayette to Washington, Feb. 6, 1786, Gottschalk, *Letters*, p. 304. See also *Mémoires*, III, 199. Sparks MSS XXXII, pp. 145–46, tells this story with more elaborate and probably less accurate detail.

23. To Alexander Ross, Oct. 5, 1785, Charles Ross (ed.), *Correspondence of Charles, first marquis Cornwallis* (London, 1859), I, 212.

24. To Ross, Sept. 9, 1785, *ibid.*, p. 202.

The grand maneuvers were engaged in by 30,000 men—
22,500 infantry in thirty-one battalions and 7,500 cavalry in
seventy-five squadrons. Lafayette, who had never commanded
more than 8,000 or 9,000 men in war, now saw 20,000 men in a
single line. They advanced into sham battle under the eye of
their wizened old king, who, surrounded by admiring French,
English, and German guests, glared at them from his saddle
through his field glasses. Lafayette later gave the benefit of his
observations to the American secretary of war. "The Prussian
troops are indeed most admirable," he granted. "Their infantry
is handsome, well exercised, and maneuvres in a line better than
I had an idea of." Their cavalry was "the best in the world,"
though mounted on "very indifferent" horses. "Habit and discipline gives them a boldness and a rapidity which is surprising." The whole army was so thoroughly drilled that "military
routine" would make it possible for a fool to "manage his corps
in the line as well almost as if he was sensible."[25]

But the marquis's instincts as a humanitarian were none the
less shocked. He had seen the king lose his temper twice and
put three officers under arrest.[26] Moreover, "the [Prussian] mode
of recruiting is despotic," he confided to Knox. "There is hardly
any provision for old soldiers, and altho' I found much to admire, I had rather be the last farmer in America than the first
general in Berlin."[27]

In his report to Knox, Lafayette did not mention the horse-
drawn artillery that he saw in Silesia and later at Potsdam.
Nevertheless it made a great impression on him and eventually,
when he reached a position of sufficient authority in the French
army, he introduced it there.[28] Cornwallis, perhaps because he
was jealous but more likely because he was a more experienced
soldier than Lafayette, was far from equally enthusiastic about
Frederick's military system. He found the Prussian infantry
slower than the Hessians and its maneuvers "such as the worst

25. Lafayette to Knox, Feb. 11, 1786, *loc. cit.*; cf. Lafayette to Washington, Feb. 6,
Gottschalk, *Letters*, p. 304.

26. Lafayette to [Frederick William?], Sept. 29, 1785, *loc. cit.*

27. Lafayette to Knox, Feb. 11, 1786, *loc. cit.*

28. *Mémoires*, III, 297.

General in England would be hooted at for practicing." Nothing could be more ridiculous, he thought, than "two lines coming up within six yards of one another, and firing in one another's faces till they had no ammunition left."[29]

On the fourth day of the maneuvers, it rained hard. Frederick, wishing to set an example for his men and "the damned cobblers" he had to employ as generals, refused to leave his saddle or to wear a cloak. For six hours, drenched to the skin, he put his troops and his own shriveled carcass through their paces. That afternoon, despite a fever, he had dinner as usual with the Duke of York, Lafayette, and Cornwallis. But he already had a cough that was to leave him only on his death. There is no evidence that Lafayette endured the rain or noticed the fever. When the party broke up, and Frederick returned to Berlin to prepare for the Potsdam maneuvers late in September, the king was a dying man, though it took him almost another year to die.[30]

Since the Potsdam maneuvers were not to come for almost a month, Lafayette determined to make a hasty visit to Austria. Still accompanied by Gouvion, he rode into the Hapsburg dominions. In so doing, he was either indiscreet or innocent. Since Austria and Prussia, inveterate enemies, were at the moment at sword's point over the question of the exchange of Belgium for Bavaria, a French general could not go from one to the other without rousing suspicion and giving offense. At Potsdam, where apparently some looked upon him as either a spy or a go-between, there was much speculation as to whether he would in fact return, and Lucchesini, offering to bet that he would, easily found takers.[31]

Traversing Moravia without making a stop, the two French officers reached Vienna on September 2.[32] They stayed at the home of Adrienne's uncle, the Marquis de Noailles, who was the

29. To Ross, Oct. 5, 1785, Ross, I, 212.

30. Nathan Ausubel, *Superman, the life of Frederick the Great* (New York, 1931), pp. 770–71; J. D. E. Preuss, *Friedrich der Grosse* (Berlin, 1834), IV, 240–41.

31. Lafayette to Lucchesini, May 22, 1786, Gardner-Ball collection; Lafayette to [Frederick William?], Sept. 29, 1785, *loc. cit.*

32. Lafayette to [Frederick William?], Sept. 29, 1785, *loc. cit.*; Lafayette to Jefferson, Sept. 4, [Weaver], *Diplomatic correspondence*, I, 435.

French ambassador. Even in the heart of a foreign empire, petitions reached Lafayette requesting his patronage in America. He wrote several letters of introduction for André M. Michaux, a well-known botanist, who was being sent to America to collect seeds like those Lafayette had requested but had not yet received.[33] He indorsed and sent to Jay the petition of a shipowner named Argaynaratz asking for a fairer compensation on a cargo shipped to America in 1778.[34] Otherwise, he devoted himself entirely to more august pursuits in the Austrian capital.

On September 3 the two French officers were presented by the Marquis de Noailles to Emperor Joseph II.[35] Their interview lasted about an hour and dealt mostly with the United States. France was mentioned but little and Prussia not at all. Perhaps, as Noailles feared, the emperor was piqued that Lafayette's visit to him should be so conspicuously sandwiched in between two visits to his rival in Prussia and deliberately avoided speaking of Frederick; or perhaps a delicacy that the less diplomatic marquis did not understand inhibited him.[36] At any rate, the conversation was largely a series of questions by Joseph and answers by Lafayette about American campaigns, the powers of Congress, the strength of the United States, American trade, and Washington. The marquis found the emperor, like many other Germans, as ill informed as he was interested. In part this ignorance (notable also in Frederick) was due to conservative prejudice, but it was also, Lafayette believed, the result of deliberate English propaganda to destroy confidence in America and to discourage emigration.[37] Lafayette tried to suggest to the

---

33. Lafayette to Thomas Bee (LC, Lafayette papers), to McHenry (Steiner, p. 624), and to Washington (Gottschalk, *Letters*, p. 302), all of Sept. 3, 1785; see above, pp. 139 and 163.

34. Lafayette to Jay, Sept. 6, 1785, [Weaver], *Diplomatic correspondence*, I, 437–38 (LC, PCC 156, fol. 436).

35. Lafayette to Washington, Sept. 3, 1785; Gottschalk, *Letters*, p. 302, and to Jefferson, Sept. 4, [Weaver], *Diplomatic correspondence*, I, 435. Both *Gazette de Leyde*, Sept. 20 (suppl.), and Noailles to Vergennes, Sept. 5, AAE, corr. pol., Vienna, Vol. 350, fol. 152, mistakenly indicate September 4.

36. Lafayette to [Frederick William?], Sept. 29, 1785, *loc. cit.*; Noailles to Vergennes, Sept. 5, *loc. cit.*

37. Lafayette to Jay, Feb. 11, 1786, [Weaver], *Diplomatic correspondence*, I, 440. Cf. Adams to Jay, Dec. 15, 1785, *ibid.*, IV, 463–64.

emperor that Austria would be wise to open her doors to American goods in exchange for Austrian goods and indicated the commodities America could furnish. Joseph, apparently not caring to promote English commerce, wanted particularly to know whether American cargoes would be carried in American vessels to Austrian ports. The whole conversation, the marquis thought, was marked by geniality and understanding.[38]

That evening[39] Lafayette had a private interview with the venerable Prince von Kaunitz, Austrian chancellor. The anxious French ambassador, having learned that his nephew's conspicuous preference for Prussia had been noted by the prince, had concocted the excuse that his two guests had made a hasty trip to Vienna only in order to seek formal permission to stay for the whole of the Austrian maneuvers the next summer. Lafayette accordingly made a special effort to bring that matter up in his conversation with Kaunitz,[40] but he also took care once more to raise the American issue. The chancellor, too, wondered whether the Americans would carry their own exports. Lafayette, for his part, urged that Austria send consuls and make business arrangements with American firms. No trade could last, he insisted, unless it were mutually beneficial. Why, then, asked Kaunitz, did not the Americans make advances to Austria? Because, Lafayette answered, they had been discouraged in the past. Kaunitz explained that their approaches had been too indirect. Lafayette rejoined that he knew the Americans to be ready for a trade agreement with Austria; if Austria would open her Italian ports to American salt fish, that would be a good beginning. When he left, he carried away the impression that the chancellor would soon instruct his ambassadors to enter into

38. Lafayette to Jefferson, Sept. 4, 1785, [Weaver], *Diplomatic correspondence*, I, 435; Lafayette to Washington, Feb. 6, 1786, Gottschalk, *Letters*, p. 306; Lafayette to Jay, Feb. 11, 1786, [Weaver], *Diplomatic correspondence*, I, 441; Lafayette to [Frederick William?], Sept. 29, *loc. cit.*

39. Lafayette to Jefferson, Sept. 4, 1785, [Weaver], *Diplomatic correspondence*, I, 435. Lafayette to Jay, Feb. 11, 1786 (*ibid.*, p. 441), says "next day" and also that it was Kaunitz who introduced the subject of America but the earlier letter gives the more reliable testimony.

40. Noailles to Vergennes, Sept. 5, 1785, *loc. cit.*; Lafayette to [Frederick William?], Sept. 29, *loc. cit.*

negotiations with Jefferson or Adams on the subject and was quite pleased with himself and Kaunitz.[41]

The self-appointed emissary lost no time in reporting his conversations to the American representatives in Europe. Since the French ambassador was his uncle, he was able to do so by private courier. But Jefferson, it proved, was not greatly impressed by Lafayette's diplomatic efforts. A treaty with Prussia had just been signed (apparently unaffected by Lafayette's visit to Berlin), and Jefferson was of the opinion that further treaties with powers that were not directly interested in American territories had better be avoided.[42] Thus a labor of love was lost.

Lafayette's time in Vienna was also occupied with military matters. He was invited to the home of the young Archduke Francis, the future emperor, and on September 6 went as the archduke's guest to review a Viennese regiment. He met Marshals Lacy, Hadik, and Laudon and the Count de Clerfayt, all distinguished generals of the Seven Years' War. He conversed freely with them about the Prussian maneuvers and (if his own account is to be credited) corrected some of the exaggerated reports that had reached Vienna. Avoiding mention of the more unpleasant aspects of Frederick's behavior, he did not attempt to conceal his admiration for the Prussian army.[43]

Lafayette also found in Vienna that his reputation as a "republican" could be quite a nuisance. While he was there, the Austro-Dutch controversy momentarily flared up again and some troops were given marching orders. The agents of Holland in Vienna sought him out "as Frenchman and republican," apparently counting upon him to use his influence in their behalf. He later admitted to one of his most aristocratic German friends that he "would greatly have preferred not to see" them.[44] Being both a "republican" and a friend of royalty

41. Lafayette to Jefferson, Sept. 4, 1785, [Weaver], *Diplomatic correspondence*, I, 435; to [Frederick William?], Sept. 29, *loc. cit.*

42. Lafayette to Jefferson, Sept. 4, 1785, [Weaver], *Diplomatic correspondence*, I, 435–36; Jefferson to Jay, Aug. 4, and to Adams, Sept. 24, Lipscomb and Bergh, V, 66–67 and 140–41. Cf. Jefferson to Jay, Oct. 11, *ibid.*, pp. 174–75.

43. *Gazette de Leyde*, Sept. 23, 1785 (suppl.); Lafayette to [Frederick William?], Sept. 29, *loc. cit.*

44. Lafayette to [Frederick William?], Sept. 29, 1785, *loc. cit.*

seemed to cause embarrassing complications sometimes. Fortunately the international crisis blew over rapidly.

When Lafayette left Vienna, he carried away pleasant recollections of Austria's statesmen and generals. He knew that Joseph II was one of the most zealous of the so-called "enlightened despots" of the day, but apparently the marquis was one of those—and they were many—who felt that the emperor's schemes were more ambitious than fruitful. His brief tour of Vienna had convinced him that Joseph's projects were "scattered to all points of the globe."[45] Several times thereafter he referred to Joseph's unstable "temper" (meaning "temperament") in a derogatory fashion.[46] One of the emperor's projects, however, he felt would be much more useful to humanity than the others. That was a model hospital—copied, Lafayette patriotically thought, from the one in Lyon.[47] The capital of Joseph II, who was perhaps the best-intentioned ruler of his day, interested the young "republican" chiefly for military and commercial reasons. That it did so revealed that his political philosophy was still largely concerned with concrete problems—to increase his military knowledge and to seek advantages for the land of his birth and the land of his adoption.

The Marquis de Noailles was relieved when Lafayette and Gouvion left Vienna. He undoubtedly remembered the time in 1777 when Lafayette had visited him in London, where he then was ambassador. He had been painfully embarrassed when it turned out that his young nephew had been engaged, while enjoying the hospitality of the English, in a conspiracy to go to the aid of the American insurgents. All the time that Lafayette was his guest at the Vienna embassy he had feared a similar contretemps. His fears were not groundless, for Austria and France were bound by an uneasy alliance and Prussia was their potential enemy. Spies had been engaged by the Prussians to follow Lafayette's movements, and apparently Noailles's com-

45. Ibid.

46. Lafayette to Washington, Feb. 6, 1786, Gottschalk, Letters, p. 309; to Franklin, Feb. 10, APS, Franklin papers, Vol. XXXIV, No. 22½, and to Jay, Feb. 11, [Weaver], Diplomatic correspondence, I, 442.

47. Lafayette to [Frederick William?], Sept. 29, 1785, loc. cit.

ments upon him came to their knowledge.[48] Noailles's report on Lafayette's finesse in keeping the good will of authorities in both countries "without anyone feeling precisely displeased with him" displayed an uncle's pleasure at the same time that it revealed an ambassador's anxiety regarding good form and protocol.[49]

Hoping to see some of the Austrian maneuvers and the battlefields of the recent German wars, Lafayette and Gouvion left Vienna in plenty of time. They went by way of Bohemia and Saxony. At Prague they saw six battalions engaged in tactical exercises, and, quite naturally, Lafayette was less impressed than he had been with five times that number at Breslau. Nevertheless, the Austrian infantry was, he thought, rather good— better than the French and better uniformed than either the Prussians or the French. Although he remained convinced that only the Prussians could move in a line so smartly as he had seen them do, he found the Austrian artillery surprisingly effective. The Austrian generals took him for a tour of the battlefields of the Seven Years' War (Prague, Kolin, and Lebositz). He would have liked to see the neighboring fortresses but felt it would be indiscreet to ask. Since, however, Frederick and other Prussian strategists had spoken to him candidly, he was able to talk about Austrian fortifications in a manner that, he thought, roused his hearers' admiration.

Escorted by the commanding general at Prague, the marquis went on to Brandeis. There he was hospitably welcomed by a number of Austrian officers, including Marshal Wallis, Generals Wurmser and Kinski, and Prince von Hohenlohe-Kirschberg, who also were heroes of the Seven Years' War. He was permitted to watch eight squadrons of carabineers engage in tactics that he thought "very well done." Although he left Austria without seeing Joseph's army in grand maneuvers, he was none the less impressed with it. It was a "beautiful and good army," he concluded[50]—though far from as well drilled as Prussia's. He had come to the conclusion, moreover, that the Austrians' "gen-

48. *Ibid.* Cf. Gottschalk, *Lafayette comes to America*, pp. 87–92.
49. Noailles to Vergennes, Sept. 5, 1785, *loc. cit.*
50. Lafayette to [Frederick William?], Sept. 29, *loc. cit.*

eral system of oeconomy is more to be admired than the maneuvres of their troops." Even if their military machine was com-
plex and inferior in training to the Prussian and the French, it
was "much more numerous than either and costs much less than
the French."[51] Austria was still, in his estimation, a formidable
military power.

Hastening through Dresden, Lafayette stopped briefly in
Berlin on September 18 and then went straight on. He occasioned a little surprise at Potsdam when he appeared because,
as the Duke of Brunswick told him, he had not been expected
to return. While Lafayette was amused that his innocent and
unofficial trip to Vienna should have excited so much speculation, Lucchesini collected his bets.[52]

A violent attack of apoplexy kept the iron-willed Frederick II
from attending the maneuvers, and he was reported to be dying
in Berlin. But they took place nevertheless under the command
of Crown Prince Frederick William. This gave Lafayette a third
chance to gauge the future king. He found the crown prince to
be "a good officer, an honest man, a man of plain good sense,"
even if he did not measure up to his two uncles.

The marquis was once more impressed by the Prussian military organization. With the Potsdam maneuvers freshest in
mind but still under the influence of the Silesian spectacle, he
reported to Washington: "Nothing can be compared to the
beauty of the troops, the discipline that is diffused throughout,
the simplicity of their motions, the uniformity of their regi-
ments. It is a plain regular machine that has been set these forty
years, and undergoes no alteration but what can make it simpler
and lighter. Every supposition in war, and every motion deriving from it, has been from a constant use so much inculcated
into their heads that it became almost a mechanic for them."
His patriotism as a Frenchman made him want to put in a good
word for his own army, but it was a lame one at best. "Were the
ressources of France, the alertness of her men, the intelligence

---

51. Lafayette to Washington, Feb. 6, 1786, Gottschalk, *Letters*, p. 305. Cf. Lafayette to [Frederick William?], Sept. 29, 1785, *loc. cit.*, and to Knox, Feb. 11, 1786,
loc. cit.

52. See above, p. 188, and n. 31.

of her officers, and national ambition and moral delicacy applied to such a constant system, we could be as superior to the Prussians as our army is now inferior to theirs—and that is saying [a] great deal."[53] It was indeed, if, besides the resources and aggressive nationalism of the Prussians, the French lacked alert soldiers, intelligent officers, and morale. But apparently Lafayette did not yet think those lacks irreparable.

At Potsdam, Lafayette met an old friend, William Stephens Smith, who had been lieutenant colonel and inspector of his Light Infantry during the American War and was now John Adams' secretary in London. Together with the Venezuelan patriot Miranda, whom Lafayette had met in Boston, Smith was making a tour of Europe. The two men had come to Potsdam to attend the grand maneuvers. Imposing English officers were greatly in evidence there. The American army, on the other hand, was represented by Smith alone (if one excepted French officers like Duportail, Gouvion, and Lafayette). Thus, as Smith and Lafayette agreed, the young republic would have cut a sorry figure indeed, "had we been unfortunate in the contest."[54]

During one of the most impressive sham battles at Potsdam (September 21), Miranda and Smith stood close to Lafayette. They watched one force of soldiers led by General von Möllendorf go through the motions of attack upon another simulating defense. Lafayette was greatly impressed by Möllendorf and came away with the conviction that he was the best officer in the Prussian service. While the sham attack was going on, Lafayette conversed with Colonel Miranda. The Spanish-American soldier, having already formed a dislike for the marquis at Boston, was suspicious when the Frenchman now expressed an interest in South America. Characteristically, Lafayette indicated that "he would much like to promote its liberty."[55] But Miranda coolly pretended to know nothing about the subject and the conversation ended. When Miranda afterward, on the insistence of the Spanish ambassador, was dogged by the

53. Lafayette to Washington, Feb. 6, 1785, Gottschalk, *Letters*, pp. 304–5.

54. *Ibid.*, p. 306; cf. Robertson, *Life of Miranda*, I, 65.

55. Robertson, *Life of Miranda*, I, 66; cf. Gottschalk, *Letters*, p. 304.

French police, his friends believed that Lafayette, incensed by Miranda's curtness, was partly responsible.[56]

Lafayette returned to the Prussian capital on September 24.[57] A tragicomic episode filled the single day he spent in Berlin. He discovered that he was being shadowed by someone whom he found to be "the most beautiful spy I have ever seen in my life." He suspected that the spy was set upon him by the Prussian intelligence department because they still thought his movements between Berlin and Vienna had some dark military or diplomatic purpose. He determined to treat the whole matter lightly. He would send a full report of his Austrian experiences to the Prussian authorities by the very spy they had put on his trail. His report would be written in a tone of friendly banter to a Prussian prince whom he would not identify but whose identity the spy undoubtedly would guess. "You know," he was to say when he finally got around to writing the report, "that, once caught, these people can be treated however one wishes; but by very great mischance, this spy, though pretty difficult, was one of those persons whom one must respect at the same time as love. We therefore arranged a capitulation and agreed that I would relieve her of the trouble of writing up my confession on condition that she would let me call on her in order to give her my letter. Thus I earn a visit and she earns nothing, since it has all along been my intention to write you, my dear prince, and, while telling you of my little journey, to thank you for all the kindness you showed me in Silesia."[58]

The rendezvous with the spy, however, had to wait a few days, for her captor had other plans. He intended to be present at the war games at Magdeburg, where Brunswick was going to

---

56. *Archivo del Miranda*, XII, xxvi n. and 182–83, n. 2.

57. Charavay, p. 126, n. 4.

58. Lafayette to "*mon cher prince*," Sept. 29, 1785, *loc. cit.* This manuscript has been mended and, in the mending, the date was changed to 1786, but, since it is from Rheinsberg, which Lafayette did not visit in 1786, the year 1785 is the only possible correct one. *Mon cher prince* seems to have been the Crown Prince Frederick William. Prince Henry is ruled out, since the letter was written from Rheinsberg and he is mentioned. The Duke of Brunswick is also mentioned. The crown prince appears to be the only other Prussian general and prince with whom Lafayette became sufficiently familiar to write in the tone of this letter. That Lafayette thanks the prince for his kindness only in Silesia may be explained by the fact that they saw more of each other there than at Potsdam.

put another group of soldiers through their paces. Since the intervening period was only a few days long, he and Gouvion set off immediately to revisit the cordial atmosphere of Prince Henry's castle and to bid him goodbye. Once more Lafayette found the lord of Rheinsberg a man after his own heart. "I don't examine who is the greater general, his brother or he," he afterward informed Washington. "[That is] a question that divides the military world. But to abilities of the first rate both as a soldier and a politician, to perfect litterary knowledge and all the endowements of the mind, he joins an honest heart, philantropic feelings, and rational ideas on the Rights of Mankind."[59] Other Prussian noblemen, even when they admired Washington and their fellow-countryman Steuben[60] or were enthusiastic regarding American military conduct during the war, were, like the great Frederick, doubtful that free institutions could long survive. Prince Henry, however, was among the few "sensible and feeling men" who were more optimistic.[61]

The intimacy of the two men was well illustrated by their discussion of the Duke of Brunswick. The misunderstanding between Lafayette and Brunswick had not diminished in their recent contacts. Prince Henry, Brunswick's uncle, did not share Lafayette's suspicions. Lafayette, however, having seen Brunswick pay court to both Henry and his royal brother though they were known to disagree thoroughly, distrusted the duke and believed that he would someday betray his uncle's confidence. Sometime later the prince (if Lafayette did not read into Henry's letters some of his own distrust) came around to the same opinion.[62]

At Rheinsberg, Lafayette found time to write the report of his Austrian tour promised to "the most beautiful spy." He apparently had no hesitation in telling what he had learned about the Austrian army, although Austria was an ally and Prussia a potential enemy of France. Actually he had learned little that

59. Feb. 6, 1786, Gottschalk, *Letters*, p. 305.

60. Lafayette to Knox, Feb. 11, 1786, *loc. cit.*

61. Lafayette to Franklin, Feb. 10, 1786, *loc. cit.*, p. 2; cf. Lafayette to Knox, Feb. 11, *loc. cit.*

62. Lafayette to Maubourg, Jan. 22, 1792, *loc. cit.*

was not already generally known. On the other hand, he did set some store by being thought well of by his *cher prince*. "I am going to leave," his long report concluded, "with heart and mind full of enthusiasm for your admirable army, deeply touched by all the attention and courtesy that I have received and very sincere in all the sentiments that your kindness has made me feel. I shall be happy indeed, my dear prince, if you deign to count for life on the feelings you have inspired in me." He requested the prince to write him, promising, as they had agreed, not to allow their letters to be seen. "I take the liberty of closing unceremoniously with the homage of my thanks and my devotion."[63] If *mon cher prince* was the future King Frederick William II (and it is hard to believe it was anyone else), that homage did little to soften the blow for Lafayette when he later became the king's prisoner of war. Whether the rendezvous with the pretty spy was ever kept, or, indeed, whether Lafayette's letter was ever delivered to its destination, remains unknown.

After about ten days at Rheinsberg, Lafayette returned briefly to the Prussian capital. He did not attempt to pay his respects to the sick king but sent him a letter of adieu instead, receiving one in turn.[64] Frederick allowed his regular French correspondent, Baron de Grimm, friend of the great Diderot, to know that he regretted not having seen more of the "several Frenchmen in this country, among them M. de La Fayette."[65] The French minister in Berlin testified to the impression the young officer had made by "his most perfect conduct" on all occasions. "Preceded here by an honorable reputation, he has received from this court all the favors that he deserves, and he has been able to win universal approval."[66]

Hastening on to Magdeburg, Lafayette attended the sham battles there and probably again encountered Cornwallis, who much against his better judgment had traveled "160 miles on

63. Lafayette to [Frederick William?], Sept. 29, 1785, *loc. cit.*

64. Lafayette to Washington, Feb. 6, 1786, Gottschalk, *Letters*, p. 305; *Gazette de Leyde*, Nov. 4, 1785 (suppl.).

65. Oct. 24, 1785, J. D. E. Preuss (ed.), *Œuvres de Frédéric le Grand* (Berlin, 1846–57), XXV, 361.

66. Esterno to Vergennes, Oct. 5, 1785, AAE, corr. pol., Prusse, Vol. CCIV, fol. 410v.

the worst roads in Europe" to get there.[67] Cornwallis' unfavorable reaction to Prussia set off in greater relief Lafayette's youthful enthusiasms. Yet, as the Magdeburg war games were little different from the ones already inspected and perhaps, too, because of his dislike of the Duke of Brunswick, the French general was now blasé.[68] From Magdeburg he returned directly home without going, as he had originally intended, by way of Holland (perhaps because the waters no longer seemed troubled there). He arrived in Paris somewhat behind schedule.

When Lafayette came to take stock of what he had learned from his three or four months in Germany, he did not regret its cost. He had met many men of stature, including an emperor, a king, and an heir apparent, as well as famous ministers and generals. He had added significantly to his military knowledge by tours of illustrious battlefields, reviews of the most modern tactics, and conversations with the most practiced officers of the finest armies in the world. He did not underestimate those benefits when he wrote to his most trusted friends in America about his German tour. Yet he knew that they would be still more interested in the prevalent German attitude toward America.

Lafayette had to admit that he had found most Germans discouraged or discouraging. In the first place, even the exalted among them were either misinformed or skeptical about liberal aspirations. "In countries so far distant, under constitutions so foreign to republican notions, the affairs of America cannot be thoroughly understood, and such inconveniences as we lament ourselves are greatly exagerated by her enemies." It would require a volume, the marquis estimated, to list the mistaken ideas he had himself set right. "It is foolishly thought by some that democratical constitutions will not, cannot, last; that the States will quarrel with each other; that a King, or at least a nobility, are indispensable for the prosperity of a nation." But these beliefs were "absurdities" and were easily refuted "by the

---

67. Cornwallis to Ross, Oct. 4, 1785, Ross, I, 212. According to Cornwallis (*ibid.*, p. 201), the Magdeburg maneuvers took place on October 10–12. Lafayette left Berlin on October 6, not 7. Charavay (p. 126) makes Esterno say *après-demain*, but he really said *demain*.

68. Lafayette to Washington, Feb. 6, 1786, Gottschalk, *Letters*, p. 305.

smallest particle of unprejudiced common sense, and will I hope be for ever destroyed by the example of America."[69]

In fact, Lafayette had discovered a few in high places, like Prince Henry, who not only had been enthusiastic about the American soldier but also had expressed "wonder and applause" for the American statesman. "To the philosopher, the philantrope they are a matter of unspeckable delights and I could say of adoration," he boasted.[70] He had found a universal regard for Franklin and particularly for Washington. "Where ever I went, my dear General," he told his famed exemplar, "I had the pleasure to hear your name pronounced with that respect and enthusiasm which altho' it is a matter of course, and I am used to it, never fails to make my heart glow with unspeackable happiness. With your eulogium began every conversation on American affairs. And to be your friend, your disciple, and your adoptive son was, as it ever has been, and will be for ever, the pride of my heart, and the most pleasing of my thoughts."[71] He could not honestly maintain that what had disturbed him most in Germany was the absence of democratic faith. It was something more serious still.

That the American experiment was the hope of the world if it succeeded, Lafayette readily believed. He saw clearly that it was not enough to verbalize liberty in documents, for in Germany he had seen that abstract liberty was given lip service by the princes but remained "little felt by the people."[72] A concrete example of government successful though free had to be furnished, and America would have to furnish it. But he was afraid that the American experiment might not succeed. He could not deny that much of the criticism he had heard was based on fact. It was not without reason that eulogies of America had generally begun and ended with Washington and the constitutions of the several states, even for those Germans who were most enthusiastic regarding the Rights of Man. When discussions had

69. Lafayette to Jay, Feb. 11, 1786, [Weaver], *Diplomatic correspondence*, I, 440.

70. *Ibid.*, p. 439 (quoted here from the original in LC, PCC 156, fol. 446).

71. Lafayette to Washington, Feb. 6, 1786, Gottschalk, *Letters*, p. 306; cf. Lafayette to Franklin, Feb. 10, *loc. cit.*

72. Lafayette to Franklin, Feb. 10, 1786, *loc. cit.*

reached the problem of federal organization, practical questions arose that were hard to answer. "I have often had the mortification to hear," Lafayette complained to Washington, "that the want of powers in Congress, of union betwen the States, of energy in their governement should make the Confederation very insignificant. The fact is that those people, generally speacking, know very little of the advantages of democratical governements, of the ressources to be found in a free nation, and the parties which are essentially deriving from the Constitution. But they cannot help being more forcibly struck with all the blemishes which we have so often lamented together."[73]

It was with the sneers of German doubters fresh in mind that Lafayette returned to France. He was now more than ever anxious to make Congress and other American leaders understand how low American prestige had fallen in Europe.

BIBLIOGRAPHICAL NOTES

On Holstein's biography of Lafayette see my *Lafayette comes to America*, pp. 84 and 147. The narrative of the 1835 edition, while far from authoritative, is not so fantastic as that of the 1824 edition.

The biographies of Frederick the Great by Preuss and Ausubel are not the "standard" ones. They nevertheless treat the maneuvers of 1785 with the greatest detail.

Robertson's biography of Miranda is careful and detailed. There is an incredible account by a later aide of Miranda (*Archivo del General Miranda*, XII, 182-83 n.) about a quarrel between Colonel Smith and Lafayette. It implies that Smith broke with Lafayette because he believed that the marquis had persecuted Miranda, but see below, pp 306-7.

Charavay (pp. 119-27) has given (with occasional inaccuracies) some of the more inaccessible documents relating to Lafayette's German tour.

Max Büdinger, "Lafayette in Österreich, eine historische Untersuchung," [Vienna] *Sitzungsberichte der philosophisch-historischen Classe der Kaiserlichen Akademie der Wissenschaften*, XCII (1878), 235, cites Gustave Brabée, *Sub rosa, vertrauliche Mittheilungen aus dem mauerischen Leben unserer Grossväter* (Vienna, 1879), p. 12, to the effect that Lafayette visited a Masonic lodge in Vienna. Mr. R. Baker Harris, librarian of the Supreme Council, Washington, D.C., has helped me to look for corroboration of this statement, but we have been unable to find any.

73. Lafayette to Washington, Feb. 6, 1786, Gottschalk, *Letters*, pp. 306-7.

CHAPTER XV

Driving Jefferson's Nails

IMPRESSING upon Americans their loss of prestige in Europe was not the first task that Lafayette faced when he got back to Paris, for shortly after his return, the difficulties of Franco-American trade were once more forcibly brought to his attention. This time it was a Boston merchant named W. N. Boylston who requested his intercession. Boylston had brought a cargo of spermaceti to Le Havre, hoping not only to sell it but also to secure good terms for future sales. He had letters of introduction to both Jefferson and Lafayette and, in the marquis's absence, had taken his problem to the new American minister. When Lafayette returned, Jefferson brought the Boston merchant to the Rue de Bourbon.[1]

Thus began the close co-operation of Jefferson and Lafayette that was to lead, first, to a series of important commercial concessions by the French authorities and, eventually, to ideas for thoroughgoing reform of the French constitution. Lafayette and Jefferson had been associated since 1781, when Jefferson was governor of Virginia and Lafayette was trying to protect that state against the ravages of British invaders. But their associations had been only official and formal until Lafayette, returning from the United States in 1785, had found Jefferson in Paris as one of the commission, along with Franklin and Adams, to negotiate trade agreements with European nations.

The news that Lafayette had brought of the death of Jefferson's youngest daughter had affected Jefferson so deeply that for some time he rarely went out into society. Consequently, in

1. Jefferson to Adams, Nov. 19, 1785, Lipscomb and Bergh, V, 213; to Jay, Jan. 2, 1786, [Weaver], *Diplomatic correspondence*, II, 465.

the few months that Lafayette spent in Paris before his departure to the Midi and to Germany, he had seldom seen Jefferson. Although Jefferson had in March formally replaced Franklin as the American minister, Lafayette continued to conduct most of his business regarding America with Franklin (or rather, because of Franklin's illness, with his grandson William) and Adams. Occasional visits at each others' homes and the interest of the marquis and his wife in Jefferson's daughter Martha had, however, brought them closer together.[2] Lafayette was among the select few to whom Jefferson sent a copy of the first printing of his *Notes on Virginia*. He inscribed in it an expression of his "friendship and esteem" for one "whose services to the American Union in general & to that member of it particularly which is the subject of these Notes, & in that precise point of time too in which they relate, entitle him to this offering."[3]

After Lafayette's return from Germany, Jefferson found the marquis "so useful an auxiliary that acknowledgments for his co-operation are always due."[4] At the close of a year or more of residence in France, Jefferson, again declaring that Lafayette had been "a most valuable auxiliary to me," explained: "His zeal is unbounded, and his weight with those in power, great. His education having been merely military, commerce was an unknown field to him. But his good sense enabling him to comprehend perfectly whatever is explained to him, his agency has been very efficacious."[5]

Jefferson never tired of paying tribute to his collaborator. Long, long afterward, when both men were worn and gray and Lafayette was an honored guest at Jefferson's home, Jefferson

2. Cf. Jefferson to Short, Apr. 30, 1785, "Letters of Thomas Jefferson to William Short," *William and Mary College quarterly historical magazine*, 2d ser., XI (1931), 243; Mrs. Adams to Lucy Cranch, May 7, 1785, *Letters of Mrs. Adams*, p. 240; Mme de Lafayette to Jefferson, [Aug. 26, 1785], J. P. Morgan Library (New York, N.Y.), Lafayette Vol. I; S. K. Padover, *Jefferson* (New York, 1942), p. 124.

3. This copy is now in the rare book collection of the University of Virginia. Ford (*Writings of Jefferson*, III, 70) implies that the presentation was made in 1786. May, 1785, seems more likely. Jefferson sent copies of the book to Madison by the Comte Doradour, who left France around May 13, 1785. See Lafayette to Washington, May 13, 1785; Gottschalk, *Letters*, p. 298; Madison to Jefferson, Nov. 15, 1785, Hunt, II, 214–15 n.; and Jefferson to Madison, Feb. 8, 1786, Lipscomb and Bergh, V, 278–79.

4. Jefferson to Madison, Dec. 16, 1786, Lipscomb and Bergh, VI, 8.

5. Jefferson to Madison, Jan. 30, 1787, *ibid.*, pp. 69–70.

told the people of Charlottesville, Virginia: "When I was stationed in his country for the purpose of cementing its friendship with ours and of advancing our mutual interests, this friend of both was my most powerful auxiliary and advocate. He made our cause his own, as in truth it was that of his native country also. His influence and connections were great. All doors of all departments were open to him at all times; to me only formally and at appointed times. In truth, I only held the nail, he drove it."[6]

Nevertheless, Jefferson's gratitude need not have been one-sided. Lafayette owed him much, too. The younger man (Jefferson was forty-two in 1785, and Lafayette twenty-eight) needed and sought, though often unconsciously, the guidance of older minds. The ebullience, the genial aggressiveness, the gallantry, the joy in wire-pulling, and the desire to please (which led sometimes to his giving to the same episode a different color when speaking of it to different persons and which sometimes looked to the less charitable like hypocrisy) were a "coverup." They were the outward second-nature compensation for an inner personality that, reared in childhood without father or male companionship, was fundamentally insecure and timid. Lafayette was to learn some day (though not yet) to be steady and sure, but he now sought almost pathetically for affection, guidance, and approval from those he respected.

Such a personality could easily be exploited by the self-seeking like the Comte de Broglie[7] or by the self-effacing like Vergennes, because it lent itself willingly to rendering services, to assuming responsibilities, and to acting as if on its own initiative. It was a personality that eagerly attached itself to older men. Washington represented in Lafayette's mind the idea of "father"—probably more beloved and respected than his own father would have been. But with his "adoptive father" far away, the young man looked to Jefferson, who, no matter how much he differed from Washington, still reflected the image of Washington and the glory of America. In everything he did,

6. *Huntsville* (Ala.) *Democrat,* Dec. 7, 1824 (courtesy of Alabama Department of Archives and History). Cf. Jefferson's "Autobiography," Lipscomb and Bergh, I, 96.

7. Gottschalk, *Lafayette comes to America,* pp. 68–76.

Lafayette was to continue, as he had once confessed to Washington, "first [to] consider what your opinion would be, had I an opportunity to consult it."[8] Jefferson presented him with that opportunity as well as anyone then in France could present it. The young man's future political education thus lay in Jefferson's hands to a degree that might have astonished both men had they realized it.

Before Lafayette had left for Germany, he and Jefferson (as we have seen) had collaborated in securing permission for Tourtille Sangrain to import free of duty a certain quantity of oil for the streetlights of Paris. Lafayette now undertook to see whether Boylston's cargo could not be included in that quantity. The bargaining that ensued gives ample reason to believe that Lafayette could have earned a living in the market place if he had not been born an aristocrat. Nevertheless, though Sangrain himself proved most amenable, the marquis was not able to persuade the officials to admit Boylston's cargo as part of the nondutiable shipment. It looked as if Boylston would have to pay the usual tariff (of 12 livres per barrel), and Lafayette undertook to put the matter before the royal ministry once more. "The oil business," he declared, "is a most favorite object to my heart, because I throughly know how far it is essential to the very subsistence of many families in New England."[9]

A new series of negotiations now began between Jefferson and the French government, with Lafayette acting as intermediary. Jefferson hoped that they would lead to the entire suppression of the duties on whale oil, and this aim was quickly joined to another of a similar nature. Tobacco was one of the principal staples of the United States. Even before Lafayette had left for Germany, he had enlisted Jefferson's aid in the effort to increase America's tobacco exports directly to France, thereby eliminating the hated England as an *entrepôt*. Jefferson believed that the major obstacle in the way of the direct importation of tobacco was the Farm; for the farmers-general, through their monopoly

8. Lafayette to Washington, June 29, 1782, Gottschalk, *Letters*, p. 253; cf. p. vii and Gottschalk, *Lafayette and the close of the American Revolution*, pp. 371–72.

9. Lafayette to Boylston, Oct. [error for Nov.] 4, 1785, American Antiquarian Society (Worcester, Mass.).

on the purchase and sale of all excisable articles, were making an enormous profit from the sale of tobacco, and American exporters preferred to ship to England, where there was no such monopoly. The tobacco trade was further complicated by a contract the Farm had recently made with Robert Morris, formerly American superintendent of finance. Since the farmers-general preferred to deal with a single importer, he had obtained such a favorable price (along with a handsome advance payment) that it gave him enormous advantages in the American tobacco market. Vigorous protests soon arose from other American merchants. To Jefferson, a Virginia planter, the tobacco trade was a personal matter. Moreover, it was easy to foresee that the favoritism showed to Morris would alienate other American merchants, tarnishing the victories won for Franco-American solidarity by earlier concessions.[10]

Even before Lafayette's return from Germany, Jefferson had suggested to Vergennes that the farmers-general were grossly exploiting their monopoly. He contended that they collected more than one-half again over what it cost to grow, ship, and prepare American tobacco for market (including the tax for royal revenue). He estimated that a 5 per cent charge for collection would be a fair remuneration to the Farm. The price could thereby be reduced one-third, more purchasers would be found, and the crown's revenue would increase despite the lowering of the consumer's tax. French commerce also would benefit, Jefferson argued, since American imports, no longer coming by way of England, would be paid for directly in French commodities instead of in specie.[11] When, therefore, Lafayette next went to pay his respects at court and took up with the foreign minister the perennial problem of American commerce, he had both the tax on whale oil and the monopoly on tobacco to talk about.

Tobacco proved the more interesting to Vergennes. The periodical contract from which the Farm derived its monopoly was shortly to be renewed, and this monopoly was an old sore.

10. Jefferson to Henry, June 16, 1785, Lipscomb and Bergh, V, 7–8; to Adams, Nov. 19, *ibid.*, p. 213; F. L. Nussbaum, "American tobacco and French politics, 1783–1789," *Political science quarterly*, XL (1925), 502–3.

11. Jefferson to Vergennes, Aug. 15 and Nov. 14, 1785, Lipscomb and Bergh, V, 68–76 and 203–13.

Time and again reforming ministers had tried to revise or abolish it, only to be defeated by powerful vested interests. The prospect of staunch support from popular figures like Jefferson and Lafayette led Vergennes to consider reopening the struggle. Having more of a reforming spirit and feeling less friendly to the farmers-general than did his colleague Calonne, the foreign minister was glad to avail himself of Lafayette's self-starting power, which would make it easier for him to appear not to have taken the initiative. Vergennes now informed Lafayette that he had already submitted Jefferson's letter to the farmers-general and had received a reply. The marquis asked for a copy of it to submit to Jefferson. "Those gentlemen," he jested, "are so formidable, despite their disinterestedness, that it is impossible to improve one's means of defense enough."[12] He begged that the section dealing with tobacco in the new contract should be delayed until Jefferson could make a rejoinder.

Lafayette soon discovered "two or three gentlemen" who were "well acquainted" with the problem of the farmers-general (and it is possible that he was unobtrusively helped to find them by the Comte de Vergennes). He brought these expert consultants and Jefferson together, and they suggested that Jefferson propose to Vergennes the appointment of a special committee to consider a new tobacco contract with the Farm. Jefferson, however, preferred to work indirectly—as Vergennes did too—through Lafayette as an intermediary.[13]

Lafayette's earlier victories on free ports and whale oil made him feel fairly confident now. Still he was not hopeful that speedy results could be achieved. Adopting Jefferson's arguments without his judicious tone, the marquis complained sarcastically: "The farmers-general, thanks to their patriotic en-

12. Lafayette to Vergennes, Nov. 16, 1785, AAE, corr. pol., É.-U., Vol. XXX, fol. 412.

13. Jefferson to Monroe, May 10, 1786, Lipscomb and Bergh, V, 330. F. L. Nussbaum, "Vergennes and Lafayette versus the farmers general," *Journal of modern history*, III (1931), 597, thinks that Dupont de Nemours and the Marquis de Condorcet were among these "two or three gentlemen." If so, they most likely were recommended to Lafayette by Vergennes, since Dupont had been engaged in preparing reports for Vergennes on this subject since 1783. Cf. *ibid.*, p. 595, and the same author's "American tobacco and French politics," pp. 504–5. That Lafayette knew Condorcet at this time is easily established (see below, p. 224), but he does not seem to have met Dupont until a little later (see below, p. 222, n. 2).

lightenment, send their money to England to buy their commodities, which, considering the heavy duties levied in America on all English vessels, they could have much more cheaply in our own ports, paying in manufactured articles." In fact, he was beginning to wonder whether the governmental administration of France was not faulty. In writing to Rabaut-St. Étienne, who could be expected to sympathize with his suspicions, he expressed himself rather freely. He had found the ministers well disposed, he confessed, and did not doubt that the ultimate outcome would be good. "But in this country of ours we are afraid of things that may have certain repercussions, we try to put them off, and any business is impeded if it branches out under different departments [of the government]."[14]

Lafayette's quarrel with the farmers-general soon reached a state that he described as "very hostile terms."[15] At the same time, his admiration for Jefferson grew. "No better minister could be sent to France," he stated. "He is every thing that is good, upright, enlightened and clever, and is respected and beloved by every one that knows him."[16] The worst stumbling block was obviously the office of the comptroller-general, whose department had jurisdiction over revenues and duties. On the matter of Boylston's whale oil Comptroller-General Calonne proved only a little more pliable than he was on tobacco. Although Lafayette gave the impression that the cargo was not actually at a French port (as it was) and could easily be disposed of in another country, Calonne at first seemed unimpressed. He still thought that France should develop its own whaling industry and therefore for the time being was unwilling to make any further concessions to American shippers.

The struggle against the whale oil tariff, nevertheless, developed rapidly. Prompted by the Boylston case, Jefferson suggested to Lafayette that instead of taking individual shipments of oil one by one to the ministers, it would be wiser to get a gen-

14. Lafayette to Rabaut-St. Étienne, Nov. 20, 1785, Bibliothèque de la Ville de Nantes, MS 667, No. 171.

15. Lafayette to Wadsworth, Dec. 3, 1785, Connecticut State Library, Trumbull collection.

16. Lafayette to McHenry, Dec. 3, 1785, B. C. Steiner, "Miscellaneous letters from the McHenry papers," Southern History Association publications, XI (1907), 44-45.

eral ruling. Realizing that it would be tactless for a diplomat to go beyond the regular channels of international negotiation openly, the two men agreed that the marquis should privately push the matter further. Lafayette was soon able to report a signal victory. Despite Calonne's hopes for the French whaling industry, he undertook in the king's name to grant another temporary favor to Americans. For one year the tax on American fish oil was to be reduced to the rate then charged the Hanseatic towns, which on that article of import were the most-favored nation. Cargoes must, however, be carried in American or French ships. Jefferson was pleased. Relying on the principle of "most-favored" nation laid down in the Franco-American treaty of 1778, he was hopeful that the temporary privilege would be extended after the first year. In that way a great commercial victory would be won for struggling American fishermen. Although Boylston, who had hoped to secure a complete exemption, was disappointed and did not sell his oil to Sangrain, his loss was a total gain for American whalers and another impressive bid for American loyalty to the French alliance.[17]

Encouraged by this new victory, Lafayette proceeded to plan a great Franco-American commercial empire. Although his motives were not economic, he was not entirely disinterested. His rewards were to be personal and political—the satisfaction and prestige that would come from being a patron of French and American merchants, the reinforcement of American allegiance to France, and the corresponding discomfiture of the British. When General Greene, who had recently purchased a large interest in the timber on Cumberland Island in Georgia, appealed to Jefferson to help him sell his live oak to the French government for naval vessels, Lafayette took the matter personally to the minister of the navy. Castries at first had some scruples about dealing directly with a private bidder abroad. Nevertheless, Lafayette felt sufficiently encouraged to write specific in-

17. Calonne to Lafayette, Nov. 17, 1785, [Weaver], *Diplomatic correspondence*, II, 492–93; Calonne to Vergennes, Nov. 24, AAE, corr. pol., É.-U., Vol. XXX, fols. 421–22; Vergennes to Jefferson, Nov. 30, [Weaver], *Diplomatic correspondence*, II, 490–91; Jefferson to Vergennes, Dec. 2, *ibid.*, pp. 491–92; Lafayette to [Breck?], [Dec. 3?], *Pennsylvania Packet*, June 24, 1786; Jefferson to Adams, Dec. 10, Lipscomb and Bergh, V, 229–30; Jefferson to Jay, Jan. 2, 1786, [Weaver], *Diplomatic correspondence*, II, 465–66.

structions to Greene on how best to impress the minister. He urged that "a very clever captain" be sent with a small quantity of timber and with full power to negotiate a large-scale contract. The captain was to report to him before seeing anyone else. He suggested that McHenry and Wadsworth also be associated with the venture.[18]

This letter was still on its way when Castries decided upon an outright order of a thousand cubic feet of American oak and cedar. Lafayette gladly forwarded this order to Greene. Since there would also be need for tar and hemp in boatbuilding, he forthwith suggested the purchase of those materials from "the house of McHenry of Baltimore." "I have long been convinced," he said, "of the quality of American naval stores and that we can pay our allies in merchandise for sure deliveries instead of our rivals in cash for uncertain deliveries."[19]

About the same time, Lafayette advised the merchant from whom he bought his own furs, "a very rich man," to get his raw materials directly from America. He soon received a request to ascertain prices, with the promise that if they proved satisfactory the merchant could order 1,000 guineas' (about 24,000 livres') worth of furs the first year and 400,000 livres' worth the next. The marquis sent the request for prices to Wadsworth, suggesting that McHenry, Constable, and others also be joined in this enterprise. He personally communicated with French merchants in the effort to find a correspondent for McHenry's firm and put himself at the disposal of Nathaniel Barrett, a Boston merchant who had come to France in order to negotiate a more general understanding regarding whale oil. He apparently looked toward a large-scale co-operation in the export-import field by Greene, Wadsworth, Breck, McHenry, Constable, Barrett, and others, most of them former companions-in-arms.[20] If

18. Lafayette to Greene, Dec. 3, 1785, LC, Nathanael Greene collection. Cf. Jefferson to Greene, Jan. 12, 1786, Lipscomb and Bergh, V, 246.

19. Lafayette to [Castries], Dec. 29, 1785, Jackson collection. Cf. Lafayette to Greene, Dec. 29, Clements Library, Greene papers.

20. Lafayette to McHenry, Dec. 3, 1785, *loc. cit.*; to Wadsworth, Dec. 3, *loc. cit.*; to Wadsworth, Dec. 7, Connecticut State Library, Trumbull collection; Jefferson to Adams, Dec. 10, Lipscomb and Bergh, V, 230–31; Lafayette to Smith, Dec. 12, K. M. Roof, *Colonel William Smith and lady: the romance of Washington's aide and young Abigail Adams* (Boston, 1929), p. 126 (with misreadings; original in Gardner-Ball collection).

he could have his way, those who had fought the War of American Independence would not find independence unprofitable.

One group of American entrepreneurs, as Lafayette had learned in Boston, had special reason to question whether independence was not regrettable. The whalers of Nantucket, finding British markets now closed to them as foreigners, had begun to wonder whether they ought not to migrate and either become British subjects again or place their talents at the disposal of the nascent French whaling industry. A crisis was reached in the fall of 1785. Two families had actually boarded ship to go to Halifax and others were on the point of embarking when it became known that Lafayette had won free importation for a large quantity of oil for the lamps of Paris. The Boston papers had carried that announcement in September. Not another family left Nantucket and the American whaling industry was saved. Lafayette was to learn of these events in a gratifying manner only some months later. For the present, however, fearing that not enough attention was being given to French generosity in America, he urged publicity upon his friends and even prepared copy for insertion in the newspapers.[21]

As the mixture of politics with trade led Lafayette more and more into bourgeois pursuits and brought him more and more into conflict with vested interests, his outlook upon social problems grew more and more comprehensive. Upon his return from Germany he continued to plan for the emancipation of Negroes and he also renewed his interest in Protestants. Unfortunately, another *cause célèbre* occupied the attention of ecclesiastical authorities, including the minister of the king's household, and many of the best legal minds of France to the exclusion of other religious affairs. Some clever crooks had imposed upon Cardinal de Rohan to buy for Queen Marie Antoinette an extravagant diamond necklace which she knew nothing about and which was never delivered to her. When the jewelers approached the queen for payment, the whole scandalous ruse had come out, and

21. *Massachusetts Centinel*, Sept. 14, 1785; Lafayette to Wadsworth, Dec. 3, 1785, and Feb. 10, 1786, Connecticut State Library, Trumbull collection; to McHenry, Dec. 3, 1785, *loc. cit.*; to [Breck?], [Dec. 3, 1785?], *Pennsylvania Packet*, June 24, 1786; Jefferson to Montmorin, [*ca.* Oct. 1, 1788], Lipscomb and Bergh, VII, 202; report dated Feb. 1, 1791, *ibid.*, III, 134. See also below, pp. 223–24 and 254.

Rohan was now being tried for his part in it. The court was so absorbed by the Diamond Necklace Affair that there was little Lafayette could do at the time for other victims of injustice.

Rabaut-St. Étienne had long been expecting the signal to come to Paris. When nothing happened, he became restless. Lafayette could afford to be more philosophical. "With patience and gentleness," he counseled, "just causes prevail."[22] Negro emancipation and Protestant toleration would simply have to mark time until a more propitious day.

Lafayette achieved greater immediate success, however, in another philanthropic gesture, which had a significance out of all proportion to its cost. Ever since he was two years old, he had been receiving an annual pension of 600 livres because his father had been killed in the Battle of Minden. Together with certain accumulations and interest, the pension now came to around 780 livres. Before he left for Germany, he had proposed to relinquish it. Feeling that the money could be spent "more usefully," he now formally begged the king to permit him "to preserve only the memory of it."[23] Along with this request, unusual at a time when pensions for court nobility were a common drain upon an overburdened royal treasury, he sent three petitions. One of them asked that a veteran soldier, the nephew of the curé who was the director of Lafayette's experimental school at St. Georges d'Aurac, should receive an annuity of 640 livres (the letter of award to mention the curé's virtues as well as the veteran's services). A second requested that the widow of another old Auvergnat soldier should receive the remaining 140 livres as a pension. A third proposed that the sum due Lafayette for the current year go to still another veteran's widow. The first two petitions were granted outright, and Lafayette was informed that, although he alone could collect the sum due for 1785, there was nothing to prevent him from disposing of it in the widow's favor.[24] He thus became the benefactor of several

22. Lafayette to Rabaut-St. Étienne, Nov. 20, 1785, *loc. cit.*

23. Lafayette to the Maréchal de Ségur, Dec. 3, 1785, Archives du Ministère de la Guerre (Paris), dossier 1261, Lafayette, L. G., June 30, 1791.

24. Lafayette to Ségur, Dec. 3, 1785, and to Melin, Dec. 17, and Ségur to Lafayette, Dec. 30, *ibid.* (The veterans' names were, respectively, De Talobre, Des Guignards, and Clappe).

victims of France's dynastic wars at the same time that he entered a mild and graceful protest against a dynastic system that,
overlooking the poor, paid pensions to the rich.

So, when the new year 1786 dawned, Lafayette was no longer
a pensioner of the king. As a good "republican," he expressed
the opinion that it was not right "to mention any day as the beginning of the year but the blessed 4th of July."[25] Nevertheless,
while the year was still quite new by the conventional reckon-
ing, he paid it the traditional deference of taking stock of his
several pet enterprises. This he did in a long letter to John
Adams. He first reported on commercial matters. He was
pleased with a six-year contract that Barrett had succeeded in
making with Sangrain for 400,000 livres' worth of oil a year.
Sangrain's purchases, he hoped, would keep the people of Nantucket satisfied. To be sure, Calonne was still uneasy about the
probable complaints from French whaling interests, but, Lafayette felt, they could not possibly fill the French demand for oil,
"and that of New England indeed smells better than that of
Great Britain." He and Jefferson were also hoping to make
American spermaceti candles popular in France and were conducting experiments to test how long they would burn. He was
satisfied also with the success of his propaganda on behalf of
American naval stores. The prejudices against American products, he found, were "drying away in France." New contracts
for timber were under consideration, and recent tests of American pitch and potash had proved favorable. "It seems to me
there may be given in this country a vent for a million sterling
worth of American produce; that to be paid in French goods, &
I wish a preference may be given to natural productions, or useful manufactures, over the extravagant trinkets of fashion &
luxury."

On the American tobacco trade, Lafayette reported, the
French government also was becoming increasingly well disposed because of Jefferson's persuasiveness. The marquis was
beginning to hope that a special committee would, in fact, be

25. Lafayette to Adams, Jan. 9, 1785 [error for 1786], Clements Library, Townshend
papers. The presence of this copy in the Townshend papers indicates that it fell into the
hands of some English agents.

appointed "to examine article by article" the difficulties arising from the tobacco monopoly of the farmers-general. Evidently the proposed scope of this committee had expanded since it was first conceived, for Lafayette now suggested that it might also prepare plans "to facilitate exportations from America into France and level every obstacle that attends the French goods from the manufacturing place to the vessel wherein they are embarked—in a word, to benefit both trades and bind together both nations on the basis of mutual advantages."[26]

Lafayette's new year's inventory ended on a note indicating that he was still mixing philanthropy with business and politics, that he was even developing the dismal practice of reading. He requested two favors. The first was that Adams send him "everything that has been written in England" on the suppression of Negro slavery. The second was that Adams become acquainted with an English humanitarian "who had travelled all over Europe to inquire into, and has written an excellent book to amend, the state of prisons." This was John Howard, whose book was entitled *The state of the prisons in England and Wales, with . . . an account of some foreign prisons and hospitals*. Lafayette had "a great desire to be honored with his correspondence."[27] The marquis did not report, but it was nonetheless a fact, that he was also engaged in transactions that were soon to cost him a huge sum in order to carry out his own experiment in gradual emancipation.

Philanthropy and politics continued to be merged when Rabaut-St. Étienne finally came to Paris. It was risky for a Protestant divine to travel to the capital to plead for toleration. Nevertheless, Rabaut-St. Étienne felt he ought to delay no longer, since Lafayette could not be expected to remain in the city for the summer. He wished, if possible, to strike a decisive blow for the "great lawsuit" before the end of the year. Under the pretext of attending to the publication of an essay in early Greek history (which, in fact, did appear in 1787), he left for Paris in January, 1786. Despite his precautions, his departure created a mild stir in Nîmes, and his father feared that he had been denounced to the local Catholic clergy. When a few days

26. *Ibid.*   27. *Ibid.*

passed without word from him, the worried old pastor gave vent to his fears in a letter to Lafayette. Shortly thereafter, however, Rabaut-St. Étienne arrived safely in Paris, and his father's mind was soon set at rest by a friendly and encouraging letter from Lafayette.[28] The incident seemed to dictate even greater caution than before, and Rabaut-St. Étienne was to grow impatient and discouraged.

As the Protestant cause became increasingly difficult to handle, the problem of the farmers-general clamored more and more loudly for attention. The chief resistance to the proposed committee to inquire into the trade obstructions between the United States and France could be expected to come from Calonne's department. The comptroller-general, who had never been so ready as Vergennes to use trade merely as a political weapon or to sacrifice the farmers-general, was now more cautious than ever. A dispute within the ministry made his tenure appear so shaky that Lafayette expected him to be dismissed any day.[29] As unofficial intermediary between Jefferson and Vergennes, the marquis felt therefore that he must address himself directly to Calonne's department as the most belligerent and, at the same time, the most vulnerable spot. He first approached Councilor of State Jean-Charles-Pierre Lenoir, who had recently been made president of the government's standing Commission of Finances. Lenoir proved not to be easily impressed with the need for a special committee. He pointed out that there already existed a Royal Council of Commerce, of which Vergennes, Castries, and Calonne were members, along with other leading experts. He seemed unwilling to recommend any extraordinary measures except to add to the existing committee some persons who might be especially well versed in American affairs. Lafayette was glad for him to do so but also insisted upon the necessity of a special committee. "Since we are in a crisis," he pleaded, "let's not give England time to

---

28. Lafayette to Rabaut-St. Étienne, Nov. 20, 1785, *loc. cit.*; *idem* to *idem*, Jan. 1, 1785 [error for 1786], collection of Dr. Max Thorek (Chicago, Ill.); Paul Rabaut to Lafayette, Jan. 11, 1786, Anon., "Les promoteurs de l'édit de 1787," *Bulletin de la Société de l'Histoire du Protestantisme français*, III (1855), 340; Lafayette to Rabaut, Jan. 21, *ibid.*, p. 341. Cf. Rabaut's report, Feb. 12, 1788, Dardier, II, 394-95.

29. Lafayette to Washington, Feb. 6, 1786, Gottschalk, *Letters*, pp. 308-9.

profit from our slowness." He urged Lenoir to intercede with
Calonne but, without waiting, went himself to see the comptroller-general. "As I find no pleasure or profit in this affair," he
explained, "I am more at my ease in pushing it."[30]

Calonne acceded to Lafayette's request faster than did
Lenoir. He promised to take the initiative in creating a committee "to examine the means of establishing the greatest possible
trade between France and the United States, of substituting the
export of our goods to our allies for that of our specie to our
rivals."[31] To make sure that he would not forget, Lafayette
again reminded him of his promise within a few days. The marquis suggested that the committee consist of two persons from
each of the three interested departments—finance, navy, and
foreign affairs. True to his word, Calonne spoke to Vergennes
and Lenoir on the subject. It was agreed that the well-known
physiocrat Dupont de Nemours, inspector-general of commerce,
Boyetet, councilor of state responsible for the commerce of the
Midi, and Montaran and Laporte, intendants of commerce,
should join with Colonia, intendant of the department of the
farmers-general, to form the new committee. Lafayette suggested
as the sixth member the banker Le Coulteux, who was already
involved in one of his American contracts.[32] That, however,
would have left no room for Lafayette himself. The velvet glove
of Vergennes thereupon appeared once more, and a reluctant
Calonne finally decided to create a committee of twelve rather
than six with Lafayette as one of the members.[33]

So it happened that when the "American Committee," as it
came to be called, met for the first time, Lafayette could state
that it had been formed "on my application." He foresaw that
the committee's assignment would not be "an easy matter, for
it tends to no less than the destruction of the tobacco farm, the
greatest barrier against the American trade," and he did not

30. Lafayette to Lenoir, Jan. 23, 1786, Albert Mathiez, "Lafayette et le commerce
franco-américain à la veille de la Révolution," *Annales historiques de la Révolution
française*, III (1926), 475.

31. Lafayette to Calonne, [between Jan. 23 and 30, 1786], *ibid.*, p. 476.

32. Lafayette to Adams, Jan. 9, [1786], *loc. cit.*

33. Jefferson to Jay, May 27, 1786, Ford, *Writings of Jefferson*, IV, 233. Cf. Nussbaum, "American tobacco and French politics," p. 505.

expect it to succeed entirely. He graciously gave part of the credit for his success so far to the American minister. "Words cannot sufficiently express to you," he wrote Washington, "how much I am pleased with Mr. Jefferson's public conduct. He unites every ability that can recommend him to the Ministers, and at the [same] time possesses accomplishements of the mind and the heart which cannot but give him many friends."[34]

Meanwhile, Lafayette had recently received several letters from Mount Vernon. They brought news of the splendid progress that had been made in financing the Potomac River Company and in launching the James River Company. Washington was even more hopeful than before that the Atlantic states and the West would thereby be drawn together. England's restrictions on American trade, he thought, would result in widespread resentment and a speedier grant to Congress of the power to regulate trade. "It is to be regretted, I confess, that democratical states must always *feel* before they can *see:* it is this that makes their government slow, but the people will be right at last."[35] Washington's letters, too, had informed Lafayette that his revered preceptor approved of his Protestant venture. "But remember, my dear friend," the American Fabius cautioned, "it is a part of the military art to reconnoitre and *feel* your way before you engage too deeply. More is oftentimes effected by regular approaches than by an open assault. From the first, too, you may make a good retreat; from the latter (in case of repulse) it rarely happens."[36] Lafayette also learned that the French hounds and a Spanish donkey he had sent to Washington had arrived and that Houdon had been at Mount Vernon.[37]

After five months of silence (his excuse was that the packets had been interrupted), Lafayette acknowledged these letters from Washington and at last addressed himself to the declining prestige of America that had been so painfully obvious in Germany. He intrusted his reply to Barrett, who was now returning to America, well satisfied with the trade arrangements he had made. It was the longest letter in the already extensive corre-

34. Lafayette to Washington, Feb. 6, 1786, Gottschalk, *Letters*, pp. 309–10.
35. July 25, 1785, Fitzpatrick, XXVIII, 208.
36. Sept. 1, 1785, *ibid.*, p. 243.   37. Nov. 8, 1785, *ibid.*, pp. 308–9.

spondence between the "beloved general" and his "adoptive son." In it Lafayette gave a detailed account of his German trip with interesting descriptions of the personages and the armies he had seen. He spoke of the joy he had experienced in finding his friend universally respected and admired. "But I have often had the mortification to hear that the want of powers in Congress, of union betwen the States, of energy in their governement should make the Confederation very insignificant." Everywhere he had encountered false reports of American affairs planted by English agents. "Numberless of these notions I have set to rights. The King of Prussia, the Emperor, the great men in both countries I found either ill informed or informed by people who had led them the wrong path. By their conduct in the Revolution the citizens of America have commanded the respect of the world but it grieves me to think they will in a measure loose it, unless they strengthen the Confederation, give Congress powers to regulate the trade, pay off their debt or at least the interest of it, establish a well regulated militia, in a word compleat all these measures which you have recommended to them."[38]

Lafayette also rendered an account of the latest developments in his humanitarian enterprises. He thanked Washington most tenderly "for the caution you give me [regarding the Protestants], which I will improve and find that satisfaction in my prudence to think it is dictated by you." A less sanguine person might have been discouraged since remarkably little progress had in fact been made in the direction of tolerance. But not Lafayette. He felt that there was reason to believe that in the course of the next winter "the affair of the Protestants will take a good turn." In another undertaking that had the paternal blessing he was proud to report more definite progress. He had at last been able to do something substantial regarding the emancipation of the Negro. "I have purchased for hundred and twenty five thousand French livres a plantation in the Colony of Cayenne and am going to free my Negroes in order to make that experiment which you know is my hobby horse."[39]

38. Feb. 6, 1786, Gottschalk, *Letters*, pp. 306–7. See also Lafayette to Barrett, Feb. 10, 1786, Connecticut State Library, Trumbull collection.

39. Feb. 6, 1786, Gottschalk, *Letters*, p. 309. Cf. the statement of Grattepain-Morizot, [ca. 1792], Chinard, *Lafayette and Jefferson*, p. 305.

Barrett also carried a letter to Franklin. Lafayette here expressed his great pleasure at the honors the returning sage had won in America. "When your friends in Paris meet together their first word is to talk of you. The wishes for your fortunate voyage and pleasing sight of your family and friends became a national sentiment. In my tour through Germany I have been asked thousand questions about you, when I felt equally proud and happy to boast of our affectionate intimacy." The many lies he had heard about America in Germany, he explained, made him all the more pleased that Franklin had been chosen president of Pennsylvania. "Nothing but that could speedily restore internal union and remove the jealousies against neighbours. You will encourage foederal measures, regulations for trade, a general system of militia, and the more I see the opinions of foreign nations, the more I wish for such arrangements the necessity of which is obvious almost to every American but want to be set a going."[40] ·

Since Washington and Franklin were not federal officers, Lafayette also sent letters by Barrett to Secretary of War Knox and Secretary of Foreign Affairs Jay. To Knox he reported at length about the Prussian and Austrian armies but limited his remarks concerning foreign affairs to a brief statement on how misinformed the best German people were, "and I wish no ground was left for our ennemies to broach those lies upon."[41] But for the secretary of foreign affairs, who, he knew, would submit his letter to Congress, he wrote a lengthy plea for greater federal power in military, commercial, and financial matters. Again he described the enthusiasm for America he had found among the more enlightened. "But to my great sorrow (and I will the more candidly tell it in this letter as it can hurt none more than it hurts myself), I did not find that every remark did equally turn to the advantage of my pride and that satisfaction I feel in the admiration of the world for the United States. . . . And it has been painfull for me to hear, it is now disagreable to mention the bad effect which the want of foederal union, of effective arrange-

40. Lafayette to Franklin, Feb. 10, 1786, APS, Franklin papers, Vol. XXXIV, No. 22½.

41. Feb. 11, 1786, Jackson collection. See above, pp. 185 and 187.

ments for the finances and commerce, of a general establishe-
ment of militia had on the minds of European nations. . . . It was
impossible for me to feel . . . unconcerned when the points were
insisted upon for which I could not but aknowledge within myself there was some ground altho' it was so unfairly broached
upon by the ennemies of the United States. . . . And while I was
enjoying the admiration and respect of those parts of the world
for the sun rise of the United States, while I was obliged to hear
some remarks which altho' they were exagerated did not seem
to me quite destitute of a foundation, I heartly adressed my
prayers to Heaven that by her known wisdom, patriotism, and
liberality of principles as well as firmness of conduct, America
may preserve the consequence she has so well acquired, and
continue to command the admiration of the world."[42]

No one in America would have hesitated to believe that Lafayette was a confirmed and outspoken republican. If he had
ever shown skepticism, it had been when addressing European
soldiers, ministers, and aristocrats. Such skepticism had come
very rarely since his last visit to America, and all hesitation was
now rapidly vanishing. The apologist easily becomes the advocate, and the advocate easily passes from the defensive to the
offensive. As the interpreter of American interests, Lafayette
had undertaken a fight in favor of freer trade against the monopoly of the farmers-general. As the advocate of American
ideals, he had become the champion of minority rights elsewhere
—for Protestants in France and for Negroes in the colonies. If
he was not yet fully persuaded that republicanism was a good
thing for Frenchmen, he nevertheless believed firmly in freedom
everywhere, and he made no effort to hide his hope that republicanism might succeed in America at least, there to become a
beacon guiding less free and less fortunate states.

It required great courage to stand forth in an absolute monarchy as an avowed champion of a foreign republic. His friends
understood the risk he was taking. With the letters that Lafayette sent to America by Barrett went one from Jefferson to

42. Feb. 11, 1786, LC, PCC 156, fols. 447–48. The version in [Weaver], *Diplomatic
correspondence*, I, 439–42, has been anglicized. See also *Journals of the Continental Congress*, XXX, 287 n. (May 17, 1786).

Madison in which the American minister expressed his fear for his young radical friend. Clearly implying that the recently completed bust by Houdon was not enough reward from Virginia to its adopted son, Jefferson wrote prophetically: "I am persuaded that a gift of lands by the State of Virginia to the Marquis de La Fayette would give a good opinion here of our character and would reflect honor on the Marquis. Nor am I sure that the day will not come when it might be an useful asylum to him. The time of life at which he visited America was too well adapted to receive good and lasting impressions to permit him ever to accommodate himself to the principles of monarchical government; and it will need all his own prudence, and that of his friends, to make this country a safe residence for him. How glorious, how comfortable in reflection, will it be to have prepared a refuge for him in case of reverse."[43] The reverse was to come, but not the refuge.

BIBLIOGRAPHICAL NOTES

The numerous biographies of Jefferson treat his relations with Lafayette before 1789 more or less amply. The best printed source on this subject is, of course, Chinard's *Lafayette and Jefferson*. (But see below.)

Nussbaum's articles have skilfully portrayed how Vergennes took friendly advantage of Lafayette and Jefferson in carrying out his policy of using trade as a diplomatic weapon. Some of the most revealing documents in that connection have been published in Mathiez' "Lafayette et le commerce franco-américain." They include the letters of Lafayette to Lenoir and Calonne relative to the American Committee.

Brand Whitlock, *La Fayette* (New York, 1929), p. 296, makes the Comte de Ségur responsible for Lafayette's interest in emancipation through his account of the horrible conditions he found on his own plantation in San Domingo (see Louis-Philippe Ségur, *Mémoires ou souvenirs et anecdotes* [Paris, 1825–27], I, 443–47). But Ségur's return from San Domingo, though much earlier than Lafayette's purchase of the Cayenne plantation, was later than Lafayette's first proposal to engage in such an experiment. Cf. my *Lafayette and the close of the American Revolution*, pp. 401–2.

Since the first printing of this work, the second volume of Dumas Malone's *Jefferson and his time* (3 vols. to date; Boston, 1948———) has appeared (1951), and it gives excellent coverage to Lafayette's associations with Jefferson during the period here examined.

43. Jefferson to Madison, Feb. 8, 1786, Lipscomb and Bergh, V, 281–82.

CHAPTER XVI

Conflict with the Tobacco Cartel

THE first meeting of the American Committee took place on February 8, 1786.[1] The chairman of the committee was Tavernier de Boullongne, who was a councilor-of-state in Calonne's department, and Lafayette was the second member. The committee included, besides, four *maîtres de requêtes* (referendaries) from the several departments, two inspectors-general of commerce, two farmers-general, and a Paris merchant named Simon Bérard, who had already written a memoir opposing the Farm's monopoly.[2] They met in Boullongne's office.

The issue of the tobacco trade arose immediately. No one was

1. Lafayette to Washington, Feb. 6, 1786, Gottschalk, *Letters*, p. 309, says "tomorrow" (i.e., Feb. 7). This letter was misdated February 8 in *Mémoires*, II, 130, and if the date February 8 were correct, *demain* would have meant that the first meeting fell on February 9. I have followed F. L. Nussbaum, "American tobacco and French politics," *Political science quarterly*, XL (1925), 505, which gives February 8. This date is supported by the letter of Lafayette to Vergennes, dated *ce mercredi* (AAE, corr. pol. É.-U., Vol. XXXI, fol. 79), which places the meeting *aujourd'hui*. February 8, 1786, fell on a Wednesday. Moreover, this letter has been dated by a contemporary hand (not Lafayette's) "8 febr. 1786."

2. Three of the *maîtres de requêtes* were probably Colonia, Laporte (who was also a councilor-of-state), and Montaran. All three *maîtres des requêtes* were also intendants of commerce. The fourth has not been identified. The two inspectors-general of commerce were Boyetet (who was also a councilor-of-state) and Dupont (see Lafayette to Franklin, Feb. 10, 1786, APS, Franklin papers, Vol. XXXIV, No. 22½). The two farmers-general were Paulze and Brac de la Perrière (F. L. Nussbaum [ed.], "Lafayette's attack upon the tobacco farm in the American Committee of 1786," *Journal of modern history*, III [1931], 606 n.). Who the twelfth member of the committee was is not clear. The correspondence with Lenoir (Albert Mathiez, "Lafayette et le commerce franco-américain à la veille de la Révolution," *Annales historiques de la Révolution française*, III [1926], 474–84) leads to the belief that it was he. Perhaps it was M. de Saint-Amand, another farmer-general (cf. Nussbaum, "Lafayette's attack upon the tobacco farm," p. 606, n. 5), but Lafayette says distinctly that there were only two farmers-general in the committee (see below, n. 3). Cf. Nussbaum, "American tobacco and French politics," pp. 505–6, and Boyd, *Papers of Jefferson*, IX, 338 (as indicated on p. 237 below).

prepared to discuss it, and so the meeting was adjourned for a week. "Since there are two farmers general in the Committee," Lafayette declared, "I doubt that there will be a unanimous opinion."[3] Although he was resolved to attend religiously, he was not yet prepared to say that the committee would be very useful. He realized that the two farmers-general, "supported by the monneyed people," had been made members "to fight the battle" with him. The "tobacco business" would thus prove "not an easy matter," but he intended to speak his mind freely.[4]

Lafayette estimated the potential exports of the United States to France at 25,000,000 livres.[5] Nothing daunted by the prospect of a tough fight on tobacco, he hastened to assure his New England merchant friends, who might not be so exercised as he about the southern planter's staple, that he also had their interests at heart. "After the commerce of the kingdom has been settled, I will try to bring on that of the [West India] Islands." He had in fact conversed at length on the West Indies trade with the Comte de La Luzerne, just before La Luzerne left to become governor of the islands.[6]

Meanwhile, Lafayette wanted all Americans to appreciate the advantages he had already won for them as well as those to come. He suggested to Wadsworth that there be inserted in the newspapers, both North and South, an item regarding Barrett's liberal contract for American whale oil. "By that gentleman," the item was also to say, "we hear that a Committee of twelve persons has been appointed to debate with the Marquis his proposals in favour of our trade. It was expected by the merchants in Paris that the principles of the Farm Generale and the obstacles to our commerce with France will be vigourously attacked by the Marquis, which it is thought will have a good effect on governement. At the same time [that] we find in every opportunity the attachement of our friend to us and his attention to our concerns, we cannot help being struck with this new instance of the contrast betwen the dispositions of France to-

3. Lafayette to Vergennes, [Feb. 8, 1786], *loc. cit.*

4. Lafayette to Wadsworth, Feb. 10, 1786, Connecticut State Library, Trumbull collection. Cf. Lafayette to Franklin, Feb. 10, *loc. cit.*

5. Lafayette to Washington, Feb. 6, 1786, Gottschalk, *Letters*, p. 309.

6. Lafayette to Wadsworth, Feb. 10, 1786, *loc. cit.*

wards us and the haughty rancour of Great Britain."[7] The item was a skilful piece of popular propaganda for both France and Lafayette. Congress, too, was asked to believe that because of the appointment of the committee, "American commerce wears a better prospect than it has hitherto done."[8]

The ensuing weeks were spent in acquiring detailed information about the tobacco trade. The Marquis de Condorcet collaborated with Jefferson to teach Lafayette the arguments and figures involved.[9] If Mazzei's somewhat melodramatic account is to be believed, the mutual admiration of Lafayette and Condorcet arose from their interest in the cause of Negro emancipation. Condorcet, best known and most democratic of the later Voltaireans, had published in 1781 a pamphlet entitled *Réflexions sur l'esclavage des Nègres* under the pseudonym of "M. Schwartz, pasteur du Saint Évangile à Brienne." A copy of it came to Lafayette's attention in 1783, and he expressed to the Duc de La Rochefoucauld the desire to know the author. A little later he received, ostensibly from Switzerland, a letter signed "Schwartz" thanking him for his interest. Lafayette and "Schwartz" continued to correspond for months through La Rochefoucauld as intermediary, since the censorship authorities were still too officious for a reforming publicist to take unnecessary risks. Finally, "Schwartz" announced that business would bring him to Paris, and Lafayette immediately invited him to his house. One afternoon "Schwartz" appeared at the Rue de Bourbon, and thus began "a friendship [in Mazzei's words] that, because of the likeness of their views, appears indissoluble."[10] Soon Lafayette associated Condorcet with his other reform projects.[11] When Condorcet

7. *Ibid.*

8. Lafayette to Jay, Feb. 11, 1786, [Weaver], *Diplomatic correspondence*, I, 442.

9. Lafayette to Benjamin Constant, [no year], Lafayette College Library; Jefferson to Monroe, May 10, 1786, Lipscomb and Bergh, V, 330. Dupont possibly also helped (see F. L. Nussbaum, "Vergennes and Lafayette versus the farmers general," *Journal of modern history*, III [1931], 600–601). See also above, p. 207, n. 13.

10. Mazzei to Maurice de Glayre, Aug. 1, 1788, Raffaele Ciampini (ed.), *Lettere di Filippo Mazzei alla corte di Polonia (1788–1792)* (Bologna, 1937), I, 8.

11. Condorcet to M***, [1790], A. C. O'Connor and M. F. Argo (eds.), *Œuvres de Condorcet* (Paris, 1847–49), I, 328–29; Lafayette to Rabaut-St. Étienne, Jan. 1, [1786], Thorek collection.

came to publish his booklet entitled *De l'influence de la Révolution d'Amérique sur l'Europe*, he dedicated it—most fittingly—to Lafayette, "who, at an age when ordinary men are hardly known to their own society, has earned the title of benefactor of two worlds."[12] Thus Lafayette became frankly allied with the *philosophes*, with whom previously his strongest link—and that quite casual—had been through Chastellux.

The second meeting of the American Committee (February 15) led only to an exchange of views and statistics. The statistics of the farmers-general, however, seemed astonishingly favorable to them, and Lafayette desired, if possible, to controvert them. There followed new consultations with his advisers. They were particularly concerned with the claim of the farmers-general that the tobacco monopoly was not highly remunerative. Jefferson, who had earlier maintained that it produced about 35 per cent profit,[13] did not believe their figures. He and Lafayette went over the Farm's calculations and at first could find nothing seriously wrong with them. But after further scrutiny, Jefferson noted that the farmers-general had failed to include in their costs the interest on their original investment. For a two-year period at 5 per cent that expenditure would come to a significant amount, and thus the farmers-general, if their figure for their gross income was right, were losing over 4,000,-000 livres a year. "The king should," Jefferson ironically concluded, "in favour to them, discontinue the bail, and they cannot ask its continuance without acknowledging they have given in a false state of quantities and sums."[14]

Jefferson sent his new calculations to Lafayette only on February 20, the day of the next meeting of the American Committee—which meant that Lafayette did not have them at his disposal during that meeting. In any case, he probably would not have accepted Jefferson's drastic conclusion, for he was not willing to propose, as Jefferson was, that the tobacco farm ought to

12. (1786), *Œuvres de Condorcet*, VIII, 1.

13. Jefferson to Vergennes, Aug. 15, 1785, Lipscomb and Bergh, V, 69.

14. Jefferson to Lafayette, Feb. 20, 1786, Chinard, *Lafayette and Jefferson*, pp. 91–92 (misdated in Ford, *Writings of Jefferson*, IV, 197). See also p. 108 above.

be abolished outright.[15] He preferred to break its monopoly and lower its profits but still guarantee it a reasonable return on its total investment if it continued in the tobacco business.

The problem of the tobacco monopoly was a major concern of the committee. It proved to be a stormy issue. The supporter of the farmers-general argued that the control on tobacco purchases gave the Farm no greater income than its expenditures justified. Since, however, the tobacco warehouses were nearly empty, they announced that the Farm would be glad to buy any American tobacco, whether it came from Morris or elsewhere.[16] Toward the end of the meeting Lafayette set forth his ideas. Citing some figures and making some rapid calculations, he came to the conclusion that the tobacco farm was receiving a profit of 13 per cent. This he considered exorbitant. He advocated instead a duty of $32\frac{1}{2}$ sous per pound of leaf tobacco, which alone might be imported. Collection of that duty might be left to the farmers-general or some other agency. The collectors, whoever they were, should not be permitted to charge more than 10 per cent of the net return for their services. They should have the support of the police to prevent smuggling and might compensate themselves for the cost of customs inspection from seizures of contraband tobacco. The duty, however, would be paid not by the American exporter, who would merely leave his shipment without tariff at designated *entrepôts*, but by the French shipper or manufacturer when the tobacco was removed from the *entrepôts*. Buying and selling tobacco and snuff should otherwise be free of impost.[17]

The two farmers-general on the committee immediately opposed Lafayette's proposal and were supported by a third member.[18] These men challenged Lafayette's figures in their turn.

15. Jefferson to Monroe, May 10, 1786, Lipscomb and Bergh, V, 331; Jefferson to Jay, May 27, Ford, *Writings of Jefferson*, IV, 233.

16. Lafayette to Vergennes, [Feb. 25, 1786], AAE, corr. pol., É.-U., Vol. XXXI, fol. 144. Cf. Nussbaum, "American tobacco and French politics," p. 507.

17. Nussbaum, "Vergennes and Lafayette versus the farmers general," p. 602, and "Lafayette's attack on the tobacco farm," pp. 605-13. See also p. 237 below.

18. Nussbaum ("Lafayette's attack upon the tobacco farm," p. 606 n.) thinks this was Saint-Amand, but see above, n. 2. If it was not Saint-Amand, it might have been Colonia, who was intendant of the department of the farmers-general in Calonne's ministry. See also p. 237 below.

The Farm had been earning less on recent tobacco sales than Lafayette had calculated, they said, and the prospective contracts would produce still less.

The ensuing discussion brought out (probably on March 6 or within the next few days) a number of other objections to Lafayette's proposal. Some of them, even at that time, must have had a familiar ring whenever restriction of monopoly was under contemplation. Exclusive privileges, it was argued, were desirable in order to promote enterprise. At the same time, enterprise was somewhat frowned upon because free manufacture would produce inferior quality and a distasteful variety of new and easily counterfeited brands. Earlier experience with free tobacco, it was contended, had not been very successful. Furthermore, customs inspection at land borders, as Lafayette's proposal would require, would be harder than at the ports; the effect would be to promote tobacco culture in countries beyond the French border. Some objected that Lafayette's scheme would encourage tobacco growing where forbidden, and others that it would discourage tobacco growing where permitted. Not only would employees of the Farm be unsettled by a new arrangement, but changing a solemn understanding with Robert Morris would be a shocking breach of contract. And anyhow the tobacco monopoly was not the most crying one; the evils of the salt monopoly were far more urgent.[19]

The arguments of the Farm's advocates, however, did not wholly convince the chairman and several other members of the committee. When Lafayette in his turn called into question some of his opponents' figures, they rectified them somewhat. It was agreed that Lafayette would present a résumé of his remarks at the next meeting and that the farmers-general would similarly present their point of view. The meeting of February 20 adjourned with the understanding that it would not meet again until sometime in March.[20]

19. Lafayette, "Résumé de mon avis au Comité du commerce avec les États-Unis lorsque la question des tabacs nous a été présentée," in Nussbaum, "Lafayette's attack upon the tobacco farm," pp. 605-13.

20. *Ibid.*, p. 607; Lafayette to Vergennes, [Feb. 25, 1786], *loc. cit.*; and Lafayette to Boullongne, June 1 [Mar. 19], 1786, Nussbaum, "Lafayette's attack on the tobacco farm," p. 605. That the date of this last letter must be March 19 and neither June 1

Unfortunately, the contracts of the Farm, already postponed six months on Jefferson's urging, were subject to renewal early in March. That meant that they might be signed and delivered before the next meeting. Lafayette had to content himself with requesting Vergennes and Calonne to see to it that the new contracts contained no "expression that directly or indirectly might check the government's plans and the committee's ideas on the tobacco matter."[21] Without waiting to know what the outcome of his request would be, he assured Adams that, though all the other contracts with the Farm would be renewed, that of tobacco would not be. "On this side of the Channel," he added, "when good deeds fail, you will at least find good intentions; in England, neither."[22]

When the contracts with the Farm were renewed, however, the tobacco monopoly was still among them. The only safeguard for possible change was a clause providing that the monopoly might be discontinued whenever the king saw fit to do so. Jefferson was of the opinion that the only hope now remaining for free trade in tobacco was to induce the king to invoke that clause. Even that little, however, could hardly be expected before the expiration of the lease at the end of the year.[23]

Just before the Farm's contract had been renewed, the American minister went off for a brief visit to England, leaving Lafayette to carry on temporarily without him. In his absence, Lafayette had a breathing spell in which to devote himself to his other projects on behalf of liberty. John Adams had not been idle regarding the marquis's request for the good English literature on the slave question. As a result a shipment by the abolitionist Granville Sharp of his own writings on that subject soon reached the Rue de Bourbon. Thus began Lafayette's association with the British abolitionists that was to last all the rest of

(the date written upon it, probably at the time it was filed in the archives) nor February 19 (as Nussbaum thought [*Journal of modern history*, III (1931), 600 and 605]) is shown by Lafayette to Jefferson, Mar. 18, 1786, Chinard, *Lafayette and Jefferson*, p. 92. See p. 237 below.

21. To Vergennes, [Feb. 25, 1786], *loc. cit.*; cf. Jefferson to Jay, May 27, 1786, Ford, *Writings of Jefferson*, IV, 232.

22. Lafayette to Adams, Feb. 22, 1786, *Works of Adams*, VIII, 377.

23. Jefferson to Monroe, May 10, 1786, Lipscomb and Bergh, V, 329–30; Jefferson to

his life. In writing to thank Sharp for his consideration, Lafayette attacked "the selfish calculations of mistaken avarice" indignantly. "And I heartily wish with you, while circumstances have made us in many respects superior to our black brethren, that we may cease to place ourselves beneath them in the pursuit of this disgraceful trade."[24] In requesting Adams to deliver this letter, he was even more outspoken. "In the cause of my black brethren I feel myself warmly interested, and most decidedly side, so far as respects them, against the white part of mankind. Whatever be the complexion of the enslaved, it does not, in my opinion, alter the complexion of the crime which the enslaver commits, a crime much blacker than any African face. It is to me a matter of great anxiety and concern, to find that this trade is sometimes perpetrated under the flag of liberty, our dear and noble stripes, to which virtue and glory have been constant standard-bearers."[25]

The efforts on behalf of Protestant toleration also benefited from Lafayette's respite from committee meetings. Rabaut-St. Étienne had been spending his time in Paris cautiously making contacts and feeling out supporters. He found in the marquis a ready accomplice. Lafayette gave him the advantage of his own information and introduced him to Malesherbes, Condorcet, and other friends. Rabaut found that caution on one side and suspicion on the other made things move very slowly indeed, but he had reason to feel that they did move.[26]

During this period of relative leisure, Lafayette also found his attention once more attracted to the United Provinces. Although war had not broken out over the Scheldt River controversy, inside Holland the old quarrel of merchant-class Republicans against landowning Royalists continued unabated. Lafayette's sympathies with the Republican party remained constant. He kept informed of Dutch politics not only through the papers but also through a steady stream of American merchants, some of whom came to France only after transacting

Jay, May 27, Ford, *Writings of Jefferson*, IV, 233.
24. Lafayette to Sharp, Feb. 22, 1786, Jackson collection. Lafayette actually wrote "heartily" this time—not, as usually, "heartly."
25. Lafayette to Adams, Feb. 22, 1786, *Works of Adams*, VIII, 376-77.
26. Rabaut-St. Étienne to the Committee of Bordeaux, Feb. 12, 1788, Dardier, II, 395; Lafayette to Rabaut-St. Étienne, Jan. 1, [1786], Thorek collection.

business in Amsterdam or The Hague. To one of these merchants, Lafayette frankly avowed his hopes for Holland. "As a
republic and an ally of France and the United States, it has a
triple right to my concern. I wish her internal disputes may be
healed, so far as is consistent with liberty."[27] Once more he began to contemplate going to Holland himself.[28]

Meanwhile, the task of preparing a résumé of the remarks he
had made at the last meeting of the American Committee occupied Lafayette's chief attention. When the résumé was finally
completed, it began and ended with a disarming gesture of
modesty. The author knew little about the details of commerce,
it declared, but he had sought information regarding the tobacco trade from better-informed persons. Although his own
estimates had been corrected "by a friend accustomed to more
profound calculations,"[29] he had adopted "almost blindly" the
figures of the Farm and he hoped allowances would be made in
his favor accordingly. To be sure, he had found their 30 per cent
discount for wastage "singular," their estimate of manufacturing costs "a little high," and their presumed price for future
sales the lowest that actually prevailed. Nevertheless, without
disputing their figures, he wished to propose a plan that would
yield an annual revenue of 29,000,000 livres for the king, ap-
proximately 5,800,000 livres for administrative costs (which he
thought high), a reasonable profit for manufacturers and dis-
tributors, and a 10 per cent commission for the farmers-
general.[30]

Then followed an argument which was an open declaration of
war upon monopolies in France—the first semipublic utterance
of Lafayette in favor of creating liberal institutions in France.
"In presenting this plan to the committee I have foreseen that
my preference for liberty would be recalled or perhaps that I
would be supposed to have a preference for impractical systems,
but . . . the rather unbridled liberty to quintuple the price of a

27. Lafayette to unknown, Feb. 26, 1786, Jackson collection.

28. Lafayette to Washington, May 24, 1786, Gottschalk, *Letters*, p. 312.

29. "Résumé," *loc. cit.*, p. 613. He perhaps meant Jefferson, but since Jefferson was
away, Condorcet seems more probable.

30. *Ibid.*, pp. 607-8.

product by a tax does not exist, and it is not being too schematic
to substitute a just and simple idea for a complicated scheme."[31]
The résumé thereupon repeated the proposal of a duty of $32\frac{1}{2}$
sous per pound of leaf tobacco upon entry. It then presented
calculations to show that such a tariff arrangement not only
would produce enough money to meet the proposed royal, administrative, manufacturing, distributing, interest, and other
charges against the tobacco industry but would even make possible a slight reduction of the current price to the consumer.

Lafayette then took up one by one the objections that had
been raised against his proposal. Conceding that special monopolies might well be granted to products of invention or special
skill in order to reward struggling genius, he ironically pointed
out that "the fortune . . . of MM. les fermiers généraux is already made and nothing is better known or easier than the
manufacture of tobacco." To the argument that free manufacture would, in fact, disgust consumers with a distasteful array
of competing brands, he retorted that "if such a new standard
of taste is generally adopted," he would give up his plan. In
reply to the thesis that earlier French experience with free tobacco had been unfortunate, he pointed to the increase in
French patriotism since then and to the contradictory experience of England. England also furnished proof, he claimed, that
a coastline was no more easily guarded against smugglers than
a land border. And he added: "Since the English are more given
to smuggling than we, since they do not even have names for
new taxes, why, if our system is so beautiful, haven't they
adopted it? Can it be that our fiscal program frightens mankind
or that in that country, where, however, money is so powerful,
the big capitalists have less influence than in ours?"[32]

Other evils that his opponents pretended to fear from his
proposal, Lafayette asserted, would not actually result or could
be properly guarded against without increasing the cost of polic-
ing. "I am neither an extractor[33] nor a planter. The Farm dis-
courages the importation of tobacco by sea and I propose to in-

<hr />

31. *Ibid.*, p. 608.   32. *Ibid.*, p. 609.

33. The French word (*ibid.*, p. 610) is *arracheur*, which usually was applied to a
"yanker" of teeth. It was a none too subtle reference to the farmers-general.

crease it. It seeks 29 millions by a monopoly that is hateful to the public, and I am trying to find it in a simple duty which restores activity to commerce and liberty to the individual." To reduce the hazards of imitation and counterfeit, he was willing to limit the warehousing of tobacco to certain towns of entry, where the factories would also be located, and to make it illegal for shipments to leave without an inspection stamp. Nor did the prospect of poor confused employees of the Farm disturb him. "They will not feel sorry, I believe, to work for themselves or for manufacturers whom they will choose themselves and who will, as a result, treat them well. Nothing will be lost but the ease with which powerful men compensate a few protégés at the expense of the public."

Any new contract that the Farm would have to make, Lafayette realized, would probably work to the disadvantage of Robert Morris. He nevertheless insisted that Morris would not object. "I am Robert Morris' friend," he announced, "and no one has had more reason than I to do homage to his talents, but if his private interest is harmful to the public interest of the two countries, he surely knows that I will oppose it." The contract, however, was already void, he argued, because the farmers-general had themselves failed to abide in several respects by its explicit or implicit terms.[34]

A few of the arguments made against the marquis's proposal, the résumé implied, were hardly worthy of serious attention. As for the suggestion, for example, that the salt monopoly needed attention more than the tobacco monopoly, "fortunately, my proposal does not interfere with that one, and my friends the farmers-general will find me ready to agree to the justice of that observation." Nor was he impressed with the contention that free trade would lead to varied and lower standards of manufacture. "One might as well demand that, to satisfy public tastes better, all wines should be made at once in the same press." Moreover, the Farm was not maintaining high standards itself; complaints about its product were increasing and the parlement of Brittany had recently condemned some tobacco to be burned for its bad quality.[35]

34. *Ibid.*, p. 611.   35. *Ibid.*

All these arguments had been based upon the figures provided by the farmers-general, Lafayette continued. Yet those figures were doubtful. The manufacturing costs and the 30 per cent wastage that the farmers claimed seemed "extraordinary," and "everybody must be struck by their exaggeration." If he took his own estimates rather than those of the farmers-general, it would be reasonable to expect as much as 40,000,000 livres for the royal treasury rather than the Farm's potential 29,000,000. Furthermore, if, as he hoped, his plan would lead to the manufacture of more common brands, the result would be less wastage and a corresponding fall in price. Thus his proposal held forth the promise of "that advantage which it is always pleasant to encounter—that is, that the whims of the rich turn to the benefit of the poor."[36]

The résumé wound up with a peroration appealing to both the patriotism and the purse of the farmers-general. If trade with America flourished, Lafayette reasoned, it would increase French commerce elsewhere. "And when I consider our alliance, our common interests, the location of our ports, the quality of our work and the past shortcomings of England, I get a double pleasure out of the thought that France can be the channel for a very great part of the trade of the United States in Europe. . . . I request my friends the farmers-general, remembering that my cause is that of the people and that I speak here in the name of public welfare and opinion, to be kind enough to improve upon my plan in every detail. . . . I know that any member of our committee, if he accepts the fundamental idea of a tariff instead of a monopoly, will be better able than I to test and affirm it; and if I am not to have the pleasure of seeing my plan replaced by a better one, I shall get satisfaction out of the thought that I presented a short rough sketch of a work that was found useful and [afterward] perfected by others."[37]

Without waiting to see the brief of the farmers-general, Lafayette finished his résumé the Sunday before the scheduled meeting of the committee and sent it to Boullongne that very day. With characteristic energy and optimism, he requested Boullongne also to instruct the inspectors of commerce, Dupont

36. *Ibid.*, pp. 611–12.   37. *Ibid.*, p. 613.

and Boyetet, to prepare the necessary information on still other matters—furs and whale oil, "which, after the disposal of the tobacco business, is to be the subject of our inquiry."[38] Even while preparing his memorandum, he had engaged in an effort to organize competition to the Farm as collector of the duty he proposed on tobacco. "But every body is so much affraid of the Farm that none dare to think of it unless I keep their names a secret—so that I stand alone." As he reported to Jefferson, who was still in London, "I am considered as one that has got a very strange idea." The dislike of financiers was all that he expected to earn by his efforts. Malesherbes, however, encouraged him, telling him that he was "sowing seeds which will bear fruit in time."[39]

At the next meeting of the American Committee[40] all the anticipated reports were not yet ready, and so no definite decision was possible. The controversy thus dragged on. In April the farmers-general, to meet the criticism of the committee, offered a bounty to merchants who, in exchange for their cargoes of tobacco, would take on a return shipment of French goods. They hoped thereby to meet the criticism that American tobacco was being bought for French cash, which was then spent in England.[41]

Between meetings of the committee, Lafayette took a step that increased his landed estates and political influence enormously. He at length bought the seigniory of Langeac in Auvergne. This seemed to some of his less friendly confreres to be a cool bid for a peerage. It was, however, probably only a gesture to meet the gratifying wishes of the inhabitants of Langeac expressed personally to him when he had been there three years earlier. The new lands cost the huge sum of 188,000

38. Lafayette to Boullongne, June 1, [Mar. 19], 1786, *loc. cit.*

39. Lafayette to Jefferson, Mar. 18, 1786, Chinard, *Lafayette and Jefferson*, pp. 92–93.

40. Lafayette to Jefferson, Mar. 18, 1786, *ibid.*, p. 92, says, "Tomorrow we meet again." If this is not an error, the meeting took place on Sunday, March 19—which seems unlikely. It probably took place on March 20, as indicated in Lafayette to Boullongne, June 1 [Mar. 19], 1786, *loc. cit.*

41. Cf. Nussbaum, "Vergennes and Lafayette versus the farmers general," p. 603, and "American tobacco and French politics," p. 507.

livres. The people of Langeac showed their gratitude by a flowery resolution addressed to both Lafayette and his aunt at Chavaniac. In his reply he promised to engage "with a constant zeal in whatever may be of use to the city."[42]

When Jefferon returned to Paris, he resumed negotiations with Vergennes on Franco-American commerce. A discontinuance of the Farm's monopoly seemed possible to him so long as the American Committee continued its meetings. Vergennes, he found, was on his side, but Calonne, struggling to bolster up his tottering position, was "under the absolute control of the farmers-general." He found, too, that the committee, though not yet ready for the total suppression of the tobacco monopoly, hoped to find some less violent restriction of the Farm. Jefferson opposed any palliative that did not wholly destroy Morris' control of tobacco sales, since it would only deprive the friends of America of arguments and support. Lafayette, on the other hand, was still anxious to find a palliative, though he shared Jefferson's principle of "absolute liberty [of sale] or nothing."[43]

All expectations came close to frustration, however. When it began to look as if the committee might propose a change in their contract with Morris, the farmers-general sought out Calonne and put pressure on him to give the contract his written approval in return for a paper proviso that they buy fifteen thousand hogsheads in the open market. As soon as the committee learned of this stolen march, they protested forcefully. They found it hard to believe, they declared, that the Farm would buy fifteen thousand hogsheads of tobacco it did not need or that Americans would find it profitable to sell that much in a market which was already well supplied by a monopoly arrangement. The bounty already proffered by the Farm to carriers of French exports "in return for a commodity which will not be imported" also seemed futile. They could conclude only that the Morris

42. Lafayette to Messieurs, June 8, 1786, Belmont, pp. 317–18. Cf. *ibid.*, pp. 315–16 and n. 2; Maurice Chanson, "L'assemblée de l'élection de Brioude (1787–1788)," *Revue d'Auvergne*, V (1888), 300; Comte d'Espinchal, "Lafayette jugé par le comte d'Espinchal," *Revue retrospective*, XX (1894), 293; Charavay, pp. 132–33 and 539; and AN, T 1640, No. 61. See above, pp. 28–29.

43. Jefferson to Monroe, May 10, 1786, Lipscomb and Bergh, V, 331. Cf. Jefferson to Jay, May 27, Ford, *Writings of Jefferson*, IV, 234. See also p. 108 above.

contract must eventually destroy the tobacco trade with the United States. "Without counting the incidental consequences, our manufacturers lose a market of six million livres, and those of England gain it, all paid for with the gold of France."[44] They unanimously begged Calonne to permit them to debate the question with the farmers-general in his presence.

In the meantime, six memoirs on the tobacco problem had been completed. They suggested varying solutions. Lafayette's brief for free sale and a duty possibly collectable by some agency other than the Farm had to vie for attention with several suggestions for mere limitation and modification of the Farm's contract as well as with the farmers' defense of the existing arrangement. Dupont reported upon these memoirs and the recent protests of the committee to Vergennes. The foreign minister now openly joined the lists against the Farm and the Morris contract.

The insecure Calonne, caught between two fires, called a session of the American Committee on May 24 at his own château. Vergennes also attended.[45] There, under Vergennes's friendly eye and without opposition from Calonne, a set of decisions was reached that Lafayette called "popular resolutions." Although they did not abrogate the Farm's contract with Morris, they broke his sales monopoly. They required the farmers-general to buy annually an additional twelve to fifteen thousand hogsheads of American tobacco on the same terms as those of the Morris monopoly. What was more important, after the lapse of the Morris contract no similar contracts were ever to be made. Thus the farmers-general were rebuked and their effort to create an import monopoly frustrated. Still they were allowed to remain the exclusive purchasers and sellers of tobacco within France, and Lafayette had to admit that that was a partial defeat. "I did vigorously attak the Farm Generale," he informed Washington, "and warmly expostulated for its destruction, but they can't be cut down, and must fall by the slower method of

44. Minutes of the meeting of May 12, quoted in Nussbaum, "American tobacco and French politics," pp. 508-9.

45. Jefferson to Jay, May 27, 1786, Ford, *Writings of Jefferson*, IV, 234. Cf. Nussbaum, "Vergennes and Lafayette versus the farmers general," p. 603.

mines."[46] Some of the American Committee nevertheless felt
that they had won a signal victory. Jefferson was satisfied that
it would at least keep the commerce between the United States
and France alive until the Farm's monopoly could be destroyed, which might be as soon as Calonne's expected resignation took place.[47]

The news of the latest concession to America's merchants was
rapidly dispatched across the Atlantic. Although not yet officially approved by the king and although quite definitely dis-
approved by Robert Morris, the restoration of even a limited
competitive market led to an immediate increase in tobacco
shipments. Dupont de Nemours proposed to continue the attack
on the contract, and Lafayette was prepared, now that head-on
collision had produced only a minor shock, to try subtler methods.[48] Undermining privileged groups was fast becoming a major
activity of the new lord of Langeac.

BIBLIOGRAPHICAL NOTES

For an understanding of the Morris tobacco contract and its consequences
Nussbaum's edition of Lafayette's "Résumé" in the *Journal of modern history*,
III (1931), 592–613, and his references to the minutes of the American
Committee in his article in the *Political science quarterly*, XL (1925), 497–516,
have been especially useful.

The Comte d'Espinchal was an Auvergnat aristocrat who eventually became a political opponent of Lafayette. His memoirs, still largely unpublished
(see above, p. 22), must be regularly discounted, but they make a good index
of what those hostile to or envious of Lafayette thought.

The *Letters of Don Juan McQueen* illustrate Lafayette's interest in American merchants. McQueen, whom Lafayette had first met when he reached
Charleston from France in 1777, was visiting Paris on business in 1786.

Since this volume was first printed, Boyd (*Papers of Jefferson*, IX, 337–38)
has argued convincingly that Lafayette's speech (pp. 226–27 above) may have
been delivered on March 6 and not February 20. I have corrected those pages
and also p. 222 as he suggested.

46. Lafayette to Washington, May 24, 1786, Gottschalk, *Letters*, p. 312. A copy of
the resolution of the committee is in the *State records of North Carolina*, ed. Walter
Clark, XVIII (Goldsboro, N.C., 1900), 633 (wrongly dated Mar. 24, 1786).

47. Jefferson to Jay, May 27, 1786, Ford, *Writings of Jefferson*, IV, 234.

48. Lafayette to McQueen, May 27, 1786, W. C. Hartridge (ed.), *The letters of Don
Juan McQueen to his family, written from Spanish East Florida 1791–1807* (Columbia,
S.C., 1943), p. 9; Lafayette to unknown, May 27, collection of Gustave Oberlaender,
Reading, Pa.; Lafayette to Bowdoin, May 27, Massachusetts Historical Society; Jefferson to Jay, May 27, Ford, *Writings of Jefferson*, p. 236; and Morris to Constable, Jan.
9, 1787, Jackson collection. Cf. Nussbaum, "American tobacco and French politics,"
p. 511.

CHAPTER XVII

A Code for American Trade

WITH the problem of the tobacco cartel settled, the American Committee protracted its meetings in order to inquire into other aspects of Franco-American trade. Lafayette continued to "drive the nails" as Jefferson held them. Believing that his colleagues were ill informed regarding American products, the marquis suggested that Jefferson formally communicate to him, as a member of the committee, the relevant statistics with appropriate suggestions, which he would thereupon submit to their attention.[1] Thus, having a willing agent within a committee that had already shown itself favorably disposed, Jefferson began to lobby in behalf of a set of general regulations of American trade.

While Jefferson's communication was being prepared, other smaller complications called for consideration. For one thing, it was discovered that the earlier concession, whereby Americans might bring in whale oil without paying more duty than the "most-favored" Hanseatic merchants, was less advantageous than had been supposed. It developed that even Hanseatic exporters had to pay a special soap duty on whale oil over and above the regular impost. Lafayette hastened to assure the Massachusetts government that he would try to have the soap duty abolished, expressing the hope that meanwhile it would not affect Barrett's contract.[2] Shortly afterward, Jefferson got himself involuntarily immersed in the effort of the citizens of Honfleur to have their harbor listed among the free ports. As an advocate

1. Jefferson to Jay, Oct. 22, 1786, Lipscomb and Bergh, V, 451.

2. Lafayette to Bowdoin, May 27, 1786, *Massachusetts Historical Society proceedings*, V (1860–62), 355.

of free trade, he favored making "every port of France and of every other country" a free port "for our interest as for that also of all the world." But following his earlier principle of not requesting favors piecemeal (for, said he, "those who have had, and who may yet have occasion to ask great favors, should never ask small ones"), he sent the Honfleur petition to Lafayette to handle.[3] Likewise, whenever American merchants required legal papers of one kind or another, he would turn to the same quarter for aid. Jefferson's "nails" thus continued to accumulate.

The summer was a bad time for business, however, since Lafayette's obligations as courtier kept him moving with the king from town to town. Recently work had started on a brilliant engineering project to build a new harbor at Cherbourg. Jefferson thought it would be "one of the safest and most commodious ports in the world," capable of sheltering the whole French navy.[4] Vast quantities of rock thrown into the sea had enabled the engineers to provide a harbor with two openings, allowing vessels to come or go with any wind. The king and his ministers of the navy and of war were now preparing to inspect the project, and Lafayette was invited to go along. The ministers started out before the king, and Lafayette went with them. They left Paris on June 19, 1786, and reached Cherbourg on the 21st.

Louis XVI arrived shortly afterward, and Lafayette was one of the distinguished persons who greeted him on his arrival, somewhat after midnight on June 23. Cherbourg was decorated and illuminated in honor of the beloved monarch.[5] At dawn the king and his retinue boarded a gilded boat decorated with the royal flag and sailed out into the harbor to watch the sinking of the eighth stone pile that was to improve the roadstead. The journey lasted all day. Artillery salutes, music, and cheers greeted the king wherever he went, and even some English sailors who happened to be in the harbor shouted their approval.

3. Jefferson to Lafayette, June 15, 1786, Lipscomb and Bergh, V, 346–47; cf. *idem* to *idem*, June 17, Chinard, *Lafayette and Jefferson*, p. 94.

4. Jefferson to Benjamin Hawkins, Aug. 13, 1786, Lipscomb and Bergh, V, 391.

5. Tourneux, XIV, 420; *Gazette de Leyde*, July 11, 1786 (suppl.); *Courrier de l'Europe*, July 18.

One man was killed and several injured when a capstan broke as the pile was sinking. The king rebuked a royal surgeon who did not hasten to the aid of the injured and ordered a pension of 500 livres for the dead man's widow. After the engineering exhibition was over, Louis XVI and his cortege sailed around the harbor. The wind suddenly changed and there was some jesting about their being carried off to England. The king proved to be a good sailor, "but M. de la Fayette was courtier enough to be very sick."[6] The next few days were spent in reviewing a sham naval battle.

On the 26th Louis left for Paris. Lafayette was graciously permitted to ride with the king and several members of the king's entourage in the royal coach. They went by way of Caen and Honfleur, where they witnessed some more naval maneuvers on June 27. Then they crossed by ferry to Le Havre, where they spent the night, reaching Gaillon and Rouen on June 28. Here Lafayette had occasion again to observe demonstrations that amply testified the popularity of Louis XVI. They got to Paris the next day.[7]

Lafayette had just witnessed one of the happiest events of Louis's whole reign. Coming as it did when the scandalous revelations of the Diamond Necklace Affair had disgraced the Cardinal de Rohan and had sullied the reputation of Marie Antoinette, the loyalty of the king's subjects was particularly gratifying. Long afterward it was related in Cherbourg that when the people shouted *Vive le roi*, the king had answered *Vive mon peuple!*[8] Neither the king nor his kingdom was ever to be so happy again.

Meanwhile Jefferson had completed his letter on the trade of America, and shortly after Lafayette's return it was delivered to him. It contained three lists. The first gave the commodities that the United States exported, with estimates of how much

6. William Eden to Lord Carmarthen, July 6, 1786, *The Journal and correspondence of William, Lord Auckland* (London, 1861–62), I, 139. Cf. Bachaumont, XXXII, 166 (July 9); *Gazette de Leyde*, July 7 and 11 (suppls.).

7. *Gazette de Leyde*, July 11, 1786; Bachaumont, XXXII, 158–60 (July 7) and 168 (July 11); Tourneux, XIV, 420–22.

8. Bachaumont, XXXII, 167 (July 7, 1786).

of each went to the West Indies and how much to Europe. The
second gave the ones that the United States imported from
Europe with an approximation of their total value. The third
enumerated those that the United States imported from the
West Indies with a similar approximation. Jefferson inclosed
with these lists a detailed letter. It explained that the exclusion
of flour and fish from the articles freely imported into the
French West Indies had obliged Americans to curtail their production of flour and to sell their fish in Europe, with a consequent decrease in their importation of coffee and sugar from the
islands. He urged the American Committee to give these subjects their attention.[9]

Thus Lafayette was provided with new ammunition for his
attack upon French mercantilist practices. His hostility to the
farmers-general was further aggravated at this juncture by another example of their monopolistic practices. He now learned
of an effort on their part to extend the salt monopoly to his native Auvergne. Most of that region was a privileged area so far
as the salt tax was concerned, being in the category of "re-
deemed provinces." Having to pay no tax, it had hitherto benefited from a low price for salt and from smuggling the commodity into neighboring areas where the tax was high. The Farm's
new departure led to an outcry from leading citizens of the
province. Lafayette and other Auvergnats met at the Paris
home of the province's governor and undertook to protest directly to Calonne. The minister explained that the purpose of
the new regulation was not to impose a salt tax on Auvergne
but only to make the farmers-general the exclusive salt agents
in a wider area in order to discourage salt smuggling. For that
privilege they recently had increased their payment to the king.
He promised, however, a postponement of three months, during
which the subject would be reconsidered. But "you cannot be
too careful about any arrangement proposed by the farmers-
general," Lafayette cautioned his Auvergnat friends,[10] and he
proposed to make a trip to Auvergne soon in order to see what

9. Jefferson to Lafayette, July 17, 1786, Lipscomb and Bergh, V, 371–76.

10. Lafayette to Gaspard-Claude-François Chabrol, July 20 [1786], Pierpont Morgan
Library, Lafayette Vol. I.

could be done about forestalling the Farm by reducing the contraband trade in salt.[11]

Meanwhile the meetings of the American Committee continued. They were now presided over by Councilor of State Lenoir. Lafayette not only kept up a steady correspondence with the new president on committee matters but also met him privately on several occasions. As previously arranged, Jefferson's statistics had been submitted to the committee. Lafayette wanted the ministry, in reply, to lay down a set of general regulations for American trade. He kept prodding Lenoir, insisting that, on the initiative of the committee, a letter be sent to Jefferson recapitulating all the concessions already granted and stating the reasons for not granting others. Since he was more interested in political than commercial results, he proposed that it be worded in a fashion "suited for reading by republicans."[12]

The committee finally unanimously agreed to do as Lafayette requested, even undertaking to compose a model draft of the proposed letter. This draft set forth the concessions made to the United States in the course of the preceding two years, indicating several other recommendations that could not be approved. In addition, it laid down the general rule that only those duties would be eliminated which hindered French industry by increasing the cost of raw materials, interfered with trade without producing revenue, or kept Americans from buying French munitions and paper.[13] Lafayette's recent experience in helping Jefferson and Barclay to buy some arms for Virginia lay behind the last provision.[14] The marquis was pleased with the committee's decision, believing the sacrifices "almost nothing" and the

11. Lafayette to Vergennes, Aug. 2, 1786, AAE, corr. pol., É.-U., Vol. XXXII, fol. 34.

12. Lafayette to Lenoir, *ce dimanche au soir* [probably July 30, 1786], Albert Mathiez, "Lafayette et le commerce franco-américain à la veille de la Révolution," *Annales historiques de la Révolution française*, III (1926), 479; cf. *idem* to *idem*, [probably July 29, 1786], *ibid.*, p. 478. Mathiez read Lafayette's date as *ce lundi matin*, but the original (AN, AJ¹336) reads *ce samedi matin*.

13. Lafayette to Lenoir, *ce lundi* [probably Sept. 18, 1786], *ibid.*, p. 481; Jefferson to Jay, Oct. 22, Lipscomb and Bergh, V, 451–52; Lafayette to Vergennes, Aug. 2, *loc. cit.*

14. *Calendar of Virginia state papers*, IV, 59, 70, and 81; William Wirt, *Sketches of the life and character of Patrick Henry* (Hartford, Conn., 1854), p. 455; Jefferson to Henry, Jan. 24, 1786, and to MM. St. Victor and Bettinger, May 12, Lipscomb and Bergh, V, 253 and 334.

advantages "very great."[15] The letter was submitted to Calonne for official confirmation.

The birth of another royal princess unfortunately obliged Lafayette to squeeze his bourgeois project in between courtly visits to Versailles, Fontainebleau, and Rambouillet. There he found occasion to report to Vergennes on the progress of the proposed letter to Jefferson and to announce that he would soon be on his way to Auvergne to look into the salt-smuggling situation. From Fontainebleau he went to the country seat of Malesherbes, only a few miles distant, where the two conspirators once more pondered the Protestant situation.[16]

Lafayette had not been idle of late in his efforts to achieve religious toleration. For nearly a year, however, the Diamond Necklace Affair had so engrossed the attention of the chancellor, the minister of the king's household, and other religious authorities in France that Lafayette had felt it inexpedient to raise the question of his own "great·lawsuit." Meanwhile he had paved the way for his eventual approach to them. He had joined forces with the Protestant financier Necker and his brilliant daughter Mme de Staël in the good cause. He had also delivered an essay on toleration by Condorcet to the Duc de Nivernais, who was well known as a liberal statesman and man of letters. Through these influential politicians he hoped to enlist the interest of Chancellor Miroménil. But he did not really expect such maneuvers to lead to a speedy success. "It is rather as a salve to my conscience that I make this effort than in the hope of getting anywhere," he owned.[17]

Rabaut-St. Étienne had constantly kept in close touch with Lafayette and Malesherbes. In the course of the summer it became clear that the marquis had outstripped his mentor Malesherbes as a champion of toleration and had become more sympathetic to Rabaut's point of view. All three men agreed that there should not be "a people within a people" and that hence

15. Lafayette to Vergennes, Aug. 2, 1786, loc. cit.

16. Lafayette to Lenoir, [probably July 29, 1786], loc. cit.; to Vergennes, Aug. 2, loc. cit.; to Jefferson, Aug. 2, [1786], LC, Jefferson papers, No. 4642; to Lenoir, Aug. 4, Mathiez, "Lafayette et le commerce franco-américain," p. 475.

17. Lafayette to unknown, (Aug., 1786) [but probably of May 31, 1786], Mémoires, II, 155–56.

there should be no state religion. But whereas Malesherbes was for "replastering" the wall that separated the two religious groups, Lafayette and Rabaut-St. Étienne were for "pulling it down."[18] Now at last the Rohan trial was out of the way and the culprits punished, and Lafayette hoped to get more speedy action. His visit to Malesherbes in August, 1786, however, led to no immediate results.

The Cayenne experiment with Negro slaves proved more encouraging. Castries was friendly toward it, and his intendant for the colony, M. Lescalier, had indicated the greatest willingness to favor it as a sort of public enterprise. In August, 1786, the title to "La belle Gabrielle," as the Cayenne plantation was called, formally passed into Lafayette's hands. A young scientist introduced to Lafayette by Condorcet, Henry de Richeprey, agreed to go to Cayenne as supervisor, and Lafayette placed him in complete charge. Richeprey soon bought additional lands. Lafayette instituted a program of gradual emancipation, paying each worker for his labor according to his deserts, absolutely forbidding the sale of any slaves, giving them a modicum of schooling, and punishing Negroes no more severely than whites for the same offenses. It was the intention of the experiment to show that the birth rate would rise among a happy population and thus the necessity for the slave trade would diminish. The first reports from Richeprey were very heartening.[19]

Shortly after his visit with Malesherbes, Lafayette started off on his previously announced visit to Auvergne. On August 13, escorted by a guard of honor from among the leading citizens of Langeac, he visited that town, of which he was now the lord, formally took possession of it, and was publicly feted. He received the keys of the city and once again drank the traditional *vin d'honneur*. Mass was celebrated and a *Te Deum* sung. A gay banquet wound up the festivities. The day's rejoicing was shortly put into verse by one of the town's poetasters, who called his

18. Rabaut-St. Étienne to Committee of Bordeaux, Feb. 12, 1788, Dardier, II, 396.

19. *Ibid.*; Lafayette to M. Murray, May 1, 1834, *Mémoires*, VI, 766; AN, T 1640, dossier 61, Lafayette; Victor Henry (brother of Richeprey) to the editor, May 12, 1791 [*sic*], *Journal de Paris*, Feb. 26, 1791 (suppl.); Thomas Clarkson, *The history of the rise, progress, and accomplishment of the abolition of the African slave trade by the British Parliament* (London, 1808), II, 123–24. See also p. 259 below.

poem "La belle journée."[20] About the same time Bayonne declared Lafayette a citizen in recognition of his part in making their city a free port.[21]

Lafayette had no time to accomplish anything with regard to the Auvergne salt problem on this trip. He was shortly obliged to join his father-in-law, the Duc d'Ayen, in Alsace for the annual summer inspection of troops.[22] He had reached Lunéville on his way there when his mail caught up with him. By a letter from Jefferson he learned that during his absence little was being done to advance his proposal for the general regulation of American trade. In fact, the American minister was fearful that Lafayette's efforts to gain publicity for earlier concessions might injure the cause. The papers in America had announced these concessions by prominently printing a letter from Lafayette on the subject, mentioning the French minister only incidentally. "It will do you just service there," Jefferson chided. "The only question is whether it may not disarm you here."[23]

Noting Jefferson's ill-concealed displeasure, the marquis tried to explain away the indiscretion as a possible plot to weaken his influence in America. Perhaps the American newspapers had been misled, he weakly suggested, "by an unfriendly hand, on purpose to set me up as a man blinded by partiality."[24] This fleeting episode, however, did not lessen the mutual regard of the two men. In fact, in Lafayette's absence, their families drew closer together. Mme de Lafayette, graciously acting in her husband's place as Jefferson's sponsor, befriended his daughter, received his distinguished American visitors, and introduced him to the polished and influential circle of her aunt, Mme de Tessé.[25]

A sheaf of letters from the United States also was in the mail

20. Belmont, "La belle journée," p. 305; Charavay, p. 133.

21. *Mémoires*, II, 147 n.

22. Lafayette to Washington, Oct. 26, 1786, Gottschalk, *Letters*, p. 314.

23. Jefferson to Lafayette, Aug. 24, 1786, Lipscomb and Bergh, V, 417. The letter in question is probably that of Lafayette to [Breck?], [Dec. 3, 1785?]. It is to be found in the *Pennsylvania Packet*, June 24, 1786.

24. Lafayette to Jefferson, Aug. 30, 1786, Chinard, *Lafayette and Jefferson*, p. 106.

25. Mme de Lafayette to Jefferson, [Aug. 26, 1786], Pierpont Morgan Library, Lafayette Vol. I, and [Aug.] 28, [1786], Chinard, *Lafayette and Jefferson*, p. 103.

that reached Lafayette in Lunéville. They contained the sad news that General Greene had died. "It is a great loss for the United States," Lafayette mourned, and a "heavy loss" to Washington and himself in particular. He was soon to find that it also interfered with the Franco-American commercial empire that he had envisaged. Only inferior samples of American timber were to be received by the French navy after Greene's death, and Lafayette was to feel called upon to seek better ones.[26]

Among the letters received in Lunéville was one from Jay indicating that American relations with Spain were growing increasingly strained because of recent frontier disputes. The Spanish envoy in America did not consider his country bound by Lafayette's friendly understanding with Floridablanca in 1783,[27] and the Spanish still held and fortified certain points east of the Mississippi. An amicable solution of the Spanish-American boundary dispute now seemed more desirable than ever because of insistent reports that the British, who refused to surrender the Great Lakes posts, were deliberately stirring up the Indians against the Americans. A renewal of war was therefore quite conceivable. In setting forth his views on this subject for Jefferson, Lafayette hoped that the Madrid authorities would prove more amenable than their envoy. In order that, meanwhile, American public opinion should not become too hostile to Spain, he suggested that his correspondence with Floridablanca be published. Such publicity might also make Spain feel "more engaged." Only "motives of personal delicacy," he explained (possibly remembering Jefferson's implied rebuke), had prevented him from recommending its publication before, as it "would have had an air of vanity."[28]

During this summer tour of 1786 Lafayette found time to do

26. Lafayette to Jefferson, Aug. 30, 1786, Chinard, *Lafayette and Jefferson*, p. 106; to Wadsworth, Oct. 8, LC, Jeremiah Wadsworth papers; to Washington, Oct. 26, Gottschalk, *Letters*, p. 315.

27. Gottschalk, *Lafayette and the close of the American Revolution*, pp. 410–11. Cf. *Journals of the Continental Congress*, XXXI, 540–43 (Aug. 22, 1786).

28. Lafayette to Jefferson, Aug. 30, 1786, Chinard, *Lafayette and Jefferson*, pp. 105 and 107. Cf. Comte de La Touche to Lafayette, July 28, *ibid.*, pp. 99–100; Jefferson to Jay, Aug. 11, Lipscomb and Bergh, V, 379–80; and Lafayette to Jay, Oct. 28, [Weaver], *Diplomatic correspondence*, I, 445–46.

some reading, which was a relatively new way for him to con-
sume energy. Jefferson's *Notes on Virginia* elicited a friendly
comment—chiefly an egocentric remark about his own career in
Virginia. The literary controversy between Chastellux and a
rising young author named Brissot de Warville over the merits
of Americans also interested him. Chastellux had just published
his *Voyages dans l'Amérique septentrionale dans les années 1780,
1781 et 1782.* Brissot, as a *philosophe* of a more radical stripe, resented Chastellux's aristocratic tone, particularly with regard
to Quakers, Negroes, and common folk, and sought to defend
them against Chastellux's random but sometimes extensive remarks.[29] Lafayette, distantly related to Chastellux, had also recently come to know Brissot. When therefore he wrote to Jefferson, who likewise knew both men, calling his attention to
this "most severe criticism popping out against our friend Chas-
telux," he discreetly avoided comment.[30]

It is highly unlikely, however, that Lafayette failed to notice
one thing that the two *philosophes* agreed upon. "There certainly is no Frenchman, no American," wrote Brissot in his
Lettre à Chatellux, "who will not reread with pleasure your por-
trayals of Washington, of the scholarly Jefferson, and of that
young and brave Frenchman whom you characterize so well as
the hope of our Nation, *spes altera Romae,* whose name will be
cited forever beside that of his father and friend Washington in
the annals of the United States."[31] Much of Chastellux's new
book, indeed, was about Lafayette, and if Lafayette had it with
him, he could easily have found the passage to which Brissot
referred: "On seeing him [Lafayette], one is at a loss which most
to admire—that so young a man as he should have given such
eminent proof of talents or that a man already so tried should
give promise of so long a future career of glory. Fortunate his
country, if she knows how to avail herself of them; more fortu-

29. Cf. J.-P. Brissot de Warville, *Examen critique des "Voyages dans l'Amérique
septentrionale de M. le Marquis le Chatellux"; ou lettre à M. le Marquis de Chatellux dans
lequel on réfute principalement ses opinions sur les Quakers, sur les Nègres, sur le peuple et
sur l'homme* (London, 1786).

30. Lafayette to Jefferson, Aug. 30, 1786, Chinard, *Lafayette and Jefferson,* p. 107.
See also p. 108 above.

31. P. 135.

nate still, should she stand in no need of calling upon them."[32] Probably Lafayette was quite familiar with the passage, whether he had the book with him or not.

Chastellux and Brissot were not the only *philosophes* who took delight in the career of the youthful general. The Baron de Grimm had recently made Lafayette a subject of his correspondence with the crowned heads of Europe. He reported that two French clergymen had just published sermons mentioning "the young friend of glory." With good-natured amusement, Grimm described the embarrassment caused the marquis by a tactless remark in one of them. In his eulogy of the late Duc d'Orléans, the Abbé Claude Fauchet had stated that Frederick the Great, in the presence of Lafayette and Prince Henry, had praised the deceased's tactical ability and military genius. "It must be so," Grimm pretended, "since it is announced from the seat of truth; but M. de La Fayette is said to have some trouble remembering the episode." As a matter of fact, the marquis had felt called upon to deny the abbé's story and to apologize to the Prussian court, explaining that he was nowise responsible for the abbé's blunder.[33] About this time, too, Condorcet's book setting forth the American influence upon Europe was published, with its flattering dedication to Lafayette. Thus in 1786 outstanding men of letters in France allied themselves with Lafayette—Condorcet, Chastellux, Brissot, Grimm.

Lesser writers had also done so. On Jefferson's suggestion, the marquis helped Jean-Nicholas Démeunier to correct his articles on the United States and the Cincinnati for the new *Encyclopédie méthodique*.[34] The new Maecenas obtained for the Connecticut poet Joel Barlow royal permission to dedicate his *Vi-*

32. Quoted in Gottschalk, *Lafayette and the close of the American Revolution*, pp. 154–55.

33. Tourneux, XIV, 342 (March, 1786); Lafayette to [Lucchesini?], [*ca.* Feb. 20, 1786?], Gardner-Ball collection. The sermon in question was *Oraison funèbre de ... Louis-Philippe d'Orléans, duc d'Orléans ... prononcée dans l'église de S.-Eustache ... le lundi 20 février 1786 ... par M. l'Abbé Fauchet*. The other was delivered at the cathedral church of Notre-Dame on February 14, 1786, by the Abbé Jean-Siffrein Maury. It is not listed in the catalogue of the Bibliothèque nationale but is identified in Tourneux, XIV, 340 and n.

34. Jefferson to Washington, Nov. 14, 1786, Lipscomb and Bergh, V, 2–3; cf. G. H. T. McKee, *Thomas Jefferson, ami de la Révolution française* (Lorient, 1928), pp. 129–30.

sion of Columbus to Louis XVI, the king subscribing for twenty-five copies and Lafayette for ten.[35] Thereby (though probably unintentionally) the marquis rebuked the French poet who had said Americans "know our Dorats [Dorat was a recently deceased poet] less than our Lafayettes . . . [and] need heroes rather than poets."[36] The men of letters were gradually annexing Lafayette. As they acquired the habit of writing about America and therefore about him, he acquired the habit of reading what they wrote and became increasingly "philosophic."

While Lafayette was in Alsace, Lenoir kept him informed on the affairs of the American Committee. Returning to Paris for about two weeks in September, the marquis threw himself once more into the work of the committee. Finding that "many prejudices" still prevailed against the American people, he appealed to his old friend Barbé-Marbois to write more fully in his diplomatic dispatches from America "on the truths that can establish confidence and harmonious relations." He was familiar, he admitted, with reproaches that might fairly be made, but "they are exaggerated," and he urged Marbois to help him correct them. In the American Committee, he said, "I shall fight for the good cause, if not with talent, at least with good lungs."[37] He was true to his word.

The general regulations that had been requested, Lafayette found, had not yet been drawn up. The shipment of arms that he had helped to buy for Virginia was still being held at Le Havre because of ancient restrictions. Once again, it seemed, the minister of finance was reluctant to incur the opposition of the farmers-general. Lafayette immediately began to call on the government for dispatch. He wanted the news of the general regulations to reach America, he said, as soon as possible, since they had already been agreed upon informally. A visit to Ministers Vergennes and Calonne convinced him that there were no insurmountable obstacles, and he urged Lenoir to press for ac-

35. Lafayette to Wadsworth, May 11, 1785, Connecticut State Library, Trumbull collection, and Feb. 10, 1786, Gardner-Ball collection; to Vergennes, Jan. 26 and Feb. 8, AAE, corr. pol., É.-U., Vol. XXXI, fols. 65 and 79.

36. [Louis Gabriel Bourdon], *Voyage d'Amérique: dialogue en vers entre l'auteur et l'Abbé **** (London, 1786), p. 21.

37. Lafayette to Marbois, Sept. 10, 1786, Charavay, pp. 134–35, n. 4.

tion. He also reminded Lenoir that the Americans would welcome a regulation substituting a single payment on whale oil for the several that were now demanded.[38] Still the matter dragged on.

Yet Lafayette's popularity neither in the United States nor in France suffered from this protracted stalemate. The young man's fame was graciously acknowledged by the joint effort of his monarch and the republic that had adopted him. The bust that Houdon had made was at last ready to be installed in the Paris city hall, as resolved by the Commonwealth of Virginia. The good intentions of Virginia republicans, however, had raised a somewhat complicated question in an absolute monarchy. In France, Jefferson found, "the King is the sole fountain of honour" and never before had a foreign country asked to put up a bust of one of His Most Christian Majesty's living subjects. But the king's friendship for America and "his personal esteem for the character of the Marquis de la Fayette" overcame all the conventions.[39] It was well over a year after the bust had been begun, however, that the Baron de Breteuil, as minister of the king's household, at last wrote to the Paris authorities giving them permission to receive it.[40]

Accordingly, Jefferson formally wrote the city fathers requesting them to accept the sculpture, which was an exact copy of one that would be placed next to Washington's (as yet unfinished) in the rotunda of the Virginia capitol. He expressed the hope that they would "place it where, doing most honor to him [Lafayette], it will most gratify the feelings of an allied nation." He took this occasion to recite the young hero's services to the state of Virginia. Lafayette had exhibited, he said, "a character so great in its first developments that they would honor the close of any other."[41]

38. Lafayette to Lenoir, undated [but September, 1786], [Sept.] 17, ce lundi [probably Sept. 18], and Sept. 25, Mathiez, "Lafayette et le commerce franco-américain," pp. 479–82.

39. Jefferson to E. J. Randolph, Feb. 7, 1787, Lipscomb and Bergh, VI, 84.

40. Sept. 10, 1786, Hippolyte Monin, L'état de Paris en 1789; études et documents sur l'ancien régime à Paris (Paris, 1889), p. 633.

41. Jefferson to Le Pelletier de Morfontaine, Sept. 27, 1786, Lipscomb and Bergh, V, 428–89.

Jefferson's petition was immediately approved by the city council, and the next day was set for the ceremony. In the Grande Salle of the Hôtel de Ville, the provost and the eschevins gathered to accept the bust. Many celebrities were present including Mme de Lafayette. Her husband, leaving with Mazzei the impression that he "sincerely regretted all that was being said and written in his honor," had himself returned to Auvergne,[42] and Jefferson, having fallen recently and injured his wrist, was represented by his secretary, William Short. The provost made an appropriate speech, after which the chief clerk read the Virginia resolution, Jefferson's letter of presentation, and the king's consent that the gift be received.

As Lafayette's still infallible luck would have it, it fell to Éthis de Corny, as the king's *procureur*, formally to accept the bust. Corny had been one of Lafayette's aides-de-camp in the American army and was now a fellow Cincinnatus, and he was indebted to the marquis for having recently tried to get him the Cross of St. Louis.[43] As a friend of the late Voltaire, he was also an advocate of the new ideas of liberty and reason. In the midst of a patriotic speech attacking the English and praising the United States and the "knight of liberty," he recalled that in 1774, when Lafayette had become a captain in the French army, it was he who had administered the oath. "Although he swore in my presence . . . never to serve a foreign power, I find it quite proper, quite just that he who tendered the oath should have reached the same destination as he who swore it. . . . Today, in accordance with the king's wishes, I am called by my present functions to see to it that his bust is placed among you, and that this memorable homage shall preserve forever the record of his glory and his merits. . . . Our august monarch confirms with his approval that of two worlds."[44] Thus was disobedience to kings made into a virtue by the servant of a king —with Jefferson in the background. When the speeches were

42. Mazzei to Poniatowski, July 8, 1791, H. R. Marraro, "Philip Mazzei and his Polish friends," *Quarterly bulletin of the Polish Institute of Arts and Sciences in America*, II (1944), 800–801; *Journal historique et politique*, No. 4, 1786, p. 63.

43. Memoranda of May 15 and 27, 1786, AAE, corr. pol., É.-U., Vol. XXI, fols. 313–14 and 385.

44. Monin, p. 634.

finished, the bust, crowned with laurel and oak, was placed on the main mantel of the Grande Salle, among the monuments of kings and other great men. The ceremony was punctuated by bursts of applause and music.

Every word uttered on the occasion had been in praise of Lafayette. Those walls were one day to hear more bitter remarks on the same subject, but that was not yet. Now he was the "hero of two worlds," "the knight of Liberty." Few episodes in all his career had yet received more attention from European journalists and aroused more general interest than this offering made by a thankful American commonwealth to Europe's greatest metropolis and approved by a magnanimous king.[45] Lafayette reported the episode to Washington with becoming modesty, declaring that he would be still more pleased when the other copy of the bust was placed in Richmond "eternally by the side of, and paying an ever lasting homage to the statue of my beloved general."[46] Somewhat later, a poem by Marmontel, another recent addition to Lafayette's circle of learned and literary friends, commemorated the occasion. It apostrophized the "hero of the New World" as "modest in the midst of success, noble and great without pride, gentle and good without weakness," joining the "valor of Achilles to the composure of Nestor."[47]

Lafayette had by this time become a favorite subject of artists as well as poets. L. Lepaon and Adrien Carpentier, French painters; William Angus, English engraver; and Charles Willson Peale and John Trumbull, Americans, were among the artists who had already made or were soon to make pictures of him.[48]

45. *Courrier de l'Europe*, Oct. 13, 1786; *Journal historique et politique*, No. 4, 1786, p. 63; *Gazette de Leyde*, Oct. 16 (suppl.); Bachaumont, XXXIII, 75 (Oct. 6); *Journal Général de l'Europe*, Oct. 14, pp. 241–42; Crèvecœur, III, 381–83. Cf. also Jefferson to Corny, Oct. 20, Lipscomb and Bergh, V, 449–50, and to Le Pelletier de Morfontaine, Feb. 17, 1787, *ibid.*, VI, 91. Mathew Carey showed his gratitude to Lafayette by printing the *Procès-verbaux des 15 et 28 septembre 1786 relatifs à la reception du buste de M. le Marquis de La Fayette à l'Hôtel-de-Ville de Paris* (Philadelphia, 1786); see S. W. Jackson, *La Fayette, a bibliography* (New York, 1930), p. 162.

46. Oct. 26, 1786, Gottschalk, *Letters*, p. 316.

47. *Journal encyclopédique*, 1787, II, 82–83.

48. *Mercure de France*, December, 1784; *The French Revolution, a loan exhibition for the benefit of Société d'Histoire de la Révolution française and l'École Libre des Hautes Études, throughout December 1943 at Wildenstein* (New York, 1943), p. 23, No. 22;

His portrait had begun to appear in several admirers' homes. Ebenezer Stevens, who had served under him as a colonel, had had one made that graced his wall.[49] Conspicuous in Washington's drawing-room hung the family picture of all the Lafayettes, sent over by Lafayette himself.[50] And at least one Irish patriot's library, that of Sir Edward Newenham, was adorned with his portrait, hanging alongside those of Washington and Franklin.[51] By the time the Richmond copy of Houdon's bust was finally placed in the Virginia capitol in 1789, there was hardly a friend of liberty in two hemispheres to whom his features were not familiar. Houdon's was the only bust, however, and it was to remain the most famous of the works of art centering around Lafayette—not only because it was the work of a great master exhibited in two copies in two far distant capitals but also because the Paris copy became a center of attraction. Placed in the focus of the city's political life, it was to witness volcanic events in the near future, during which it was itself to be smashed to bits.

But no revolutionary wave was ever to shatter the image of Lafayette that, already imprinted on the hearts of Americans, was still more deeply engraved by his recent benefactions. In a thoughtful letter expressing the belief that "the benefits of a

---

André Girodie, *Musée national historique de Blérancourt, Haute-Picardie, coopération franco-américaine, catalogue sommaire* (Blérancourt, 1928), p. 52, and *Les États-Unis et la France au XVIIIe siècle, exposition organisée par la Société des Amis du Musée national de Blérancourt (Aisne) ... Catalogue raisonné* (Paris, 1929), p. 63; H. W. Sellers, "Engravings by Charles Willson Peale," *Pennsylvania magazine of history*, LVII (1933), 170; "Notes and queries," *Publications of the Southern History Association*, I (1897), 324–25; John Andrews, *History of the war with America, France, Spain, and Holland; commencing in 1775 and ending in 1783* (London, 1785–86), II, facing 422; John Trumbull, *Autobiography, reminiscences and letters, 1756–1841* (New York, 1841), pp. 150–51; Fogg Museum of Art, Harvard University, *Exhibition, Washington, Lafayette, Franklin, etc.* (Cambridge, Mass., 1944), No. 133; T. T. Waterman, "Notes on a portrait of Lafayette," *Gazette des beaux-arts*, 6th ser., XXVIII (1945), 379–80. The Carpentier portrait is now the property of S. W. Jackson, Gloucester, Va.

49. Anon., "An historical portrait," *Magazine of American history*, I (1877), 252. The portrait is now the property of the New York Historical Society and is said to have been painted in 1784.

50. See above, p. 73; Anon., "An account of a visit made to Washington at Mount Vernon, by an English gentleman in 1785," *Pennsylvania magazine of history*, XVII (1893), 81.

51. Washington to Newenham, Nov. 25, 1785, Fitzpatrick, XXVIII, 324.

liberal and free commerce will, pretty generally, succeed to the devastations and horrors of war," Washington gave the stamp of his approval to his protégé's commercial endeavors. "Be assured the measures which have lately been taken with regard to the two articles of *oil* and *tobacco* have tended very much to endear you to your fellow citizens on this side of the Atlantic."[52] Jay wrote to him that people all over the United States commonly remarked "that wherever you go, you do us good."[53] The whalers of Nantucket, whose livelihood had been saved by the new concessions that Lafayette had won for American oil in France, were particularly "penetrated with gratitude for so signal a service." They resolved "in corporation assembled" that each of them should contribute the milk from one of his cows for a whole day, that the milk thus obtained should be manufactured into a cheese weighing five hundred pounds, and "that the same should be transmitted to the Marquis de Lafayette as a feeble, but not less sincere, testimonial of the affection and gratitude of the inhabitants of Nantucket."[54] A five-hundred-pound cheese may not be "a monument more enduring than bronze" but it is probably rare among heroic trophies.

When Lafayette returned to Paris from Auvergne, it was just in time to learn that France had signed the Eden Treaty with England, which provided for tariff reciprocity on the basis of the "most-favored" European nation. Vergennes and Calonne, following the new physiocratic principles, had undertaken, despite protests from certain commercial spheres, to build up a friendly understanding with England through a mutually profitable trade agreement. Lafayette had had no hand in the negotiation, but when he learned of it, though continuing to distrust England, he somewhat unenthusiastically approved. He was anxious lest it should appear to Americans to be a betrayal of their interests. The Eden Treaty, he explained, gave to England the rights only

---

52. Aug. 15, 1786, *ibid.*, pp. 520-21.

53. Jay to Lafayette, June 16, 1786, Johnston, III, 201-2.

54. *New Plymouth Gazette*, Sept. 19 [27], 1786, [Davis], *Complete history*, pp. 154-55; *Mémoires*, II, 147; Crèvecœur, III, 385.

of "most favoured *European* nation," and would have no effect whatsoever upon American concessions.[55]

In fact, if the Eden Treaty had any influence at all on American affairs, it was only to hasten the understanding between France and the United States. While the court was once more residing in Fontainebleau, Lafayette finally learned of Calonne's formal approval of the regulations that the American Committee had drafted. It took the form, as had been agreed, of a letter to Jefferson reviewing all the concessions which the French government had made since 1784, when Calonne had announced that four free ports would be open to Americans instead of two. It once more declared that duties on brandies were suppressed. It indicated that no change was contemplated in the tobacco trade other than those recently adopted. It enumerated the concessions made to Tourtille Sangrain and Nathaniel Barrett, thus at last giving them formal royal confirmation. It extended the "most-favored" treatment enjoyed by the Hanseatic cities to American merchants for a period of ten years, carefully pointing out that further concessions on whale oil would conflict with the king's obligations to other countries. It suppressed all further duties on potash, pearlash, beaver skins, raw leather, masts, yards, keels, red cedar, live oak, and, "in a word, all kinds of wood fit for shipbuilding," and on shrubs, trees, and seeds if they were produced in America and shipped in American or French vessels. It permitted the free import of all ships built in America. It made all arms and powder bought in France by American states subject to only a small duty if carried in French or American ships, while all books and paper were completely exempted if similarly transported. It renewed the hope that duties payable upon the arrival of American vessels in French ports might be reduced to a single payment estimated on the basis of the number of masts and draught in place of the "uncertain estimations" hitherto in force. It promised to encourage the importation of Carolina rice. And as a postscript to an al-

55. Lafayette to Washington, Feb. 6, May 24, Oct. 8, and Oct. 26, 1786, Gottschalk, *Letters*, pp. 307–8, 311–12, 313, and 314; to Wadsworth, Oct. 8, *loc. cit.*; to McHenry, Oct. 26, LC, James McHenry collection; and to Jay, Oct. 28, [Weaver], *Diplomatic correspondence*, I, 446.

ready lengthy letter came Calonne's confirmation of a set of recent decrees (copies of which were inclosed) granting specific
exemptions from or reductions of export duties on wines from
certain parts of France.[56]

Jefferson apparently received this long-awaited document
from the hands of Lafayette himself.[57] Although the American
minister still hoped for a better solution of the tobacco tangle
and noted the absence of any stipulation regarding the West
Indies trade, he was greatly pleased. "Indeed," he declared, "I
must say that, as far as I am able to see, the friendship of the
people of this country toward us is cordial and general, and that
it is a kind of security for the friendship of ministers who cannot
in any country be uninfluenced by the voice of the people. . . .
It is their interest, as well as ours, to multiply the basis of
friendship between us." He sent the letter that very day to Jay,
explaining the various maneuvers by which it had finally been
extracted from the reluctant minister of finance. He gladly admitted his indebtedness to the marquis: "The assistance of M.
de La Fayette in the whole business, has been so earnest and so
efficacious, that I am in duty bound to place it under the eye of
Congress as worthy of their notice on this occasion. Their
thanks, or such other notice as they think proper, would be
grateful [sic] to him without doubt. He has richly deserved and
will continue to deserve it, whenever occasions shall arise of
rendering service to the United States."[58]

Lafayette was no less pleased with Jefferson and made his
satisfaction clear in the first long letter he had found the time to
write to Washington in five months. While in Lunéville he had
received several affectionate communications from Washington.
They had informed him, among other things, that some new
gifts had reached Mount Vernon. Among them was another
donkey for breeding purposes, a present from the king of Spain.
Washington reported of "Royal Gift," as he had named the

---

56. Calonne to Jefferson, Oct. 22, 1786, [Weaver], *Diplomatic correspondence*, III,
160–74.

57. *Ibid.*, p. 164.

58. Jefferson to Jay, Oct. 22, 1786, Lipscomb and Bergh, V, 452–53.

animal, that, though he was "fine in appearance," yet "his late royal master, tho' past his grand climacteric, cannot be less moved by female allurements than he is; or when prompted, can proceed with more deliberation and majestic solemnity to the work of procreation."[59]

Lafayette had also learned that his revered friend approved of his many recent activities. Although Washington lamented that "one man should tyrannize over millions" in Prussia and that "thousands of gallant spirits" had fallen on the battlefields that Lafayette had seen in Germany only "to satisfy . . . ambition . . . or to support their sovereigns . . . in acts of oppression or injustice," yet he believed that the reception Lafayette had received from German royalty was "as indicative of their discernment as it is of your merit." He was sorry to learn that a bad opinion of the United States prevailed in Europe. "Unhappily for us, though their accounts are greatly exaggerated, yet our conduct has laid foundation for them. It is one of the evils of democratical governments, that the people, not always seeing and frequently misled, must often feel before they can act right; but then evils of this nature seldom fail to work their own cure." Washington hoped that Congress would soon receive power from the several states to remedy some of its weaknesses. The various state legislatures were even then, he said, considering a commission to draw up trade regulations, and a general convention for correcting the defects of the confederacy was being widely talked about.[60]

Washington also approved of Lafayette's colony in Cayenne, as "a generous and noble proof" of his humanity. "Would to God a like spirit would diffuse itself generally into the minds of the people of this country; but I despair of seeing it."[61] As a token of his and his wife's affection he was sending the Lafayettes a barrel of Virginia hams. "You know the Virginia ladies

59. Washington to Lafayette, May 10, 1786, Fitzpatrick, XXVIII, 423; to Mme de Lafayette, May 10, ibid., pp. 417-19. Cf. Lafayette to Jefferson, Aug. 30, Chinard, *Lafayette and Jefferson*, p. 105.

60. Fitzpatrick, XXVIII, 421-22.

61. *Ibid.*, p. 424.

value themselves on the goodness of their bacon," and he remembered that Lafayette was fond of it. He would have sent with its "an anchor of old peach brandy" but had found none good enough.[62]

One of Mrs. Washington's hams had already been consumed three days before Lafayette acknowledged them and the several letters he had received. It had graced the Lafayette table at one of their regular Monday dinners attended largely by "Americans," of whom Chastellux was one. Perhaps the homely reminder of Virginia accounted for the nostalgic touch in Lafayette's letter of thanks. "Never, on any part of the globe, even in his own house," he stated, could he "feel himself so perfectly at home as in your family. . . . I beseech you in the name of our friendship, of that paternal concern of yours for my happiness, not to miss any opportunity to let me hear from my dear General." He then went on to give a chronicle of events in Europe. Foremost among them was the news of Calonne's recent regulation of American trade, of which he inclosed a copy. He graciously gave a good share of the credit for the committee's success to the American minister. "Mr. Jefferson is a most able and respected representative, and such a man as makes me happy to be his aid de camp."[63] And he echoed this opinion in writing to a member of Congress: "Mr. Jefferson . . . is one of the most amiable, learned, upright and able men who ever existed, and is much beloved in France for his amiable disposition and much respected for his abilities."[64]

The work of the American Committee was not yet over, however. Lafayette expected it to continue through the winter, "and," he promised, "I will endeavour to propose such measures as may be thought advantageous."[65]

BIBLIOGRAPHICAL NOTES

The originals of the correspondence of Lafayette with Lenoir are in the Archives national, AJ^{1}336 (not 526, as cited by Mathiez). Though Mathiez

62. Washington to Lafayette, June 8, 1786, *ibid.*, p. 457.

63. Oct. 26, 1786, Gottschalk, *Letters*, pp. 313–16.

64. Lafayette to McHenry, Oct. 26, 1786, *loc. cit.*

65. To Washington, Oct. 26, 1786, Gottschalk, *Letters*, p. 314.

made some errors of transcription, they are negligible, except as indicated above (n. 12). It is now possible also to date these letters more precisely than he did.

T. W. Gillard, "Lafayette, friend of the Negro," *Journal of Negro history*, XIX (1934), 358-64, tells the story of "La belle Gabrielle" but is somewhat too dependent upon inferior secondary sources.

The iconography of Lafayette is full of pitfalls. There are several "Lafayettes" that are questionably attributed. I have tried above (pp. 252-53) to cite only verifiable items.

The version in the first printing of p. 244 above has been corrected in accordance with comments upon it by M. H. Guilhamon (Lycée Victor Duruy, Mont-de-Marsan) in a letter to me dated February 6, 1952. See also G. Debien, "Les colons des Antilles et leur main d'œuvre à la fin du XVIIIe siècle," *Annales historiques de la Révolution Française*, XXVII (1955), 279-80.

CHAPTER XVIII

Benevolence and the Tsarina

UCH was wrong in the world in the years that followed the War of American Independence. Though Lafayette had begun only in recent years to be concerned about the defects of human institutions, he had long befriended their victims. Even now that he had started the dangerous habits of reading and writing, he continued to add cubits to his political stature less by taking thought than by acting as advocate in individual cases. Rather than systematic philosophy, haphazard experience, assisted by his own benevolent nature, was still his principal teacher.

Much of this experience (as we have seen) took the form of helping the weak, the oppressed, and the needy. Sometimes, however, it was nothing more than a courteous gesture in behalf of a friend seeking favors. He still continued to help more or less deserving acquaintances. The Chevalier de Barré, who claimed to have suffered hardship in the American naval service, was a subject of Lafayette's correspondence with American officials until it was finally determined that Barré had served on a French privateer and not an American warship.[1] Finding that some Frenchmen had lost property when the Americans retreated from Canada in 1776, the marquis interested himself in furthering their claim for compensation.[2] When he learned that "an orphan lady" of Martinique had lost heavily in Continental currency, he appealed to "the justice of Congress."[3] Individu-

1. [Weaver], *Diplomatic correspondence*, I, 422–32.

2. Lafayette to Franklin, Mar. 15, 1785, APS, Franklin papers, Vol. XXXIII, No. 54; Lafayette to Pierre du Calvet, Mar. 11 and 22, British Museum (London), Add. MSS 21866, fols. 38–39; Calvet to Lafayette, Apr. 1, *ibid.*, fols. 47–48.

3. Lafayette to Jay, Apr. 18, 1785, [Weaver], *Diplomatic correspondence*, I, 425 (on behalf of Mlle Thomas).

als, sometimes only slightly known to him personally, who emigrated to America in order to better their lot, received letters of introduction to his American friends.[4] When one of them, the Chevalier d'Anterroches, got into debt, he undertook to transfer credit for the young man from his family, at the same time cautioning mutual acquaintances not to lend any more.[5] He advanced money to his friend Littlepage and tended to side with him against his "protector" John Jay in the public scandal over their financial affairs.[6] He wrote letters to businessmen in America seeking favors for businessmen in France,[7] and to businessmen in France seeking favors for businessmen in America.[8] Likewise, all public servants of America found him generous, whether it was in trying to collect money due for past efforts (as in the case of C.-F.-W. Dumas, American agent at The Hague) or in getting new posts (as for Mazzei) or in raising money for new ventures (as for Paul Jones).[9]

4. Consult, e.g., index of Gottschalk, *Letters*, under "Beaune," "Chastel de la Vallée," "Doradour," "Ducher," "Duplessis," "Fontenille," "Lampert," "La Terrière," "Le Coulteux," "Lotbinière," "Sailly," and "Wengiersky"; Lafayette to Wadsworth, Feb. 10, 1786, Connecticut State Library, Trumbull collection (introducing a peddler named Eszra), May 11, *ibid.* (emigrant not named), and Oct. 8, LC, Wadsworth papers (Le Coulteux); Lafayette to Bowdoin, Aug. 1, [1786], Massachusetts Historical Society (Mme Grégoire); Mme Melin Dutartre to Franklin, Apr. 19, 1785, APS, Franklin papers, Vol. XXXIII, No. 52 (Comte de Polaresky).

5. Comtesse d'Anterroches to Franklin, June 6, 1785, APS, Franklin papers, Vol. XXXIII, No. 128; Lafayette to [General Dayton?], Feb. 8, 1787 (courtesy of S. W. Jackson); Feb. 13 (Gardner-Ball collection) and May 27, 1786 (Oberlaender collection). Cf. E. G. Pierson, "Some records of the French in Elizabethtown," *New Jersey Historical Society proceedings*, 2d ser., XIII (1895), 165 and 168.

6. Lafayette to Washington, Feb. 6, 1786, Gottschalk, *Letters*, p. 307; Washington to Lafayette, May 10, Fitzpatrick, XXVIII, 423; Littlepage to Jefferson, Sept. 12, Hayden, p. 413.

7. Cf. Nicolas Bergasse to Henri Bergasse, Feb. 21, 1786, Étienne Lamy (ed.), *Un défenseur des principes traditionnels sous la Révolution: Nicolas Bergasse, avocat au parlement de Paris, député du tiers état de la sénéchaussée de Lyon aux États-généraux (1750–1832)* (Paris, 1910), n. 39; Crèvecœur to Franklin, July 1, 1786, Mitchell, p. 149 n.

8. In addition to the merchants and ship captains already mentioned, there were Messrs. John Banister, John B. Church, John Paul Jones, Thomas Ridout, and Nathaniel Tracy; cf. Lafayette to Wadsworth, Feb. 10, 1786, *loc. cit.*; Lafayette to unknown, Feb. 26, Jackson collection; Jones to Jefferson, [ca. 1785], [R. C. Sands (ed.)], *Life and correspondence of John Paul Jones including his narrative of the campaign of the Liman: from original letters and manuscripts in the possession of Miss Janette Taylor* (New York, 1830), p. 366; J.-A. Brutails (ed.), *Inventaire du fonds de la chambre de commerce de Guienne* (Bordeaux, 1893), p. 112 (Sept. 9, 1786).

9. Lafayette to Washington, Jan. 13, 1787, Gottschalk, *Letters*, p. 319; Jones to Estaing, [August or September, 1785?], [Sands], *John Paul Jones*, p. 366; Lafayette to

The Society of the Cincinnati also continued to excite Lafayette's sentimental interest. Any French officer who felt that he had a claim to membership was likely to look to the marquis to help him establish it—usually with success.[10] Furthermore, when Major l'Enfant, having passed out the eagles of the Cincinnati in France, claimed that he could not collect payment for them and refused in turn to pay the jeweler, Lafayette helped meet the bill and waited until the society reimbursed him.[11] He was too jealous of the good name of the order to allow it to become involved in a common scandal. On the other hand, when some aristocratic members hesitated about changing the hereditary character of the French Cincinnati, Lafayette did not hedge upon his own "republican" principles. Nevertheless, he repudiated the suggestion that the society be "all abandonned," proposing at least the preservation of the badge and the annual Fourth of July meeting as "a way to renew old friendships without hurting the people and being embarrassed with the foreigners."[12]

Two large classes of society also continued to exert a special claim on Lafayette's sympathy—the French Protestants and the Negro slaves. In these philanthropies he had the loyal support of his wife. "La belle Gabrielle" especially claimed the interest of Adrienne de Lafayette. Emancipation appealed to both her heart and her religious principles, and she gradually assumed more and more responsibility for it. She entered into correspondence with the Seminary of the Saint Esprit, which had a mission in Cayenne. "Her charity was warmed by the

---

Jefferson, [February, 1786?], LC, Jefferson papers, fol. 4605; Lafayette to Jones, [1786?], Gardner-Ball collection.

10. In addition to those already mentioned, De Coste, Menonville, St. Simon, and Gimel; see Lafayette to unknown, June 4, 1785, *Yale University Library gazette: Lafayette centenary number*, VIII (1934), 146; Lafayette to Franklin, June 6, APS, Franklin papers, Vol. XXXIII, No. 129; Lafayette to Washington, May 13, 1786, Gottschalk, *Letters*, p. 299; Washington to Lafayette, May 10, Fitzpatrick, XXVIII, 424; Lafayette to Chevalier de Gimel, Jan. 30, 1787, LC, Washington papers.

11. Jefferson to Washington, Jan. 17, 1786, Fitzpatrick, XXVIII, 447 and n. 72; Lafayette to Knox, Feb. 11, Jackson collection; Washington to Jefferson, Aug. 1, Fitzpatrick, XXVIII, 505; L'Enfant to Washington, Apr. 15, 1788, Hume, *Washington's correspondence concerning the Cincinnati*, p. 328; Girodie, *Exposition du centenaire de La Fayette*, p. 49; Hume, *La Fayette and the Cincinnati*, p. 19.

12. Lafayette to Wadsworth, Feb. 10, 1786, *loc. cit.*

hope of teaching to Negroes how to know and love God, and to philosophers friendly to the Negroes how much the success of their efforts depended on religion."[13] The land belonging to the plantation was again increased by new purchases at the close of 1786,[14] and reports from "La belle Gabrielle" for a long time continued to be encouraging.

Lafayette's personal interest in the success of his experiment remained unabated as his wife's increased. He was able also to befriend individual victims of the slave system. He already had provided a religious education for one Negro lad, whom the Noailles family then had had baptized.[15] Now, when an American merchant returning home had some difficulty getting a passport for his Negro boy, Lafayette volunteered, "if he is a black and of a likely appearance," to buy him and "have him educated in my family, taking him on such terms as you think proper," so as to "rid you of the incumbrance, without exposing him to bad treatment."[16] The record does not show whether the marquis ever acquired this servant.

A gleam of hope even for French Protestants began to appear to Lafayette's benign vision in the summer of 1786. Rabaut-St. Étienne had heard that the queen was now an advocate of toleration and that she had pressed the subject warmly in her conversations with the king. The court's annual visit to Fontainebleau seemed the right moment to settle the question once and for all. Malesherbes invited Rabaut-St. Étienne to come to his château to present his case to some friends, and Lafayette took him there. Among others there were present Pierre-Louis Lacretelle, already famous as a liberal writer, and M. de Bretignières, a member of the Paris parlement who had long championed toleration. Several heartening conferences took place. But once more the champions of liberty learned that they must proceed slowly and quietly. The Baron de Breteuil personally

13. Lasteyrie, p. 208; cf. MS description of Fabius collection (Paris), carton No. I, Terres en Guyane (courtesy of Walter P. Gardner).

14. AN, T 1640, dossier 61, Lafayette.

15. S.-P. Hardy, *Mes loisirs, ou journal d'événemens tels qu'ils parviennent à ma connoissance* (Apr. 15, 1782), Bibliothèque nationale (Paris), fonds français 6684, fol. 144 (LC photostats).

16. Lafayette to Harris, Oct. 23, 1786, Jackson collection.

called on Malesherbes and elicited from him a promise not to see Rabaut again.[17] Yet Lafayette was not dismayed. The forces favoring toleration seemed to be growing. He confided to Washington, "I have great hopes to see the affairs of the Protestants in this kingdom put on a better footing, not by far as it ought to be, but much mended from the absurd and cruel laws of Lewis the fourteenth."[18] And this time he did not try to hide his bold language by cipher or subterfuge.

The cause of liberty and philanthropy continued to smoulder too, though with brightness dimmed, in other countries in which Lafayette was interested, and he continued to look upon every sign of popular action as a personal challenge. Although he hoped that "the affairs of Ireland have a chance of getting once more embroiled,"[19] the Irish were to remain temporarily quiescent. But the old conflict between Republicans and Royalists in Holland was still rife and might yet present him with an opportunity to play a heroic role. Dumas kept him informed of developments. "It is strange to see so many people, so angry, on so small a spot, without bloodshed," the marquis thought. It appeared that a favorable outcome was for the moment assured, since "the Republicans are so strong and the State Holder is such a block head."[20] Still, he felt, Dutch affairs required the attention "of all republican souls."[21] Furthermore, there was always the prospect of an American flareup with England over the frontier posts or with Spain over the Mississippi navigation, and he repeatedly reminded his American friends of his readiness to serve once more against either foe.[22]

Old causes thus appeared possible, if remote, doors to glory. Besides, new ones seemed to open readily to Lafayette's impor-

17. Rabaut-St. Étienne to Committee of Bordeaux, Feb. 12, 1788, Dardier II, 399.

18. Lafayette to Washington, Oct. 26, 1786, Gottschalk, *Letters*, p. 315.

19. Lafayette to Smith, Jan. 16, 1786, Roof, p. 143.

20. Lafayette to Washington, Oct. 26, 1786, Gottschalk, *Letters*, p. 314.

21. Lafayette to Dumas, Nov. 24, 1786, H. H. Morse (ed.), *The Lafayette letters in the Bostonian Society* ("Bostonian Society publications," N.S., Vol. IV, [1924]), pp. 164–65.

22. Cf. Lafayette to Washington, Oct. 26, 1786, Gottschalk, *Letters*, p. 314; Lafayette to Jay, Oct. 28, LC, PCC 156, fol. 452.

tunate knock. The latest scheme that he had hatched dealt with the Barbary corsairs. These Moslem seamen, dashing in and out of North African ports, long had made trade in the Mediterranean a great hazard for Christian sailors, who ran the risk not only of losing their ships and cargoes but also of ending their lives as the slaves of some Tripolitan master or as prisoners in some Moroccan dungeon. Two American vessels had been captured by Algerian corsairs in 1785 and their crews and passengers held for ransom. Adams and Jefferson had offered $200 per man, but the bey of Algiers thought Americans worth many times that. At the same time, the bey of Tripoli offered Congress peace—in return for an enormous annual tribute. This was exactly the sort of situation to rouse Lafayette's indignation. He was ready once more to gird on his sword in defense of oppressed Christians against infidel enslavers.

John Adams made this problem somewhat the official business of the marquis by requesting Jefferson to consult him upon it. Lafayette soon brought forward a proposal that years later he admitted "appeared romantic."[23] It was to create a common pool from among some of the smaller states that traded in the Mediterranean—Naples, Portugal, Rome, Venice, the Hanseatic cities—and to build a fleet for which the United States would provide the naval stores and the sailors, Naples the marines, and Malta and Sicily the naval bases. He was himself to be "chief to the Antipiratical Confederacy."[24] Adams, fearing that the Southern states would oppose expenditures for vigorous steps against the corsairs, was in favor of buying them off, but Jefferson preferred an armed patrol of the Mediterranean. Lafayette took it upon himself to urge Congress to give its ministers in Europe the authority to commit the United States to some such scheme of international action as he proposed. He also tried to interest the Swedish and Sardinian envoys.

Before anything could be done to implement Lafayette's plan, however, it was checked. As he had feared, the French govern-

23. *Mémoires*, VI, 5; Adams to Jefferson, July 3, 1786, *Works of John Adams*, VIII, 407.

24. Lafayette to Jefferson, [October, 1786], LC, Jefferson papers, fol. 9047 (incomplete version in Chinard, *Lafayette and Jefferson*, p. 101).

ment did not want him "to meddle with that war."[25] Vergennes, learning of his newest scheme, invited him to dinner and bluntly advised him to desist. His project, the minister declared, was foredoomed to failure because neither France nor her competitor England wanted an international patrol of the disputed Mediterranean. Lafayette was led to believe that the big naval powers did not object to the hardships inflicted upon smaller rivals by the corsairs so long as they were strong enough to defend themselves. Nevertheless, he felt obliged to yield. Shortly afterward he declared himself pleased with the understanding reached with the corsairs by two of his acquaintances, Thomas Barclay and Lieutenant-Colonel David S. Franks, who had been sent by the United States government to negotiate with the sultan of Morocco.[26]

Another chance to win glory had meanwhile appeared. This time opportunity took the attractive guise of the Tsarina Catherine II of Russia. The tsarina, like her contemporaries Frederick of Prussia and Joseph of Austria, was eager to appear before the world as an enlightened ruler. She kept abreast of recent literary and artistic achievements in France and the rest of western Europe by subscribing to several *nouvelles à la main* of the day, which often noted the achievements and popularity of Lafayette. Among them Baron de Grimm's *Correspondance littéraire* was the most influential. Grimm, now a sort of unofficial representative of the tsarina in Paris, had of late become one of the growing circle of Lafayette's friends among intellectuals. Lafayette soon had occasion to turn Grimm and Catherine to his service.

Among the Americans in Paris there was a young explorer named John Ledyard. Ledyard had already accompanied Captain James Cook on one of his voyages of discovery and was now contemplating new expeditions. In Paris (as we have seen) he had made the acquaintance of Lafayette just before the marquis

25. *Ibid.* See also Adams to Jefferson, July 3, 1786, *Works of John Adams,* VIII, 406–7; Lafayette to Washington, Oct. 26, Gottschalk, *Letters,* p. 315; to McHenry, Oct. 26, LC, McHenry collection; to Jay, Oct. 28, LC, PCC 156, fols. 451–52; to Washington, Jan. 13, 1787, Gottschalk, *Letters,* p. 317.

26. Sparks MSS XXXII, pp. 105–6; *Mémoires,* III, 222–23, and VI, 5; Lafayette to Washington, Jan. 13 and Feb. 7, 1787, Gottschalk, *Letters,* pp. 317 and 320.

set off for Germany in the summer of 1785. The French nobleman's liberalism intrigued the young explorer. "He has planted
a tree in America," Ledyard wrote, "and sits under it at Versailles." Ledyard considered the marquis "one of the most growing characters in this kingdom," rivaled only by Vergennes and
Jefferson for "political fame."[27] On Lafayette's return from
Germany, his relations with Ledyard became quite cordial.

Upon Jefferson's suggestion, Ledyard had begun to plan a
daring exploration. He proposed to traverse Russia and Siberia,
go by way of the Pacific to the west coast of America (then
claimed by Russia), cross the American continent from Nootka
Sound to Virginia, and eventually return to St. Petersburg to
make his report. Lafayette persuaded him not to go to Russia
directly but to wait until he was sent for. He and Jefferson
sounded out the Russian ambassador in Paris as well as Baron
de Grimm, and Grimm advanced money to Ledyard in the expectation of being reimbursed by Catherine when she approved
of the exploration. Lafayette supplemented Grimm's advance.
Meanwhile, he also spoke to Castries and Vergennes about his
intrepid friend, apparently hoping that France, too, might support the venture.[28]

This was not the first time that Lafayette, at Jefferson's in-
stigation, had approached the government on behalf of Americans interested in the arts and sciences. A few days before Ledyard's bizarre request, a less strange one had come from Lafayette to the director-general of royal buildings. It asked that
Charles Bulfinch, a young Boston architect, be given a general
pass to whatever might interest him in the French metropolis[29]
—with results that are still visible in the Capitol at Washington.

Ledyard's success was to be less conspicuous. Vergennes and
Castries hesitated to encourage his project. Meanwhile, Baron
de Grimm had proceeded to sound out the tsarina. For that purpose Jefferson had written to Lafayette a formal recommenda-

27. Ledyard to Isaac Ledyard, [1785], Sparks, *Ledyard*, p. 161.

28. Lafayette to Vergennes, Feb. 8, 1786, AAE, corr. pol., É.-U., fol. 79; Ledyard to
Isaac Ledyard, Apr. 8, Sparks, *Ledyard*, p. 165; Jefferson's "Autobiography," Lipscomb
and Bergh, I, 101–2; Lafayette to Jefferson, Aug. 2, [1786], LC, Jefferson papers, fol.
4642.

29. Lafayette to Comte d'Angivillier, Jan. 26, 1786 (courtesy of S. W. Jackson).

tion of Ledyard's project, and Lafayette had sent it to the baron, who, in turn, had forwarded it to St. Petersburg.[30] Lafayette also wrote to the French ambassador in Russia, who happened to be his friend and relative, the Comte de Ségur. Ségur eventually got a passport for Ledyard.[31] Communication between Paris and St. Petersburg, however, was slow in the days when coaches had to stop about every ten or twenty miles for a change of horses. Spring and summer came and went without word from Catherine.

Ledyard meanwhile grew more attached to Lafayette. "He is a good man, this same Marquis," he wrote. "I esteem him, and even love him, and so we all do, except some few, who worship him."[32] While waiting for an answer from Catherine, Ledyard practically had to live on Jefferson's and Lafayette's bounty. He finally went off to London, expecting to take part in what at first promised to be another exploration of the American northwest. From London he wrote acknowledging his indebtedness to "the amiable la Fayette." He promised, "If I find in my travels a mountain as much elevated above other mountains as he is above ordinary men, I will name it *La Fayette.*" He was disappointed about this American expedition, too, and it was only in December, 1786, that he finally set out for Russia and Siberia. Before he left London, he wrote to Jefferson, "I shall never wish to die while you and the Marquis are alive." And from St. Petersburg he wrote again, "I hardly know how to estimate the goodness of the Marquis de la Fayette to me, but I think a French nobleman of the first character in his country never did more to serve an obscure citizen of another than he has done for me, and I am sure that it is impossible . . . that an obscure citizen can be more grateful than I am."[33] Unfortunately, Ledyard's exploration was not approved by the tsarina, and his travels in

30. Lafayette to Vergennes, Feb. 8, 1786, *loc. cit.* Copies of Ledyard's petition, Jefferson's letter to Lafayette, Feb. 9, and Lafayette's to Grimm [Feb. 9 or 16, 1786?] are now all in the Tsentralnoye Archivnoye Upravleniye (Moscow). See also Chinard, *Lafayette and Jefferson,* pp. 90–91.

31. Ségur to Lafayette, August, 1823, Sparks, *Ledyard,* pp. 283–84.

32. To [Isaac Ledyard], Aug. 8, 1786, *ibid.,* p. 171.

33. [*Ca.* August, 1786], [*ca.* December, 1786], and March 19, 1787, *ibid.,* pp. 173, 177, and 188.

Russia ended in his unexplained arrest and expulsion in 1788. The relations of Lafayette and Catherine nevertheless seemed to improve as his friend's good fortune diminished. At almost the same time that the marquis had asked the tsarina's favor for the young explorer, Catherine sought his, also using Grimm as intermediary. Among Catherine's varied projects was included a universal dictionary. In the search for the American Indian equivalents for some of the words in the dictionary, she enlisted the aid of Lafayette. His personality and situation made him more accommodating than Catherine proved to be toward Ledyard. He immediately requested Washington to get the desired knowledge from officers and missionaries among the Indians of the Ohio country, and Franklin to do the same among the tribes along the Delaware. Both men did what they could to comply.[34] Even before the philological resources of American soldiers and clergymen could be exploited, Lafayette, using the Indian lore available to him in France, sent Catherine the first instalment of his vocabulary.[35]

Ledyard's proposed explorations and Catherine's proposed lexicon conspired to increase the Russian autocrat's interest in the French liberal. It was further piqued by the French ambassador in St. Petersburg. Ségur, who, like Lafayette, had fought in America and had become imbued with American ideals, had made a favorable impression upon Catherine, who was susceptible to bright young men. He was anxious to correct a bad impression recently left on the tsarina by the improper behavior of some young Frenchmen in Russia. Knowing her interest in "the cause of liberty if in another hemisphere,"[36] he sought permission for several heroes of the American War to come to Russia. Upon discovering that Ségur "loved and esteemed the Marquis de La Fayette," she expressed the hope that the mar-

34. Lafayette to Washington, Feb. 10, 1786, Gottschalk, Letters, pp. 310-11; Lafayette to Franklin, Feb. 10, APS, Franklin papers, Vol. XXXIV, No. 22½; Washington to Lafayette, May 10, Fitzpatrick, XXVIII, 425; Washington to Thomas Hutchins, Aug. 20, ibid., p. 525; Washington to Richard Butler, Nov. 27, ibid., XXIX, 88-89; Franklin to Lafayette, Apr. 17, 1787, Smyth, IX, 571.

35. Catherine to Grimm, Apr. 14, 1785 [1786?], Sbornik Imperatorskago Russkago Istoricheskago Obshchestva, XXIII (1878), 329.

36. Ségur, Mémoires ou souvenirs, III, 50.

quis would be among the visitors. He would be, she thought, "a highly pleasant acquaintance to make."[37]

When Lafayette learned of the tsarina's indirect invitation, he was ready to comply. Only the Barbary project, still in the wind, and the possibility that America might go to war with England seemed more attractive. Knowing that Catherine was planning to make a triumphal procession through the Crimea in 1787, he arranged for her to understand that he would accept an invitation to be one of her numerous guests during her tour. The invitation was quickly extended. Lafayette immediately made preparations to be in the Crimea in the spring. He urged his American friends to rush their plans either for a league against the pirates or for an attack upon the British posts, for, unless he found some other more interesting occupation, he intended to go to Russia as soon as the thaws set in.[38]

Something more interesting did occur, and Lafayette never became one of the celebrities who accompanied Catherine and her guest of honor, the Emperor Joseph, on her gala procession through the Crimea. Instead of paying court to Europe's two imperial crowns, Lafayette was destined to play the role of tribune in France. France was fast approaching a crisis. Prices and taxes were mounting, industrial unrest was becoming more and more threatening, land hunger was increasing, the desire for freedom from traditional restrictions and regulations was growing, resentment against legal and social inequalities was rising higher and higher, and the demand for religious liberty sounded ever louder and louder, while, at the same time, confidence in the government and the privileged élite was diminishing and the treasury deficit passed from bad to worse. The distress of the people of France and the protests of writers and reformers had already reached the point where it was commonly realized that something must be done to effect a change. What to do or how

37. Catherine to Grimm, June 20, 1785 [1786?], *Sbornik Istoricheskago Obshchestva*, XXIII (1878), 342.

38. Lafayette to Washington, Oct. 26, 1786, Gottschalk, *Letters*, p. 314; to McHenry, Oct. 26, *loc. cit.*; to Jay, Oct. 28, *loc. cit.*, fol. 452; to Wayne, Dec. 20, Historical Society of Pennsylvania, Wayne papers (incomplete version in "Notes and queries," *Pennsylvania magazine of history*, XXIX [1905], 372).

to do it was not equally well understood. Whether to diminish the control of politics by the aristocracy, granting the middle class a wider arena for its talents and influence, or to abolish the surviving feudal levies of the landlords, allowing the peasants a cheaper and less encumbered use of their lands, or to embark upon an unlimited laissez faire program, eliminating tariffs and octrois and special mercantile privileges, or to limit the power of the king and the church, recognizing the fundamental rights of man and the sovereignty of the people, were issues which had long been debated and on which there was little agreement. Members of the aristocracy—Lafayette conspicuous among them—growing more and more conscious that privileges for the few were made possible only by hardships for the many, had begun to talk like *philosophes*.

A conservative government, however, for all the good will of reforming ministers like Vergennes, Calonne, and Castries, found it hard to act effectively. The church and its devotees thought it un-Christian to extend liberty to pagan and heretic. The king, his family, and his court preferred that reform should come from the royal bounty and not be wrung by popular demand from too lenient ministers. The aristocrats were unwilling that relief should come through the increase in the taxes, the loss of the feudal income, or the surrender of the political power of the privileged classes. The bourgeoisie, anxious to pick up whatever influence the nobility might drop, were nevertheless apprehensive of an alliance with peasants and artisans to achieve their ends and were not always enamored of freedom. And, so, little was done even by a popular and well-intentioned king, although for different reasons the different groups grew increasingly insistent that something must be done.

Meanwhile, in all too human fashion, trusting that an eruption would somehow be forestalled, French court society continued to live a pleasant life on the brink of the volcano. The fall of 1786 was thus a pleasant one, in which most courtiers either ignored or misread the many hints of the fiery time ahead. For all his mounting reputation as a champion of reform, Lafayette never was more welcome at court. Time and again, he was invited by Louis XVI to dine and to play cards at the royal table.[39] Rumors began to spread that he would soon be made governor of His Majesty's dominions in the East, and it was several months before they were denied.[40]

Judging from the idyllic excitement created at Mount Vernon by some gifts of livestock, no one would have guessed that great political events likewise were brewing in the United States. One day three Maltese donkeys (one male and two females) arrived from Lafayette. They were followed shortly by some pheasants and partridges, gifts from Louis XVI's aviary sent through Lafayette's intercession, but the birds were less exhilarating since they drooped and died.[41] The donkeys, however, were destined to bear a new breed of draft and carriage animal. They were "the most valuable things you could have sent me," Washington wrote gratefully by the first vessel that passed his door.[42] In order to contradict the rumor that they were expensive gifts, he immediately offered to pay for them, but he was not permitted to do so.[43] With that humor which his relations with the Rue de Bourbon frequently evoked, Washington gave Lafayette's jackass the name "Knight of Malta," and when a fine son, combining the size and strength of the sire with the courage and activity of the dam, was born to "Royal Gift" by one of Lafayette's jennies, Washington called the offspring "Compound."[44]

For Lafayette little serious business, whether commercial or political, marred the pleasantness of that last calm autumn before France was rent asunder by stormy assemblies and conven-

39. Comte de Beauchamp, *Comptes de Louis XVI* (Paris, 1909), pp. 315, 316, and 322.

40. *Gazette de Leyde*, Nov. 24, 1786 (suppl.), and Nov. 28; *Courrier de l'Europe*, Nov. 28.

41. Washington to McHenry, Nov. 29, 1786, Fitzpatrick, XXIX, 94. Cf. *The diaries of George Washington, 1748-1799*, ed. J. C. Fitzpatrick (Boston, 1925), III, 136 (Nov. 11) and 138 (Nov. 16), 138 n. and 139 n.; Washington to Arthur Young, Dec. 4, 1788, Fitzpatrick, XXX, 151-52.

42. Washington to Lafayette, Nov. 19, 1786, Fitzpatrick, XXIX, 74.

43. Washington to McHenry, Nov. 29, 1786, *ibid.*, pp. 94-95; Washington to Lafayette, Nov. 19, *ibid.*, p. 75; Lafayette to Washington, Feb. 7, 1787, Gottschalk, *Letters*, p. 320; Washington to Lafayette, Aug. 15, Fitzpatrick, XXIX, 260.

44. Custis, *Recollections*, pp. 455-56.

tions. One of his rare letters between October, 1786, and January, 1787—breaking an otherwise almost complete and unprecedented silence of nearly three months—spoke casually of the recent trade settlement with England and the United States and of the receding prospect of war in Holland and America. It was intended chiefly, however, as another token of his loyalty to old comrades. On learning of General Greene's death, John McQueen, a mutual friend, had written from Holland stating that he would like to join with Greene's son to carry out the lumber deals which the late general had made. Lafayette not only gave that suggestion his blessing but also undertook to propose to General Anthony Wayne, who now also lived in Georgia, that he unite with McQueen and young Greene. "I don't know if you middle with commercial affairs—but this might be a temptation," he wrote. Far from suspecting the seething times ahead, he closed his letter by inviting himself "most certainly before the end of the next winter:" to Wayne's house for "some fresh punch."[45]

Lafayette's interest in Americans led him that Christmas again to show his good-natured indifference to religious nuances. He gathered from the newspapers—erroneously, it proved—that Dr. Griffith had gone to England to be consecrated bishop of Virginia. Remembering their cordial associations in the Battle of Brandywine, the huts of Valley Forge, and Mount Vernon, he wanted to be the first to congratulate Griffith; for, he thought, it would be "singular enough," if, "after you have been presented by a presbiterian plenipotentiary minister, the first American officer whose congratulatory letter reaches you is one who is himself suspected of a very strong tincture of presbiterianism."[46] It was proper that Griffith should be consecrated, he jested, since it was "a dignity to which you have been not a little prepared by our dissertations on Mrs. Washington's Bible." He now invited Griffith and his fellow-clergymen to visit him. Griffith, however, was not in England and so never

45. Lafayette to McQueen, Nov. 20, 1786, *Letters of McQueen*, pp. 10–11; to Wayne, Dec. 20, *loc. cit.*

46. Lafayette to Griffith, Dec. 25, 1786, Lafayette Memorial, Inc. (Chavaniac). The version in Brydon, "David Griffith," p. 230, has been "Englished."

availed himself of the invitation. Still, the Catholic marquis's letter to the American clergyman had a significance he probably did not appreciate. It made a striking close for his epistolary activity of the year 1786. At a time when Protestants in France were not yet civil persons, Lafayette's first letter that year had been the one addressed to the Huguenot Rabaut-St. Étienne and his last this invitation to the Episcopalian Griffith.

The final social event of the year was the wedding of the Marquis de Condorcet to Sophie de Grouchy on December 28. Lafayette was one of the groom's witnesses. The bride was a lady of great wit and charm. It was sometimes said that others were implanted in her heart more deeply than her husband, and Lafayette among them. This, however, was probably little more than a figment of romance.[47]

The next day Louis XVI announced that the Assembly of Notables would convene in February. That meant the end of the elegant, peaceful regime which had prevailed among the old aristocracy of Louis XVI's court, though few of them realized it. The Assembly of Notables had not met for one hundred and sixty years. In earlier days it had been a council of celebrities that the king sometimes consulted in preference to the even longer defunct Estates General, which had represented the people of France on a wider, if also inadequate, basis. The reason for reviving the long-dead institution was that Calonne, still striving both to retain his post and to meet the increasing demands upon the royal treasury, hoped to solve his predicament by a bold stroke. The normal expenses of an extravagant court and government had been augmented by the enormous cost of the American War, in which France had subsidized her allies as well as maintained an army and a navy that had fought victoriously all over the world. For a few years after the war the prestige of victory and an enlightened commercial policy had enabled Calonne to meet the growing deficit by loans. Lafayette and his friends could recall how pleased the court nobility had once been with Calonne's genius.[48]

47. Antoine Guillois, *La Marquise de Condorcet, sa famille, son salon, ses amis (1764–1822)* (Paris, 1897), pp. 67–68 and 71–72.

48. Ségur, *Mémoires ou souvenirs*, II, 23.

Vergennes's pacific international program had at first helped to bolster the government's shaky credit. Sometimes, however, he had had to buy peace with cash payments that added to Calonne's fiscal problems. In addition, the recent trade agreements with England and the United States had met with opposition from some quarters. At the same time, mounting difficulties in Holland, where the French supported the Republicans while the Prussians and English supported the stadholder, made it desirable to shore up the royal revenues against impending international crises.

Turgot, Necker, and other predecessors of Calonne had long ago indicated how that could be done. One of the things they had proposed was a more uniform collection of taxes whereby the privileges and exemptions of the clergy and the nobility would be circumscribed, requiring them to pay contributions corresponding more nearly to their ability to pay. That proposal, however, had during the past met in the parlements sufficient opposition to defeat it. Calonne, hoping to profit from his predecessors' experience, had now persuaded the king to circumvent the parlements and put it before an Assembly of Notables. In that way, he believed, the nobles would themselves be brought to consent to a more equitable system of taxation. Few perceived that this concession to the nobility was the first tiny leak that would soon crumble the dike of royal absolutism in France. But that it was a great event was universally recognized. Jefferson reported that it was "deemed here the most important one which has taken place in their civil line during the present century."[49]

The Notables were designated by the king from among the outstanding men of the realm—princes of the blood, prelates, marshals, peers, dukes, councilors, magistrates, provincial deputies, and municipal officers. Lafayette was named on the initial list of one hundred and forty-four members, but when it was publicly announced, he was not among them. It soon began to be rumored that he had apparently been considered either too young, too obscure, or too radical to be designated as one of the thirty-nine representatives of the nobility (other than

49. Jefferson to Edward Carrington, Jan. 16, 1787, Lipscomb and Bergh, VI, 56.

princes of the blood). He and some of his friends were naturally quite disappointed and "his ardour did not permit him to be quiet."⁵⁰ But before he could take the matter up formally, Calonne decided to drop the Marquis de Noailles, Adrienne's uncle, and to designate Lafayette in his stead. When the final list of Notables was published, Lafayette's name was among them as the last but one of the nobles.⁵¹

This awkward episode gave unfriendly observers a pretext for believing that to rid himself of Lafayette's importunities, Calonne had consented to drop the Marquis de Noailles.⁵² That it was Noailles, however, who was dropped to make room for Lafayette suggests that it was to avoid naming too many from the Noailles family that one was thus substituted for the other. Those who sought an ulterior motive did not know or chose to forget that at this moment there were few men who enjoyed the king's respect more or were more regularly in attendance at court than Lafayette. On January 16 he played cards with the king for the fourth time in about ten weeks.⁵³ In some quarters it was even believed that he would be altogether too docile a follower of royal policy in the Assembly of Notables.⁵⁴

That Lafayette's name should have been put on, taken off, and then put on again struck even his friends as having some sinister significance. "This shows," Jefferson surmised, "that his character here is not considered as an indifferent one, and that it excites agitation." But Jefferson hoped that the event would pass without crisis.⁵⁵ And a contemporary journalist de-

50. Rochambeau to Washington, May 12, 1787, quoted in L. M. Sears, "George Washington and the French Revolution—the first phase," *Essays in honor of William E. Dodd*, ed. A. O. Craven (Chicago, 1935), p. 21 and n.; *Mémoires*, II, 191 n.

51. APS, Breck MSS, pp. 65–67; Charles Breck, "Samuel Breck," *Memorial biographies of the New England Historic Genealogical Society*, V (1894), 104; *Courrier de l'Europe*, Jan. 16, 1787, p. 35; *Gazette de Leyde*, Jan. 29, 1787; Lafayette to Washington, Jan. 13, 1787, Gottschalk, *Letters*, p. 318; *Procès-verbal de l'Assemblée de Notables, tenue à Versailles en l'année MDCCLXXXVII* (Paris, 1788), p. 11.

52. "Lafayette jugé par le Comte d'Espinchal," *Revue retrospective*, XX (1894), 294–95; Allonville, I, 225; Bachaumont, XXXIV, 184–85 (Feb. 21, 1787); Marquis de Clermont-Gallerande, *Mémoires particuliers pour servir à l'histoire de la révolution qui s'est opérée en France en 1789* (Paris, 1826), I, 20–21; Bertrand de Moleville, IX, 333–34.

53. Beauchamp, p. 322.

54. Bachaumont, XXXIV, 184–85 (Feb. 21, 1787) and 301 (Mar. 19).

55. Jefferson to Carrington, Jan. 16, 1787, Lipscomb and Bergh, VI, 56.

clared, "The king could certainly have made no choice that was more applauded than that of a lord who has devoted the finest period of his life to the defense of the rights of man and the citizen and whose generosity equals his valor."[56] Obviously, whether Calonne's final preference for Lafayette over his uncle was dictated by Lafayette's clamor, his hope of winning Lafayette's vote among the Notables, or his desire to court popular favor, the choice was a carefully studied one.

Lafayette's personal triumph in being chosen a member of the Assembly of Notables was all the greater because he was the youngest man among them, except for one who served ex officio.[57] It necessitated, however, dropping the quest for glory elsewhere. He now had to inform the Comte de Ségur that he would not be able to go to Russia in the spring. The tsarina made no effort to hide her disappointment. Over a year later she still let Grimm understand that "if the Marquis de La Fayette were to come, he would be welcome,"[58] and John Paul Jones, then an admiral in her service, assured Lafayette that if he came and paid his "court once more to Bellona," he could be sure that he would be received "as her favorite."[59] But by that time Lafayette was incensed by her unexplained treatment of Ledyard, which he described as "illiberal and narrow minded" and "particularly ungenerous."[60] And as time wore on, Catherine changed her mind about Lafayette. He was soon to become notorious for bringing revolutionary American ideas to the European continent and, since that was uncomfortably close to home, Catherine came to look upon him as a rebel and a criminal.[61]

BIBLIOGRAPHICAL NOTES

The letters of Catherine II to Grimm have been published in Volume XXIII of the collections of the Imperial Russian Historical Society by Ya.K. Grot in French mixed with occasional German (as she wrote them). Ségur's *Mémoires* provide an excellent background for them.

56. *Ma correspondance*, No. 6, p. 47 (Feb. 9, 1787).

57. Jefferson to Carrington, Jan. 16, 1787, Lipscomb and Bergh, VI, 56.

58. *Sbornik Istoricheskago Obshchestva*, XXIII, 345. Cf. pp. 433–34 and 450.

59. June 26, 1788, [Weaver], *Diplomatic correspondence*, VII, 384.

60. Sparks, *Ledyard*, p. 288.   61. Ségur, *Mémoires ou souvenirs*, III, 49–50.

Guillois's biography of the Marquise de Condorcet, unfortunately inadequately footnoted, is about the only reliable source on her relations with Lafayette.

The caution that has already been expressed with regard to the memoirs of Espinchal must be extended also to Allonville's.

With regard to the *Mémoires secrets*, it should be recalled that they were continued after Bachaumont's death by others, who were even less critical of their sources than he had been.

Sparks's *Ledyard* is an excellent biography. Unfortunately his sources are not always indicated and it may be taken for granted that he "doctored" the texts of the letters he quotes (as was his wont). K. Munford, *John Ledyard: an American Marco Polo* (Portland, [Ore.], 1939), and Helen Augur, *Passage to glory: John Ledyard's America* (New York, 1946), add nothing to our knowledge of Ledyard's relations with Lafayette.

CHAPTER XIX

The Council of "Not Ables"

ALLING together a round gross of distinguished gentlemen to discuss a change in the royal fiscal system
could hardly be regarded as a throne-shaking decision.
Nor need it have been if the throne had not already been under-
mined. The Assembly of Notables was to reveal unmistakably
what many had already suspected—that the very groups which
benefited most from the system of aristocratic privilege and
should have been most tightly united to preserve it were in
fact sharply divided.

That division was only in small part due to the seepage of reform ideas to aristocratic levels. Many of the nobility were unaffected by the *philosophes*, and to those who had been
affected, the evils of society appeared not so deeply imbedded
but that a few reforms in favor of the middle class and the
oppressed would suffice to remove them. If the nobles did not
rally to the support of the monarchy before it was attacked by
overwhelming forces, it was because they were themselves
opponents of absolutism. They were *Frondeurs*, spiritual and
biological descendants of the seventeenth-century aristocrats
who had fought the civil war known as "the Fronde" against the
court of the infant Louis XIV. As they read the history of
France, the good old days were the ones before the Bourbons had
subordinated the feudal lords and centralized a governmental
system in which the local aristocracy had once been strong.
These gentlemen did not intend to yield their remaining privileges in return for nothing. If they were going to surrender tax
exemptions, it would be only in return for a more formal voice
in the government of France. Lafayette understood this line of
reasoning only when it was too late.[1]

1. Lafayette to M. d'Hennings, Jan. 15, 1792, *Mémoires*, III, 224–26.

An assembly controlled by the upper estates was no new demand of the French aristocracy. Since the days when Louis XIV's predecessors had suppressed the Estates General and the Assembly of Notables and subdued the parlements, France had been an absolute monarchy. The king, to be sure, had generously distributed emoluments, distinctions, and offices among the nobility and they still ruled France, but now it was only as his agents speaking with royal authority. There were those—especially since the time of Montesquieu—who thought that a system of legislation and judicial review largely controlled by the aristocracy would be the best check on absolutism. In several quarrels over new royal decrees during the eighteenth century the parlements had maintained that France had a fundamental law by which even the king was bound and which could be changed only by popular will. More and more, they used the phrase "the Estates General," although the thing itself had been defunct since 1615.

Louis XVI knew that it was dangerous to call together a body of men who might utter that phrase in unison. He also knew that if they did utter it, they would mean by it an assembly representing the three estates of France—the Clergy, the Nobility, the Commoners—organized along the historical lines that guaranteed control to the aristocracy. He ran the risk, therefore, of adding to the parlements' demands for an Estates General of that description the similar demands of the new Notables. It was not, as events proved, a negligible risk, but it was a carefully calculated one. It seemed better to run that risk than to make fundamental reforms by royal decree, which, as long experience showed, would be challenged by the parlements, who would win popular and possibly violent support. It also seemed better to run that risk than to call the Estates General directly. Perhaps it might prove unnecessary to call the Estates General at all. So the first minced step was taken toward a public admission that the king must consult the general will if he contemplated a serious change in the fiscal structure, in the hope that bolder steps might thereby be precluded.

Thus Frenchmen became divided into three distinct groups. The first was the court party, which meant to maintain royal absolutism by making unavoidable concessions and no more, meanwhile manipulating the other two groups so as to win support from each against the other. The second was the aristocratic party, which hoped to profit from public repugnance to arbitrary power by obliging the monarch to return, part of the way at least, toward an ancient decentralization. And, finally, there was a nascent popular party—sometimes called "the Americans" and sometimes "the Patriots"—who looked to the "laws of Nature and of Nature's God" for inspiration. As France waited for the Notables to assemble, La Rochefoucauld wrote to Franklin: "I speak often of America with Mssrs Jefferson and Mazzei, and especially with the Mis de La fayette, with whom I have, since your departure, contracted a very intimate relationship which pleases me more every day, and I see with interest and pleasure that, although your states do not always do as well as possible, they nevertheless often win the right to serve as models for Europe and to restore the full lustre, sometimes on one point and sometimes on another, of the rights of mankind."[2]

The prospect of an Assembly of Notables roused conflicting expectations. Lafayette reflected them when he notified Washington that he was a member of the assembly. He recognized that the king's purpose was nothing more ambitious than a mere discussion of the most patently needed concessions—"an examination of the finances to be adjusted, of the means to alleviate the taxes of the people, and of many abuses to be redressed." He understood, too, that the government's motive in permitting this mere discussion without authority to act was "at bottom a desire to make monney some how or other, in order to put the receipt on a level with the expenses." Nevertheless, he himself had a program in mind that would have shocked the king and many among the Notables, had they known it. The unbalanced budget of France, he believed, was due to "the sums squandered on courtiers and superfluities" (forgetting the great cost to the French treasury of the American War). That belief made him an advocate of economy as well as of tax reform. He had in mind, however, a program that was more than fiscal. "My

2. Feb. 14, 1787, APS, Franklin papers, Vol. XXXV, No. 16.

earnest wish and fond hope is that our meeting will produce popular assemblées in the provinces, the destruction of many schlakles of the trade, and a change in the fate of the Protestants." Nor did he intend to be satisfied merely with idle discussion of these abuses. He proposed to promote them into actualities "by my friends as well as my feeble endeavours with all my heart."

Freedom of trade and toleration for Protestants had long formed part of Lafayette's program. Local assemblies had become of interest to him only recently. But all three principles together, no matter how much they would have shocked king or Notables, did not constitute a republican program even when joined to protests against court squandering. Lafayette, although much more aware of the shortcomings of monarchy than some, even among the *philosophes*, and although much more ready to improve the lot of the middle and lower classes and of minorities than most of his peers, was still a monarchist. The best reformers, in his opinion, were enlightened rulers. "There was no way more patriotic, more candid, more noble to effect those purposes," he declared, than through the calling of an Assembly of Notables. "The king and M. de Calonne his minister deserve great credit for that—and I hope a tribute of gratitude and good will shall reward this popular measure." He proposed to keep Washington informed of the Notables' doings, "not only because what concerns me cannot be stranger to my dear General, but also because every thing is interesting which influences the happiness of 26 millions of people."[3]

Colonel Smith, now John Adams' son-in-law as well as secretary, also was the recipient of the marquis's confidences on the new departure in French politics. Lafayette took an obvious delight in imagining Adams' surprise "that we turn out such republicans as to have assemblies." This delight was tempered, however, by the realization that the Notables were not a thoroughgoing representative body; "but such as it is, I confess I would not have fore told it twelve months ago."[4]

Smith and Adams were not indifferent to Lafayette's elation

3. Jan. 13, 1787, Gottschalk, *Letters*, p. 318.
4. Lafayette to Smith, Jan. 16, 1787, De Windt collection; cf. Roof, pp. 142–43.

over French affairs. Yet they were probably more interested in his reactions to some startling new developments in the United States. Congress, they had all recently learned, was raising a federal army in Massachusetts. This step had been taken the preceding October ostensibly out of fear of an Indian war. Reports of it arrived in France, however, at the same time as the first accounts of an uprising of Massachusetts taxpayers and debtors that was soon to become known as "Shays' Rebellion." The two events did not appear merely coincidental. Lafayette's sympathies were against the rebels in this instance. After all, they were not rebelling against England, and that made a great difference. He was not so heated in his scorn as Mrs. Adams, whose spelling got worse than usual as she fumed against them.[5] Neither was he quite so philosophical as Jefferson, who took this occasion to remark that "a little rebellion, now and then, is a good thing, and as necessary in the political world as storms in the physical."[6]

Yet Lafayette too wished the American government to be circumspect in its treatment of the rebels. He preferred that the proposed Continental force should be used not against misguided citizens, but against foreign enemies in the effort to achieve that destiny of the United States which was already manifest to him. "I hope the banner of liberty shall be, thank God, planted from the Eskimaux country down to Cape Horn," he wrote Smith. "I know that business is the very thing for me, and there is no doubt but what English men must have a dance in Canada before we go to Mass with the Spaniards."[7] In fact, he had already requested Washington to count on him and Smith in case of war with England.[8]

Yet the marquis could not help fearing that Congress' real purpose was "to middle with the riots in New England." That, he felt, would be unfortunate. "I trust more to the exertions of each [state] governement, and the good sense of the people, than to any Continental measure in this business."[9] He did not doubt

5. A. Adams to Jefferson, Jan. 29, 1787, LC, Jefferson papers, fols. 4761–62.
6. Jefferson to Madison, Jan. 30, 1787, Lipscomb and Bergh, VI, 65.
7. Jan. 16, 1787, *loc. cit.*   8. Jan. 13, 1787, Gottschalk, *Letters*, p. 319.
9. Lafayette to Smith, Jan. 16, 1787, *loc. cit.*

"the disposition of the people to put things to right when the evil is demonstrated to them." Meanwhile, however, premature action by Congress might "arm the people against foederal ideas." What bothered him still more was the injury that internal dissension would cause to the foreign prestige of the Americans. "They hurt their consequence in Europe to a degree that is very distressing, and what glory they have gained by the Revolution, they are loosing by little and little."[10]

With one eye trained on the critical situation in America, Lafayette was no less aware that what was simultaneously taking place in France was also critical. He found himself in a difficult position, championing the American ideal of local freedom for France and the French ideal of centralized government for America. To Americans he appeared French—the only foreigner, to be sure, who could be trusted in these times of European intrigue in America but a foreigner none the less.[11] To Europeans he appeared romantically American. A young German officer who visited his home felt as if he were "in America rather than Paris." The marquis's guests were Englishmen or Americans or *philosophes*. He spoke English almost as readily as French, though Gallicisms still crept into his speech and writing. His children also spoke a halting English, and he taught them to sing the war songs he had learned in America. Young Kayenlaha, dressed in native costume and calling Lafayette "Father," served him as a page.[12] Peter Otsiquette, the half-breed Oneida warrior, had by this time come from America and now also formed a part of his household.

And so Lafayette's reputation as an "American" grew—with all the revolutionary undertones carried by that word in the days when the United States stood in a monarchic world for a new kind of middle-class democratic philosophy. Few had as much reason to understand this portent as Thomas Jefferson. Lafayette's character, he noted, excited agitation in certain quarters in France: "His education in our school has drawn on him a

10. *Ibid.* and Lafayette to Washington, Jan. 13, 1787, Gottschalk, *Letters*, p. 319.

11. Cf. Rufus King to Elbridge Gerry, Nov. 5 1786, Burnett, VIII, 496–97.

12. Xavier de Schonberg to his mother, Jan. 14, 1787, Agénor Bardoux, *Études sociales et politiques: la jeunesse de La Fayette, 1757–1792* (Paris, 1892), pp. 193–94; Lafayette to Smith, Jan. 16, 1787, *loc. cit.* See below, p. 434 and n. 8.

very jealous eye from a court whose principles are the most absolute despotism."[13] Although the young man had "a great deal of sound genius" and was "well remarked by the King, and rising in popularity," he had against him "the suspicion of republican principles."[14] Still, Jefferson thought that Lafayette's difficulties at court would pass. "The King, who is a good man, is favorably disposed towards him, and he is supported by powerful family connections and by the public good will."[15] Despite the doubt regarding his political principles, Lafayette would "one day be of the ministry." What seemed to Jefferson more likely to stand in the marquis's way was another weakness. "His foible is a canine appetite for popularity and fame," but this, too, Jefferson thought, the marquis would "get above" as he grew more experienced.[16]

The American envoy, though he looked upon France as a "government of wolves over sheep,"[17] did not understand, for all his political astuteness, that the time had come when an ambitious young man would find it hard to enjoy both popularity and a ministerial post. He did not yet realize that Lafayette had embarked upon a journey that was soon to come to a fork in the road. On the one hand, it would lead to the ministry and, on the other, to popular acclaim. The traveler would have to choose which fork to take. Lafayette's "republican principles" would make the choice inevitable but not easy.

The Assembly of Notables was to have met in January, 1787, but the illness of three of the king's ministers led to its postponement. Vergennes was one of them, and he never arose from his sickbed. When he died, Lafayette suffered a great personal loss. Without ever having been friendly to republican ideas, Vergennes had nevertheless, in his effort to rebuild French prestige, played the role of a godfather to the American Revolution. His wisdom, experience, and political skill were to be sorely missed in the trying times ahead. Perhaps, if he had lived, reform might have been achieved by timely concessions rather

13. Jefferson to Carrington, Jan. 16, 1787, Lipscomb and Bergh, p. 56.
14. Jefferson to Madison, Jan. 30, 1787, *ibid.*, p. 70.
15. Jefferson to Carrington, Jan. 16, 1787, *ibid.*, p. 56.
16. Jefferson to Madison, Jan. 30, 1787, *ibid.*, p. 70. See p. 108 above.
17. *Ibid.*, p. 65.

than by revolutionary compulsion. His exit left Jefferson as Lafayette's chief political adviser in France, and Jefferson was neither so oblique nor so cautious as Vergennes would have been.

While waiting for the Notables to assemble, Lafayette became a little less hopeful of them. The public, it proved, was somewhat amused by the new venture in politics. Enough puns circulated about the Notables, Jefferson found, "to make a larger volume than the Encyclopédie,"[18] and "wicked people," Lafayette informed Washington, called them "*not able.*" The marquis's expectations by this time had been modified in one important regard. They still included local assemblies and freedom from internal duties, but he now doubted whether the assembly would take up the matter of religious toleration. "The reclamations of the clergy and a bigoted party," he apprehended, "might hurt the business." What the Notables would not advise, however, the king might ordain, if he were not swayed by opposing intrigues and complaints; for public opinion in general, Lafayette maintained, was in favor of greater toleration, and the majority of the clergy, if they were not obliged to express themselves in an open assembly, would not object. That was not the democratic way to proceed, he recognized, but "since we have the inconveniences of power, let us in this instance have the benefits of it."[19]

As Lafayette waited for the chance to help his countrymen toward greater freedom, he received reports from America indicating that there at least the onward march of liberty was steady. The disturbances in New England were subsiding, he was informed, and a convention at Annapolis of delegates from five states had suggested a federal convention to consider revision of the Articles of Confederation in the interests of a more effective, centralized government. Both developments filled him with satisfaction. "May every Americans know the blessings of their own Constitutions," he prayed, "and from comparison, judge that if they are to correct, it would be madness in them to destroy! . . . Each state has within itself the means

18. Jefferson to Richard Peters, Feb. 26, 1787, *ibid.*, p. 100.
19. Feb. 7, 1787, Gottschalk, *Letters*, p. 320.

fully sufficient to set to rights the opinions of mistaken citizens
—and those means seem to me principally founded on the good
sense, knowledge, and patriotic liberality of the people. Every
wrong measure of theirs would hurt not only the consequence of
the United States, but also the cause of liberty in all part of the
world."[20]

After a suitable postponement on account of Vergennes's
death, the Assembly of Notables prepared to hold its first meeting. Lafayette was invited by the king to take up his residence
at the royal château of Versailles, one of only twenty-two
gentlemen so honored. The less favored Notables found lodgings elsewhere.

The opening of the assembly took place in the Hôtel des
Menus Plaisirs at eleven o'clock on the morning of February 22.
With more than the usual pomp that every public appearance
of the king demanded, the Notables listened respectfully and
ceremoniously to the address from the throne. Lafayette found
himself seated at one of the two benches set aside for nobles
sans rang (that is to say, neither princes nor peers) to the left of
the king.[21] The assembly remained standing, and the ushers and
heralds knelt as His Majesty spoke. The king's speech indicated,
as had been expected, that he wanted a more equitable distribution of taxes, greater freedom of internal commerce, and relief for his most indigent subjects. Then, amid much bowing and
kneeling, the royal keeper of the seals received and announced
the king's permission for the assembly to be seated. Out of the
goodness of his heart, Louis XVI also allowed the ushers and
heralds to rise, though strict etiquette required that they stay
on their knees all through a royal session.[22] Then the keeper of
the seals made a speech urging the Notables to co-operate in the
king's endeavors.

Calonne's turn came next. He set forth at considerable
length what he thought to be the core of the nation's difficulties:
the annual deficit in the royal treasury. That deficit had reached

20. Lafayette to Jay, Feb. 7, 1787, [Weaver], *Diplomatic correspondence*, I, 449–50.

21. *Procès-verbal de l'Assemblée de Notables tenue à Versailles en l'année MDCCLXXXVII* (Paris, 1788), diagram between pp. 38 and 39.

22. *Ibid.*, p. 52.

37,000,000 livres at the end of 1776, he said. Since that time, largely because of the "national war," it had been necessary to borrow 1,250,000,000 livres. While a prosperous nation of around 25,000,000 people could stand such a debt, the accumulated deficit showed every prospect of becoming worse before it could be expected to become better. All palliatives had been tried and either were insufficient or had been exhausted of their possibilities for good. Only one remedy remained. That was to abolish "abuses."

By "abuses," Calonne then made apparent, he did not mean so much the seignorial survivals still burdening the peasants or the special privileges still enjoyed by the clergy and aristocracy. Rather, he meant the commercial and financial prerogatives of certain groups and areas in the kingdom—"in short, whatever interferes with production, whatever diminishes the sources of credit, whatever makes revenues insufficient, and all the unnecessary expenditures that absorb them."[23] Nevertheless, he set forth a program of reform that must have seemed to many of his listeners extreme and to Lafayette encouraging—local assemblies in which all the propertied should be represented, a uniform land tax in place of the existing uneven ones, freedom of trade in grain, amelioration of the *corvée* (the commoners' obligation to work or pay for workers on government projects), and the abolition of internal customs frontiers. Probably no part of Calonne's long speech won his hearers' approval more than his eulogy of Louis XVI as "a young, virtuous king, who had no other desire than to achieve the welfare of his subjects who adore him" and who, having at last brought about peace inside and outside his realm, found it "possible to think of reforming what is vicious in the constitution."[24] The magistrate and the bishop who arose to speak on behalf of the Notables when Calonne was done re-echoed this note of gratitude to an enlightened monarch.

It immediately became obvious, however, that the king's enlightment did not extend to approval of rule by unhampered majority, even if a majority of hand-picked Notables. The keeper of the seals now announced that the Assembly of No-

23. *Ibid.*, p. 73. 24. *Ibid.*, p. 75.

tables would meet not as a single body but in seven bureaus, or committees, each under one of the seven princes of the blood. Lafayette found himself assigned to the Second Bureau, presided over by the younger of the king's two brothers, the Comte d'Artois, destined in future years to become Charles X of France. He was named ninth of the twenty-two members of that bureau, last of the prelates and nobles but ahead of the magistrates and representatives of the provinces and cities. This division into bureaus, whether such was its purpose or not, made it possible for a minority of higher aristocrats to veto any action of the Notables. Since ten or eleven Notables would form the majority within each bureau, and four bureaus would form a majority of the assembly, forty-four votes would be enough to veto radical proposals even if the remaining hundred favored them.[25]

The next day a joint session of the Notables was presided over by the elder of the king's brothers, the Comte de Provence. Here the nobles *sans rang* sat in front of the king's brothers, about halfway between the princes and peers above them and the clergy, civil officers, magistrates, provincial and municipal deputies below.[26] The meeting was devoted entirely to the reading of detailed memoirs on Calonne's proposals of the preceding day. When the Notables adjourned, it was understood that they would thereafter meet regularly in bureaus.

Had there been a disposition on the part of the Notables to sacrifice their own privileges for the national welfare, Calonne's program might have somewhat ameliorated the abuses that were all too soon to lead to impatience and violence. Only a small group among them, however, understood that reform is sometimes no less necessary to prevent revolution than surgery to prevent gangrene. Lafayette was one of the few who were prepared to make the necessary sacrifices. His bureau was presided over by a prince who was rapidly to win notoriety as a leader of the most reactionary court party. The Duc de Laval,

25. Cf. Jefferson to Lafayette, Feb. 28, 1787, Chinard, *Lafayette and Jefferson*, p. 109; Condorcet, *Essai sur la constitution et les fonctions des assemblées provinciales* in *Œuvres*, VIII (Paris, 1847), 372; and Paine, pp. 337-38.

26. *Procès-verbal*, diagram between pp. 94 and 95.

once a guest at Washington's headquarters, sat on one side of
the marquis and, on the other, the ambitious councilor of
state, Laurent de Villedeuil. Loménie de Brienne, the enlightened and intriguing archbishop of Toulouse, was the first member of the bureau, and after him came the Bishop of Langres,
who was a worthy relative of Malesherbes. The presence of
these liberal or aspiring figures gave the Second Bureau more
than its share of prominence.

Lafayette zealously attended the frequent meetings of his
bureau. The first subject discussed was the problem of local assemblies. It soon became clear that Calonne's indifference to the
preservation of the traditional three estates in the proposed
provincial assemblies so long as all the propertied were represented was not shared by the Notables. The Second Bureau
proved one of the most liberal. It advocated elective provincial
assemblies in which, though the three estates should remain
distinct, the Third Estate, representing the commoners, should
have more than half the total membership. The distribution of
membership among the three estates was to become a sore
point. It inevitably raised the question of how the provincial assemblies were to vote, for obviously there would be small advantage to the commoners in the greater number of their
deputies if majority decisions in the Third Estate could be
vetoed by unfavorable majorities in the two smaller ones. The
Second Bureau also proposed that members of the provincial
estates be chosen by voters who qualified for the franchise by a
certain tax payment rather than by a certain income, thus
allowing more people to vote. Moreover, it was proposed to
make the new provincial assemblies an effective public instru-
ment by granting them enough power to restrict the local royal
intendants. Lafayette made several cautious comments in the
bureau in favor of this program. Although he conceded that "a
monarchy ought not to be exclusively popular," he did not intend, if he could help it, that the provincial assemblies should be
mere puppets of either king or aristocracy.[27]

27. "Procès-verbaux du Second Bureau de l'Assemblée des Notables 1787," Bibliothèque de l'Arsenal (Paris), MS 3978, fol. 150. Cf. ibid., fols. 37, 38, 42, 45, 49, 50,
57, 59, 94, 108, and 160. See also Pierre Renouvin, Les assemblées provinciales (Paris,

The bureau next considered the problem of taxation. Lafayette, apparently becoming more accustomed to debate, expressed emphatic dissatisfaction with some parts of the existing system, and at length. A discerning observer might have detected the future revolutionary in him. At the eighth meeting (March 6) he was appointed one of the five members of a committee on the *taille* (tax on servile lands), the grain trade, and the *corvée*. This committee's proposals were submitted to the bureau at the next meeting. They recommended that the *taille* be lowered and (except for laborers) equalized and that, if the reduced revenue be found insufficient for the king's charitable and other purposes, it be left to the contemplated provincial assemblies to take the proper measures. They also suggested that the *corvée* be abolished, leaving the building of bridges and roads to the provincial assemblies or, in the frontier provinces, to the royal commandants. At the tenth session of the bureau (March 10) further suggestions for the efficient administration of the *taille* and its use for local relief were discussed and approved. The committee's indorsement of the royal plan for abolishing some of the restrictions on the grain trade was likewise adopted, with thanks to the king for his "wisdom and philanthropy" in formulating it. So were the committee's recommendations on the *corvée*. The bureau thus manifested a generous intention to alleviate some of the distress of the poor without increasing onerously the burden of the rich.[28]

The Notables were called together again as a single body on March 12, the Comte de Provence presiding. Again Calonne held forth. He congratulated the bureaus on their recommendations and promised that His Majesty would weigh them all carefully. Every bureau, however, had made some criticism of his plans. In general, the Notables had not only thought his proposed tax system impractical but had also questioned the accounts he had presented and had demanded further informa-

---

1921), pp. 83–87; *Mémoires*, II, 191 n.; A. Goodwin, "Calonne, the Assembly of French Notables of 1787 and the origins of the 'révolte nobiliaire,'" *English historical review*, LXI (1946), 343.

28. "Procès-verbaux du Second Bureau," *loc. cit.*, fols. 254, 273, 405, 438–40, and 502; MS minutes of the Second Bureau, AN, C2, liasse 4.

tion. Although Calonne could not have been ignorant of this growing opposition, he chose to ignore it. He went on, instead, to make new proposals. This time the fiscal privileges of certain localities of France were the object of his attack.[29]

The minister's cavalier dismissal of the Notables' criticisms, however, created new irritation. His reform program was now largely forgotten, the bureaus spending the next few days protesting against his having implied a greater approval of his proposals than in fact existed. Each of them drew up a request to the king that its disapproval be recorded in the formal minutes of the assembly. The protest of the Second Bureau was briefer but no less incisive than those of the others. It stated simply that, lest agreement with the comptroller-general be inferred, "it is important to the Notables that their sentiments be transmitted in their entirety to the king, the nation, and posterity."[30] The action of the bureaus was a signal rebuke to Calonne. Although the proceedings of the Notables were supposedly secret, he suffered greatly in the public eye. There grew up a feeling, which had frustrated other reform ministers in the past, that he was trying to ram through a new fiscal policy without due regard for the rights of the nation.

At first Lafayette did not join the hue and cry against Calonne. The impression spread abroad that he was one of the military figures in the assembly who, having distinguished themselves in the American War, had become so imbued with respect for discipline that they were blindly submissive. But another explanation seems more probable. The protests of the bureaus were directed against the status quo only in the interest of the aristocracy. Lafayette's support of Calonne while others raised their voices against him indicated merely that he had his doubts about the motives of those who attacked the minister.[31]

The rumor about his submissiveness must have bothered

29. *Procès-verbal*, pp. 136–218.

30. *Ibid.*, p. 220.

31. Bachaumont, XXXIV, 272 (Mar. 19, 1787); M. de Lescure (ed.), *Correspondance sécrète inédite sur Louis XVI, Marie Antoinette, la cour et la ville, de 1777 à 1792* (Paris, 1866), II, 119 (Mar. 18); A. Sayous (ed.), *Mémoires et correspondance de Mallet du Pan pour servir à l'histoire de la Révolution française* (Paris, 1851), I, 139. Cf. *Mémoires*, II, 191 n.

Lafayette less than another that circulated at about the same time. Word had come from the provinces that the Comte de Simiane had just committed suicide, and gossip in Paris society had it that he had done so in a fit of jealousy of Lafayette.[32] Jefferson apparently believed the rumor. He was in doubt, he wrote Short, "whether to condole with, or to congratulate, the Marquis on the death of M. de ————." But, traveling in the Midi at the time and finding the weather much more to his liking than that of Paris, he concluded that "the man who shoots himself in the climate of Aix must be a bloody minded fellow indeed."[33]

The Notables meanwhile continued their debates relentlessly. The question of customs duties was now under discussion. Lafayette began to think again of the possibility of making American commerce a matter of public concern. Not content merely with presenting his views to his fellow-Notables, he called the new foreign minister's attention to the need for better enforcement of Calonne's regulations and requested Lenoir and William Short (since Jefferson was still touring southern France) to second his efforts.[34] He was also at least partly responsible for a recent work entitled *De la France et des États-Unis, ou de l'importance de la révolution d'Amérique pour le bonheur de la France.*[35] It was by a well-known financier named Étienne Clavière, assisted by the young writer who had already attracted Lafayette's attention, Brissot de Warville. This book analyzed Lafayette's memoir on the tobacco farm at length. It showed so detailed a knowledge of the discussions in the American Committee as to lead to the suspicion that it was furnished by Lafayette himself. Amid glowing praise for the marquis's trade

32. Bachaumont, XXXIV, 259 (Mar. 14, 1787); Espinchal, *Journal*, p. 222; *Lettre d'un correcteur des comptes à M. le Marquis de L[a] F[ayette]* (Paris, [*ca*. May, 1787]), Jackson collection.

33. Mar. 27, 1787, "Letters of Thomas Jefferson to William Short," *William and Mary College quarterly historical magazine*, 2d ser., XI (1931), 246. See p. 108 above.

34. Lafayette to Montmorin, Mar. 17, 1787, AAE, corr. pol., É.-U., Vol. XXXII, fol· 228; Lafayette to Short, [Mar. 21, 1787], LC, William Short papers.

35. Clavière in *Reflexions addressées à l'Assemblée nationale*, etc. (Nov. 19, 1790), p. 25, gives the date of publication as March 20, 1787. The place of publication was given in the original edition as London, but that was probably to deceive the French censors. More likely it was Paris.

proposals, the authors felt called upon to "stop for a moment and contemplate the new and affecting spectacle" of a "young and generous Frenchman" giving his attention to such matters, and they offered him "the homage of that peaceful philosophy which never admired any thing in military exploits but the only praise worthy end, that of favouring liberty, and with it the progress of light and reason."[36]

So far Lafayette had done little that was startling in the Second Bureau. On March 20 (sixteenth session), acting as a Breton, he read without comment a statement by the Notables from Brittany formally recording their intention to preserve intact their local rights and privileges. As a province that had come into the French monarchy only by a marriage contract, Brittany was one of the most privileged, and its deputies wanted it understood that they had no authority to adopt any changes. If Lafayette's noncommittal behavior on this occasion had any import, it was apparently in support of the status quo. Nor was there any greater significance in his brief comment the next day regarding customs duties collected at Bordeaux.[37]

This uncharacteristic restraint is in part explained by a siege of illness. Winter, hard work, loss of sleep, and, presumably, the scandal over M. de Simiane's death had collected their toll in the form of an illness that suggests tuberculosis. His chest hurt, he coughed, he lost weight. His family was greatly alarmed. "I am a woman," wrote Mme de Tessé to Jefferson, "and so my interest in public affairs is subordinated, overwhelmed by my private interests. I have seen in the assembly nothing but a source of calamity, and for a week, I have had no other wish than to see it end." But her illustrious nephew was apparently better by the end of March, and Mme de Tessé "once more became a good citizen."[38]

It was not until March 28 that the marquis gave further indication that he was to become one of the few stormy petrels of

36. Clavière and Brissot, *Considerations on . . . France and the United States* (Eng. trans.; London, 1788), p. 175.

37. Minutes of the Second Bureau, *loc. cit.*

38. Mar. 30, 1787, Gilbert Chinard, *Trois amitiés françaises de Jefferson d'après sa correspondance inédite avec Mme de Bréhan, Mme de Tessé et Mme de Corny* (Paris, 1927), pp. 102–3.

liberty among the Notables. On that day he joined in the discussion of the much-hated salt tax. Advocating that the unequal indirect tax be "repurchased" by a direct tax, he declared, "It would enhance the king's humanity and justice to free from the galleys all those who are today locked up in them for smuggling."[39] This suggestion met with general approval. That day Lafayette also read a proposal of another bureau in favor of "repurchasing" the tax on leather, but since none of the memoirs submitted to the Notables had mentioned this point, it was dropped from consideration.

Meanwhile, the rift between Calonne and the assembly that he had conjured out of a forgotten past had become irreparable. Having found the Notables unwilling to proceed drastically with the problem of tax revision, Calonne, who, like earlier reform ministers, was now looked upon by the public as a monster who wished to squeeze new money out of an already hard-pressed people, sought to justify himself. Accordingly, he published a *Collection des mémoires présentés à l'Assemblée des Notables*. In the introduction, written by one of Calonne's partisans, it was claimed that if Calonne's plans were adopted, the privileged classes would pay more in taxes but the total collected from the poor would be much less. Thereupon the bureaus unanimously protested. They wanted, they declared, only to maintain the old constitution of France, which required frank consultation with the three separate orders for important legislation. If the Notables had withheld their consent so far, it was not because they wished to preserve their privileges but simply because Calonne would not give them the necessary information on which to act intelligently. The king permitted these protests of the bureaus also to be published.[40] Thus the quarrel between the minister and the Notables became a major public scandal in which one side or the other was bound to lose face.

Easter was now approaching. The Notables would have to

39. Minutes of the Second Bureau, *loc. cit.* Cf. *Mémoires*, II, 164, where date is given as March 24, with a quotation that is now not to be found in the Minutes.

40. Lafayette to Hamilton, Apr. 12, 1787, *Works of Hamilton*, I, 433–34; cf. Goodwin, pp. 357–60, and M. B. Garrett, *The Estates General of 1789, the problems of composition and organization* (New York, [1935]), pp. 6–7.

take a holiday, and Lafayette suspected that if Calonne dared to risk popular displeasure and the subsequent blow to royal credit, he would dismiss them altogether.[41] The next full meeting of the assembly (March 29) was charged with an ill-concealed hostility. This time Calonne submitted proposals to reorganize the administration of royal lands so as to yield a greater revenue and at the same time improve the lot of the peasants living on them. These proposals led to new attacks on the minister intended to show that he had hitherto mismanaged the king's domain. A debate took place on the subject on March 31 in Lafayette's bureau. President Nicolay of the Chambre des Comptes contended that recent deals in royal lands had profited certain individuals more than the royal treasury, and he was supported by the Bishop of Langres and by Lafayette. The marquis declared that purchases had lately been made in the king's name at prices that were exorbitant and charged that millions of revenue were being wasted. That was a serious charge—all the more so since the Comte d'Artois, who presided over the Second Bureau, was known to be one of Calonne's partisans. When the meeting was over, Artois took the matter directly to the king. Louis XVI was displeased. Such charges, he declared, were so serious that they ought not to be made unless the persons who made them were ready to put them down in black and white and sign them.[42]

The royal displeasure, Calonne's friends expected, would be sufficient to intimidate his opponents.[43] Nicolay did, in fact, consider it wise to remain silent.[44] Discretion, however, made up only the lesser part of Lafayette's valor. Moreover, he had now begun to doubt that Calonne was the best man for the post of comptroller-general. He decided to challenge him openly at the next meeting of his bureau. Over the intervening Sunday, he wrote a speech dealing with those transactions in royal real estate that he thought particularly shameful. They involved

41. Lafayette to Washington, May 5, 1787, Gottschalk, *Letters*, p. 323.
42. *Mémoires*, II, 164.
43. Lafayette to Hamilton, Apr. 12, 1787, *Works of Hamilton*, I, 434.
44. *Mémoires*, II, 164; cf. p. 191 n.

well-known noblemen and could hardly have taken place without Calonne's connivance.

It is not clear where Lafayette got this information. Some of it apparently came from the recent *Dénonciation de l'agiotage au roi et à l'Assemblée des Notables* by the now notorious publicist Comte de Mirabeau, who was displeased with Calonne for personal reasons.[45] Some was perhaps also provided by a party of liberals, among them Mme de Tessé and the former minister Necker, who had determined to replace Calonne by Lafayette's colleague, the Archbishop Loménie de Brienne, who had a reputation for being a *philosophe.* The archbishop was believed to be ambitious to become prime (*premier*) minister, an unusual post in the French king's councils, and had made his home the headquarters of Calonne's enemies. Lafayette was sometimes found among them. He had gone so far as to propose to Brienne that, although the Notables had no legal authority to do so, they should nevertheless grant the king the necessary tax relief in return for a formal proclamation of constitutional principles. Brienne, without committing himself to anything, had encouraged him, possibly intending both to use the marquis's support against Calonne and to exploit the existence of an "insurgent faction" as a reason for demanding a prime minister. Again it looked as if Lafayette were being made the willing spearhead of an attack planned by older heads.[46]

The marquis was not a great orator. One who would hear him often when he had acquired greater skill was to say of him that he spoke in a familiar conversational tone, "without metaphor or colored images but with the precise word to express the precise idea, without passionate verve but with a flow of words that stirred because of their apparent conviction."[47] The speech he now prepared to deliver on recent land speculations was to be Lafayette's first significant political address in France. Pre-

45. Welschinger, p. 41, n. 1.

46. Weber, p. 104; cf. *Mémoires*, II, 167, and III, 225. See also Ségur, III, 228; *Journal historique et politique* (1787), II, 185–87; Bachaumont, XXXV, 166–67 (Nov. 15, 1787); *Lettre d'un correcteur des comptes.*

47. Timon [pseud. of Vicomte de Cormenin], *Livre des orateurs* (Paris, 1867), II, 39. Cf. Lameth, p. 113, n. 1.

viously, except for his comments in the Second Bureau, his oratory had consisted almost entirely of pretty speeches at banquets, receptions, and powwows before audiences of admiring Americans or Indians. This one was to be delivered before a hostile prince and was fraught with personal danger.

At the next meeting of the bureau Lafayette asked permission to read his speech, requesting that it be presented to the king as coming from him alone. Permission was granted, but Lafayette had not read far when he reached the challenging words, "The monster of speculation must be attacked instead of fed." Thereupon the Comte d'Artois interrupted. The tone of the memoir, he objected, was too strong and too personal. Lafayette was not intimidated, however. As a gentleman, he insisted, he had the right to carry his protests directly to the throne. A bitter discussion ensued. One of Lafayette's impassioned supporters, addressing him directly, proclaimed that, although the marquis's exploits in America had already given him the right to be considered one of the country's heroes, "now you especially deserve that glorious title." The speaker regretted that there was no sculptor present to preserve forever his young colleague's likeness "at this moment when your patriotic zeal puts you in the ranks of His Majesty's most faithful servants."[48]

Artois at length yielded and permitted Lafayette to proceed. The marquis then asked for an impartial investigation into the management of the royal domain in order to correct abuses. Repeating the charge that the king had paid exorbitantly for properties recently bought or exchanged, he named some of the persons he thought had benefited. He wanted to know why

48. "Discours de M. le Marquis de La Fayette ... le 24 avril 1787," in [L. P. de Bérenger], *Mémoires historiques et pièces authentiques sur M. de La Fayette pour servir à l'histoire des révolutions* (Paris, [1790]), p. 158. The correct date is April 3; see p. 320 below. The copy in Hardy (VII, 53–54) is so dated. Bachaumont (XXXV, 53–56) gives April 21. See also *Mémoires*, II, 164–66. The event was also reported in four separately published pamphlets: *Dénonciation des abus et des charges, par le Marquis de La Fayette, 18 avril 1787; Discours adressé à M. le Comte d'Artois* (in *Mémoire sur l'état actuel des finances de la France* [1787]); *Discours de M. le Marquis de La Fayette, prononcé au Bureau des Notables présidé par Monseigneur le Comte d'Artois, le 24 avril 1787;* and *Mémoire présenté au roi par les députés du bureau de Mgr le Comte d'Artois le 28 mars 1787, suivi de la dénonciation de M. le Marquis de la Fayette.* See below, pp. 300, 320.

ministers made deals that profited only private individuals and why they bought certain parcels of land at the same time that they sold others. He admitted that he might be misinformed. "But my patriotism is roused and requests a serious investigation. And since this open statement signed by me is to be submitted to His Majesty, I repeat with redoubled confidence . . . that the dissipated millions have been raised by taxation and that taxation can be justified only by the genuine need of the state; that the many millions granted to corruption or selfishness are the fruit of the sweat, the tears, and perhaps the blood of the people."[49] The Bishop of Langres, when Lafayette was done, arose to support him, stating that after the Easter recess, he would present proof of all the statements that Lafayette had made. The bureau formally indorsed Lafayette's behavior.[50]

The meetings of the Notables were not public, but it was not long before Lafayette's speech was published in newspapers and pamphlets and became widely known at home and abroad. That could hardly have happened without his knowledge and consent. The cry that he had raised (probably a cliché even in his day) about "the sweat, the tears, and perhaps the blood of the people" did not have the dramatic defiance or clear-cut simplicity of the "blood, toil, tears, and sweat" of a later and greater orator. It did not become the heartening slogan that a future generation was to find it. Lafayette's generation was one that sought "liberty and equality" not "blood, toil, tears, and sweat." But that a great noble had defied the minister and the brother of the king to carry his complaints to the foot of the throne and had personally appealed to "the justice and goodness that we know to be the natural sentiments of His Majesty"[51] was soon learned wherever men gathered to read pamphlets and newspapers or to talk politics. Lafayette, of course, with a pride that he tried hard to conceal, sent a copy of his speech to Washington.[52] Another found its way into the library

49. [Bérenger], pp. 160–61. See above, n. 48.

50. [Bérenger], pp. 156–57; Lafayette to Hamilton, Apr. 12, 1787, LC, Hamilton papers (with errors, in *Works of Hamilton*, I, 434).

51. [Bérenger], p. 161.

52. May 5, 1787, Gottschalk, *Letters*, p. 324.

of Loménie de Brienne.[53] It was republished with a crude English translation in the bilingual *Gazette de Québec*.[54] The Swedish ambassador reported universal approval of "the patriotism" that Lafayette had shown—"a virtue so little known in this country."[55] Even the queen noted Lafayette's activity, although she disparaged his opinions as based "upon what happens at Philadelphia."[56]

The Assembly of Notables, after two more days of bureau meetings, adjourned for the Easter holidays. Calonne had now become a scapegoat for conservatives and liberals alike.

BIBLIOGRAPHICAL NOTES

The manuscript minutes of the Assembly of Notables at the Archives nationales differ only in slight details from the published *Procès-verbal*. The minutes of the bureaus have never been published. The two different manuscript versions in the Archives nationales and the Bibliothèque de l'Arsenal have been used above.

Chinard's *Trois amitiés de Jefferson* consists largely of the letters of Mme de Tessé to Jefferson and is the best available source on this favorite aunt of Adrienne de Lafayette.

The four separately published pamphlet versions of Lafayette's speech of April 3 (cited above, n. 48) vary only in minor details except for the date, introductory materials, and some figures. The differing dates are to be accounted for as guesses made necessary by the secrecy of the bureau's meetings. The first three pamphlets are in the Andrew Dickson White Library of Cornell University. The *Mémoire présenté au roi ... le 28 mars 1787* is in the Jackson collection. The Bérenger version is that of the *Discours ... prononcé au Bureau des Notables*. The version in the *Mémoires* is apparently likewise based on this *Discours*.

Lafayette's statement that he had been suspicious of Calonne "since the affair of the famous La Chalotais" (*Mémoires*, II, 191 n.) is not borne out by the available testimony. The La Chalotais affair began in 1765, when Lafayette was eight years old.

Jean Egret, "La Fayette dans la première Assemblée des Notables (fevrier-mai 1787)," *Annales historiques de la Révolution Française*, XXIV (1952), 12, dates the meeting mentioned above (pp. 294–95) as of March 24, but see p. 295, n. 39, above. See also p. 320 below.

53. *The French colonization of America as exemplified in a remarkable collection of French administrative acts (1581–1791), mainly from the library of Cardinal E. C. de Loménie de Brienne,* Maggs Brothers catalogue No. 8, French ser. (Paris, 1936), p. 134, Item 639.

54. Oct. 4, 1787.

55. Apr. 8, 1787, L. Léouzon le Duc (ed.), *Correspondance diplomatique du Baron de Staël-Holstein, ambassadeur de Suède en France, et son successeur comme chargé d'affaires le Baron Brinkman: documents inédits sur la Révolution (1783–1799)* (Paris, 1881), p. 50.

56. To Duchesse de Polignac, Apr. 11, [1787], F. S. Feuillet de Conches, *Louis XVI, Marie-Antoinette et Mme Elizabeth, lettres et documents inédits* (Paris, 1865), I, 185–87.

CHAPTER XX

Should France Have a National Assembly?

THE Easter vacation of 1787 was a blessing to Lafayette. It gave him a much-needed respite. Mazzei, greatly alarmed by his friend's bad health, begged Jefferson to urge the young man to slow down.[1] A brief rest was all that the marquis would permit himself, however, since he now had to be on his guard against Calonne. The still powerful minister had been so directly implicated in Lafayette's accusations that he must either retort or by his silence appear to admit malfeasance. The marquis, when the assembly reconvened, could therefore expect to be engaged in a hot debate, and he began to collect proofs of his charges. The king, too, Lafayette feared, was on Calonne's side and was very angry with detractors. What if Calonne should persuade Louis to put them in the Bastille or to banish them?[2]

This apprehension, in the end, proved groundless, but only after a bitter ministerial crisis; for Brienne as well as Calonne had partisans in the king's councils. At first, the king decided to support Calonne against his opponents, but when the more conservative ministers won Marie Antoinette to their side, Louis XVI was persuaded to change his mind.[3] Without waiting for the Notables to reconvene after the Easter recess, he asked for Calonne's resignation. It was a great victory for the Brienne faction and, incidentally, for Lafayette.[4]

1. Apr. 17, 1787, Garlick, p. 109.

2. Lafayette to Hamilton, Apr. 12, 1787; *Works of Hamilton*, I, 435; Lafayette to Washington, May 5, Gottschalk, *Letters*, p. 323; Jefferson, "Autobiography," Lipscomb and Bergh, I, 98; *Gazette de Leyde*, Apr. 20.

3. Cf. Goodwin, p. 362.

4. *Ma correspondance*, No. 30 (Apr. 14, 1787), p. 245; Lescure, II, 128 (Apr. 12).

The vacation of the Notables lasted two weeks. Lafayette used his leisure to reorient his attitude toward impending developments in France. When an absolute monarch dismissed a minister who had been attacked as corrupt or incompetent by apparent champions of the people, important innovations might be expected. Unfortunately, Lafayette did not yet recognize that the opponents of Calonne were really not primarily concerned with the welfare of the people. They had made the comptroller-general a scapegoat chiefly to gain a stronger voice in the government of France. The victory of the Notables under Brienne's quiet leadership with Lafayette's conspicuous support was a victory only for the concept of a traditional constitution by which the aristocracy might share with the king in making policy. It was not intended to be a blow for the principle of monarchy limited by popular consent.

Only subsequent events were to make clear to the youthful champion of the poor, not yet thirty years of age, that he was participating in a sort of aristocratic revolt. He fully understood, however, that something very important was happening —that in fact France was in the process of becoming a constitutional monarchy. The *philosophes* had long held that France's constitution should be based upon the principles of Natural Justice and Right most recently exemplified in the American constitutions. Lafayette, as his acquaintance among the *philosophes* grew, had become more and more familiar with those principles. Yet his hostility to Calonne and his admiration for Brienne now led him temporarily to a more conservative point of view. As he took stock of what had happened since the first session of the Notables, he thought that the outcome might well be only to restore the old aristocratic constitution of France. That alone seemed quite worth while, however, since France's ancient constitution was, in his opinion, "pretty much what it was in England before it had been fairly written down and minutely preserved."[5]

Calonne's indifference to class distinctions in the proposed provincial assemblies now appeared to Lafayette to have been too much a "mixture of democracy and despotism." Such as-

5. Lafayette to Hamilton, Apr. 12, 1787, *Works of Hamilton*, I, 432.

semblies might easily result in the growth of royal power in the provinces, annihilating "those checks and graduations that are necessary evils where ever there is a king." He hoped that the amendments proposed by the Notables in favor of retaining the old forms of representation would strengthen the new assemblies and "lay a foundation for a good building." Apparently the obvious fact escaped him that if the three-class representative system of France prevailed, no assembly could really be an effective channel of the "popular measures" he desired.[6] So long as the Clergy (dominated by prelates from aristocratic families) and the Nobility controlled two of the three houses in each assembly, the Commoners could be systematically outvoted.

Brienne's influence upon Lafayette thus momentarily led him to favor Tradition rather than Reason as the source of French constitutional principles. But the younger man did not mean thereby to desert his quest for popular acclaim. In the state of public opinion then predominant, royal absolutism was the common enemy of both the people and the aristocracy. Decentralization through independent provincial assemblies might easily be looked upon as a means toward a more popular form of government, where noblemen and commoners, though acting through discrete bodies, might unite against tyranny. Thus Lafayette temporarily played into the hands of older and more sophisticated politicians who did not hesitate to exploit his popularity in the effort to restore to the aristocracy some of its lost political power.

The work of the Second Bureau was resumed at its twenty-seventh session on April 16, 1787. It was devoted chiefly to a discussion of the administrative reform of the royal domain, which by this time was an issue with which Lafayette was inescapably identified. He did not speak on that issue again until the next session of the bureau (April 17). By the time the bureau adjourned that day, twenty-one speeches had been made, which the Comte d'Artois found characterized by "diversity." President Nicolay, who had been among the first to attack Calonne, now stated that while he believed it was patri-

6. *Ibid.*, pp. 433-34.

otic to speak as Lafayette had spoken, some of the marquis's assertions would not stand up under rigorous scrutiny.[7] Several critics of Lafayette's behavior found great satisfaction in this repudiation of the marquis.[8] A pamphlet soon made its appearance in which his knowledge of financial affairs, as well as his personal integrity, was so roundly impugned that one of his admirers found it impossible to read it to the end.[9] The way of the reformer is hard.

The ministerial crisis induced Louis XVI to take the lead again in the deliberations of the Notables. At a plenary session on April 23 he announced that he would prepare a law providing for provincial assemblies where they did not already exist but preserving the rights of the upper two orders. This was a complete victory for Calonne's opponents. The king likewise promised to consider abolishing the salt tax. In return for these concessions, he asked the Notables to give their attention to the concrete suggestions already made for a new system of revenue. The meeting adjourned after the appropriate bowings, kneelings and risings, and dull speeches on the subject of taxes and deficits.

The next day, however, the Second Bureau continued to discuss His Majesty's domains. Outright sales of royal properties were generally opposed as a means of raising revenue, but some advocated sales at public auction of the usufruct of the king's lands. How completely the conservatives had won out was illustrated by the insistence upon the temporary retention of old tolls and payments still due to Louis XVI as landlord. These opinions were unanimously adopted as the bureau's recommendation, not even Lafayette voting in the negative.

On April 25 the marquis addressed himself to the question of

7. *Gazette de Leyde*, May 1, 1787. Cf. *Lettre d'un correcteur des comptes*, which gave specific details regarding which Lafayette was said to be misinformed.

8. Cf. Bachaumont, XXXV, 53 (Apr. 30, 1787), and *Mémoires du Baron de Besenval* ("Bibliothèque des mémoires relatifs à l'histoire de France pendant le 18ᵉ siècle," ed. Fr. Barrière, Vol. IV) (Paris, 1882), p. 287.

9. Comtesse de Damas to Crèvecœur, Oct. 24, 1787, Robert de Crèvecœur, *St. John de Crèvecœur, sa vie et ses ouvrages, 1735–1813* (Paris, 1883), p. 370. Cf. Bachaumont, XXXV, 213–14 (June 13). The pamphlet in question may be the *Lettre d'un correcteur des comptes*. The countess says, however, that she could read only the first twenty pages, and the *Lettre d'un correcteur des comptes* contains six pages in all.

the stamp tax, proposing that an excise on paper be adopted in its stead.[10] It was only on April 27, however, that the Second Bureau got down to discussing the deficit in earnest. Dividing the bureau into five subcommittees to consider the best method of keeping royal accounts, Artois named Lafayette first of the third subcommittee.[11] Thereafter the marquis found himself immersed almost daily in reports, accounts, and interviews in an earnest attempt to determine how to raise more revenue without increasing taxes. The business of the assembly, Lafayette wrote, kept him occupied "from morning until late in the night."[12] "If we should get into the good use of such meetings, I think we ought not hereafter take it so much in earnest as to employ our whole time from the rising hour untill we go to bed."[13] Every day except Sundays was taken up with meetings. Such activity was "a pretty extraordinary sight at Versailles," Lafayette conceded, "the more so as a great deal of patriotism and firmness has been displayed."[14]

An issue on which Lafayette could speak with greater authority than any other member of the Notables arose in his bureau on May 2. With the assets of the French government under discussion, it was inevitable that the debt owed to France by the United States should be mentioned. The irregular payments of interest on that debt led some members of the bureau to suggest that America might be an undependable source of revenue. Sensitive to the implied rebuke, Lafayette felt called upon to defend his adopted country. No other country's debts, he explained, could be equally good, for American credit was based not only upon the magnanimous character of the American people but also upon immense tracts of rich land, for which the demand was constant. If there had been some tardiness in meeting obligations, it was due, no doubt, to the need to rebuild the country after a glorious but dearly purchased revolution. The debt to America's unpaid

10. Charavay, p. 145.
11. Minutes of the Second Bureau, AN, C2, liasse 5.
12. Lafayette to Jay, May 1 [?], 1787, Johnston, III, 245.
13. Lafayette to Knox, May 5, 1787, Massachusetts Historical Society.
14. May 5, 1787, Gottschalk, *Letters*, p. 322.

soldiers was even more sacred than that to foreign countries. Still, the United States, already contemplating a federal convention, needed only time to build up an effective central regime. Furthermore, part of the blame lay on the French side. Had the Americans not been subjected in France to certain commercial prejudices and restrictions—and Lafayette specifically mentioned the farmers-general—they would have been better able to meet their obligations. Before his speech was done, as his dutiful friend Gouvion reported,[15] he made his colleagues feel quite apologetic for having brought up the matter at all.

Nevertheless, Lafayette's pride in America having been wounded, he took immediate steps to heal it. He appealed for action directly to Short in France and to Washington, Jay, and Knox in America.[16] Gouvion sent off a stirring account of the marquis's noble defense of American honor for American consumption, nevertheless questioning how "our American bretheren" could "reconcile it to their feelings to be so deficient in their punctuality."[17] Colonel Smith, who happened to be in Paris, was immediately enlisted in the marquis's propaganda campaign. Lafayette invited him to dinner and, carefully excluding the servants, spent an hour and a half in private conversation with him on American affairs. Directly afterward Smith wrote to his wife, the former Abigail Adams, to communicate to her "papa" what "a disagreeable sensation" had been produced in France by America's defaults.[18]

By this time, Brienne had won a complete political triumph. On May 1 he had been named Vergennes's successor as head of the royal council of finances, and Laurent de Villedeuil, also a member of the Second Bureau, had been named Calonne's successor as comptroller-general. Lafayette was anxious to have Americans understand that this meant no reversal of Calonne's friendly policy toward the United States. Colonel Smith was

15. Gouvion to unknown, [May, 1787], Maine Historical Society.

16. Lafayette to Short, May 7, 1787, LC, Short papers; to Washington, May 5, Gottschalk, *Letters*, p. 323; to Jay, May 1 [?], Johnston, III, 246; to Knox, May 5, *loc. cit.*

17. Gouvion to unknown, [May, 1787], *loc. cit.*

18. May 5, 1787, *Journal of Miss Adams*, I, 132–33.

given the distinct impression, which he thereupon conveyed through his wife to his father-in-law, that Brienne's triumph would be to America's advantage. The new ministers were all well disposed to the United States, Smith announced, and "they all respect and esteem Lafayette."[19] And Lafayette reciprocated this esteem. He described Brienne as "a man of the most upright honesty and shining abilities" and Villedeuil as "a clever man."[20]

As the strenuous work of the Notables continued, Lafayette became increasingly optimistic. "We are going to have good houses of representatives in each province," he forecast, "not to vote the taxes but to divide them [i.e., help apportion them among the provinces]. We have got the King to make reductions and improvements to the amount of forty millions of livres a year. We are proposing the means to insure a better and more public method of administration [of taxes]. The assembly have acted with firmness and patriotism. The walls of Versailles have never heard so many good things."[21] Unfortunately, this optimism proved largely ill founded. It was based on the assumption, which a more astute politician would not have made, that the opposition to Calonne had been altruistic. Now that Calonne was gone and an unselfish patriot was in his place, Lafayette naïvely thought, a series of reforms could be quickly outlined by well-intentioned Notables and submitted to a willing monarch for speedy enactment. In that expectation, he submitted a program of budget reform to his bureau. It was contained in two memorials formally addressed to the Comte d'Artois.

The first memorial argued that new taxes would be both unwise and inhuman. The actual deficit, it reasoned, was neither so great nor so irremediable that a "virtuous and enlightened administration" could not meet it—possibly by simple expedients such as small loans or the postponement of less pressing payments. If changes in the system of taxation nevertheless be-

19. *Ibid.*, p. 135.

20. Lafayette to Washington, May 5, 1787, Gottschalk, *Letters*, p. 323. Cf. Lafayette to Jay, May 1 [?], Johnston, III, 246; to Knox, May 5, *loc. cit.*; to Short, May 7, *loc. cit.*

21. Lafayette to Washington, May 5, 1787, Gottschalk, *Letters*, p. 323. Cf. Lafayette to Knox, May 5, *loc. cit.*, and to Short, May 7, *loc. cit.*

came necessary, they could be made, Lafayette insisted, only by the "representatives of the nation or, in their absence, of the sovereign courts" (the thirteen parlements and four sovereign councils of France) and not by the Notables. Yet he did not despair of seeing the deficit substantially reduced. "I do not know, Monseigneur, how this reduction will compare with the squandering and luxury of the court and of the highest classes of society, but follow these millions [of taxes] as they are distributed among the rural huts, and you will recognize them as the widow's and orphan's mite, the final burden that forces the farmer to abandon his plow or a family of honest workers to take to beggary." Humanity alone dictated a strenuous effort to avoid imposing new taxes on an exhausted people.[22]

The second memorial indicated how economies could be effected. It declared that the expenditures of the government in Louis XV's time had been 398,000,000 livres and had since grown by nearly 200,000,000. "All would be lost, even honor, if the king were not determined upon every saving and improvement that may relieve an already overburdened people of new exactions." Lafayette then went on to propose a reduction of expenditures for the armed forces; for the households of the king, the queen, and the royal family; for unused royal buildings and hunting lodges; for royal gifts and sinecures; and for the private exploitation of government properties. Adrienne and a few friends had recently visited some of the state jails, [23] and it was probably on their testimony that he now announced that ghastly prison conditions likewise involved waste of government funds. "The king's heart would disavow [these prisons] if he fully understood their uselessness and danger." The memorial further advocated a more uniform system of bookkeeping for the several departments of government, with provisions for regular audit and report to the public (except for the department of foreign affairs). The department of war must not, however, effect its savings at the expense of the soldiers' food, which was already insufficient. And royal pensions and grants

22. [Bérenger], pp. 146–49.

23. Cf. Anon., *Anne-Paule-Dominique de Noailles, Marquise de Montagu* (Paris, 1872), pp. 42–43.

ought to be continued "for services rendered" or for works of genius. In fact, the publication of such awards would "double their value" and would be welcomed by "the grateful hearts" of those whom His Majesty so honored. But otherwise a program of strict economy should be followed. Once again Lafayette stressed the advisability of borrowing only within known and prescribed limits, advocating strict police measures to control and punish officials and bankers who made profit out of the manipulation of government loans. While the king effected the necessary savings, he concluded, "we [the Notables] shall try, in the excess of our zeal, to meet the remainder of the deficit by the unhappy miracle of an increase in taxes." He hoped, however, that the new taxes would be for a limited period only.[24]

In pleading thus for redress of grievances before supply, Lafayette was following the tactics traditionally used by parliamentary bodies in the struggle against royal prerogative. As yet he had no violent revolutionary motives. He was concerned only with saving the poor from new taxes to be squandered by the rich. So far he had encountered no vehement opposition among his colleagues in the Second Bureau because even the more conservative of them saw in his plea for royal economy in advance of new taxes a program that might increase the power of the aristocracy by impeding the king. The resentment came rather from Bourbons like Artois. "The King and family and the great men about court, some friends excepted," Lafayette reported, "don't forgive me the liberties I have taken, and the success it had among the other classes of the people."[25]

Brienne was thought to be sympathetic with the principle of aristocratic check upon royal absolutism. But after only a few days in office, the new minister too discovered that increased taxes were necessary if the government's credit was to be maintained. Accordingly, he called together a group of leading Notables (of whom Lafayette was not one) and requested their support of a new tax proposal. It was remarkably similar to that of the disgraced Calonne and contained no compensating constitutional concessions. The Notables had expected better things

24. [Bérenger], pp. 150–55.

25. Lafayette to Washington, May 5, 1787, Gottschalk, *Letters*, p. 323.

of him. The ensuing discussions led, on May 10, to a new subdivision of the Second Bureau into committees to consider the deficit. Lafayette this time was named second on the fourth committee.[26]

By now, the marquis had begun to recognize that the traditional institutions of France offered only small chance of salvation. Not only was his head, to use Jefferson's pun, "full of notable things,"[27] but recently he had also been mingling with outspoken radicals. He had been invited, as the patron of the United States in France, to join the new Gallo-American Society, of which the writers Clavière and Brissot, along with the lawyer Nicholas Bergasse, an outstanding champion of mesmerism, were the founders. Crèvecœur, now in France preparing another edition of his Americanophile Lettres, which was to devote a large share of its pages to Lafayette, was also a member. The Gallo-American Society, without being republican, was in favor of thoroughgoing change in the French monarchical system.[28]

Perhaps even more unsettling than the radicalism of Brissot was an eloquent letter received at this juncture from the roving Jefferson.[29] Though that inveterate champion of the downtrodden found the people of the French countryside less miserable then he had expected, he informed Lafayette that they nevertheless were the victims of short-term leases, which did not give them time enough to improve their holdings, and that they had to work too hard to pay for their food, clothing, and shelter. He urged Lafayette to make a trip into the provinces to see for himself how the French peasants lived. "It will be a great comfort to you to know, from your own inspection, the condition of all the provinces of your own country, and it will be interesting to them at some future day, to be known to you. This is perhaps the only moment of your life in which you can acquire that knowledge. And to do it most effectually, you must

26. Minutes of the Second Bureau, loc. cit.

27. Jefferson to Lafayette, Apr. 11, 1787, Lipscomb and Bergh, VI, 106.

28. Brissot to Lafayette, Mar. 8, 1787, C. Perroud (ed.), J. P. Brissot, correspondance et papiers (Paris, [1912]), p. 126. Cf. p. 125 and Brissot, Mémoires, II, 54.

29. Jefferson to Lafayette (from Nice), Apr. 11, 1787, Lipscomb and Bergh, VI, 106-10.

be absolutely incognito, you must ferret the people out of their hovels as I have done, look into their kettles, eat their bread, loll in their beds under pretence of resting yourself, but in fact to find if they are soft. You will feel a sublime pleasure in the course of this investigation, and a sublimer one hereafter, when you shall be able to apply your knowledge to the softening of their beds, or the throwing a morsel of meat into their kettle of vegetables." Thus the lord of Monticello appointed the lord of St. Romain (as Lafayette sometimes called himself in jest)[30] the champion of the poor.

Other prominent men also spoke to the young paladin about the rights and aspirations of mankind. At Mme de Tessé's house in Chaville, at the home of the newlywed Condorcets, and at the select salon of Mme Suard, sister of the celebrated publisher Panckoucke and wife of the one-time editor of the *Gazette de France*, he frequently met old pundits like Morellet and Garat and rising young stars like the Comte de Volney and Benjamin Constant.[31] These men were *philosophes*. They looked to Reason to solve man's problems. "Gallo-Americans" and *philosophes* alike had small faith in the power or good will of the Notables to solve France's problems.

Under these American and philosophic influences Lafayette now prepared a third memorial on the subject of taxes.[32] He made it crystal clear that in opposing new taxes he was no longer concerned with the power of the aristocracy but with the welfare of the people. And this time, when he read his memorial to his colleagues, he encountered startled opposition and open reproof. He began by repeating his conviction that precautions against future recurrence ought to be provided before taking steps to meet the existing deficit. He still counted, he said, on the king's good will to prevent further "dangers of arbitrary administration." Yet a sad and costly experience had shown that good intentions were not enough. The nation could be "reassured only by a new order of things," to be based upon

---

30. *Mémoires*, II, 156 n.

31. Gustave Rudler, *La jeunesse de Benjamin Constant, 1767–1794* (Paris, 1909), pp. 150–51; Guillois, pp. 75–76; D.-J. Garat, *Mémoires historiques sur la vie de M. Suard, sur ses écrits, et sur le XVIIIe siècle* (Paris, 1830), II, 308–9 and 333.

32. [Bérenger], pp. 133–44.

"the constitutional rights of the state rather than upon the demands of the bureaus." The king had proposed only new loans and new taxes. Yet it must be frankly admitted that "no matter how great the love of the people may be for His Majesty, it would be dangerous to believe that their resources are inexhaustible." In Lafayette's own Auvergne, "the farmers were leaving their plows and the workers their shops, and the most industrious citizens, deprived of their earnings at home and abroad, will soon have no other alternative than beggary or emigration." New taxes would reduce them to misery and despair. "Let us hope that this disastrous crisis, presenting as it does an inescapable contrast with the wasteful luxury and thoughtless squandering of the court, may make as deep an impression on those who can prevent this evil as on those who are its innocent victims!"

By this time the Second Bureau was roused. The youthful orator was saying things that one simply did not say in polite society. Fortunately, continued Lafayette undismayed, the Notables would not have to make any decisions. "The imprescriptible right of determining the public taxes belongs to the representatives of the nation alone." The Notables ought at least to abide by their earlier conviction that new tax proposals must go through the constitutional procedure, although at present that would mean nothing more than approval by the sovereign courts.

The proposed taxes, Lafayette recognized, would distribute the burden more equitably. Still they would increase rather than diminish the total load.[33] Furthermore, the stamp tax on legal documents seemed likely to make justice expensive for the poor. But "since there is no evil in taxing things that are themselves a great evil," he had no objection to placing a tax "upon those royal certificates that vanity seeks, upon those appointments in the court which change hands, it is said, fifteen hundred times a year, and upon the litigations of the royal hunting preserves, which within the jurisdiction of Paris alone cost agriculture around 10,000,000 livres."

33. The editors of Lafayette's *Mémoires* omitted this passage, possibly because subsequent experience showed Calonne's proposals to be an improvement on the existing taxes. Cf. *Mémoires*, II, 174, with [Bérenger], pp. 138–39.

At this point the outraged Comte d'Artois could contain himself no longer. He burst in to express his doubt regarding the accuracy of Lafayette's figure. Lafayette replied simply that he had got it from the royal intendant of Paris.[34] Then he went on to list the things that the bureau ought still to insist upon before the proposed taxes nevertheless became law: details of future economies sufficient to save at least 40,000,000 livres, a carefully revised estimate of the deficit, a precise schedule for the gradual reduction of taxes, and the audit of receipts from the stamp tax by the provincial assemblies. These precautions were necessary not because of any lack of confidence in the present administration, "which would be even less permissible to this bureau than any other," but because "men pass, Monseigneur, and the sacred trust of the public welfare should be superior to such vicissitudes." And here Lafayette inserted a note that betrayed distrust even of Brienne. "Have we not too often seen the government, by changing administrators, confirm and deny in turn the same assertions, the same promises, and the same principles!"

The marquis then went on to recommend to the king's "paternal solicitude" certain changes. He attacked the salt tax and internal customs duties. He criticized royal lotteries and the leather impost. But he reserved his harshest words for the *taille* as "unequal, arbitrary, and ruinous." The people of the country districts upon whom it worked the greatest injustice, he boldly declared, "have no representatives in this assembly," but "we ought at least to prove to them that they have not lacked friends and protectors." To meet the emergency, he suggested a luxury tax and a fairer distribution of tax quotas among the provinces.

Lafayette's plain language obviously annoyed some of his colleagues and probably distressed others. Yet so far he had proposed no conspicuous departure from the program that the leaders of the Notables had adopted. They too had pitied the poor taxpayer and bewailed the injustice of increased taxation no less than had Lafayette. They too, pleading incompetence to give advice on fiscal matters, preferred the traditional proce-

34. *Mémoires*, II, 174 n.

dure through royal edicts "verified" by the sovereign courts, since they knew from experience that such a procedure led to new revenues only at the expense of royal prestige and power.

In a peroration, however, Lafayette now made his meaning clear. He was engaged in no maneuver to rally the people against the king on behalf of the aristocracy but, on the contrary, was interested in an alliance of a benevolent king with his grateful people. "In any case," he said, "the assembly's work, the salutary influence of the provincial assemblies, the talents and virtues of the present administration must lead to a new order of things." A thorough change in the credit system, interest rates, and collection methods of the government was unavoidable. "It seems to me," he concluded, "that we have reached the point where we ought to beseech His Majesty once more to assume responsibility for all measures and to assure their happy outcome forever by convoking a national assembly."[35]

The effect of the phrase "national assembly" was electric. The boldest opponents of royal absolutism among parlementarians and *philosophes* had hitherto dared to suggest only the revival of the historic Estates General. In fact, a demand for the Estates General had already been made in the Second Bureau.[36] But Lafayette now called for a "national assembly." The word "national" in his vocabulary meant "popular." A *national* assembly would be one controlled not by the upper two orders of society, as would the Estates General, but by the nation at large.

The Comte d'Artois again lost his patience. Did Lafayette mean to ask for an estates general, he demanded. Lafayette was anxious not to be misunderstood. "Yes, Monseigneur," he answered, "and even better than that." Would Lafayette put his request in writing so that Artois might take it to the king? "Yes, Monseigneur." An awkward silence followed. No one indorsed Lafayette's request, and he was led to conclude that his colleagues thought that he had spoken without due regard

35. The version in the *Mémoires* (II, 177) puts the phrase "assemblée nationale" in capitals, but that makes it more specific and emphatic than it probably was.

36. C.-L. Chassin (ed.), *Les élections et les cahiers de Paris en 1789* (Paris, 1888–89), I, 2.

for the seriousness of his proposal. One day he would be able to boast that he had had greater insight than they.[37]

By this time the Notables had been in session almost three months. Brienne, at last recognizing, like his predecessors, that an aristocratic body would not grant tax reform without compensating political advantage, determined to get rid of them. The final full session was set for May 25.

The Second Bureau now began to prepare a summary of its work. It used for this purpose Lafayette's former collaborator, Dupont, who was one of the assembly's secretaries. Dupont's first report (May 23) was approved in general, but a committee, of whom Lafayette was one, was appointed to recast certain details.[38] This gave Lafayette a pretext for calling attention to a point that had been barely touched upon in Calonne's opening address and had not been raised since. He moved that His Majesty be petitioned to grant civil rights to Protestants. He also proposed a thorough revision of the criminal code. Having prepared an address to the king on these subjects, he requested and received permission to read it. This was a courageous act, for, as Lafayette afterward informed Jay,[39] "So far are we from relligious freedom that even in asking for tolerance, we must measure our expressions."

When Lafayette finished reading his address, the punctilious Artois again objected. The subject was so irrelevant to those submitted for the bureau's consideration, he said, that they would be exceeding their power as Notables to take it up. In fact, as was afterward revealed, a similar motion made by the Duc de La Rochefoucauld in the First Bureau had been ruled out of order for the same reason.[40] Nevertheless, Artois said, he would volunteer to speak to the king about it if the Second Bureau so desired. Again the "learned and virtuous" Bishop of Langres came "admirably" to his young colleague's support.[41]

37. *Mémoires*, II, 177.

38. Minutes of the Second Bureau, *loc. cit.*

39. May 30, 1787, [Weaver], *Diplomatic correspondence*, I, 452 (erroneously dated May 3 in *Mémoires*, II, 199–202).

40. *Gazette de Leyde*, June 5, 1787.

41. Lafayette to Jay, May 30, 1787, [Weaver], *Diplomatic correspondence*, I, 452. Cf. Comte de Boissy-d'Anglas, *Essai sur la vie, les écrits et les opinions de M. de Malesherbes* (Paris, 1819), I, 385.

Lafayette, he said, had talked as a *philosophe*, but he himself, as a bishop, liked temples better than meeting houses and ministers better than pulpiteers. His meaning was unmistakable. Enlightened clergymen, it was clear, preferred an authorized to a clandestine Protestant church.[42] Thereupon the bureau indicated overwhelmingly[43] that they were in favor of Lafayette's motion and expressed the further opinion that his request for revision of the law should be extended to include not only the criminal law but also the civil code, the commercial code, and the regulations on woods and streams. Artois set aside the next evening for discussion of the petition.[44]

At the next meeting the bureau indorsed Lafayette's address with some slight revisions. The changes included not only several amendments designed to broaden the scope of the proposed legal reform but also "many compliments to the Roman creed to appease priests and devotees."[45] The marquis's own version had contained a left-handed appeal to clerical prejudice: "The clergy, inspired by the great principles that the church fathers have honored themselves in professing, will undoubtedly approve this act of justice." But this reference sounded too ironical to some and was ruled out.[46] Other shorter phrases friendly to the Catholic church were inserted. Although Lafayette thought that these complimentary phrases "clogged" the resolution, he accepted the revisions.[47]

These recommendations on tolerance and legal reform were then incorporated in a petition to be formally submitted to Louis XVI. While admitting that the new proposals were foreign to the bureau's agenda, the petition nevertheless expressed

---

42. *Mémoires*, II, 178.

43. Lafayette to Jay, May 30, 1787, [Weaver], *Diplomatic correspondence*, I, 451, says, "I may almost say unanimously." Lafayette to Rabaut-St. Étienne [*ca.* May 24, 1787] says, "à peu près unanimement" (see n. 49 below). The minutes of the Second Bureau, *loc. cit.*, say, "unanimes." Cf. Dedieu, II, 262–63.

44. Minutes of the Second Bureau, *loc. cit.*

45. Lafayette to Jay, May 30, 1787, [Weaver], *Diplomatic correspondence*, I, 452.

46. *Mémoires*, II, 178. The version in [Bérenger], p. 145, retains this statement. That in *Mémoires*, II, 180, omits words like "la religion" and "bonnes mœurs." For the most part, I have borrowed the version given in the translation in LC, PCC 156, fols. 416–17. This translation was made from the copy of the original apparently inclosed in Lafayette's letter to Jay, May 30, 1787, *ibid.*, fols. 458–61.

47. Lafayette to Jay, May 30, 1787, [Weaver], *Diplomatic correspondence*, I, 452.

"a lively and respectful confidence in the king's equity and goodness" with regard to matters "so significant to humanity, justice, the state's welfare, and His Majesty's glory." The bureau was convinced "that His Majesty, desirous of rendering the true religion beloved by all his subjects, whose common Father he is, and knowing that Truth supports itself through its own strength and that only Error requires the aid of constraint, joins to all those virtues which have gained him the nation's love the kindly trait of toleration." If religious freedom were granted, a large number of His Majesty's subjects "would be relieved from the oppression of a proscription contrary alike to the general intention of religion, to good order, to population, to national industry, and to all principles of morality and politics." The bureau further recommended that the outworn civil, criminal, and commercial codes and the old regulations of woods and streams of Louis XIV's day be re-examined with a view to "the changes which the antiquity alone of these laws and the difference of times and manners may require, and which the greater enlightenment of our day will surely make worth while." When the proposed petition was read to the Second Bureau, it was greeted with a burst of applause. Artois then announced that, true to his promise, he had already taken up the matter with his brother the king and that His Majesty had entertained it graciously.[48]

It now looked as if the struggle for toleration upon which Lafayette had embarked two years earlier was about to be won. Rabaut-St. Étienne and he rejoiced together. They sent a copy of the Second Bureau's resolution to the Academician Target, who was preparing a royal memorial in favor of toleration.[49] When Lafayette reported this success to his American friends, he did not trouble to conceal his elation. He was all the more pleased, he admitted, because recently a similar petition in the Paris parlement[50] had not been well received. It was now per-

48. Minutes of the Second Bureau, *loc. cit.*; Lafayette to Jay, May 30, 1787, [Weaver], *Diplomatic correspondence*, I, 452.

49. Lafayette to Rabaut-St. Étienne, [*ca.* May 24, 1787] and [*ca.* May 25, 1787], Bibliothèque de la Ville de Nantes, MS 661, Nos. 134 and 135.

50. Lafayette to Jay, May 30, 1787, [Weaver], *Diplomatic correspondence*, I, 452. Cf. A. Chérest, *La chute de l'ancien régime* (Paris, 1884), I, 389, n. 1.

missible to hope that "the affair of the Protestants will soon be settled."[51]

The Assembly of Notables met for the last time in full session on May 25. The king, amid the usual ceremony, made a short speech of thanks. The keeper of the seals made a longer one, promising economies, efficiency, reforms, and the creation of provincial assemblies where they did not already exist.[52] Then Brienne detailed the changes that the government proposed. He revealed, among other things, that the new provincial assemblies might in fact be controlled by the Third Estate, since it would have as many representatives in each assembly as the upper two orders combined and voting would not be by order (each house having one vote) but by head (thereby almost assuring the lowest order of a majority). "The present crisis will become the starting point of a new splendor," Brienne concluded.[53] And this theme was politely repeated by the subsequent speakers, who briefly thanked the king on behalf of their colleagues. Then the king requested each of the Notables to sign the minutes of the assembly. Lafayette signed fifty-first, using only the name "Lafayette," though nearly all the other nobles gave their titles.[54] The king having meanwhile retired to his cabinet, the Notables, in the order of their places in the assembly, then filed past him to make their adieus as the queen and her children looked on. Later each bureau called upon the king's brothers in a body. And each finally escorted its chairman to his home.

President Nicolay invited all the members of the Second Bureau to his house for dinner a few days later. When the Comte d'Artois hesitated to accept the invitation, Nicolay reminded him that Henry IV had so honored his great-great-grandfather on a similar occasion.[55] Artois thereupon accepted but in the end did not go to the dinner. Lafayette was there, however, and made a lasting impression on the fourteen-year

51. Lafayette to Washington, Aug. 3, 1787, Gottschalk, *Letters*, p. 325.

52. *Procès-verbal*, p. 296.

53. *Ibid.*, pp. 307–8.

54. *Ibid.*, pp. 322–23.

55. *Gazette de Leyde*, June 5, 1787.

old daughter of the house. She thought him very handsome (though few of her older contemporaries did), impeccably dressed, with an air "as distinguished as possible" but spoiled by a colorless face and an annoying tic of the eyes (which must have been the temporary result of overwork, since no other witness seems ever to have noticed it).[56] "He was already the hero of one part of the world," the young lady remembered; "we had no doubt that he would become the hero of ours."

The Assembly of Notables of 1787, now ended, seemed to portend a new world even to those contemporaries who had at first been somewhat skeptical. Lafayette revealed his own sanguine hopes on the occasion of a visit to the Duc d'Harcourt, a colleague in the Second Bureau, who had recently been named the tutor of the Dauphin. When the question was raised as to what history books the young prince should study, Lafayette solemnly declared, "He will do well to begin his history of France with the year 1787."[57] This was at a time when the marquis still thought of Brienne as "the ablest and one of the most honest men that could be put at the head of the administration," as a man who was "equally enlightened and liberal."[58] He was to change his mind within the year.

BIBLIOGRAPHICAL NOTES

Meade Minnigerode, in his *Lives and times, four informal American biographies: Stephen Jumel, merchant; William Eaton, hero; Theodosia Burr, prodigy; Edmond Charles Genêt, citizen* (New York, 1925), page 162, and in his *Jefferson, friend of France, 1793: the career of Edmond Charles Genêt . . . 1763–1834* (New York, 1928), page 81, tells an anecdote for which I have been able to find no confirmation. He states that young Genêt condemned the proposed stamp tax before Artois's bureau and that Lafayette said to him, "You are very young, but you behaved yesterday like a man." It is unlikely that young Genêt would have had any direct association with the Second Bureau.

Brissot's *Mémoires*, written in the shadow of the guillotine as justification of his career, probably exaggerates his republicanism before the Revolution. He does not, however, ascribe republicanism to Lafayette even when he mentions him as a member of societies definitely committed to political reform. See below, pages 380–81.

56. "Souvenirs d'enfance et de jeunesse de la Marquis de Villeneuve-Arifat," *Revue des études historiques*, LXVII (1901), 158.

57. *Mémoires*, II, 183.

58. Lafayette to Jay, May 30, 1787, [Weaver], *Diplomatic correspondence*, I, 452.

The memorials that Lafayette read before the Second Bureau in May, 1787, are given in [Bérenger], pages 133–55, out of chronological order. They are also given, with editorial changes calculated to make Lafayette appear wiser than he was, in *Mémoires*, II, 167–80. It must be recalled that the *Mémoires* were compiled by the marquis's family and suffer from filiopietistic shadings. The order of the speeches in the *Mémoires* is, however, correct.

Lafayette in later years was under the impression that he had proposed the abolition of *lettres de cachet* in one of these memorials (see *Mémoires*, VI, 6). Lady Morgan, *France* (London, 1818), II, 289, and [Gabriel Lucas de Montigny (ed.)], *Mémoires biographiques, littéraires et politiques de Mirabeau, écrits par lui-même, par son père, son oncle et son fils adoptif* (Paris, 1841), IV, 444 n., probably derived their testimony to the same effect from him. I can find no direct reference, however, in any of these memorials to *lettres de cachet*, though Lafayette may have had them in mind when he made his sharp comments on state prisons and the criminal law.

About and since the time this volume was first printed, Jean Egret has written several works which deal with the Assemblies of Notables. In addition to his "La Fayette dans la première Assemblée des Notables" (see p. 300 above) he has published *La Révolution des Notables: Mounier et les Monarchiens, 1759* (Paris, 1950) and *La pré-révolution française (1787–1788)* (Paris, 1962). Without reference to this volume but using many of the same sources, Egret has given a narrative of Lafayette's role in the Assemblies that essentially confirms the one told here.

Pierre Chevallier has edited the *Journal de l'Assemblée des Notables de 1787 par le comte de Brienne et Etienne Charles Loménie de Brienne, archevêque de Toulouse* (Paris, 1960), which provides several pieces of evidence hitherto unknown. On the basis of an entry in this *Journal* (p. 49) I have corrected the date of Lafayette's attack on Calonne (pp. 298, n. 48, and 300 above). Chevallier gives also Brienne's mixed reaction to Lafayette's attack on Calonne (pp. 93–94), a variant text of Lafayette's *Dénonciation des abus* (pp. 118–19), and a letter of Lafayette to Louis XVI, May 25, 1787, justifying his actions as a member of the Assembly of Notables (pp. 136–38).

CHAPTER XXI

"Political Notions Widen"

THE Assembly of Notables marked a turning point in Lafayette's career. Hitherto he had been looked upon as the stuff out of which ministers and marshals were made. But now that he had shown himself a champion of a written constitution and popular assemblies and the castigator of court extravagance, small hope remained that he would ever receive promotion in the army and still less that he would be appointed to any civil office. Regal displeasure was not immediately obvious, but in the course of two or three months it became easy to recognize. He believed this hostility to be due chiefly to the resentment of the royal family over his remarks about gifts and pensions to favorites at public expense. "I can't say," he admitted somewhat ruefully, "that I am on a very favourable footing at Court, if by Court you understand the King, Queen and King's Brothers."[1]

If, however, the young reformer had made "a great number of powerfull and inveterate enemies," he found that he was "very well come to the Nation" and "very friendly with the present administration," particularly with the great Brienne.[2] The smaller his chance of becoming a minister in a government where the king named the ministers, the bigger the chance that he might exercise power by his hold upon the popular imagination and his consequent influence with the ministers. He was therefore all the more hopeful that the Assembly of Notables would mark the beginning of a popular regime in France. When he came to sum up the benefits that France had derived

1. Lafayette to Washington, Aug. 3, 1787, Gottschalk, *Letters*, p. 325.
2. *Ibid.*

from the assembly, he was optimistic: "A more equal repartition of the taxes, including the clergy, who hitherto had escaped them, and the powerfull ones among the Noblesse who were not very exact—provincial assemblies on an elective principle, which by the bye are big with happy, very happy consequences that will come to light as we go on—oeconomies to the amount of forty millions at least—the destruction of interior custom houses—a modification of the gabelle—an annual publication of the account of the finances—the printing of all pensions, gifts, etc.—more proper arrangements within some departements— and a more general instruction, habit of thinking of public affairs, etc., etc., are the good effects of this Assembly, which altho' it was not National, since we were not representatives, behaved with great propriety and patriotism."[3]

Several of the reforms the marquis thus listed were not in fact to develop beyond the stage of ineffectual promises. Others were to prove futile after being put into operation. But at this juncture the next step for Lafayette seemed obvious if he was to continue to play an active part on the political stage. He must become a member of one of those provincial assemblies that he envisaged as "big with happy, very happy consequences."

From this time on, Lafayette was to feel more and more conscious of appearing to his friends at court as too "republican." Although much of this feeling was due to his outspoken advocacy of reform, which roused genuine concern among shocked and disdainful courtiers, some of it resulted merely from his own self-consciousness upon finding himself becoming gradually estranged from the people with whom he had usually been identified. In any case, if the details, firmly impressed upon his mind, had not been recorded by him (probably with adornments) in after years, several of the anecdotes that bear testimony to a self-righteous, even flamboyant "republicanism" in the midst of a staid monarchical conservatism would have been forgotten.

Lafayette indeed provided abundant evidence of a critical attitude toward certain French institutions, but remarkably

3. Lafayette to Jay, May 30, 1787, LC, PCC 156, fols. 458-59, and (with slight changes) [Weaver], *Diplomatic correspondence*, I, 451.

little of it showed an antimonarchical bias. It must have been about this time (if the event in fact occurred as Lafayette remembered it) that the Comte de Provence tried to embarrass Lafayette about his "republicanism." One day, at a royal dinner party, the future ruler of France suggested that the marquis probably approved of the execution of the English king Charles I by rebellious subjects. Lafayette was put thereby under the awkward necessity of explaining that he did not sympathize with injustice of any kind, but he did so in terms that still must have sounded strange at a royal dinner table.[4] It was probably at this time, too, that the Duc de Castries and other friends at court indulgently ridiculed him for believing that monarchical authority was not so firmly rooted in France as to make all opposition a waste of effort.[5] But if princes and ministers looked askance at Lafayette's "republicanism," there were those who felt that he was not "republican" enough. At a future date, when the word "republic" came to mean a kingless state in France, Brissot was to testify that whenever he heard Lafayette speak of a republic, the marquis made clear that he did not believe the French people were yet prepared for one.[6]

The fact was that Lafayette, like nearly every political writer and thinker of his day, did not think that a country as large as France could dispense with a monarchy. So far he felt nothing but the most loyal, even affectionate, regard for Louis XVI. To be sure, he believed that in America "the far greater proportion of the people are happier than any where else on the globe,"[7] but the favorable conditions of America did not prevail in France. On the rare occasions when he used the word "republic" in connection with his own country, he did not mean to convey any antiroyalist sympathies. He meant merely to advocate more popular institutions within a monarchical regime.

For America, however, he was more "republican" than many Americans. He hoped that the United States would disprove the

4. *Mémoires*, III, 198.

5. *Ibid.*, VI, 5.

6. Speech of Oct. 25, 1793, *Moniteur*, XVIII, Oct. 27, 1793, suppl., 235. See also Brissot, *Mémoires*, II, 54.

7. Lafayette to Jefferson, June 6, 1787, Chinard, *Lafayette and Jefferson*, p. 113.

current conviction that democracies could not be strong. The association of what was happening in France with its centralized government striving for more popular support and in the United States with its popular leaders striving for more centralized government was so plain to him that every mention of the one called to mind the other also.

Washington and Franklin soon confirmed earlier reports that a federal constitutional convention was to take place in Philadelphia in May.[8] That was especially welcome news at a time when the American government's inability to pay its debts had but recently aroused unfavorable attention in France. "May the Convention," Lafayette prayed, "be the happy epocha of foederal, energic, patriotic measures! May the friends of America rejoice! May her ennemies be humbled, and her censors be silenced at the news of her noble exertions in continuance of those principles which have placed her so high in the annals of history and among the nations of the earth!"[9]

Well might a friend of liberty be prayerful. The day on which the Assembly of Notables adjourned was the very one on which the Constitutional Convention was formally organized at Philadelphia, with Washington as its president. Lafayette felt certain "that every thing will come to right" in America. It was mere ignorance, he claimed, that caused Europeans "to repeat that every thing there is in confusion." He nevertheless sounded more convinced of a happy ending when he talked of France. Brienne still evoked enthusiasm as "truly great and good" and "the very man to manage the affairs of a great empire." The new ministry as a whole appeared "very able and virtuous." And when in June, Malesherbes again became a minister and the enlightened Duc de Nivernais was called to the council of state, Lafayette's confidence in the future of his country grew.[10]

At this juncture death almost deprived the hopeful champion of his chance to behold the better world he was striving to pre-

8. Washington to Lafayette, Mar. 25, 1787, Fitzpatrick, XXIX, 184; Franklin to Lafayette, Apr. 17, Smyth, IX, 570.

9. Lafayette to Jay, May 30, 1787, [Weaver], *Diplomatic correspondence*, I, 452 (with corrections above).

10. Lafayette to Jefferson, June 6, 1787, Chinard, *Lafayette and Jefferson*, pp. 112–13.

pare. The old chest complaint that had dogged him since the early days of the Assembly of Notables again laid him low—this time for nearly two months. Adrienne had to furnish an apartment in the royal château at St. Germain to keep the children away.[11] Only toward the end of June was Mme de Simiane's sister-in-law able to announce to his American friends that "this precious young man will live to continue to be the honor and glory of his country, the treasure of yours, the delight of his friends and the admiration of the world."[12] But for another month he had to remain inactive. Not until August was he well enough to resume a vigorous political career.

During his convalescence Lafayette found time to acknowledge some of the literature that had been piling up on his desk, the gifts of admiring authors. A few of them were works of more than ephemeral interest. The Dutch poetess, Lucretia Wilhelmina Van Winter, having just published a French translation of her poem *Germanicus*, had presented him with a copy of it.[13] John Adams had sent an inscribed copy of his *Defence of the constitutions of government of the United States of America*, published that year in answer to certain criticisms of the American state constitutions.[14]

Lafayette also continued to be himself the subject of aspiring writers. The paean which had begun earlier that year with the book of Clavière and Brissot was swelled by a poem in his honor written by Hilliard d'Auberteuil.[15] In England an anonymous author wrote *Remarks on the "Travels of the Marquis de Chastellux in North America,"* which, while denying that Lafayette had any unusual military ability, credited him with great political influence.[16] In America, Joel Barlow's *Vision of Columbus* at last appeared, with passages in praise of Lafayette and

11. AN, T 333.

12. Comtesse de Damas to Crèvecœur, June 22, 1787, Robert de Crèvecœur, *Crèvecœur*, p. 363; cf. Gimel [not Gimat] to Washington, June 2, Hume, *Washington's correspondence concerning the Cincinnati*, p. 314.

13. Lafayette to Van Winter, June 25, 1787, S. C. Bosche Reitz, "An unpublished correspondence of George Washington," *Journal of American history*, XXIV (1930), 56–57.

14. Parke-Bernet Galleries, catalogue No. 73, sale of Dec. 6, 1938, item No 1.

15. Jefferson to Hilliard d'Auberteuil, Jan. 27, 1787, Lipscomb and Bergh, VI, 62.

16. Cf. *Gentleman's magazine*, LVII, Part 2 (July, 1787), 606.

other French heroes of the American Revolution.[17] He was also designated one of four honorary members of the Connecticut Society of Arts and Sciences.[18] Thus even when sickness rendered the youthful idol inactive, he remained the subject of public adoration.

As soon as he became strong enough, Lafayette resumed his political maneuvers. This time his attention was called to two distant areas—the United Provinces and Egypt. The Dutch were still involved in a civil struggle, which had begun to look strangely reminiscent of the American Revolution. While England (supported by Prussia) threw her weight on the side of the Orange party, which sought to make the Stadholder William V king of the Dutch Netherlands, France, hopeful of keeping Holland out of her enemies' orbit without going to war, intrigued with the Republican party. Dutch Republicans in Paris had kept in constant touch with Lafayette, and he had given them reason to believe that he would help.[19]

In June, as the marquis lay dangerously ill, the situation in Holland had reached a dramatic climax. The Dutch Republicans made the fatal error of placing Princess Wilhelmina, wife of the stadholder and sister of Frederick William II of Prussia, under temporary arrest. The Prussian ruler immediately made clear that he resented this insult. Counting on the moral support of England, he sent an army to the border, ready to invade the United Provinces unless proper restitution were made. The French became uneasy and mobilized a corps of soldiers for a possible counterinvasion. Nevertheless, because France had just embarked upon a program of local and tax reform that might yet produce internal conflicts, the Comte de Montmorin, Vergennes's successor in the French foreign office, preferred to temporize and appease. During all this crisis Lafayette's illness had obliged him to remain inactive, and other French officers, particularly the Rhinegrave of Salm, had come forward as champions of the Dutch.

17. Book VI, p. 181.

18. F. B. Dexter (ed.), *The literary diary of Ezra Stiles, D.D., president of Yale College* (New York, 1901), III, 277 (Aug. 22, 1787).

19. Lafayette to Washington, Oct. 9, 1787, Gottschalk, *Letters*, p. 331; *Mémoires*, II, 214-15 n.; Weber, p. 104.

While Lafayette's Dutch affair thus marked time, he found compensation in planning a daring coup in the eastern Mediterranean. Comte Mathieu Dumas, one of his companions in the American War, had recently returned from a diplomatic post in the Near East. Dumas had been impressed with the defenselessness of Crete and the consequent vulnerability of Egypt. His impression led Lafayette to concoct a glorious expedition against the Moslem states of North Africa through Crete and Egypt. In addition to the punishment of the Barbary corsairs, Lafayette believed that such an expedition would lead to the introduction of sugar cane into the eastern Mediterranean, thus promoting the gradual emancipation of the Negro in the West Indies. Besides, it would keep the area from falling to the dreadful English if the Dutch crisis should lead to a general war.[20] He spoke to several of his friends about this scheme. Among them were Mazzei, Grimm, and the Comte de Saint Priest, former French ambassador to Turkey. He had often met Saint Priest at Mme de Tessé's and knew that the ambassador had secretly proposed that the French government send an expeditionary force to occupy Egypt. Mazzei wrote to Madison, and Grimm wrote to Catherine II, about Lafayette's latest endeavor. Madison maintained a discreet silence; Saint Priest came to look upon Lafayette as an ambitious young adventurer ready to risk his neck on any mission that promised glory; and Catherine showed a feminine curiosity mixed with a desire to keep her skirts clear of anything this "tête à révolution" might fancy.[21] Lafayette's illness slowed down this eastern Mediterranean venture, too, and it made no great progress after his recovery.

The first sign that Lafayette had regained his characteristic vigor was, fittingly enough, the resumption of his reports to Washington. The venerated general had written briefly but

20. Comte de Saint Priest, *Mémoires, règne de Louis XV et de Louis XVI*, ed. Baron de Barante (Paris, 1929), I, 234–35; Lafayette to Washington, Oct. 9, 1787, and Aug. 20, 1798, Gottschalk, *Letters*, pp. 329 and 375; *Mémoires*, III, 223.

21. Saint Priest, I, 234–35; Mazzei to Madison, Aug. 6, 1787, Garlick, p. 112; Catherine to Grimm, Dec. 1, *Sbornik Istoricheskago Obshchestva*, XXIII (1878), 433. Cf. also the cryptic reference regarding "an ambitious project" in Smith to Mrs. Smith, May 5, [1787], *Journal of Miss Adams*, I, 135.

affectionately from Philadelphia. He had explained that, contrary to his wishes, he was once more engaged in public life "to determine whether we are to have a government of respectability under which life, liberty, and property will be secured to us, or are to submit to one which may be the result of chance or the moment."[22] Recently, too, though Washington knew nothing of Lafayette's illness, gifts had come from Mount Vernon— two braces of wood ducks (which died at Le Havre) and some sides of bacon.[23]

Lafayette, without mentioning that he had been ill, replied with the usual professions of "filial love and respect." It was not surprising, he wrote, to learn that Washington was in attendance at the Convention. "On the success of this meeting the very existence of the United States may depend. And you well know that your name will add a great weight to its proceedings." The declining prestige of America had made him unhappy, he repeated. "It gives pleasure to her ennemies. It hurts her interest even with her allies. It furnishes the opponents of liberty with anti-republican arguments. . . . Good God! Will the people of America, so enlightned, so wise, so generous, after they have so gloriously climbed up the rugged hill, now stumble in the easy path? I the more heartly wish well to your meeting as I feel that the happiness of my life would not with[s]tand a disappointement in my fond hopes for the prosperity of our good United States."[24]

With his old-time vigor, Lafayette expressed his "great anxiety" for the Convention to other influential Americans also. He wrote to Jay, "[I] am too deeply wounded by any circumstance that does not come up to my ideas of the future greatness, prosperity, and internal happiness of the United States, that I don't only wish them to be well, but as perfectly well as it is possible for a nation to be."[25] If "our fellow citizens" should lack "that glory and happiness" which their "liberality, wisdom and patriotism" would lead one to expect, he confessed to Madi-

22. Washington to Lafayette, June 6, 1787, Fitzpatrick, XXIX, 229.

23. Washington to Lafayette, Mar. 25, 1787, *ibid.*, p. 186; Lafayette to Washington, Aug. 3, Gottschalk, *Letters*, p. 325.

24. Lafayette to Washington, Aug. 3, 1787, Gottschalk, *Letters*, pp. 324–25.

25. Aug. 4, 1787, Johnston, III, 253 n.

son, "I feel that the tranquillity of my life would be poisoned." But he foresaw "a more pleasant prospect."[26]

He continued to be still more hopeful for France. "The spirit of liberty is prevailing in this country at a great rate. Liberal ideas are cantering about from one end of the kingdom to the other." To be sure, his attack upon court favorites had cost him the friendship of the royal family and powerful figures at court, but he took solace in the reflection that there never had been a better king's council than the present one[27] or an "abler and honester man in the world than the Archbishop of Toulouse [Brienne]."[28]

During Lafayette's illness the struggle for the reform of French institutions had gone on. Brienne had tried to incorporate into law some of the promises made to the Notables. He secured the ready consent of the courts to the alleviation of internal customs and the *corvée*. The creation of new provincial assemblies encountered no opposition either. His effort, however, to win approval for the proposed land and stamp taxes led only to a renewed demand by the parlements for the old Estates General.

Lafayette was pleased with this turn of events. Although he did not believe that the king would soon consent to "a general assembly of the Nation," he anticipated that the government would yield when the provincial assemblies had "taken a proper weight and felt their strength."[29] But again he underestimated the court's conservatism. When the king finally announced the composition of the provincial assemblies, it was clear that he did not intend to lose control of them. To be sure, a great victory was won for the popular cause by the king's granting not only "double representation" for the Third Estate but also—what was more important—"vote by head" rather than "vote by order." That victory, however, was offset by the decision that the king would himself designate half the members of each assembly, as well as the presiding officer, who had to be either

26. Aug. 5, 1787, Historical Society of Pennsylvania, Dreer collection.

27. Lafayette to Washington, Aug. 3, 1787, Gottschalk, *Letters*, p. 325.

28. Lafayette to Madison, Aug. 5, 1787, *loc. cit.*

29. Lafayette to Washington, Aug. 3, 1787, Gottschalk, *Letters*, p. 325.

a noble or a cleric. These royal nominees were to co-opt the remainder of their colleagues. By that method of selection the provincial assemblies were highly unlikely to become truly representative bodies. Yet, Lafayette thought, they were "good seeds of a popular governement," since "political notions widen a great deal."[30]

Meanwhile, Lafayette's efforts on behalf of needy Americans and Frenchmen continued. The most crying case was that of Barclay, who had been arrested at Bordeaux, despite his consular immunity, for debts incurred by an American firm. The local courts quickly released him, and Lafayette successfully interceded with the ministers to defend him from further molestation.[31] On behalf of the dramatist-adventurer Beaumarchais, who had long been trying to collect money that he believed due him from Congress and the state of Virginia, Lafayette appealed to Madison as a member of the Virginia legislature. He urged Beaumarchais to carry his case to Jefferson as well, but it was to drag on and on. When Crèvecœur, worried by the radical change in the French ministry, began to fear for his job as consul in New York, Lafayette was able to win him reassurance from the proper authorities.[32] The marquis also kept on supporting the petitions of French officers who sought to join the Society of the Cincinnati;[33] and he endeavored to win for Nîmes manufacturers (some of whom were Protestants) special trade privileges in Spain.[34]

For a sick man without official status this benevolence alone might have constituted a sufficiently full life, but not for Lafayette. Shortly after Jefferson's return to Paris he bore eloquent witness once more to his young friend's renewed vigor. Outlining his latest negotiations, he reported, "The Marquis de la Fayette goes hand in hand with me in all these transactions, and

30. Lafayette to Madison, Aug. 5, 1787, *loc. cit.*

31. Lafayette to Short, May 31, [1787], LC, William Short papers; cf. Myrna Boyce, "The diplomatic career of William Short," *Journal of modern history*, XV (1943), 98.

32. Mitchell, p. 269.

33. Gimel to Washington, Feb. 16 and June 2, 1787, LC, Washington papers; André Lasseray, *Les Français sous les treize étoiles (1775–1783)* (Mâcon, 1935), II, 356 (on behalf of the Chevalier de La Neuville).

34. Laurent de Villedeuil to Lafayette, June 20, 1787, AN, F^{12}156.

is an invaluable auxiliary to me. I hope it will not be imputed either to partiality or affectation, my naming this gentleman so often in my dispatches. Were I not to do it, it would be a suppression of truth, and the taking to myself the whole merit where he has the greatest share."[35]

Official occupation began again for Lafayette when the king formally designated the members of the provincial assemblies. At one time Lafayette thought that he might himself be named president of the provincial assembly of Auvergne,[36] but the Vicomte de Beaune, father-in-law of one of Adrienne's sisters, was given that honor.[37] This slight might have been an outward sign of royal displeasure, but Lafayette himself attributed it to his open declaration that he did not want the post. "The president, being named by the King, is not so free in his motions as a private member,"[38] he explained, apparently forgetting that most of the "private members" would also be appointees of the king. Lafayette was one of the six nobles whom the king appointed to the Auvergne assembly—the last among them, since they were listed in the order of their age.

Before leaving for Auvergne to attend the assembly's meetings, Lafayette was called upon to devote some of his crowded hours to an awkward situation resulting from the ancient rivalry between the towns of Clermont and Riom. Clermont, being more centrally located, had been chosen for the meeting place in preference to Riom, which was the capital of the royal administrative unit (*généralité*) that corresponded to the province of Auvergne. The inhabitants of Riom, still resentful that the mayor of Clermont rather than their mayor had been chosen to represent the cities of Auvergne in the Assembly of Notables, were incensed by this new snub to their fair city. Since the beginning of the year they had sent letters of protest to Auvergnats in the capital who were believed to have influence

---

35. Jefferson to Jay, Aug. 6, 1787, Lipscomb and Bergh, VI, 242. See p. 108 above.

36. Lafayette to Washington, Oct. 9, 1787, Gottschalk, *Letters*, p. 331.

37. Regulations, July 8, 1787, *Procès-verbal des séances de l'assemblée provinciale d'Auvergne tenue à Clermont-Ferrand dans le mois d'août 1787* (Clermont-Ferrand, 1787), p. 30; Montagu, pp. 33–34.

38. Lafayette to Washington, Oct. 9, 1787, Gottschalk, *Letters*, p. 331.

with the government. Among them was Lafayette.[39] Chabrol, again delegated to plead for Riom, came to see him several times. Lafayette obligingly took the appeal to the authorities. He found their attitude to be, however, that it was up to each provincial assembly to decide its own meeting place. He therefore explained to Chabrol that the question could not be settled until the assembly had in fact first met at Clermont. He pleaded for greater unity meanwhile. "I lament local rivalries that always end by serving despotism at the expense of popular interest."[40]

About the same time, Lafayette came to the conclusion that any high adventure in Egypt and Holland would also have to await future developments. The Egyptian proposal had won no encouragement in official circles, and Brienne's pacific attitude made it appear that the Dutch war would probably be limited to skirmishes between the local factions. Consequently, when, early in August, the marquis left for Chavaniac, he had lost interest in Egypt and expected the Dutch conflagration to smoulder down to mere embers. Adrienne, now suffering herself from a chest complaint and seeking a warmer climate, had preceded him to the south.[41]

The marquis's visit to Chavaniac was cut short by the obligation to go to Clermont. On the morning of August 14, 1787, the first meeting of the twenty-five appointive delegates to the Auvergne provincial assembly opened in the main hall of the Clermont college. According to the king's regulations, this session of the assembly was to be devoted exclusively to electing the remaining members of the provincial assembly and the assemblies of the province's subdivisions (*élections* and municipalities). The first meeting was given over entirely to organization and the verification of credentials. The next day the members attended mass at the college chapel.

39. François Boyer (ed.), *Inventaire sommaire des archives communales antérieures à 1790, ville de Riom, département du Puy-de-Dôme* (Riom, 1892), p. 6. Cf. Francisque Mège, *L'assemblée provinciale (1787–1790)* ("Chronique et récits de la Révolution dans la ci-devant Basse Auvergne") (Paris, 1867), p. 10, and *Les premières années de la Révolution dans la Basse-Auvergne (1787–1789)* (Clermont-Ferrand, 1896), pp. 16 n. and 20 n.

40. Lafayette to Chabrol, [*ca.* July–August, 1787], Pierpont Morgan Library.

41. Lafayette to Washington, Aug. 3, 1787, Gottschalk, *Letters*, p. 326.

It was not until the 16th that the choice of new members began. Lafayette's godfather and "uncle" the Abbé de Murat was chosen a member for the clergy on that day, and on the next his Riom friend Chabrol was chosen for the Third Estate. Then the assemblies of the elections were organized. On the 17th Lafayette was named to the assembly of the election of Brioude but preferred not to accept the honor. He assigned as his reason that his interest in American affairs would require him to return to Paris soon.[42]

Before the assembly ended, Lafayette stood out as one of the leaders. Apprehension of the authority retained by the king in the provincial assemblies persisted among conservatives as well as liberals. Lafayette proposed therefore that nothing be done to indicate that the assembly surrendered any of the rights of Auvergne's ancient estates, though they had not met since the time of Louis XIV. The old provincial privileges, he thought, having once furnished the justification of local resistance to royal centralization, might again become an effective rationale of opposition.[43] This suggestion appealed to noble *frondeurs* anxious to restore aristocratic partnership with the king in local government as well as to those who, like Lafayette, favored an alliance of the monarchy with "the nation." "There is a very good understanding between the Ancient Noblesse and the last order," Lafayette reported to Jefferson.[44]

Consequently, general approval was expressed when Lafayette introduced a resolution on the subject. While the assembly owed a unanimous gratitude to the king, the resolution stated, for his "salutary and truly patriotic" creation of the provincial assemblies, and while, for personal and patriotic reasons, they were grateful to have been chosen delegates, they hoped for "a free scope for their zeal" and for "a becoming dignity." Re-

42. Rouchon, VI, 236; cf. Maurice Chanson, "L'assemblée de l'élection de Brioude (1787–1788)," *Revue d'Auvergne*, V (1888), 288; *Procès-verbal de l'assemblée d'Auvergne*, pp. 36–37 and 40; Lafayette to Washington, Oct. 9, 1787, Gottschalk, *Letters*, p. 331.

43. Espinchal's memoirs, quoted in Charavay, p. 152; Lafayette to Washington, Oct. 9, 1787, Gottschalk, *Letters*, p. 327.

44. Aug. 27, 1787, Chinard, *Lafayette and Jefferson*, p. 114. For the opposition of some nobles to Lafayette and the provincial assemblies see *Mémoires de M. le Comte de Montlosier sur la Révolution française, le Consulat, l'Empire, la Restauration, et les principaux événements qui l'ont suivie, 1755–1830* (Paris, 1830), I, 167–69.

minding the king of the differences between the new assembly and the old provincial estates, the resolution urged His Majesty to declare that the new regulations would in no way jeopardize "the primitive and imprescriptible rights of Auvergne."[45] It was an open bid to the king to make the new assemblies at least as significant as the old estates still retained by those provinces whose local autonomy had not yet completely disappeared. The cry for these "imprescriptible rights" was to be taken up by other provincial assemblies.[46]

When the assembly adjourned (August 21), Lafayette was satisfied with its "zeal and good harmony." There was reason to believe, he held, that "many abuses may be distroyed, liberal principles be adopted, and great deal of good be done." He was especially pleased with the dignity that the Third Estate had shown. The scions of the more ancient noble houses, he found, were better liked by the Third Estate than by the newer nobility. Vaguely perceiving that the more recently ennobled magisterial families in some ways acted as an irritating barrier rather than as a link between the nobility and the middle class élite, he apprehended that the "disgust" of the Third Estate "may produce some embarassements."[47]

After returning briefly to Chavaniac, Lafayette set out on August 28 to make a tour of the province.[48] According to one of his most suspicious colleagues in the Auvergne assembly, the Comte d'Espinchal, he deliberately sought the support of the poorer nobles and lowly bourgeoisie. "He would announce in advance his arrival in the cities where he knew he was likely to receive an honorable reception." And, indeed, Lafayette's tour was far from the detached investigation of the peasant's lot that Jefferson had recommended. Several towns received him with a pomp that Espinchal, obliged to recognize his popularity, nevertheless considered "as ridiculous as it was extraor-

45. Aug. 20, 1787, Procès-verbal de l'assemblée d'Auvergne, pp. 47-48; Mémoires, II, 185-86.

46. Lafayette to Washington, Oct. 9, 1787, Gottschalk, Letters, p. 327.

47. Lafayette to Jefferson, Aug. 27, 1787, Chinard, Lafayette and Jefferson, pp. 113-14.

48. Ibid.

dinary."[49] Lafayette himself felt that "all classes of the inhabitants" of the province showed "the most affecting marks of love and confidence."[50] The citizens of Aurillac, for example, summoned early in the morning of September 1 by the rumble of drums, met him on the road, each guild arrayed under its flag and trying its best to look military. Amid repeated cheers and the zealous efforts of the local band, they escorted him along the carefully swept streets, accompanied by the greatest dignitaries among the nobility and clergy that the neighborhood could provide. Several times the procession had to stop as Lafayette was called upon to dismount and listen to speeches of welcome. Several more speeches were pronounced after he got to his hotel. At night the streets were lighted up in his honor, and wherever he appeared, he was greeted by manifestations of joy. A grand ball was tendered him, but to the consternation of the ladies, he talked with local celebrities instead of dancing. When he attended Sunday mass the next day, he was seated in an armchair especially set aside for him by the curé. A round of visits to the best homes of the town ended the day. On Monday he departed, the population of Aurillac once again conducting him in triumph a good distance along his way.[51]

On the 4th he was at St. Flour, where the Masonic Lodge Sully, of which several local nobles, magistrates, and clergy were members and the town's mayor was the venerable, solemnly received him as an honorary member. This ceremony closed with a banquet at which a local poetaster read a series of verses in honor of the illustrious guest, who by his "noble exploits, unendingly narrated in two hemispheres, had learned to regard without discrimination all humans as his brothers" and who lived "for the eternal welfare and glory of the land . . . as well as for the honor of Masonry."[52]

49. "Lafayette jugé par le Comte d'Espinchal," *Revue retrospective*, XX (1894), 293–94.

50. Lafayette to Washington, Oct. 9, 1787, Gottschalk, *Letters*, p. 331.

51. Contemporary chronicle, quoted in Auguste Garnier, *Notice sur le général Baron Delzons* (Paris, 1863), pp. 236–38.

52. Jean Delmas, *Les loges maçonniques de Saint-Flour au XVIIIᵉ siècle* (Clermont-Ferrand, 1897), p. 10; Francisque Mège, "Les populations de l'Auvergne au début de 1789," *Bulletin historique et scientifique de l'Auvergne*, 2d ser., 1904, p. 214 n.; Charavay, p. 153 and n. 1.

When he returned to Chavaniac, Lafayette received word that a change of ministers had again occurred in Versailles. Ségur, Castries, and Laurent de Villedeuil had resigned, and M. de Lambert, another colleague of the Second Bureau, had been named comptroller-general. This development seemed to present a fitting opportunity to act again on behalf of American commerce. Recently some American vessels had come to France expecting to benefit from Calonne's concessions, only to find that the necessary regulations had not yet been delivered to the port authorities. The ships were therefore embargoed by the agents of the farmers-general.[53] Lafayette, constituting himself once more the American advocate, wrote the new comptroller-general a long letter of congratulation and advice. No Jefferson or Condorcet or Brienne prompted him this time.

The glorious but costly war that France had fought for American independence, he said, ought to have led to many advantages. Among them "one of the principal ones was undoubtedly that of bringing here the commerce of the United States." Commerce in this instance was "essential to politics," he contended, "since the merchants of those republics have great influence on the decisions of each state and of the federal body." This commerce, already worth around 80,000,000 livres, was bound to increase as the population of "that new and fortunate country" increased. Because American raw materials would be exchanged for French finished goods, the balance of trade would be favorable to France. "The advantages of this commerce ought to be counted double for us since each of our gains in the United States is a political and mercantile loss for a rival nation."

So far, Lafayette continued, this question had failed of satisfactory settlement for several reasons. Among them were prejudice, greed, privilege, and paper money, "but above all the sinister spirit of finance and the pressure of business that daily absorbs the attention of the ministers." It would be "ignorance or bad faith to assign as reasons differences in religion or loyalty to the English in a country where all religions are equal and England is hated by seven-eights of the population." Language

---

53. Lafayette to Lambert, Sept. 10, 1787, Chinard, *Lafayette and Jefferson*, p. 117; cf. Lafayette to Jefferson, Aug. 27, *ibid.*, p. 114.

difficulties, custom, and old debts, though somewhat better explanations, would not be great enough to last against the passage of time, serious effort, and "particularly the single, great rule of all commerce, *profit*."

If not deliberately obstructed, American commerce was bound to come to France, Lafayette went on. All the commodities that England could furnish and some that England's climate made it impossible for her to produce could be picked up in France at ports that were more strategically placed for Americans. Sharp English merchants, however, had profited from the errors of overprudent French merchants, naval officers, and fiscal agents, who were responsible for "vexations, discussions, and procrastinations worse than the duties." Whenever an American tries to buy anything in France, "the internal customs barriers, the language of finance which he has to learn in addition to the ordinary French language have discouraged his good intentions." The farmers-general have added to the complications by giving Robert Morris a monopoly in another hemisphere "like the one they have in this one" and paying him, not in French merchandise, but in London drafts. They had no right to complain, as they did, that "the Americans must not like France since there are so few of their ships in our harbors."

Lafayette then proceeded to outline the history of the American Committee up to the point where Calonne had formally notified Jefferson of the regulations on American trade. He urged that those regulations at last be given the full force of law. Two hours of Lambert's time would suffice to convince him that delay "is extremely harmful to our interests"; for, the letter concluded, the matter will "become still more important when the United States will have acquired the preponderant position for which they are destined."[54]

Despite invitations to visit other cities of Auvergne, Lafayette followed this letter to Paris. He stopped at Clermont on September 15,[55] and on the 18th he was at Fontainebleau,

54. Lafayette to Lambert, *ibid.*, pp. 114–18 (the contemporary translation on pp. 118–22 is not accurate).

55. Lafayette to the municipality of Thiers, Sept. 15, 1787, Archives municipales de Thiers, AA3–72.

where Louis XVI's retinue was now assembled. Shortly after his arrival, he wrote to Jefferson that he intended to see some of his friends at court, hoping not to return "without some decision or other respecting American affairs." He then planned to go on to Paris and stay about two weeks before returning to his native mountains again.[56]

Something Lafayette learned, however, when he visited his friends at Fontainebleau resulted in a mysterious burst of energy that was extraordinary even for him. He found that the Dutch civil conflict had again flared up. The Prussian king, when no satisfaction was offered by the Dutch "patriots" for the insult to his sister, had forced the issue. He had sent a contingent of his much-feared army under the Duke of Brunswick across the Dutch border. This surprise movement caught the French unprepared. They had just recalled the Marquis de Verac from his post as ambassador at The Hague and had sent Lafayette's acquaintance, the Comte de Saint Priest, in his stead. Saint Priest was no farther on his way to his post than Antwerp when he learned of the Prussian offensive.

The Dutch Republicans, having decided to resist the invasion, counted on France to support them, since the English would undoubtedly support the Prussians. But the glorious days of Vergennes were over. The French government, hampered by its deficit and its domestic politics, remembered Vergennes's intrigues but forgot his readiness to back intrigue by force. Its part in the Dutch dispute thus became a feeble imitation of French intrigue in America. For some time now, Brienne and Castries (still acting as minister in the absence of his successor) had allowed French agents, in much the same fashion as had worked so successfully in America, to encourage the "patriots" of Holland to resist. The Republicans had been secretly promised a French auxiliary corps under a prominent French commander and trained officers to lead their own forces.

Among the French agents in Holland was the Chevalier de Ternant, once an officer under Lafayette in the American army and now a colonel in the Dutch Republican army. Ternant was

56. Lafayette to Jefferson, Sept. 18, [1787], Chinard, *Lafayette and Jefferson*, p. 122. Cf. p. 114.

in favor of making Lafayette commander of that army and had been using his influence toward that end. Lafayette was not, however, the only French general who hoped that he might be selected for that honor, although he was probably correct in thinking that he was the one whom the Dutch would have preferred if they had not been discouraged. Up to the moment of his recall, the Marquis de Verac had put forward his own candidate in the person of the Rhinegrave de Salm, maintaining that the French court favored his candidate.[57] In view of Lafayette's recent political behavior, that was easy to believe.

Verac's opposition, added to the general feeling all through August that the crisis would pass amicably, had led Lafayette to give little heed to Dutch affairs. Now, however, when he went to visit his friends at court in Fontainebleau, he discovered that not only had a personal friend been named to replace the unfriendly ambassador at The Hague but that Frederick William's unexpected offensive had reopened the entire issue. These new developments led to a sudden change in Lafayette's plans. He immediately hastened to Paris, arriving there the same day. After a hurried interval in Paris, he pushed on toward Holland, spurring his horses throughout the night and most of the next day. At the end of a grueling journey of almost one hundred and fifty miles, he reached Varennes.[58] He confidently expected that through Ternant's influence he would be put in charge of a corps of twenty thousand Dutch volunteers and would no doubt, as soon as affairs grew more critical, be given command of all the Republican forces.[59] He might also be able to enlist the new French ambassador on his side. He entered into communication with Saint Priest even while they were both on their separate ways toward Holland.[60]

Lafayette, however, was doomed to frustration. Unpleasant

57. Lafayette to Washington, Oct. 9, Gottschalk, *Letters*, pp. 329 and 331–32; *Mémoires*, II, 214–15 n.

58. This itinerary is inferred from the dating of his letters to John Adams (Sept. 18, 1787 [from Paris], *Works of John Adams*, VIII, 449–50) and to an unidentified American merchant, Sept. 19 [from Varennes] (Gardner-Ball collection). Cf. Saint Priest, I, 200–203.

59. Lafayette to Washington, Oct. 9, 1787, Gottschalk, *Letters*, p. 331.

60. Saint Priest to Lafayette, Sept. 26, 1787, *Mémoires*, II, 498.

reports stopped him en route. It developed that the Dutch patriots had already chosen as their leader the Rhinegrave de Salm, and he was rapidly being pushed back by the Prussians. A letter to Lafayette from Saint Priest at Antwerp soon made clear that it was now too late to do anything effective by secret maneuvers. The Prussians were moving too fast. They were already at Utrecht and only large-scale operations could check them. "Watch carefully whether our troops march," Saint Priest advised. "You are wanted in Holland, and our movements might bring forth a decision there. Ternant commands at Amsterdam and would joyfully serve under you. But if we do not march, your errand will be useless to you." Amsterdam could not hold out long, Saint Priest warned, and France, by leaving the patriots in the lurch, had become the bête noire of both parties. But "if I find an opening some day, I shall let you know."[61]

The French army did not move, and Lafayette was back in Paris on October 3. Fuming over the humiliation the French nation had suffered, he nevertheless postponed his scheduled trip to Auvergne to await further developments.[62] But a week later the Prussians entered Amsterdam and all chance of successful intervention disappeared. Lafayette was bitterly disappointed with "the dismal event." He blamed "the indecision" of the ministry, "the blunders" of Verac, and the "rascality" of the "cowardly advanturer" Salm. The Dutch Republicans, he now found, "could never agree in any plan and were almost as much opposed to each other as they were to the state holder." He also thought that the king of Prussia had acted "contrary to the laws of honour" and in a fashion that was bound to cement the alliance of France with Austria. "We have been surprised, he mislead, the Dutch ruined, and England is the only one that gained in the bargain." Far from averting war, he reasoned, France's action had only increased the danger that,

61. *Ibid.*, pp. 498–99. Cf. Lafayette to Washington, Oct. 9, 1787, Gottschalk, *Letters*, p. 329.

62. Lafayette to an unidentified count, Oct. 3, 1787, Albert May Todd Library, Mentha, Mich. (courtesy of Mrs. E. L. Woodhams).

if it came, it would be a general world conflagration, in which even America would become involved because of a vengeful British king and her treaty obligations to France.

A general European war still seemed imminent when Lafayette sat down to write Washington one of those long letters he called "gazettes." Though he dealt with other matters first, even a less perspicacious man than Washington could easily have guessed from his self-righteous indignation, the amount of space he gave to the episode, and the way he dropped it and then went back to it that the fiasco in Holland had hurt him deeply. It was everyone's fault, he implied, but his own. The court had been "infatuated" with Salm. Salm "spoke great wonders but did nothing but to run a way." Verac "knew nothing of what was doing, said nothing of what was to be said." The ministers had been "slow in their preparations, dilatory in recalling their ambassador, and compleatly deceived in their negotiations." His own "wishes and advantage" had been "spoiled by the very men who ought to have supported" them. He was, however, prepared to believe the ministers' claim that they had been "deceived by the absurdity of the French ambassador and the knavery of the Rhingrave."[63]

Lafayette was no more severe in his judgment of Salm and the French government than were other contemporaries. Jefferson, for example, called Salm "a prince without talents, without courage, and without principle" and believed the French ministers had been outwitted.[64] Lafayette himself held the royal family more responsible for his disappointment than Brienne and Castries. "Altho' I am not on very good terms with the crowned heads," he announced, "it does not in the least lessen my influence with the ministers."[65]

Bitterness toward the court increased Lafayette's revolutionary ardor. After the Dutch fiasco he became more outspoken than ever. His wishes now seemed more fervent for real

63. Lafayette to Washington, Oct. 9, 1787, Gottschalk, *Letters*, pp. 329–32.

64. "Autobiography," Lipscomb and Bergh, I, 114; Jefferson to Jay, Oct. 8, 1787, *ibid.*, VI, 315–17. See also p. 108 above.

65. Lafayette to Washington, Oct. 9, 1787, Gottschalk, *Letters*, p. 331.

constitutional change to come out of Philadelphia. "I hope to God," he wrote Washington, "this opportunity may be made use of, so as to give solidity and energy to the Union, without receding however from the principles of democraty, for any thing that is monarchichal or of the aristocratical kind is big with evils." Distrust of the easygoing, inefficient ways of democracy, he feared, might lead to granting too much power to a central authority. But he was hopeful that "so many enlightened, experienced, and virtuous senators will have hit the very point where the people will remain in possession of their natural rights, of that perfect equality among fellow citizens, and yet [where] government, with the powers freely and frequently invested in them, will be able to provide with efficacy and act with vigour."

Recent cogitation on monarchy in France and Holland had led Lafayette also to feel still more friendly than before to the prospect of revolution nearer home. He found that "the ideas of liberty have been, since the American Revolution, spreading very fast" and that "combustible materials have been kindled by the Assembly of Notables." Brienne was having no less trouble with the fiscal problems of France than had Calonne. He had tried to impose reform by royal decree but had encountered continued resistance from the parlement of Paris. That had led him to exile some of the judges. The people thereupon had plainly shown where their sympathies lay by hissing the Comte d'Artois and burning some of the ministers in effigy. The queen, known to be a leader of the conservative court group, did not dare to go to Paris for fear of unfriendly popular demonstrations. All these events fortified Lafayette's hope for eventual reform. "We shall at least obtain the infusion . . . into every body's head . . . that the King has no right to tax the Nation, and nothing in that way can be stipulated but by an Assembly of the Nation." He did not, however, look for a thorough and speedy change. "Powerfull people will put bars in the wheels." The king himself had a "Turkish power." He was "all mighty," having "the means to enforce, to punish and to corrupt." Besides, the ministers "have the inclination and think it their duty to preserve despotism." The court also swarmed with "low and effeminate courtiers," serving despotism by their "intrigues and servility." Moreover, "the influence of women and love of pleasure have abated the spirits of the Nation, and the inferior classes are ignorant."

Yet some change was bound to come, Lafayette felt. "The genius of the French is lively, enterprising and inclined to contempt of their rulers. Their minds are getting enlightened by the works of philosophers and the example of other nations." Although the people are slaves, they "don't like to confess that is the case," since they have a "becoming sense of honour." Especially in the provinces could disgust with despotism and courtly extravagance be found. Despite spies, the Bastille, and the censorship, "the spirit of criticism and patriotism" was spreading. Even the highest classes of the nation, many of them close to the king, were becoming infected by the new philosophy, although it was "mixed with a fear to loose their stations and pensions." But if change was certain, it would also be peaceful; for although "the mob in the city was restless, their dissatisfaction expressed itself in a "frolicking insolence" and they were "ever ready to give way to a detachement of the Guards." The "country people" had "more serious discontents," but they lived in "the remote provinces." And so only "by little and little, without great convulsions" would an independent body representative of the people be called into existence, bringing with it a diminution of royal power.[66]

Lafayette was shortly to discover how mistaken he was, for the time was not far off when the Guards would either give way to or join the mob, and by that time the "insolence of the mob" would no longer be "frolicking."

BIBLIOGRAPHICAL NOTES

For the local affairs of Auvergne the books and articles of Francisque Mège are invaluable. They are based upon a careful combing of the local archives and sometimes provide data not otherwise available. The printed Procès-verbal de l'assemblée provinciale d'Auvergne is very rare. Lafayette's part in that assembly is described much less completely in his Mémoires.

66. Ibid., pp. 326-28.

The *Mémoires* of Saint Priest were written after the author had become hostile to Lafayette. They therefore give the impression that Saint Priest was suspicious of the marquis even before the French Revolution. He fails altogether, for example, to mention Lafayette's part in the Dutch crisis. Since, however, he wrote to him in a most amicable fashion during that episode (see above, p. 340), these *Mémoires* may be considered to convey his later unfriendliness rather than his true contemporary attitude. In any event there is no reason to doubt that Lafayette thought of him as being well disposed.

Philip S. Foner (ed.), *The complete writings of Thomas Paine* (New York, 1945), suggests (II, 621) that Lafayette might have been one of the Frenchmen who induced Paine to write his *Prospects on the Rubicon*, the first draft of which was dated August 20, 1787. That is possible, but it lacks substantiation, and in view of Lafayette's illness during the summer of 1787, Paine probably did not even see him until they both returned to Paris later in the year. See below, page 374.

CHAPTER XXII

Defiance in Auvergne

THE conflict of France and Prussia in Holland coincided with a renewal of the inveterate dispute of Russia and Turkey in the Near East. In that dispute Austria could not be counted upon to remain indifferent long, and if England supported Prussia and Turkey, France could be expected to go to the aid of Austria, the Dutch Republicans, and Russia. Thus the century-old series of world wars, of which the War of American Independence had been only the most recent, would be renewed. Salm's collapse did not immediately remove the danger.

If war came, Lafayette, as a general in both the French and the American armies, could feel certain of employment. That was why he broke his engagement to return to Auvergne early in October and remained in Paris.[1] A general European conflict, he reasoned, might afford the Americans a long-deferred opportunity to take the disputed frontier forts. Such a move would probably result in an answering attack from England, which in turn would be counteracted by an American invasion of Canada and Newfoundland. Reasoning thus, Lafayette (probably not without having previously consulted Brienne and Jefferson) wrote his views to the American government. "A cooperation against a proud and rancourous ennemy would equally please my politics as a French man, my feelings as an American, my wiews as an individual." Nine years before, he recalled, he had had the honor of being chosen by Congress to take command in a proposed invasion of Canada, "and never have I ceased to enjoy the prospect of its enfranchisement." A victorious war

1. Lafayette to an unidentified count, Oct. 3, 1787, Todd Library.

might also lead to favorable decisions on disputed fishing rights and the navigation of the Mississippi.

The United States, Lafayette argued, would thus have much to gain by remaining loyal to the French alliance. Yet much might be lost, too. "Are not the United States so circumstanced for the present as to render a war too expensive for them and too dangerous to their commerce? Convinced as I am that it is the case, I think myself bound in duty and love for them not to indulge my ambition farther than a neutrality useful to them and favourable to their allies." Therefore, if the United States could not avoid involvement altogether, he advised that they stay neutral as long as possible. This opinion arose, he pointed out, from "the unbounded zeal which shall ever rank me among the most devoted servants of the United States."[2] In fact, his own personal interests, he thought, would probably have been better served by America's active participation in the war than by the friendly neutrality he was recommending.[3]

Had France and the United States become involved in war in 1787, crucial effects could hardly have been averted in both countries. In the United States the proposed constitution had already been submitted to the states for approval. Yet it was perhaps not too late, despite America's remoteness, for a new world war to have modified the course of the federal revolution under way there. And, in France, had the government seen fit to concentrate its efforts on war instead of on internal reform, domestic strife might easily have come temporarily to a close as Lafayette and other liberal leaders rallied around the king in the common struggle against the hated English.

That possibility was not absent from Lafayette's mind when he ventured the guess that despite the "great progress" of "the main body" along "the right road," a struggle of twelve or fifteen years might now be necessary for France to arrive at "a pretty good constitution." It might even eventually become

2. Lafayette to Jay, Oct. 15, 1787, LC, PCC 156, fols. 463–65 (with modifications in [Weaver], *Diplomatic correspondence*, I, 454–56). Cf. Lafayette to Washington, Oct. 9, Gottschalk, *Letters*, pp. 329–30; to Adams, Oct. 12, *Works of John Adams*, VIII, 457; to Hamilton, Oct. 15, LC, Hamilton papers (with modifications and omissions in *Works of Hamilton*, I, 445–46); and Jefferson to Carmichael, Dec. 11, Lipscomb and Bergh, VI, 379–80.

3. Lafayette to Hamilton, Oct. 15, 1787, *loc. cit.*

"the best [constitution] perhaps that can be framed but one," and "may *that one*, the only one truly consistent with the dignity of man, be forever the happy lot of the sons of America."[4] He seemed to see a certain dramatic justice in the parallel struggles for constitutional government in France and America. To Alexander Hamilton, who had played a less prominent role at Philadelphia than his own at Versailles, he wrote: "While you have been attending your most important Convention, debates were also going on in France respecting the Constitutional Rights and matters of that kind. . . . Amidst many things that were not much to the purpose, some good principles have been laid out, and altho' our affairs want a proper arrangement, the nation will not in the last be the looser." Unfortunately, he owned, there was reason to fear that war might wipe out all that had so far been gained.[5] But whether or not reform were frustrated in France, he counted on the Philadelphia Convention to "add a lustre and a proper weight" to America's prestige in Europe, while assuring "internal happiness and prosperity" and baffling "the invidious wishes" of the unfriendly.[6]

The threat of war led the French government to take precautionary measures. It created a special war committee, regarding which Lafayette hastened to inform American generals.[7] Besides, a new envoy was dispatched to Philadelphia—the Marquis de Moustier, whom Lafayette introduced to influential persons in America in most friendly terms. The fact that young Victor-Marie Dupont, son of the reputed inspector of commerce, was attached to Moustier's staff gave Lafayette the opportunity to point out that the elder Dupont was zealously engaged in preparing a further report on Franco-American commerce.[8]

4. Lafayette to Adams, Oct. 12, 1787, *Works of John Adams*, VIII, 456.

5. Lafayette to Hamilton, Oct. 15, 1787, *loc. cit.*

6. Lafayette to Jay, Oct. 15, 1787, *loc. cit.*

7. Lafayette to Washington, Oct. 9, 1787, Gottschalk, *Letters*, p. 328; to Knox, Oct. 15, Massachusetts Historical Society; and Gouvion to "Dear General," Nov. 5, Maine Historical Society.

8. Lafayette to Washington, Oct. 9 and 15, 1787, Gottschalk, *Letters*, pp. 332–33; to Hamilton, Oct. 15, *loc. cit.*; to Jay, Oct. 15, *loc. cit.*; to Knox, Oct. 15, *loc. cit.*; to Sullivan, Oct. 15, O. G. Hammond, *Letters and papers of Major-General John Sullivan, Continental Army* (Concord, N.H., 1930–39), III, 548–49.

Lafayette also wanted his American friends to understand that his confidence in the good will of France's principal minister, Brienne, remained unshaken. "I confess he haş committed errors since he is in place. Yet do I think him a man of the first rate. He has been twisted of in the two storms of interior and foreign politics. But should a more calm weather come on, I am sure he would be able and disposed to do great things." High among these "great things" would be a friendly arrangement of American affairs. Delays in implementing the old concessions had been due to the "subterraneous chicanes of the Farm" as well as to the prevailing political turmoil.[9] Now, however, the splendid co-operation of young Dupont's father and the favorable disposition of the ministry led Lafayette to expect not only the indorsement of Calonne's regulations by formal royal decree but also "additional favours" in the near future.[10]

Lafayette's dual citizenship thus continually led him to the role of propaganda agent in his adoptive country at a time of international crisis for his own. In fact, he appeared to be more concerned for America's advantage than for France's. Several years before the formal announcement of America's desire to avoid entanglement in Europe's conflicts, he argued in favor of a friendly American neutrality in preference to active participation on the side of France. He even thought that the United States might "enrich themselves with a free trade with both [belligerent] nations, at the same time that they maintain their own tranquillity and help their allies."[11] The reason for this perhaps unnatural preference was betrayed in his nostalgic confession to Washington: "What is become of the happy years, my beloved General, when, before my sentiments were formed, I had time to model them after your judgement! This comfort at least remains for me, to endeavour guessing what your opinion will be on every case that occurs."[12]

9. Lafayette to Washington, Oct. 9, 1787, Gottschalk, *Letters*, pp. 328 and 330.

10. Lafayette to Washington, Oct. 15, 1787, *ibid.*, p. 333. Cf. Lafayette to Washington, Oct. 15 (another letter), *ibid.*, p. 332; to Hamilton, Oct. 15, *loc. cit.*; to Jay, Oct. 15, *loc. cit.*; and Jefferson to Jay, Nov. 3, Lipscomb and Bergh, VI, 360.

11. Lafayette to Jay, Oct. 15, 1787, *loc. cit.* Cf. Lafayette to Washington, Oct. 9, Gottschalk, *Letters*, p. 330.

12. Lafayette to Washington, Oct. 15, 1787, Gottschalk, *Letters*, p. 333.

In this instance, Lafayette's guess was not altogether right. When Washington eventually had to decide how the United States would act in a renewal of war between France and England, he chose a stricter neutrality than his disciple now envisaged. Nor was this to be the only time that Lafayette was to miss the mark in guessing how his mentor would have acted in his place. Nevertheless, consciously and unashamedly, even proudly, he continued to model his behavior on Washington's, and his imitation of his idol became so obvious that others easily recognized who his model was.[13]

In the end, France peacefully accepted her humiliation, and the Dutch crisis passed sooner than some of the wisest observers had forecast. Lafayette remained in Paris, however, until November, despite the forthcoming meeting of the Auvergne provincial assembly. Meanwhile, Jefferson, Lambert, Dupont, and he labored on the contemplated royal decree dealing with American commerce. It was probably on this occasion that Dupont discovered that Lafayette's proposals regarding the tobacco trade were not practical. Lafayette had calculated that a duty on leaf tobacco of $32\frac{1}{2}$ sous would suffice to guarantee the regular royal revenue as well as a reasonable profit to dealers. But Dupont's calculations persuaded him that tobacco could produce a royal revenue of 28,000,000 to 30,000,000 only at the prohibitive wholesale price of 52 sous a pound.[14] Before Lafayette left for Auvergne, it became clear that, although Lambert was favorably inclined, conflicting interests over tobacco as well as whale oil were going to be stumbling blocks in the way of any new commercial arrangements.[15]

This defeat was counterbalanced by the surmounting of an important rampart that had blocked another phase of Lafayette's struggle for freedom. In the fall of 1787 Rabaut-St. Étienne became impatient. He went to see Lafayette first and then Malesherbes. It was eighteen months, he protested to each

13. Augustin Barruel, *Mémoires pour servir à l'histoire du jacobinisme* (Lyon, 1818–19), II, 339; Talleyrand, Mazzei, and Mme de Staël, as cited in Gottschalk, *Lafayette and the close of the American Revolution*, pp. 391 and 421–22.

14. Dupont's speech, Apr. 23, 1790, T. Madival, E. Laurent, *et al.* (eds.), *Archives parlementaires de 1787 à 1860*, etc., 1st ser. (Paris, 1862–1913), XV, 267.

15. Jefferson to Jay, Nov. 3, 1787, Lipscomb and Bergh, VI, 360.

gentleman in turn, since, on Lafayette's suggestion, he had come to Paris to begin his uphill struggle. Now a parlement and an Assembly of Notables had interceded for the Protestants and still the king did nothing. He threatened to return home and circulate a general Protestant petition, which he hoped would rouse public opinion to the point where the royal court would have to act. Lafayette, being obliged to leave soon for Auvergne, went to see Brienne. Rabaut, he warned, might have difficulty in preventing a general wave of protest if something were not done quickly.[16]

The warning was well timed, for Brienne was already fully absorbed in the dispute between the throne and the parlements over legislative authority and wished to avoid further complications. Despite his persistence, the new prime minister had been unable to get the courts to register his proposals for a stamp and a land tax. At last, he had resorted to the king's absolute power as chief judge of the land. In a solemn ceremony known as a *lit de justice* Louis XVI had peremptorily ordered that parlement cease its protests and sanction his decrees. Parlementary opposition had seldom before been known to continue after a *lit de justice*, but this time it did, because the Paris parlement counted upon the support of the public and of their provincial colleagues. The monarch's answer to this unwonted defiance was (as we have seen) to exile parlement, but before the end of September they were allowed to return, a compromise having meanwhile been effected. Parlement agreed to prolong the period during which a new *vingtième* (5 per cent income tax) might be collected, while the king consented to hold Brienne's other tax proposals in abeyance. The new *vingtième* immediately became the object of popular protest.

That was the situation when Lafayette, having delayed his departure as long as he reasonably dared, went off to Clermont. Shortly after he left, Brienne's reluctance with regard to religious toleration was at last overcome, and on November 19 the king proposed certain limited civil rights for the Protestants of France. The marriages of "non-Catholic" French were thenceforth to be regarded as valid and their children as legitimate.

16. Rabaut to the Committee of Bordeaux, Feb. 12, 1788, Dardier, II, 408-9.

Their dead might be lawfully buried, though only in specially designated places. They were granted the full right to own property, but certain exceptions were made in the businesses and professions that they might follow. They were permitted to worship privately according to the dictates of their consciences, although no public ceremonies were allowed. Jefferson found in the proposed decree only "an acknowledgement (hitherto withheld by the laws) that Protestants can beget children, and that they can die and be offensive unless buried." He was indignant because it did not "give them permission to think, to speak, or to worship," and he concluded that "the most illiterate peasant" of his own country was "a Solon compared with the authors of this law."[17] Still it was a signal, if incomplete, victory—an indication that a dying regime was too weak either to withstand change or to make it wholeheartedly.

When the second session of the Auvergne assembly began on November 8 at the college of Clermont, an uneasy truce existed between the crown and the courts. As the meetings continued, the political atmosphere throughout the country grew more tense. Pamphlets, remonstrances of parlement, and public declarations by influential men maintained that new taxes like the *vingtième* could be levied only if the representatives of the "nation" consented. Lafayette arrived at Clermont two days late, not putting in his appearance until November 10. He was listed on the roll of this local assembly by only his Auvergne titles—"Marquis de la Fayette, Seigneur Baron de Chavaniac, Vissac, St. Romain & Marquisat de Langeac."[18] No mention was made of his American army rank and Breton holdings, but his position and influence were more than local.

It was not until the 13th that the assembly began seriously to consider the major question before it: Auvergne's quota of the national taxes. To do so more expeditiously, it created a series of committees, and Lafayette was designated a member of the Committee on Public Welfare, Agriculture, and Commerce. That day the assembly also learned that its resolution of the

17. Jefferson to William Rutledge, Feb. 2, 1788, Lipscomb and Bergh, VI, 418. See also p. 108 above.

18. *Procès-verbal des séances de l'assemblée provinciale d'Auvergne, tenue à Clermont-Ferrand dans le mois de novembre 1787* (Clermont-Ferrand, 1787), pp. 9-10.

preceding August 20 insisting upon the preservation of the rights of Auvergne's ancient estates had not been formally presented to the king. Those who should have brought it to the royal attention had regarded it as out of order because the opening sessions of the assembly had been granted authority only to elect new members. The assembly, now considering itself a fully organized body, reconfirmed its previous action.[19]

Thereafter the hard work was done largely in the committees, the plenary sessions being devoted to deliberations upon committee recommendations. On November 21 the committee on taxes reported on the moot problem of the *vingtième*. The king had asked the province to provide the enormous sum of 2,038,000 livres by this tax. The committee could see no way of raising more than 1,297,784 livres (not counting income from royal and other special appanages). The next day's meeting was entirely devoted to this issue, and it resulted in the naming of a special committee to draw up a report upon the *vingtième*. Lafayette was named one of that group.[20]

The next afternoon the committee on the *vingtième* proposed a resolution that was largely the marquis's work.[21] After thanking the king for what he had already done, the resolution expressed a mild hope that assemblies might in the future be "created by the vote of the people" and should express "a more national appreciation." It then proceeded to direct the king's attention to the "deplorable and truly critical situation of this province." There was "a disproportion—incredible, to be sure, but none the less real—between the means of the inhabitants and their excessive burden." The king was asked to view "the picture, frightening but accurate, of abandoned estates, deserted shops, unhappy farmers reduced to the alternative of begging or permanent emigration."

The resolution then went on to speak of the *vingtième* in particular. The assembly, it stated, had had only nine days to examine "a question on which the government, after seventy-seven years of work, had not yet formed clear opinions." It

19. *Ibid.* (Nov. 13, 1787), pp. 107 and 161-62.
20. *Ibid.* (Nov. 22, 1787), pp. 175-76 and 179. Cf. p. 80.
21. *Mémoires*, II, 186.

therefore did not understand how the government had derived its "exorbitant calculation." On the bases, however, of the number of parishes in the province, previous experience, the best-informed opinion, the government's private conviction, and comparison with the proceeds from other taxes, no increase in the *vingtième* seemed justified. Therefore "the Assembly, believing that it is incompetent to venture a decision consenting to new taxes, . . . is of the unanimous opinion that it would exceed its powers and would do violence to the king's beneficent intentions if it required a figure beyond the already excessive and disproportionate sum of the existing *vingtièmes*, and it therefore would prefer to limit itself to recommending the unfortunate taxpayers to the kindness and justice of His Majesty and to the protection of the laws." The committee's proposed resolution thus boldy implied that in France there were "laws" independent of "the justice of His Majesty"! It then went on, in accordance with this concept of justice, to suggest that the net annual revenue to be raised in the province should be fixed at 1,298,493 livres (slightly more than the previously mentioned figure). "Not only would an increase in taxes be physically impossible but the continuation of the present taxes of Auvergne would be obviously unjust and destructive." The resolution closed, however, with assurances of loyalty to the king.[22]

The assembly adopted the committee's report. In so doing, it followed Lafayette's leadership in what was unmistakably an act of defiance of the royal will. The report once more raised the question whether the king was not obliged to consult the taxpayers in determining how much they were to pay. The Auvergne assembly thus identified itself with the parlements and other groups throughout France that advocated the revival of the Estates General. No member could have been naïve enough to suppose that the government would not resent such defiance.

Meanwhile, in Paris, after a brief lapse, the truce between the king and the parlements had been broken again. The ministry, still driven by the need for money, had decided to float a loan. On November 19, the very day that the king had proposed at

22. *Procès-verbal* (Nov. 23, 1787), pp. 179–85.

last to give to the French Protestants limited civil rights, he had also presented the suggested loan for parlement's consideration. This was done in a "royal session" (considered less awesome and binding than a *lit de justice*). With studied casualness the king, in the hope of rendering the loan more palatable, made a still more far-reaching announcement: he would call the Estates General sometime before 1792, when the proposed five-year period of borrowing would end. But again parlement balked. This time several of its leaders were arrested and immediately became public heroes. The resolution of the Auvergne assembly protesting against the *vingtième* thus reached Versailles at a tense moment.

While waiting to learn what the effect of its resolution would be, the assembly at Clermont continued its work. Lafayette's Committee on Public Welfare, Agriculture, and Commerce made its report on December 3. Again the voice was Lafayette's voice, but the hand was the hand of the committee.[23] It was a voice that, thanks to speaking out for favors to American merchants, was familiar with the problems of agriculture and commerce.

The report showed that, although the liberal minds of Auvergne wanted change, they yet saw no need for, or indeed hope in, quick and violent revolution. Agriculture and cattle-raising, it began, were the chief occupations of Auvergne despite the existence of some industry and commerce in a few of the towns. All occupations, however, were in need of encouragement. "But how promote competition among men overwhelmed by poverty and accustomed to see all the profits of competition arbitrarily stifled by taxes?" Moreover, the Auvergne peasant, "made distrustful by experience, does not like innovations." Education must, therefore, go hand in hand with incentive. "While steering a middle course between the spirit of theory, often proved false by practice, and the spirit of routine, always alien to progress, we believe that good develops only slowly, that a small improvement is a sufficient reward for hard work, and that truth, even when demonstrated, still needs the help of persuasion."

23. *Mémoires*, II, 485-89.

Auvergne, the report continued, had reason to be grateful for the new law that permitted the free export of its wheat. "It would have greater effect, Gentlemen, if the province had not been so thoroughly forgotten in the planning of roads that, upon examining the post map, one were not tempted to believe that this part of the realm was uninhabited." The result of this neglect was that merchants and travelers sought other areas to do business. Internal tariff duties still further increased the merchant's burden, since Auvergnats, so placed as to be able to reach Paris only by paying fees at some intervening towns, could not compete with those more fortunately located. "But if this cutworm of all commerce, breeding in the heart of the kingdom, attacks all the products of our soil without distinction, it is no less harmful to those of our industry." It would be a "beautiful undertaking honoring the king's reign" if he would execute his announced intention to abolish internal customs barriers.

The report then proceeded to discuss the several products of Auvergne. The improvement of the hemp and rope industry, it maintained, would give employment to the poor and foundlings. Linen could be perfected by prize competitions and the suppression of market fees. Sheep-raising could be promoted by provincial subsidies for selective breeding, inclosures, and pens, by the careful choice of herdsmen, and by the systematic hunting of wolves. Wool manufacture, following the actual experience of certain regions, might be efficiently carried on in more farmers' homes if custom could be overcome and funds advanced. Livestock could be made more profitable if more veterinarians were trained and if the navy bought more Auvergne cheese and salt meat.

The mention of salt opened the way to an attack upon the farmers-general. The recent increase in the salt tax of Auvergne, the report contended, had raised the cost of manufacturing cheese and feeding animals. Thus cattle-raising enterprises had been ruined and the province's inhabitants had been given new incentives to emigrate. Tanning, once a flourishing business in Auvergne, was declining, because of the tax on leather, which was "no less immoral than burdensome" and was "an everlasting source of fraud and injustice." Tanneries would flourish again if this tax, along with other commodity taxes, were abolished.

The government had already provided a good example of horse-breeding in the province; the committee recommended further experiments with donkeys and mules. Good wood, too, was scarce in the province largely because of burdensome taxes. "Trees grown in good soil, being rarely useful to poor farmers, in the end fall into the hands of the rich, whither in moving, and die in the bad soil to which they are transplanted." This tree famine could be rectified by distributing young trees at little or no expense to the farmer and scattering nurseries generously through the province. Coal, abundant in the center of the province, was kept from market by tolls. Paper, hardware, and lace also were victimized by taxes and indifferent methods.

Finally came an attack upon the inadequate system of communications in Auvergne. The committee complained that the postal service suffered from insufficient couriers, indirect routes, and defunct stations and called for improvement. They also suggested the revival of several old projects for canals. Attention to public welfare, the report concluded pointedly, was so new in Auvergne that precise information and planning were not yet possible. The committee would be pleased, however, if its "feeble sketch" of the province's needs might help to "prepare gains for our country, which for a long time has been able to show only losses.[24]

When the reading of the report was over, the assembly decided to postpone discussion of it until later, for meanwhile it had learned that the royal commissioner of the province had a communication to deliver from the king. Escorted into the assembly room with the fanfaronade that his position as the royal representative demanded, the commissioner brought a message that robbed Lafayette's committee of much of its thunder and demonstrated that the government was well aware of the need for reform. After recalling that the *corvée* and internal tariffs on breadstuffs had been abolished, the king's

24. *Procès-verbal* (Dec. 3, 1787), pp. 281–300.

memorial expressed the hope that a new era had dawned for farmers. It asked the assembly to consider a more equitable distribution of the tax load, new roads and canals, improvements of soil crops, and livestock, and the education of farmers in better methods of grain storage and milling. No less concerned than Lafayette's committee about the conservatism of the peasant, the king declared that "they are led to practice what is useful only by persuasion and they are persuaded only by their eyes." The rich landlord must therefore set them an example. The memorial also urged the assembly to give some thought to the relatively simple problem of diminishing the number of deaths due to accident and ignorance.[25]

The king's generous program simplified the procedure of the session that evening to consider the report of Lafayette's committee. A set of resolutions was adopted thanking His Majesty for what he had already done and requesting that he take further steps. On the basis of the committee's report, the king was petitioned to promote the hemp, woolen, and linen culture of Auvergne, improve its textiles and livestock, free it from the usurpations of the salt farm, cancel the tax on leather, enlarge its forests, and increase its postal facilities.[26]

Nothing, however, was said about the victims of accident, since that was a matter which the Committee on Public Welfare had not previously considered. It now, however, took that problem under advisement, and for several days the marquis and his colleagues discussed the question of how to save the people of Auvergne from avoidable deaths. One of Lafayette's colleagues was Robert Heyrauld, a country surgeon who had won the love and respect of his fellow-Auvergnats by his kindness to the sick and poor. Under Heyrauld's guidance the committee turned its attention to poverty as a killer of men.[27] The king thus became a prime mover in a profounder investigation than he probably had intended.

Meanwhile, the assembly, expecting soon to adjourn, designated four honorary members to the intermediary commission that was to act in its name between sessions. The reason for

25. *Ibid.*, pp. 301–14. 26. *Ibid.*, pp. 314–17.
27. Cf. Mège, *Assemblée provinciale*, pp. 25 and 93.

this move was obviously to lend a prestige to the commission it might otherwise not have in the event of a crisis during the interim period. Thereby the assembly again went beyond the royal regulations and again ran the risk of incurring official displeasure. Lafayette was one of the four honorary members.[28]

On December 6 the Committee on Public Welfare was ready to report on the subject of the preservation of human life. Once more Lafayette acted as spokesman.[29] The report looked the problem of poverty straight in the face. "If the king's paternal wishes and our own were fulfilled, Gentlemen," it began, "the people would soon cease to look upon population increase as a multiplication of victims. But we can as yet offer only a distant hope; and . . . [meanwhile] . . . poverty that crushes, hunger that oppresses, every consideration, in short, makes them loathe to hand on an existence that is always unhappy and too often humiliating." The poor, the committee continued, must be encouraged to overcome "this sterilizing sense of their misfortunes." The old law of Louis XIV exempting from taxes the father of twelve children should be revived. Steps should also be taken for the better training of midwives in the local hospitals and for raising the prestige of the profession. Since smallpox was still common in Auvergne, ambulant inoculators and free hospitalization should be provided and the people educated to take advantage of them.

The "most important, most far-reaching, and most difficult" scourge, however, was beggary. Despite the efforts of the government, assemblies, courts, and learned and literary societies, it got worse rather than better as more and more farmers were driven by poverty from their homes and tax-ridden landlords could not employ them in the villages. "But it is beggary, Gentlemen, and not the beggars that you must destroy. . . . We have no right to forbid them their sorrowful trade until we have assured them other means of support." The committee confessed, however, that it was easier to indicate the objective than to chart the course to reach it. "We know that we must attach the poor man to his village by work suited to his strength,

28. *Procès-verbal* (Dec. 4, 1787), p. 337; cf. Mège, *Assemblée provinciale*, p. 29 n.
29. *Mémoires*, II, 485 and 489-91.

provide food for the old and sick, and be definitely certain that the beggar has enough to eat if we are to dare refuse him alms." The whole question stood in need of further investigation. The king should therefore be petitioned to make a grant to the province to enable local governments and charitable societies to study it more carefully. The committee recommended that meanwhile its colleagues give their individual support to the efforts of prisons, hospitals, and orphan asylums to solve their institutional problems. Emigration and militia service were also included on the list of evils requiring attention.

The committee then went on to eulogize private charity. "The true recompense of virtue is to be found undoubtedly in the inner consciousness, which teaches us that man is tranquil when he is just, that he is happy when he is good, and that wrongdoing hurts the one who does it more than those who are the victims of it. But it is none the less fitting that every governmental authority should encourage emulation and impart to appreciative souls the pleasure of a virtuous act by giving it public recognition." Thereupon the committee, without mentioning his name, described the self-sacrificing philanthropy of one of its colleagues. No one had any difficulty in recognizing Robert Heyrauld.

In closing its report, the committee admitted that its ideas were not thoroughly formulated. Yet it saw room for hope that the assembly would become a center for further projects whereby local authorities, "good citizens," and "friends of humanity" might contribute to a "revitalizing influence on all classes of society and particularly that of the poor." When Lafayette finished reading the report, the assembly accepted the major points in the committee's recommendations, and it also requested the king to make Robert Heyrauld a knight of St. Michel "as a mark of honor so well merited by this virtuous citizen."[30]

That was the assembly's last constructive act. Just as it was ready to adjourn for the day, a courier delivered to the president, the Vicomte de Beaune, an ominous dispatch from Comptroller-General de Lambert. It stated that the king's

30. *Procès-verbal* (Dec. 6, 1787), pp. 372-80.

commissioner would immediately give the reasons for the government's insistence upon the *vingtième* against which the assembly had protested. Accompanying it was a letter from the commissioner making known the comptroller-general's dissatisfaction. The letter revealed that the government, detecting defiance on the part of Auvergne, meant to nip it in the bud lest it be introduced into other provinces and grow too strong. If the assembly, the letter stated, had limited itself to presenting a picture of conditions in the province, the king would have heeded its representations. Without altogether crediting some of the exaggerated details, he "would in his wisdom have considered at what point it might be just to grant to this generality a favor that would not take effect in other provinces"; for His Majesty could be counted on to take account of his people's needs with goodness, justice, and charity. But the assembly, "forgetting the only purpose of its existence" (a blunt reminder of the king's primary interest in new taxes), had permitted itself to doubt the king's intentions, to twist his meaning, and to misinterpret his decrees. "That is something His Majesty is bound to regard with as much astonishment as disapproval and will never tolerate."

The comptroller-general then went on to explain the recent decree on the *vingtième*. Denying that the increase of the sum to be collected was arbitrary and insisting that any such assertion was "false and contrary to fact," he accused the assembly of "having sought to destroy public confidence" in the government's calculations. Nothing was wrong with them, however, except perhaps the fact that they did not make sufficient allowance for "several landlords who have disguised their incomes by trick leases." The small landholders in general paid their proper share of the taxes. "His Majesty knows the classes of his subjects who, in the province of Auvergne, have managed to avoid part of the taxes that they ought to pay, but he will see that the law is administered with regard to all landlords indiscriminately." And, as if recognizing the possibility of forceful resistance, Lambert continued, "He will protect all the government's agents required to carry on this work and will make his authority respected." The proposed taxes in fact would alleviate the burden of the province since they required the more favored and the exempt to pay a fair share of the total revenue.

The comptroller-general then practically dismissed the assembly. The king's commissioner was instructed to state that the assembly "had exceeded the powers that the king had granted to it, subject to his own authority, and that it should hereafter devote greater attention and effort to earning his confidence and that of the province whose true interests it might have represented better." Moreover, the assembly was required to adjourn a month after its formal opening (which gave it only a few days more of life but time enough to redeem itself by approving the government's assessment). The royal displeasure could have been more pointedly expressed only by outright and immediate dismissal.[31]

Lambert's letter betrayed the dilemma in which the Brienne ministry found itself trapped. As enlightened governors, the ministers recognized the need for reform of the most crying abuses and were willing to make concessions, particularly since that was also the best way to win popular approval of the necessary tax revision. Yet, although an alliance of the king with his people was obviously good strategy, no one must be allowed to think that the king had abdicated any of his absolute authority to court popular favor. And so, in the three-cornered fight of king, aristocracy, and people for political power, the royal government attempted to play one of its opponents against the other. Lambert's letter, for example, at the same time that it peremptorily required the Auvergne assembly not to depart from its agenda in the direction of popular protest, rebuked landlords who did not pay their fair share of the nation's taxes. Thus, while upholding royal autocracy and endeavoring to play the people against the nobles, the ministry ran the risk of encouraging the people and the nobles to unite in a joint effort to limit royal autocracy.

31. *Ibid.*, pp. 381–85. The minutes (p. 381) read: "ne termine ses séances que le trentième jour à compter du 12 novembre." See also p. 385. November 12 was the date on which the commissioner had presented the king's opening address to the assembly (p. 92). Renouvin (p. 168 and n. 1) thinks that this meant an almost immediate dismissal of the assembly by the king, but he overlooked the fact that the king's order began counting the thirty days from the formal opening of November 12 rather than from November 8, thus giving the assembly plenty of time to wind up its affairs.

The assembly took the several days remaining to it to consider its response to Lambert. On December 10, the day before adjournment, a committee of six was appointed to put this response into final form. Lafayette was one of them. The next day he read the address to the throne that the committee had drafted.[32] "The assembly," it declared, "encouraged up to the end of its labors by the fond hope of winning the king's approval, could not receive the unexpected marks of his displeasure without being struck with profound consternation." The deputies had, however, done no more than obey the dictates of their consciences. Anxious to stay within their powers but torn by fears that they desired to calm, they had trusted to the king's paternal indulgence. They regretted that they had said anything that might have displeased His Majesty, "but they owe it to the country and to the king himself that they persist in the sentiments that lay behind their resolution."

No doubt, the proposed address went on, a redistribution of the taxes would help "taxpayers illegally assessed," but it was dubious whether increasing the tax quota would do so, and the figures that the assembly had seen did not justify any such expectation. Accordingly, the assembly took the liberty to observe "that the total tax of Auvergne is beyond all proportion and already deprives the people of an essential part of their livelihood, so that any increase, since it would also augment the number of abandoned farms and migrant farmers, would result in detriment to His Majesty's finances and would wring his heart as well." Therefore the assembly, "at the feet of a beloved king, to whom it owes its existence, which it will make every effort to devote to His Majesty's glory and satisfaction, which are inextricably linked to his people's happiness,"[33] confidently repeated its earlier resolution.

The assembly accepted the committee's draft. Then, without approving a single sou of taxes, it proceeded to adjourn its session with appropriate ceremonies and speeches. Despite the complimentary tone of the royal commissioner's valedictory and of the Vicomte de Beaune's reply and despite the reference in

32. *Mémoires*, II, 187.
33. *Procès-verbal* (Dec. 11, 1787), pp. 396–98.

Beaune's own valedictory to the "paternal views of the king," tension filled the air. The passage in these closing ceremonial addresses that must have sounded most significant to the delegates was Beaune's peroration:

"I do not doubt, Gentlemen, that, though scattered, you will meditate as individuals upon the problems of public welfare, that you will collect local data which personal observation alone can provide, and that you will come back armed with several useful conclusions, ready to put them together into a single fund of which the next assembly will be able to perfect the details. May our unalterable wish, Gentlemen, to execute His Majesty's instructions strictly and our devotion to the welfare of the province convince our fellow-citizens of the indefatigable effort that we shall always devote to anything that may offer them relief."[34]

It was clear that the king's frown had not sufficed to quell defiance in Auvergne. Lambert's maneuver had resulted only in lending a greater semblance of truth to the claim of the aristocracy to be the natural buffer between royal tyranny and popular distress.

BIBLIOGRAPHICAL NOTES

The *Procès-verbal* of the November–December, 1787, meeting of the Auvergne provincial assembly was the source from which the editors of Lafayette's *Mémoires* took their versions of his reports (II, 184–88 and 485–91). They frequently omitted passages, however, but without creating any serious misapprehensions of Lafayette's role and opinions.

Renouvin's *Assemblées provinciales* and Léonce de Lavergne's *Les assemblées provinciales sous Louis XVI* (Paris, 1864) contain brief accounts of the session of November–December, 1787, in Auvergne. The account of Mège is devoted entirely to the Auvergne assembly and so gives more complete details. All these accounts fail to give an adequate impression of Lafayette's leadership.

34. *Ibid.*, pp. 309–406. Cf. Lafayette to Washington, Jan. 1, [1788], Gottschalk, *Letters*, p. 335.

CHAPTER XXIII

A National Assembly Awaited

ON LAFAYETTE'S way back to Paris his mail from America caught up with him at Nemours. It included a copy of the eagerly awaited constitution of the United States of America. He read it avidly. What struck him first was that the Philadelphia Convention, in its anxiety to avoid governmental weakness, had given wide authority to the executive. That was what he had been afraid would happen. Yet, he reflected, General Washington would probably be the first president and "I know him too well." As a great statesman, Washington would sense the danger that lay in the possible abuse of power and would employ no more than was absolutely necessary.

Otherwise, Lafayette at first saw no defects in the document. Despite his long and so far ineffectual wait to place a French declaration of rights alongside his framed copy of the American Declaration of Independence, he was not yet impressed unfavorably by the absence of a bill of rights from the Philadelphia charter. He promptly sent his copy of the proposed constitution to Jefferson, expressing his own apprehension of executive usurpation and asking for Jefferson's opinion. He also— for he regularly associated constitutional reform in America with that in France—asked for advice regarding the process by which deputies should be chosen to the Estates General that the king had promised to convoke.[1]

Lafayette reached Paris before the New Year.[2] Stirring

1. Lafayette to Jefferson, [probably before Dec. 15, 1787], Chinard, *Lafayette and Jefferson*, p. 123.

2. Lafayette to Knox, Dec. 26, 1787, Massachusetts Historical Society. Mme de Lafayette arrived on December 15, and her husband probably was with her (see Mme de Lafayette, "Duchesse d'Ayen," in Lasteyrie, pp. 92–93).

events had taken place in the metropolis during his absence. The opposition of the parlement to the king's new tax program had passed from discreet protests to open defiance. As a result, neither the loan proposed by the ministers nor the new status of the Protestants had been formally registered by the courts, and the promise to call the Estates General had only stiffened parlement's unwillingness to make concessions in the meantime. But in another field Lafayette's efforts had helped to promote the desired result. Under the able guidance of Jefferson, and with the friendly co-operation of Lambert, the problem of American trade with France was moving along toward a satisfactory solution.

In fact, the desire to keep the United States loyal in the continuing international rivalry led France to make some new concessions. A few days after Lafayette's return, the regulations for Franco-American commerce, which Calonne had set forth well over a year before, were at last given the dignity and stability of formal law. In reporting this happy event, Jefferson added, "We have obtained some new articles of value, for which openings arose in the course of the regulations. I say *we* have done it, because the Marquis de Lafayette has gone hand in hand with me through this business, and has been a most invaluable aid."[3] Lafayette, in turn, again expressed his admiration for Jefferson: "His abilities, his virtues, his temper, every thing of him commands respect and attracts affection. He enjoys universal regard, and does the affairs of America to perfection."[4]

To be sure, Jefferson and Lafayette had hoped for more than they actually got. No change, for instance, was effected in the existing arrangements with the tobacco farm, and the duty on whale oil was not entirely removed. On the other hand, a French monopoly of spermaceti candles had been suppressed; a liberal right of *entrepôt* was granted ("almost the same thing as making all their ports free ports for us"); and all privileges enjoyed by Frenchmen were extended to Americans in all French possessions in Asia (which, however, would be meaningful only

3. Jefferson to Jay, Dec. 31, 1787, Lipscomb and Bergh, VI, 405.
4. Lafayette to Washington, Jan. 1, 1788, Gottschalk, *Letters*, p. 336.

in the anticipated event that the French East India Company's monopoly were liquidated). What was still more important, as Jefferson pointed out, all the concessions were made by one side, and there was reason to look for more. Apparently the French did not propose that American commerce should "become a nursery for British seamen."[5] Lafayette urged his American friends to take advantage of the new regulations. He had promised the French government an increase in American trade and wanted to make his promise good.[6]

New Year's Day, 1788, seemed to Lafayette the proper occasion to account to Washington for his recent activity. So young was the year when he sat down at his writing table that habit led him to date his letter "1787." "The first moments of the day" went to remind the beloved leader of his "adoptive son and most affectionate, devoted friend."

Lafayette spoke first of the "bold, large and solid frame" of the American constitution. The bicameral legislature and the methods by which it was to be chosen seemed good to him. But now he saw three things instead of one to fear (perhaps because the author of the Declaration of Independence had pointed the other two out to him). His apprehension that the president had been granted potentially dangerous power persisted. In addition, he had also grown fearful that the president might succeed himself term after term, thus "one day or other" becoming "a State Holder"; and he had at last become aware also of the conspicuous absence of a declaration of rights from the proposed constitution. These weaknesses, however, could quickly be remedied, he believed. A bill of rights could be added if the people wished, and "my other comfort is that you cannot refuse being elected President, and that if you think the public vessel can stir without such powers, you will be able to lessen them, or propose measures respecting the permanence, which cannot fail to insure a greater perfection to the constitution and a new crop of glory to yourself." In the name of America, of mankind at large, and of his "dear General's" own fame, he besought

5. Jefferson to Jay, Dec. 31, 1787, Lipscomb and Bergh, VI, 405–9.

6. Lafayette to Washington, Jan. 2, 1788, Gottschalk, *Letters*, p. 336; to Wadsworth, Jan. 2, Connecticut Historical Society.

Washington to accept the office of president. "You only can settle that political machine, and I foresee it will furnish an admirable chapter in your history."[7] His faith in America's future remained firm when he wrote to other Americans as well. "Notwistanding a few blots, it [the proposed constitution] is an admirable frame for such an extensive governement," he declared, "and I hope those parts may be altered which make me a little uneasy."[8]

Reflection on what America must do then led Lafayette to reflect upon what France had done. He went on to report to Washington that he had just experienced "the happiness to please the people and the misfortune to displease governement to a very great degree." Auvergne had refused to increase her tax burden, "and she expressed herself in a manner which has been taken very much amiss." The internal situation of France, he declared, was "very extraordinary." It was characterized by "a great degree of fermentation, but not without a mixture of levity and love of ease." And he now gave evidence of understanding more clearly than ever before that the struggle in which he was engaged was not a two-cornered fight between an aristocracy championing the people, on the one hand, and royal absolutism, on the other, but a three-cornered one in which the people were only a temporary ally of the aristocracy against absolutism. He admitted that the resistance of the parlements to the king's program was "unrational" and beyond their constitutional authority, but they "are sure to be approuved by the Nation when . . . they have the good policy to call for a General Assembly." The government, seeing "that the power of the crown is declining," was trying to "retrieve it by an ill-timed and dangerous severity." It might be temporarily successful in such a course because it had money enough to last for another year. But "for my part, I am heartily wishing for a Constitution and a Bill of Rights." He still wanted to avoid violence, hoping that the French constitution would be "effected with as much

7. Gottschalk, *Letters*, pp. 334–36. Cf. Jefferson to Madison, Dec. 20, 1787, Lipscomb and Bergh, VI, 386–93.

8. Lafayette to Wadsworth, Jan. 2, 1788, *loc. cit.*

tranquillity and mutual satisfaction as it is possible."[9] Nevertheless, "a spirit of freedom in the people . . . will occupy the stage untill it is filled by a National Assembly."[10]

Thus Lafayette stood boldly forth as the advocate of a constitution and a bill of rights in both America and France at the same time. The interplay of events in both countries focused upon him in a manner that singled him out from his countrymen. His conversations with Jefferson had played an important part in improving his political education since the time when Jefferson had first found it inadequate. But they were not the only manifestation of his increasing devotion to liberal principles in two worlds. He had of recent years become an avid reader, and his favorite subject was America. The published journals of Congress, some works of Turgot on America, Barlow's *Vision of Columbus*, Adams' *Defence of the American constitution*, and Jefferson's *Notes on Virginia* were among the books now on his library shelves. And William Gordon's four-volume *History of the rise, progress, and establishment of the independence of the United States of America*, to be published in London that year, with several references to Lafayette, was soon to join them. In fact, he had several copies of some of these books, having become a sort of propaganda agent of American ideas.[11]

As Lafayette's interest in American political theories grew, practical associations with America likewise continued, as before, to occupy his time. The Society of the Cincinnati again and again demanded attention. The importunities of worthy French officers to be admitted into the American branch of the society had not diminished.[12] He now felt called upon to sum-

9. Lafayette to Washington, Jan. 1, 1788, Gottschalk, *Letters*, pp. 334–35; cf. Lafayette to Wadsworth, Jan. 2, *loc. cit.*

10. Lafayette to Washington, Jan. 2, 1788, Gottschalk, *Letters*, pp. 336–37.

11. Inventory of the sale of Lafayette's books (confiscated during the French Revolution), Apr. 30—May 7, 1794, Archives de la Seine, DQ 10, 792.

12. Cf. Washington to Lafayette, Sept. 1, 1785, Fitzpatrick, XXVIII, 243–44, and Lafayette to Washington, Feb. 6, 1786, Gottschalk, *Letters*, p. 307; Gimel [not Gimat] to Washington, June 2, 1787, Hume, *Washington's correspondence concerning the Cincinnati*, pp. 314–15; Lafayette to Washington, Feb. 4, 1788, Gottschalk, *Letters*, p. 339, and to Knox, Feb. 4, 1788, Massachusetts Historical Society (on behalf of the Marquis de Bouillé).

mon a meeting of Paris members of that branch in order to consider a number of such petitions, and a favorable decision was reached on several of them.[13] It was also decided to continue the lamented General Johann Dekalb's son on the society's rolls, since young Dekalb had been admitted before it was determined that membership was not to be hereditary.[14] In consequence, the marquis's friends once more found it necessary to defend him against the charge of wishing to make the Cincinnati an aristocratic tool.[15]

The shower of Lafayette's philanthropies upon Americans also continued. For example, he helped Mazzei to publish his *Recherches historiques et politiques sur les États-Unis*.[16] For this act of patronage he was amply repaid, however, for reviewers commented favorably upon the book's glorification of his associations with Washington[17] and quoted Mazzei's opinion that Lafayette made it "a law to imitate General Washington in everything he did" as if it cast great credit on the younger man.[18] Americans entering the French armed services or Frenchmen seeking office and lands in America counted on the marquis for friendly support, and he hastened to see ministers or society matrons in their behalf.[19] Shocked by news of a big fire in Boston, he wrote to Samuel Breck to transfer from his Boston account 300 guineas for the victims.[20]

Lafayette early became an international figure in the move-

13. Jan. 11, 1788; see Contensori, "L'ordre américain de Cincinnatus," *Revue d'histoire diplomatique*, XXVII (1913), 527–28; Lafayette to Knox, May 30, Massachusetts Historical Society.

14. Lafayette to Knox, [1788], Contenson, *Société des Cincinnati*, p. 77.

15. Mazzei, *Recherches sur les États-Unis*, IV, 121–24. This passage was translated into French by Condorcet (see *Memoirs of the life and peregrinations of the Florentine, Philip Mazzei, 1730–1816*, trans. H. R. Marraro [New York, 1942], p. 298).

16. Mazzei to Madison, Feb. 5, 1787, Garlick, p. 108.

17. *Journal de Paris*, Feb. 13, 1788; *Journal Général de l'Europe*, Feb. 21, 23, and 26.

18. *Journal de Paris*, Feb. 15, 1788; cf. Mazzei, *Recherches sur les États-Unis*, IV, 11 n.

19. Jones to St. Clair, 1787, W. H. Smith (ed.), *Life and public services of Arthur St. Clair* (Cincinnati, 1882), I, 609; I. W. Near, *The history of Penet Square and herein a brief sketch of the life, character and operations of Peter Penet* (Hornell, N.Y., 1906), p. 7; Washington to Alexander Spotswood, Aug. 26, 1787, Fitzpatrick, XXIX, 263; Lafayette to Knox (on behalf of the Chevalier Lambert), Dec. 26, *loc. cit.*; Comtesse de Damas to Crèvecœur, Jan. 28, 1788, Robert de Crèvecœur, *Crèvecœur*, pp. 142–43.

20. *Massachusetts Centinel*, Feb. 6, 1788; cf. *Recollections of Samuel Breck*, p. 123.

ment to abolish Negro bondage. When he learned of the formation in London of a society for the suppression of the slave trade, he let them know that he approved of what they were doing, hoped he might be associated with them, and intended to create a similar society in France. The example of two great nations like England and France, he said, inevitably would induce other European countries to follow "in this human and Christian work."[21] The London society named him, as well as the Chevalier de Ternant, who had carried his message, to honorary membership.

Lafayette in fact soon became instrumental in creating the first French society for the abolition of the slave trade, though the initiative was not his. The moving spirits in that society were Brissot and Clavière, fervent admirers of Lafayette and America. These two men, out of fear of becoming compromised with the government, at first decided not to invite any prominent court nobles to join their group. Abolition was neither a wholly respectable nor a popular movement as yet, and the ministers could not be expected to look with friendly eye upon efforts to interfere with the vested interests of planters or the revenue therefrom. But Brissot and Clavière did not extend that caution to include Lafayette. From the very start they associated him with their enterprise. They went to see him and invited him personally to attend their inaugural meeting. On that occasion, he told them that he was already affiliated with the London abolition society and promised them his loyal support.

Lafayette was not, however, among the group of nine gentlemen that on February 19 met under Clavière's presidency to form the French Society of the Friends of the Negroes. Only at a subsequent meeting was Brissot authorized to ask him to join. When Brissot and Clavière again went to see him (March 19), he said that he already regarded himself as a member. He also promised to seek for the society the support of the government and other prominent persons.[22]

21. Lafayette to the society, [ca. January, 1788], quoted in Clarkson, I, 466–67; cf. Prince Hoare (ed.), Memoirs of Granville Sharp, esq. (London, 1820), pp. 399 and 417–18.

22. Brissot to James Philips, Mar. 19, 1788, Perroud, Correspondance de Brissot, pp. 169–70. Cf. Brissot, Mémoires, II, 77, and Claude Perroud, "La Société française des Amis des Noirs," Révolution française, LXIX (1916), 122–23.

Lafayette soon sent the society a gracious letter formally accepting the honor they had conferred. He was glad, he wrote, to see an organization in Paris like the one in London, "of which the first examples were founded in America," and he regretted that "the National Assembly" was "too far off to share the glory with which the Parliament of England is going to cover itself" by abolishing the slave trade. The best way to succeed in the abolition movement, he cautioned, was to be practical—"not to take refuge in philosophical reflections but to seek to conciliate the interests of humanity with those of commerce and even of the colonies—which is not impossible." He pointed to his own experiment in Cayenne as an example of how a scheme of gradual emancipation might improve "not only the prosperity of the farmhand but also the income of the actual landlords."[23]

Shortly afterward Lafayette was mustered into American antislavery ranks as well. He asked Hamilton to enrol him in the emancipation movement of the United States,[24] and the New York Society for Promoting the Manumission of Slaves soon responded by admitting him to membership.[25] And when Franklin as president of the Philanthropic Society of Philadelphia sought to enlist France's aid in the abolition of "the cruelest of civil oppressions," he naturally looked to Lafayette to promote their petition at the French court.[26]

Thus Lafayette's prominence as a friend of the Negroes was known, approved, and exploited in England and America no less than in France.[27] The French society's prestige grew as Lafayette brought into it prominent humanitarians like Condorcet and La Rochefoucauld, who in turn attracted others. Adrienne de Lafayette also became a member. Arrangements were soon made with the English society to extend reciprocal membership

23. [*Ca.* March, 1788], Brissot, *Mémoires*, II, 76–77.

24. Lafayette to Hamilton, May 24, 1788, LC, Hamilton papers.

25. Jay to Lafayette, Sept. 1, 1788, Johnston, III, 356; *Mémoires*, V, 539 n.; cf. G. W. Williams, *History of the Negro race in America from 1619 to 1880* (New York, 1883), p. 167.

26. Franklin to Lafayette, May 27, 1788, [Charles Malo (ed.)], *Correspondance inédite et sécrète du Docteur B. Franklin* (Paris, 1817), I, 288–89 n.

27. Clarkson, I, 492–93; Sharp, p. 400; *Thomas's Massachusetts Spy*, Aug. 7, 1788.

and to exchange literature.[28] True to his promise, Lafayette spoke to Brienne about the society. The minister urged caution to avoid unnecessary public hostility but pledged protection from open molestation.[29] The philanthropic marquis, as perhaps the only man who was associated with the antislavery movement in all three countries where it had now become significant, gave it a kind of international prestige that it might otherwise have lacked and thereby became involved in another humanitarian attack on the status quo that reached beyond national frontiers.

Lafayette's philanthropic interests were not, however, limited to transatlantic problems. On his request, steps were taken to improve the danger signals off the Isle of Saints.[30] He tried to introduce Irish wolfhounds into Chavaniac to guard the sheep of Auvergne.[31] He subscribed 12,000 livres for new hospitals in Paris.[32] And his benevolence at home was now crowned with a satisfaction that, although long in sight, had been much delayed. Impressed by the scruples of some devout Catholics, among whom one of the most conspicuous was Adrienne's grandmother, the Maréchale de Noailles, the Paris parlement had been reluctant to register the king's decree of toleration for Protestants. At last, however, at the end of January, 1788, it did so. Despite continued opposition by many members of the Paris parlement as individuals and by some provincial parlements as bodies, a limited toleration finally became the formal law of the land.

Jefferson—with his eye perhaps too closely fixed on the law's negative aspects—was not elated. He found in it only a reluctant recognition that Protestants were subject to biological laws, along with a humiliating enumeration of "the burthens to

28. Brissot, *Mémoires*, II, 83 and n. 3; Perroud, "La Société française des Amis des Noirs," pp. 124–37; Brissot to Philips, Mar. 19, 1788, Perroud, *Correspondance de Brissot*, pp. 168 and 171.

29. Brissot, *Mémoires*, II, 76–77; Eloise Ellery, *Brissot de Warville, a study in the history of the French Revolution* (Boston, 1915), pp. 186–87.

30. AN, Marine G 140.

31. Washington to Charles Carter, Feb. 5, 1788, Fitzpatrick, XXIX, 401.

32. *Gazette de France*, insert between issues of Mar. 16 and 20, 1787.

which they shall continue to be unjustly exposed."[33] Yet Lafayette had reason to be thankful and proud for the little that the law did grant. He took the grateful Rabaut-St. Étienne to Versailles on the next Sunday and personally presented him to the king's ministers. "You easely guess," he wrote Washington, "that I was well pleased . . . in introducing to a ministerial table the first Protestant clergyman who could appear at Versailles since the Revolution of 1685" (the year that Louis XIV had revoked the Protestants' civil rights).[34] "It is only the begining of relligious tolerance," he assured Knox. "More may be done at the time of a National Assembly . . . but will, I hope, take place sooner."[35]

The royal promise of the Estates General within a few years seemed to hold forth the possibility of cure for many social and political ills. Still Lafayette did not propose that Frenchmen should stand by, idly awaiting the realization of their hopes. Believing that the provincial assemblies could be converted into effective channels of public pressure, he took seriously his obligations as honorary member of the intermediary commission of Auvergne and engaged in a steady correspondence with his colleagues that was to last the whole of 1788. During the winter and spring his communications dealt with the questions of the poor, the beggars, the excessive taxation, and the inadequacy of roads and bridges in Auvergne. He also urged the commission to express themselves fearlessly on the changes they deemed necessary and advocated establishing a cheap semiweekly newspaper at Clermont to air local questions. "Our demands are just," he wrote, "our needs urgent, our powerlessness unfortunately too real, and our situation altogether peculiar, but the government wants an increase in revenue, and the necessity of a decrease, although geometrically demonstrated, is the worst problem for which to get a hearing in the present state of finances."[36]

33. Jefferson to William Rutledge, Feb. 2, 1788, Lipscomb and Bergh, VI, 418. Cf. Read, pp. 5–6, n. 2.

34. Lafayette to Washington, Feb. 4, 1788, Gottschalk, *Letters*, p. 338.

35. Lafayette to Knox, Feb. 4, 1788, Massachusetts Historical Society.

36. Lafayette to the commission, Feb. 23, 1788, Archives départementales du Puy-de-Dôme, série 4C, cote 6, pièce no. 3. The correspondence of Lafayette with the com-

The commission received these communications gratefully and confidently counted upon Lafayette's co-operation. When questions arose such as Chavaniac's demand for independence from the community of Aurac or appropriations for the commission's own expenses, they did not hesitate to appeal to him for advice and help. Nor did he disappoint them. Together with the Vicomte de Beaune, he constituted himself the Paris agent of the commission and pressed their problems upon the attention of government officials and other personages time and again.

Meanwhile, the conversations with Jefferson on the changes simultaneously taking place in France and America continued. In the informal seminar on political theory that the American minister thus conducted for Lafayette's benefit, he had a distinguished assistant. Thomas Paine, author of *Common sense*, whom Lafayette had once met in Philadelphia, had recently visited Paris. He had invented a kind of iron bridge and hoped to be able to find some French customers for it. Upon the marquis's return from Auvergne, Paine easily enlisted his patronage, and Lafayette tried to help him sell one of his bridges to the Royal Botanical Garden.[37] Paine joined Lafayette and Jefferson in their talks about America. "Mr. Jefferson, Common Sense, and myself are debating [the proposed constitution] in a convention of our own as earnestly as if we were to decide upon it," Lafayette notified Knox.[38] They had no doubt that Washington would be chosen the first president; "and he must by all means accept," Lafayette insisted, "as it is the best way to carry to perfection a work nearer to it than any of the kind that ever was framed, altho' it is not in my opinion free of a few objections that have been perhaps by this time removed."[39]

---

mission is in the Departmental Archives of Puy-de-Dome, série 4C, cotes 6, 8, 23, and 290. It is calendared in Rouchon, VI, 225–26, 244–45, 250–51, and 381–82. Cf. Mège, *Assemblée provinciale*, pp. 102–3 n., and *Premières années de la Révolution*, p. 79.

37. Lafayette to Corny, Apr. 7, 1788, Yale University Library. Cf. Paine to Franklin, Mar. 31, 1787, and to Jefferson, Feb. 19, 1788, Foner, II, 1261 and 1267–68.

38. Feb. 4, 1788, *loc. cit.*; cf. Paine, *Rights of man*, p. 322.

39. Lafayette to Knox, Feb. 4, 1788, *loc. cit.*

Lafayette had meanwhile learned what the enlightened minds of Europe thought of the American constitutional draft. He reported that it was "much examined and admired by European philosophers." According to him, they found exactly the same shortcomings in it as he did—"the want of a declaration of rights" (particularly the right of trial by jury) and "the extensive powers of the executive." He continued to believe, however, that, if there were "a necessary rotation of the president," the fear of executive power might be removed. Although he advocated a set of amendments to appease "the dissidents," he was himself now ready to accept "the powers and the possible permanency of the president," because he foresaw that it would be "a glorious sheet in the history of my beloved General"; for, as president, Washington would reduce those powers "to what is necessary for energy" and take from them "every dangerous seed." In relaying these comments on European public opinion to Washington, he made clear that he spoke for Jefferson as well as for himself.[40]

Humane as well as diplomatic considerations' also caused Lafayette to chafe over the aftermath of one of his earlier liberal ventures. He kept returning to the humiliation of the Dutch Republicans. The conduct of the Orange party following its success was "horrid," he thought, and was responsible for continued unrest. France's role in the Dutch fiasco still tormented him: "The late affair in Holland is a blot which it will be difficult to wash out, because perfidy in other nations is not a sufficient apology, and those who cheat in politics have a right to laugh at those who have been cheated until they are able to take a revenge." The king of Prussia, Lafayette surmised, had begun to repent his recent misconduct. And well he might, for Near Eastern complications still looked as if they might lead to a war, in which case he would find himself with only England and Turkey on his side against a formidable alliance of France, Russia, Austria, and Spain. It was simply the internal crisis in France, Lafayette thought, that made the preservation of peace probable. His concern for French prestige abroad conflicted somewhat with his desire to fix attention on

40. Lafayette to Washington, Feb. 4, 1788, Gottschalk, *Letters*, p. 338.

domestic problems. "France wants peace above every thing," he explained apologetically. "Her deranged finances, the spirit of popular opposition that is prevailing are so many reasons for her ministers to keep clear of a war." Nevertheless, "her immense ressources and the readiness of her citizens would soon place her much above the idea which her rivals now entertain."[41] In fact, "the moment she gets a National Assembly, she will leave far behind every thing in Europe."[42] Even after fighting actually started between Russia and Turkey, he still thought, "France wants peace at any rate."[43]

France's confirmed pacifism left the Dutch Republicans without even a broken reed to lean upon. Dutch patriots—among them outstanding men like the Baron van der Capellen and Pierre Paulus—had fled from persecution to Paris, and there Lafayette befriended them. But their situation was hopeless, as Jefferson, upon a visit to Amsterdam, soon confirmed.[44] Some Dutch patriots began to think of America as a refuge, and Lafayette helped at least one of them, Francis Adrian van der Kemp, to find an asylum there. The marquis was long to feel apologetic for France's pusillanimous conduct.[45]

The increasing complexity of international affairs now induced Lafayette to hope that the peaceful revolution he was awaiting in France might come more quickly than he had at first dared to believe. The emergency had led to a reorganization of the French army and helped to increase the persistent fiscal stringency. Since the parlements were still deaf to royal demands, however, and the provincial assemblies were not yet in a position to voice public opinion, the marquis concluded that "the king will be obliged to assemble the Nation sooner than is

41. Lafayette to Knox, Feb. 4, 1788, *loc. cit.*; cf. Lafayette to Washington, Feb. 4, Gottschalk, *Letters*, pp. 337–38.

42. Lafayette to Washington, Feb. 4, 1788, Gottschalk, *Letters*, p. 337.

43. Lafayette to Washington, Mar. 18, 1788, *ibid.*, p. 340.

44. Jefferson to Short, Mar. 13, 1788, "Letters of Thomas Jefferson to William Short," *William and Mary College quarterly*, 2d ser., XI (1931), 340.

45. Lafayette to Washington, Mar. 6, 1788, Gottschalk, *Letters*, p. 339; to Knox, Mar. 6, Massachusetts Historical Society; to Moustier, Mar. 6, Gardner-Ball collection; to Franklin, Mar. 6, Historical Society of Pennsylvania. Cf. *Mémoires*, II, 215 n.; and H. L. Fairchild (ed.), *Francis Adrian van der Kemp, 1752–1829* (New York, 1903), p. 105.

expected by his Ministers." He nevertheless perceived the danger that the government might try to overcome popular demand by a vigorous repression of the parlements.[46]

Meanwhile, constitutional reform in America also, so far as Lafayette knew, was doing no more than marking time. The whole winter had passed without word from Washington. It was a nostalgic young disciple who penned the next "gazette." "I wish I could begin this letter," he wrote, "with the acknowledgement of a late favour from you, but none having come to hand, I have no other comfort but to attribute it to ill fortune and not to any fault of yours. I am so happy to hear from you, my beloved General, and so uneasy when I do not, that I hope you will never willingly deprive me of a satisfaction so dear to me, yet so short of the happy habits I had taken in America."[47]

In fact, it was not Washington's fault that Lafayette had received no letters from him recently. He had written twice since the New Year. One of his letters showed that he was no less a *philosophe* than his "adoptive son." Inclosing the long-awaited vocabulary of the Shawnee and Delaware Indians that the Tsarina Catherine had requested, he speculated upon the international character of the project. Well might an American republican philosophize upon sending Indian words to a French aristocrat for a multilingual dictionary sponsored by a Russian empress. "To know the affinity of tongues," Washington mused, "seems to be one step toward promoting the affinity of nations. Would to God, the harmony of nations was an object that lay nearest to the hearts of Sovereigns: and that the incentives to peace (of which commerce and facility of understanding each other are not the most inconsiderable) might be daily encreased! . . . If the idea would not be considered visionary and chimerical, I could fondly hope that the present plan of the great Potentate of the North might, in some measure, lay the foundation for that assimilation of language which, producing assimilation of manners and interests, . . . should one day remove many of the causes of hostility from amongst mankind."[48]

The other of Washington's still undelivered letters had ana-

---

46. Lafayette to Washington, Mar. 18, 1788, Gottschalk, *Letters*, pp. 340–41.
47. *Ibid.*, p. 339.   48. Jan. 10, 1788, Fitzpatrick, XXIX, 374–75.

lyzed the proposed American constitution in even greater detail than had Lafayette. In Washington's opinion, the Philadelphia charter gave the executive only the power that was necessary for good government. Authority was otherwise sufficiently divided among the legislative, executive, and judicial branches to avoid despotism or oppression "so long as there shall remain any virtue in the body of the people." Corruption of morals or usurpation might yet flourish on the "ruins of liberty." Those were contingencies against which no human prudence could effectually provide. "We are not to expect perfection in this world, but mankind, in modern times, have apparently made some progress in the science of government. Should that which is now offered to the people of America be found on experiment less perfect than it can be made, a constitutional door is left open for its amelioration." These thoughts would probably have consoled Lafayette about the shortcomings of the American charter. He would have found solace, too, in Washington's imperturbability over the Dutch fiasco: "I think it was rather fortunate than otherwise that the incaution of an ambassador and the rascality of a Rhinegrave prevented you from attempting to prop a falling fabric."[49]

But these two letters had not yet arrived in France. They had been delayed until they could be delivered personally by John Paul Jones, who was on his way to join the Russian navy.[50] Lafayette thus had good reason to lament the inadequacy of the postal methods of his day. Largely dependent upon irregular sailings and the favor of friendly travelers, correspondence from overseas was sometimes months late in delivery. And a third letter that Washington wrote somewhat later to his devoted disciple seems never to have reached him at all.[51]

The marquis might have derived even greater solace from that third letter than from the others if he had been able to read it. First of all, it carried assurance of Washington's continued affection. "The frequency of your kind remembrance of

49. Feb. 7, 1788, *ibid.*, pp. 410–12.

50. Washington to Lafayette, Jan. 10, 1788, *ibid.*, pp. 373–74.

51. Cf. Gottschalk, *Letters*, p. 345 n.

me," Washington gratefully owned, "and the endearing expressions of attachment are by so much the more satisfactory as I recognize them to be a counterpart of my own feelings for you. In truth, you know I speak the language of sincerity and not of flattery when I tell you that your letters are ever most welcome and dear to me."

That letter also revealed a reassuring optimism concerning American affairs. Washington indicated that the ratification of the proposed constitution was making good progress. He took up, one at a time, the objections that Lafayette had raised, recognizing that he was addressing not only Lafayette but Jefferson as well. No opposition had been voiced in the Convention, he explained, to a bill of rights and trial by jury, but it had been regarded as wise to leave such matters to future adjustment. On the issue of the re-eligibility of the president, Washington differed with Jefferson and Lafayette: "There cannot, in my judgment, be the least danger that the President will by any practicable intrigue ever be able to continue himself one moment in office, much less perpetuate himself in it, but in the last stage of corrupted morals and political depravity, and even then there is as much danger that any other species of domination would prevail. Though, when a people shall have become incapable of governing themselves and fit for a master, it is of little consequence from what quarter he comes." Therefore he could see "no propriety in precluding ourselves from the services of any man who on some great emergency shall be deemed universally most capable of serving the public."

Lafayette's remarks about Washington's becoming the first president of the United States then led the American Cincinnatus to some sober reflections upon political ambition. The prospect, Washington declared, "has no enticing charms, and no fascinating allurements for me." Yet it would be inappropriate for him, he feared, "to refuse to accept or even to speak much about an appointment which may never take place: for in so doing, one might possibly incur the application of the moral resulting from that fable in which the fox is represented as inveighing against the sourness of the grapes because he could not reach them." His "decided predilection," nevertheless, because of "the encreasing infirmities of nature and the growing love of retirement" was to entertain no wish "beyond that of living and dying an honest man on my own farm." And he ended his observations on a note of deep resignation: "Let those follow the pursuits of ambition and fame who have a keener relish for them or who may have more years in store for the enjoyment."[52]

Washington perhaps did not have Lafayette in mind when he wrote of those who relished "ambition and fame," since he was talking of American affairs. Yet the still young Frenchman might have taken them as meant at least in part for him. They would have seemed like a paternal blessing upon his newest aspirations. But even without them he had to go on, as he had begun, seeking for France a covenant that would set forth "the laws of nature and of nature's God." No turning back was possible now. Events that he probably could not have successfully resisted if he had tried had already marked him as a leader in a course that it was not at all clear he could control.

BIBLIOGRAPHICAL NOTES

Despite the hortatory nature of Read's *Lafayette, Washington et les Protestants de France,* his account of the opposition to the decree may be regarded as dependable since it is based upon reliable documents derived from the articles he cites from the *Bulletin de la Société de l'Histoire du Protestantisme français.*

The idea that the Société des Amis des Noirs was part of a widespread revolutionary conspiracy hiding under the pretext of being an abolitionist group still persists. Bernard Faÿ (*La franc-maçonnerie et la Révolution intellectuelle du XVIII* siècle [Paris, 1935], pp. 242–46), naming the society as only one of the numerous affiliations of Lafayette, makes the Freemasons responsible for the Revolution. The chief source of this idea as applied to the Amis des Noirs is Barruel (II, 334–39). Barruel, however, was overwrought on the subject and based most of his story on hearsay evidence. Since he wrote his book, the records of the society have been examined not only by Perroud and Ellery as students of Brissot's career but also by L. Cahen as a student of the career of Condorcet in "Les Amis des Noirs et Condorcet," *Révolution française,* L (1906), 481–511. I have gone through the ones at the Bibliothèque de l'Arsenal myself. There seems to be nothing in them that would justify a careful historian in concluding that the Amis des Noirs was anything more than it pretended to be. Its members, however, for exactly

52. Washington to Lafayette, Apr. 28, 1788, Fitzpatrick, XXIX, 475–80.

the same reason that made them desirable members of such a society, were also peaceably and legitimately engaged in other reform movements. See Brissot, *Mémoires*, II, 54.

L. de Cardenal (*La province pendant la Révolution, histoire des clubs jacobins* [*1789–1795*] [Paris, 1929], pp. 146–47) cites a work appearing in Hamburg in 1795 that speaks of a plan discussed by Rabaut-St. Étienne and Lafayette to create a Calvinistic federated republic in France. Cardenal does not credit this allegation, and no contemporary evidence has been found to substantiate it.

CHAPTER XXIV

Brittany Resists

ANOTHER attack of the same illness that had forced Lafayette to take to his bed the preceding year once more in the spring of 1788 diminished his characteristic vigor. This time he attributed his bad health to disgust with politics. "The people, my dear General," he reported to Washington, "have been so dull that it has made me sick, and phisicians have been obliged to cool my inflammed blood."[1] Since the approved way of cooling inflamed blood—that is, reducing fever—in Lafayette's day was to bleed the patient and since that was not done lightly, Lafayette had apparently been quite ill. He was ill enough, in fact, not to take his post that spring as a *maréchal de camp* in the Duc d'Ayen's command.[2] A recurrent fever that twice in about a year put a young man of thirty in bed for weeks was more likely to have been tuberculosis than disgust with politics.

Whatever the disease was, it made Lafayette for a time play the unaccustomed role of observer rather than actor. The more he observed, however, the more unhappy he became. The prospect of peaceful reform by the fiat of an enlightened government seemed to retreat farther as one went to meet it. In March the ministers had made an effort to win confidence for honesty and efficiency by publishing the fullest accounting of government funds that had yet been made. But as it showed a deficit that was larger than many had feared—too large to be covered

1. Lafayette to Washington, May 25, 1788, Gottschalk, *Letters*, p. 343.

2. Charavay (pp. 157–58) implies that he did, but Lafayette attended a meeting of the Friends of the Negroes on April 8 (see Claude Perroud, "La Société française des Amis des Noirs," *Révolution française*, LXIX [1916], 124 and 131), and his letters to Washington of May 4 and 20 are dated from Paris (see Gottschalk, *Letters*, pp. 341–42).

merely by loans—it further weakened the government's credit
and thereby increased the hope in parlementary circles that
continued opposition might wring significant concessions from
an impecunious king.

In the crisis, Brienne decided upon a royal coup d'état. It
strikingly resembled the one that the unpopular Louis XV had
effected in the closing years of his reign but which the more
enlightened Louis XVI upon his accession had countermanded.
Brienne proposed to abolish the parlements, create a more systematic hierarchy of justice in their place, and limit the new
courts to judicial functions. Only the highest or "Plenary
Court" was to have the right, until then the object of bitter disputes between kings and parlements, to register royal decrees.

In normal times judicial reform might have been welcome,
introducing efficiency into a system that had grown confused
and disruptive. But coming in the midst of parlementary
clamors for the revival of the Estates General and accompanied
by the arrest of parlementarians who had made themselves too
conspicuous by their loud demands for the nation's rights, it
looked more like a maneuver to suppress the legal champions
of the people than a step toward juridical improvement. The
parlement of Paris refused to register a decree that would have
been its own death warrant. Even after the king in a *lit de
justice* (May 8) obliged registration, opposition continued and
was supported by the lower courts and the provincial parlements. By the end of the month court after court throughout
the land had protested the royal measures. Despite the patent
need for a new judiciary system, public opinion lined up behind
the law courts, and in some towns violence broke out. A vigor-
less government did nothing either to implement its own program or to dampen the growing defiance.

Agitation was still afoot when Lafayette finally recovered
from his illness. At first it appeared that the king would have to
yield. The peers of France refused to accept service in the new
Plenary Court. The appeal of the parlements to the nation, the
solidarity of the lower courts, the support that they received
among the lawyers and even among the clergy, had created a
political crisis of the first magnitude. The king's governors had

in a few instances been hooted and even stoned when they demanded registration of the new law. "And [in] the midst of these troubles and anarchy the friends of liberty are daily reinforced, shutt up their ears against negociations, and say they must have a National Assembly or nothing."[3]

It soon became clear to Lafayette, however, that the resistance to the royal coup, coming largely from upper-class groups and the legal profession, lacked robustness. Popular resistance, except in spoɪadic outbursts, had simply not materialized. Indeed, disappointment at the continued apathy of the people, he felt, had brought on his sickness.[4] The government had "struck a great blow, and . . . the people could not be roused." Slowly Lafayette was forced to recognize that the struggle for power in France so far had been between the royal court, on the one hand, and the aristocracy, on the other, with the people looking on more or less passively. He understood that resistance to the government's high-handedness had reached so critical a point that there was a "revolution now going on in this country."[5] Yet he could not delude himself into thinking that it was a popular movement. If anything, it was made "more difficult to manage as the people in general have no inclination to go to extremities." They flaunted no popular device like that of "Liberty or Death" to which the Americans had rallied. "All classes are more or less dependant. . . . The rich love their ease, and the poor are depressed by want and ignorance."[6] For a short while Lafayette was indeed discouraged. Sickness and the prospect of political defeat left him momentarily without his usual resilience. "I have for a few days thought we were gone," he wrote to Hamilton.[7]

In the midst of this political turmoil, Brissot left for America. He had decided to study the history of the United States on the spot, and Lafayette was called upon to write him several letters

3. Lafayette to Washington, May 25, 1788, Gottschalk, *Letters*, pp. 342–43.

4. *Ibid.*, p. 343.

5. Lafayette to Hamilton, May 24, 1788, LC, Hamilton papers.

6. Lafayette to Washington, May 25, 1788, Gottschalk, *Letters*, p. 342.

7. May 24, 1788, *loc. cit.*

of introduction to outstanding Americans. That obligation induced the discouraged convalescent to report on events in France and, in doing so, to re-examine his own position. As he reflected on contemporary events, his natural buoyancy returned. There still seemed to be a way to defeat the government's "levity," he decided. That was "to reason or persuade the Nation into a kind of passive discontent or non obedience."[8] French domestic affairs must soon reach a crisis. "Despotism or liberty (*monarchical liberty*, I mean) must conquer," he declared (and since these words were meant for the rather royalistic Hamilton, he underlined the words "monarchical liberty"). Meanwhile, the people of France must be educated into "a passive discontent, non obedience, and a kind of quacker [i.e., Quaker] resistance." Such tactics, he hoped, would "suffice to undo the [government's] fatal scheme."[9]

Thus by the spring of 1788 Lafayette had been forced to take one more reluctant step in the direction of open revolt. No longer confident that royal despotism could be circumvented altogether peacefully, he nevertheless hoped to avoid armed conflict and bloodshed by a program of passive resistance. To be sure, it was "rather inconvenient to have so many thousand bayonnets in our way."[10] Still, the government so far had been worsted, and its effort to raise money without calling the Estates General had failed. "I now expect that a National Assembly will be the only means for governement to get rid of the strings that have been laid in their way."[11] And if that were true, it was possible to "begin to hope for a Constitution." A "bettering situation" might lead to another disappointing postponement of his return to America. "I don't live one day," he wrote Washington, "without grieving for this hard separation which deprives me of the blessed sight of what is dearest to me, and leaves me so few opportunities to tell you, my dear General, with all the love of a devoted heart that I am forever, with the

8. Lafayette to Washington, May 25, 1788, Gottschalk, *Letters*, p. 342.

9. Lafayette to Hamilton, May 24, 1788, *loc. cit.*

10. Lafayette to Bowdoin, May 25, 1788, *Massachusetts Historical Society proceedings*, V (1860–61), 356.

11. Lafayette to Hamilton, May 24, 1788, *loc. cit.*

most affectionate respect, your filial, grateful friend."[12] Yet it was pleasant for him to contemplate that before long he would be either "in an Assembly of the Representatives of the French Nation or at Mount Vernon."[13]

Lafayette realized that the road to true political happiness for France was beset with many obstacles. The French constitution might itself in the end prove to be far from satisfactory. Even if it were "to become as good or better than that of England," it would still "bear no comparison with the worst constitution that may be pointed out within the United States." Any conceivable French charter was bound to be "poisoned with abuses which it is impossible, and perhaps improper for the present to eradicate." That was why he thought France would have to have "monarchical liberty," it if had any liberty at all;[14] for it was an axiom in eighteenth-century political thought that liberty was possible in a monarchy only if the king and the aristocracy shared in the preservation of the law.

It was comforting, Lafayette confessed, to turn from France's troubles to "the happy prospects that oppen before my adoptive country." All reports from America indicated to him that "the best Constitution that has been hitherto heard of" would soon be accepted.[15] While he still was worried about those parts of it which were not "quite free of some danger," he felt reassured regarding even them, because the United States had "the good fortune to possess their Guardian Angel" in Washington. Not having learned of the "angel's" reluctance to become president (though it probably would not have changed his mind if he had), Lafayette repeated his entreaty that Washington accept the presidency. That would give the new Solon the opportunity, for which he alone was fitted, to weigh "the advantages and inconveniences of every article" of the new constitution. Thus he "will be able, before he retires again, to ascertain to what degree governement must necessarily be energic, what powers might

12. Lafayette to Washington, May 25, 1788, Gottschalk, *Letters*, p. 345.

13. *Ibid.*, p. 343.

14. Lafayette to Hamilton, May 24, 1788, *loc. cit.*

15. Lafayette to Bowdoin, May 25, 1788, *loc. cit.*; cf. Lafayette to Knox, May 30, [1788], Massachusetts Historical Society.

be diverted into a bad use, and to point out the means to attain that perfection to which the New Constitution is already nearer than any past or present governement."[16]

Even as Lafayette was writing these words, however, things had started to promote liberty in France faster than he expected. They centered around the aristocratic indignation over the effort to suppress the parlements. The marquis had already begun his own program of passive resistance by severing relations with Brienne. His visits to the principal minister had suddenly ceased. "The more I have been connected with him and the Keeper of the Seals, the greater indignation I have professed against their infernal plan," he told Washington.[17] It was not long before it was rumored that Brienne had told the king's council that Lafayette was "the most dangerous of our opponents, because his policy is all in action."[18]

The opportunity for a particularly daring action came even while Lafayette was in the midst of expounding for Washington's benefit his comparative reflections on the two contemporary revolutions. Brittany was one of the French provinces in which the aristocracy had been most insistent upon retaining local privileges. The Breton nobles found their justification in the fact that their land had become a possession of the crown only by marriage contract. That contract was well over two hundred and fifty years old, and the Bretons still demanded the special rights which they thereby enjoyed. Among those rights was that of retaining their own provincial estates and their own laws, interpreted by their own parlement at Rennes. When, therefore, the king's representatives had sought to register the new edict creating the Plenary Court, the Rennes parlement had resisted, and the royal officials were roughly handled by the people. Thereupon the king exiled the members

16. Lafayette to Washington, May 25, 1788, Gottschalk, *Letters*, p. 342. An unpardonable error has crept into this version of this letter. Somehow, the words "will be able, before he retires again" have been rendered "will not be able, before he retires again."

17. Lafayette to Washington, May 25, 1788, Gottschalk, *Letters*, p. 344; cf. Mazzei to Poniatowski, Aug. 4, 1788, Ciampini, I, 10.

18. *Mémoires*, II, 95; cf. pp. 201 n. and 233; and B. Barère, *Mémoires* (Paris, 1843), IV, 279.

of the Rennes parlement by *lettres de cachet*. Although the magistrates soon submitted, the local nobles took up their fight. They drew up a resolution denouncing as "infamous" anyone who should accept service in the new courts, and more than three hundred Breton noblemen signed it. Since Lafayette had recently identified himself with the nobility of Brittany, the resolution was sent to him to sign. He received it at almost the very moment when he was writing Washington that he would soon be either in a French National Assembly or at Mount Vernon. Before he turned his letter over to Brissot to deliver, he added a postscript telling of the Bretons' defiance. His closing words were, "I very plainly have given my consent. Adieu, my dear general."[19] A few days later, he wrote to Knox, "We are in a critical situation."[20]

Lafayette had in fact given his consent in unmistakable terms. In reply to the requests for his support of the Breton petition, he wrote, "I associate myself with every opposition to arbitrary acts, present or future, which threaten or may threaten the rights of the nation in general and those of Brittany in particular."[21] He expected that something critical might happen any day and threw discretion to the winds. He renewed his calls on Necker, who was the logical candidate to replace Brienne, taking with him the Dutch refugee, Pierre Paulus.[22] This was plainly keeping subversive company.

Meanwhile, a deputation of Breton nobles had come to Paris instructed to deliver their resolution to the king wherever they should find him.[23] They presented it to Louis XVI at Versailles, but he returned it unread. He did not wish to see the signatures, he said, since he did not want to know whom to punish for the document's violent tone. He sternly added, however, that the privileges of Brittany would be continued only at the price of obedience.

This rebuff seemed to Lafayette to end the outburst of

19. Lafayette to Washington, May 25, 1788, Gottschalk, *Letters*, p. 345.
20. Lafayette to Knox, May 30, [1788], *loc. cit.*
21. *Mémoires*, II, 183.
22. Lafayette to [Mme de Simiane?], *mardi soir* [June 3, 1788?], *ibid.*, p. 233.
23. *Ibid.*

open resistance to the throne. Once more only "a passive non obedience" appeared possible if there were to survive any hope of defeating "the anti national plans." Lafayette failed to perceive, however, that the Breton nobles would be satisfied with no such passive program. They were fighting the king's ministers for reasons entirely different from his. They wished to preserve local aristocratic authority; he meant to win a new national constitution. For him the opposition to the government was uniform—the nation against tyranny. "There is such a difference in our claims and those of the ministry," he wrote, "that one hardly believes those assertions, so contradictory, are stated in the same country and century. One side is mere despotism—with us a Constitution." The now inevitable chamber of representatives would, however, "restore dignity, energy, wealth, and every thing that is good both for the country and the prince."[24]

But if Lafayette, fondly nursing the delusion that the issue was merely that of despotism versus constitutional law, was satisfied with "non obedience" until a national assembly could set things aright, the Breton nobility were not. Time was plainly on the side of the popular cause, but for that very reason it was not on the side of the nobles. The royal rebuke only increased their concern for their privileges, and soon an even more outspoken protest signed with many more names was sent to Versailles. It denounced the king's ministers for leading him astray, thereby unmistakably suggesting the dismissal of Brienne.

The Brienne ministry was in fact fighting a losing fight. The challenge of Brittany was re-echoed in other provinces, and the government, wavering between weakness and good will, showed neither the ruthlessness needed to crush the opposition nor the wisdom to make concessions. At length a step was taken that was calculated to dampen fevered spirits, but it only revealed the ministry's bewilderment. The royal council issued a decree (July 5) asking officials and scholars to delve into the history of the Estates General, since its organization and pro-

24. Lafayette to Carmichael, June 2, 1788, LC, House of Representatives collection, Carmichael papers, No. 105.

cedure had long been forgotten, and to send reports of their re-
searches to the keeper of the seals. The intention of this measure
was at least in part to show that the king meant soon to keep
his promise to call the Estates General. To the parlementary
party, however, it sounded like an appeal over their heads
directly to the people, and particularly to the worst of them—
the writers. And to liberals like Lafayette it was likewise a disappointment because it looked like temporizing. "A late *arrêt
du conseil*," the marquis wrote to Jefferson,[25] "missed his
[i.e., its] object, because there was no time fixed for the meeting
of the National Assembly."

In any event, the decree came too late to appease the opposition. Already a commission of twelve Breton noblemen had
arrived in Versailles to present the new Breton petition.[26] The
king simply refused to see them. Thereupon the commission decided to call a protest meeting of all the Breton nobles in Paris
and Versailles. They called on Lafayette and asked him to
attend. He unhesitatingly agreed to do so and, in preparation
for the meeting, helped them to perfect their petition.[27]

The meeting took place on the evening of July 12 at the
quarters of the Breton deputies. Over sixty Breton noblemen
were present. They were asked to add their signatures to the
protest, and nearly all of them did so.[28] Although a few were
afterward to claim that some of the remarks made on this
occasion, especially by Lafayette, were seditious,[29] the prevailing tone was entirely respectful of the king.[30]

Nevertheless, by openly approving a petition upon which the

25. [July 12, 1788?], LC, Jefferson papers, No. 7780. Chinard, *Lafayette and Jefferson*,
p. 123, misreads this passage. See also p. 108 above.

26. Jefferson to Jay, Aug. 3, 1788, Lipscomb and Bergh, VII, 105.

27. Weber, p. 146.

28. Lafayette to Jefferson, [July 12, 1788?], *loc. cit.*; Mazzei to Poniatowski, July 18,
Ciampini, I, 3–4; *Gazette de Leyde*, July 25; Jefferson to Cutting and to Jay, July 24 and
Aug. 3, Lipscomb and Bergh, VII, 87–88 and 105; *Journal Général de l'Europe*, III
(1788), No. 72, 336 (June 17).

29. G. M. Sallier, *Annales françaises depuis le commencement du règne de Louis XVI
jusqu'aux États généraux, 1774 à 1789* (Paris, 1813), p. 181; Chérest, I, 562; and "Lafayette jugé par le Comte d'Espinchal," *Revue rétrospective*, XX (1894), 293–94 (which,
however, is mistaken in saying that Lafayette went to Brittany).

30. Mazzei to Poniatowski, July 18, 1788, Ciampini, I, 3–4.

king was known to frown, the Breton nobles became guilty of encouraging defiance. Account of their boldness reached Versailles at the same time as official repoɪts of serious disorder in Brittany. The court was persuaded that unmistakable severity was called for. The twelve Breton deputies were arrested and sent to the Bastille by *lettres de cachet*. Within a few days four court figures who had important civil and military assignments were deprived of their posts—"disgraced," said Jefferson, "in the old-fashioned language of the country."[31] Among the four was Lafayette. Rumors spread through Paris that he too had been arrested,[32] but the court contented itself with a lesser sign of its displeasure. Although he was allowed to keep his military rank, he was deprived of his command in the army of the Duc d'Ayen in Languedoc and Roussillon.[33]

The court's action was exceptionally severe. Jefferson thought that it would produce an insurrection in Brittany, but it did not. Despite popular fury, the intermediary commission of the Brittany estates contented itself with sending a new deputation to Versailles. The king received these men because they came from a constituted authority, but he insisted that they present their grievances through their provincial estates.[34] It was not long before the Breton estates too showed their sympathy with the victims of royal displeasure. They sent letters of appreciation to Lafayette and the other nobles who had been "disgraced."[35] "I am honored more than I deserve for having done nothing but my duty," the marquis told his friends.[36]

Some of the court nobility at Versailles found it hard to understand why a leading figure like Lafayette should go out of his way to identify himself with provincial troublemakers.

---

31. Jefferson to Cutting, July 24, 1788, Lipscomb and Bergh,VII, 88. Cf. Mazzei to Glayre, July 21, 1788, Ciampini, I, 5. See also p. 108 above.

32. Mazzei to Poniatowski, July 18, 1788, Ciampini, I, 4; Hardy, VIII, 19 (July 16).

33. Jefferson to Cutting and to Jay, July 24 and Aug. 3, 1788, Lipscomb and Bergh, VII, 87–88 and 105–6; Lafayette to the Comte de Latour-Maubourg, [July] 24, [1788], [Charles Nauroy], "Dix-huit lettres inédites de La Fayette," *Le curieux*, I (1884), 91; *Mémoires*, II, 183.

34. Jefferson to Cutting and to Jay, July 24 and Aug. 3, 1788, Lipscomb and Bergh, VII, 87 and 106; Weber, pp. 146–47.

35. Mazzei to Poniatowski, Aug. 8, 1788, Ciampini, I, 12.

36. Lafayette to Latour-Maubourg, Aug. 12, [1788], [Nauroy], pp. 91–92.

Some put it down to the desire to be the French Washington. It was reported to Lafayette that the queen herself wondered why an Auvergnat should take part in Brittany's quarrels. To the implied question Lafayette replied that he was "Breton in the same way that the queen was Austrian"—in other words, because of the origin of his mother's family.[37] The innuendo was probably intended.

Jefferson approved of what Lafayette had done. In his opinion, the government's treatment of the Breton nobles, although it "dishonors them at court, and in the eyes and conversation of their competitors for preferment," probably would "honor them in the eyes of the nation."[38] He believed that Lafayette's "disgrace," which at any other period of French history would have had bad consequences for him, "will, on the contrary, mark him favorably to the nation at present"; for, though Lafayette could expect nothing from the incumbent ministers, "it may save him with their successors,"[39] and a change of ministers seemed not far off. Jefferson was certain that a revolution could not be postponed much longer. "Peace or war, they cannot fail now to have the States General, and I think in the course of the following year."[40] He hoped, nevertheless, that "the appeal to the sword will be avoided, and great modifications in the government be obtained without bloodshed."[41]

Lafayette's disgrace meant that he stayed on in Paris during the critical summer months of 1788. A wiser government might have obliged him to go into the exile of his army post. Compelled to remain in Paris, he kept up his political activity. He frequently exchanged visits with Mme de Tessé, the Condorcets, Jefferson, Marmontel, Morellet, and Mazzei—philosophes and "Americans" all.[42] Distinguished foreign guests came to see him —among them Sir Samuel Romilly, English lawyer and writer;

37. Mémoires, II, 183 n.; cf. Weber, p. 146.
38. Jefferson to Cutting, July 24, 1788, Lipscomb and Bergh, VII, 88.
39. Jefferson to Madison, July 31, 1788, ibid., p. 94.
40. Jefferson to Adams, Aug. 2, 1788, ibid., p. 103.
41. Jefferson to Jay, Aug. 3, 1788, ibid., p. 106.
42. Mazzei to Poniatowski, Aug. 25, 1788, Ciampini, I, 17.

Étienne Dumont, Swiss divine and writer; Joel Barlow, who had come to Paris to sell American lands to willing immigrants; and John Ledyard, who was on his way to Egypt to seek compensation for his frustration in Russia.[43]

Lafayette's enforced sojourn at home was not unwelcome to his family—particularly since Mme de Thésan, Adrienne's sister, died in childbirth that August while her father and her husband were away with their troops. Though Adrienne afterward confessed that she found the unceasing activity of their life both "fatiguing" and "inconvenient," she nevertheless considered herself happy both as parent and spouse. She was proud that "her children were already beginning to show some of the qualities that her mother admired so much in their father."[44] Yet it might have been better for Adrienne as well as for the government if Lafayette had been allowed to join his troops that summer; for he drew closer to Mme de Simiane. The beautiful widow had left Paris for the summer, and Lafayette found time to send her several bulletins of his activities, revealing the need he felt for her approbation.[45]

Meanwhile, Brienne's position became more and more precarious. Breteuil resigned from the ministry, and Malesherbes was expected to do likewise. Although only the latter was motivated by disapproval of Brienne's domestic policy, the loss of two keymen weakened the government. To make matters worse, a tremendous hailstorm had destroyed a large part of France's crops and fear of famine was widespread. Brienne began to cast about for allies. He sent for Lafayette to come to see him, and they were closeted together for an hour on August 1. Why had the marquis avoided him for three months? he asked.

43. *Memoirs of the life of Sir Samuel Romilly*, etc. (London, 1840), I, 97–99; Étienne Dumont, *Recollections of Mirabeau, and of the two first legislative assemblies of France* (London, 1832), p. 19; Lafayette to Jefferson, [July 12, 1788], *loc. cit.*; C. B. Todd, *Life and letters of Joel Barlow* (New York, 1886), p. 82; Sparks, *Ledyard*, p. 303.

44. Mme de Lafayette, "Duchesse d'Ayen," in Lasteyrie, pp. 102–5.

45. *Mémoires*, II, 232–40. The recipient of some, if not all, of these letters must have been Mme de Simiane, since the only other ladies to whom Lafayette at this time was close enough to write as affectionately as he did here were Mme de Tessé, whom he regularly addressed as *ma cousine*, and his wife Adrienne, whom he regularly addressed as *mon cher cœur* or *chère Adrienne*. Besides, neither Mme de Tessé nor Adrienne was away from home that summer (see Chinard, *Trois amitiés de Jefferson*, p. 104, and Mme de Lafayette, "Duchesse d'Ayen," in Lasteyrie, pp. 102–4).

The answer led to a discussion of national politics, and before Lafayette left he had been led to believe that the Estates General would be convoked for May 1, 1789.[46] It looked as if the king's minister had thrown his weight on the side of popular reform.

Lafayette told at least one friend—Mazzei, but in the strictest confidence—of this interview, and if he did not himself tell Jefferson about it, Mazzei did. At any rate, Jefferson soon was sufficiently informed to feel sure that "a bill of rights, a civil list, a national assembly meeting at certain epochs," would come up for consideration in the projected Estates General and to think it probable that France would "within two or three years be in the enjoyment of a tolerably free constitution . . . without its having cost them a drop of blood." If that happened, it would be, Jefferson perceived, because the clergy and nobility of France were divided and the king would side with "the real patriots"—those who were trying to free the nation from the despotism of both parlements and king. It is not hard to guess who was the source of Jefferson's insight into the royal policy or to gather from his optimism that Lafayette had once more become optimistic likewise. Moreover, Jefferson's reports (derived, as they were, indirectly from Brienne through Lafayette) indicated that the king's minister was fully aware that what was going on was a three-cornered struggle—parlements vs. king vs. people.[47] For the moment, at least, it seemed that Brienne was intending to see whether he could wean the people from their alliance with the parlementary nobility. That was why he wanted Lafayette on his side; and Lafayette was ready to join him.

The promised decree stipulating that the Estates General would meet in 1789 was not long delayed. It was formally issued on August 8, and on August 11 the more exact date of May 1, 1789, was fixed. At the same time, the Plenary Court was suspended. It looked like a great victory for the policy of

46. Mazzei to Poniatowski, Aug. 4, 1788, Ciampini, I, 10.

47. Jefferson to Monroe and to Crèvecœur, Aug. 9, 1788, Lipscomb and Bergh, VII, 113 and 114. Jefferson does not mention Lafayette as his source, but it could hardly have been any other; see Mazzei to Poniatowski, Aug. 4, 1788, Ciampini, I, 10.

peaceful reform. The decree gave Lafayette "a keen pleasure," he admitted. He foresaw the return of calm. "Good citizens are going to be permitted to be peaceful and happy."[48] Jefferson, too, thought that the decree would "have a great effect toward tranquillizing the nation."[49]

Enthusiastically, Lafayette requested all his correspondents to drop their opposition and join the ministers in working for the common good.[50] He went to see a friend who was a councilor of parlement[51] and urged that parlement temporarily withdraw its opposition to Brienne's tax proposals, thus giving the government revenue enough to carry on until the opening of the Estates General. To any nobleman who he thought would value his opinion, he declared, "You must without delay withdraw from every kind of opposition that reflects *esprit de corps.*" (If he had been writing in a later age he might have said "class-consciousness.") Thus, he definitely committed himself to the union of court and nation against the particular interests of the nobility.[52]

The hope of an exemplary national unity, however, was premature, for it proved too late for parlement to make concessions. The financial difficulties of the state had already created so much apprehension that stocks had fallen on the market "in the most alarming manner."[53] In consequence, a desperate government had determined upon a foolhardy palliative. On the very day (in fact, at almost the very moment) that Lafayette returned home from his visit with his parlementarian friend he learned of a new decree of the royal council. It announced that the government would pay half its debts in paper, and, as compensation to the Caisse d'Escompte, from which it had borrowed freely during the recent period of financial stress, it gave to that bank's notes the right to circulate as money. To

48. Lafayette to Latour-Maubourg, Aug. 12, [1788], [Nauroy], pp. 91–92.
49. Jefferson to Jay, Aug. 11, 1788, Lipscomb and Bergh, VII, 121.
50. Lafayette to [Mme de Simiane], *ce mercredi* [Aug. 20, 1788], *Mémoires*, II, 235.
51. For some reason Lafayette did not name this councilor, but it might have been Adrien Duport. See *ibid.*, p. 235, and Georges Michon, *Essai sur l'histoire du parti feuillant, Adrien Duport* (Paris, 1924), pp. 4–5 and 25–26.
52. Lafayette to [Mme de Simiane], [Aug. 20, 1788], *Mémoires*, II, 235–36.
53. Jefferson to Jay, Aug. 11, 1788, Lipscomb and Bergh, VII, 122.

Frenchmen who had heard or read about the disaster that had followed experiments with paper money about seventy years earlier, this was tantamount to a declaration of insolvency. Lafayette considered himself disgraced, since he had recently identified himself with Brienne's policies. He called the government's declaration "demi-bankruptcy." "I felt almost as ashamed of it," he wrote to Mme de Simiane, "as if I had done it myself."[54]

After two days' thought on the subject, Lafayette was still indignant. The government's action looked like a ruse to make it appear that the proposal to call the Estates General—his proposal—had caused the bottom to drop out of the market. The price of bread rose, there was a run on the Caisse d'Escompte, and the muttering in the streets became so vehement that the police had to be doubled. "The ministers said that I was republican and the wiseacres that I was too hasty," Lafayette confided to Mme de Simiane, half in gloating, half in bitterness. "Now they have had to recognize that opposition has been national. . . . But there is this difference between my suggestion, so lightly disregarded, and the government's conduct—that the announcement of the Estates General, which, eight months ago, would have turned everyone's head, has seemed forced, that the parlements, with which there was general discontent, have fallen heir to the court's prestige, and that by virtue of having to wait for the Estates General to meet, the council's decree [convoking it] is tied to that on partial bankruptcy."

Thus Lafayette rationalized that, if disaster had come, it was not his fault. The king would have done better by following his advice. Had the Estates General been called a year earlier, as he had proposed, before the quarrel with the parlements and the sacrifice of French honor in Holland had raised doubts about the government's intentions, the king would have appeared a "Charlemagne in the midst of his nation voluntarily assembled." "You will reflect," he wrote Mme de Simiane, "on the danger there is in this country in being a little more precocious in one's ideas than the people with whom one is surrounded."

54. Lafayette to [Mme de Simiane], [Aug. 20, 1788], *Mémoires*, II, p. 236.

Even the king's tardy convocation of the Estates General could have saved the country had it not been for the declaration of "demi-bankruptcy." "I speak of it, I confess, with anger and grief. I flattered myself that calm would return, that the ministers would regain confidence, that everyone would unite to work with them for the public good." Now he was ashamed that he had talked such nonsense. "I have said and written things for which I would be mocked, for which I would be suspect, if I were not I."[55]

The new decree even looked to some like an effort on the part of the royal council to avoid calling the Estates General. Lafayette, however, thought that suggestion absurd. "I am fully persuaded that that is not what they intend, that they would not even dare to propose it to a king as sincere as ours, that they could not get away with it, that the very suspicion of it would put an end to tax collections throughout the realm. Nevertheless, that is what will be said, and it will rekindle discontent and double defiance." The only way he now saw to renew public confidence was quickly to reconfirm that the Estates General would meet.[56]

All these hopes and fears were set forth in a lengthy letter to Mme de Simiane. Realizing that he had written entirely about himself and his politics, Lafayette felt called upon to apologize to his confidante before he closed. "You share in so amiable a fashion everything that interests me, and this interests me so much, that I love to open my heart to you. Those who think it turbulent know it ill, but those who think it firm render it justice." And finally came a few words of endearment, undoubtedly welcome for all their self-consciousness: "I should like to see you once more before entering my thirty-second year, for, young though I am thought to be, I shall, on September 6, have lived three hundred and seventy-two months."[57]

Writing the same day to Carmichael, Lafayette likewise betrayed his anxiety not to be blamed for the way things had

55. *Ibid.*, pp. 234–36.
56. *Ibid.*, pp. 235–36.

57. *Ibid.*, p. 236. It is possible, of course, that the *Mémoires*, which avowedly give only extracts (see p. 232 n.), omit some of the more sentimental passages.

developed. Since the Assembly of Notables, he said, he had "pointed out evils" and "asked for constitutional remedies, which at court was termed Republicanism, and elsewhere Exageration." The long deferment of the Estates General had led him in his "private capacity" to oppose those who had been his "personal friends" (such as Brienne). "So did my conduct, consistent with the principles I ever gloried to profess, take a course in which I would thread every same foot step, was I to begin again." Only gradually had his opinions prevailed. Had the government determined upon a National Assembly earlier, it could have avoided the "unhappy suspension of one half of the payements that has lately been announced." The long deferment of constitutional measures, however, had proved harmful to the true interest of the country and the king. Nevertheless, he still felt that the wise way for the nobility to proceed was to rally behind the government's reform measures. "Now, my dear Carmichael, I think that my friends and myself ought to clear ourselves from any thing like party spirit and *esprit de corps*, and with the same steadiness that we would have laid down our lives rather than desert our principles, we must endeavour to assist and support the ministers, as far as lays within the limits of our power, in promoting a spirit of wisdom, tranquillity, disinterestedness and forgiveness, in order that the National Assembly may quietly attend to the plans of governement, and to the framing of a proper constitution."[58]

A constitution, Lafayette implied, was proper to the degree that it resembled the constitution of the United States. He recognized, however, that France's problem was somewhat more complicated than that of the United States. The possibility of presidential usurpation still seemed to him about the only serious flaw in the American constitution, and it was a flaw that would be easily remedied. Hence he concluded that "with a few amendments such as the rotation in the presidency," the American charter would "make the best constitution that may, I think, be imagined by the human mind." Since he now knew that more than nine states of the union had ratified the Phila-

---

58. Aug. 20, 1788, LC, House of Representatives collection, Carmichael papers, No. 106.

delphia document, he expected it soon to be put into successful operation. "It has the advantage to work a new ground, uninfluenced by all the circumstances which in Europe necessitate calculations very different."[59] In France, he once more implied, well-intrenched institutions, traditions, prejudices, and interests would make reform somewhat more difficult.

Lafayette need not have been so discouraged. Within a few days Brienne's maneuvers turned out well for him and ill for Brienne. Of all the likely candidates for the post of comptroller-general, Lafayette's friend Jacques Necker alone had the confidence of French financial circles. The desperate state of the government's finances, the threat of panic on the market, and the tense atmosphere in Paris and the provinces at length induced Louis XVI to overcome his personal dislike of Necker. The king and, more particularly, the queen at first tried to get Necker to accept a post under Brienne, but Necker was unwilling to bear the additional onus of an unpopular chief. Protestant, Swiss, and middle class though Necker was, his demands had to be met. So Brienne and Lambert were packed off, and Necker was called to the ministry.

Lafayette, having meanwhile kept up his correspondence on social and economic problems with the intermediary commission of the Auvergne provincial assembly, reported this victory the day after it occurred. A little later he was asked to present the commission's congratulations to the new minister.[60] His spirits rose as rapidly as they previously had fallen. "Our internal affairs are in good train," he now announced. Brienne had been foiled in his attempt "to establish despotism worse than it ever had been," and "every thing that had been established is now undoing and we shall have a National Assembly in the winter."[61] The king might even be obliged to call the Estates General together as early as January. "It is believed," Lafayette explained, "that M. Necker will get along till then

59. *Ibid.* Cf. Lafayette to Jefferson, [July 12, 1788?], *loc. cit.*

60. Mège, *Assemblée provinciale*, pp. 106–8, gives the minutes of a special meeting of the commission, August 29, 1788. Cf. Mège, *Premières années de la Révolution*, p. 67 n.; and Charavay, p. 159. See also Rouchon, VI, 224 and 253.

61. Lafayette to Wadsworth, [*post* Aug. 25, 1788], Connecticut State Library, Trumbull collection, No. 188.

without a new loan by borrowing the full amount of the old ones and employing *tours de force* of talent and public opinion."[62]

The most crucial question now became how to organize the Estates General. Should they be modeled upon ancient precedents—in which case they would be controlled, as they formerly had been, by the privileged classes? Or should they be made to conform to those "Laws of Nature" which were glibly cited in the numerous studies that poured from the presses in response to the king's invitation? Lafayette himself hoped for a skilful mixture of the two. He was still enough of an aristocrat to respect Tradition and yet also enough of a child of his age to have faith in "the Laws of Nature." "We must wait," he wrote in one of his frequent bulletins to the absent Mme de Simiane, "to see what forms he [Necker] is going to propose for the convocation of the Estates General—which is not an impossible question, as once was said, but which is not an easy one if you want to ally custom with reason."[63]

Mme de Simiane was a serious lady with a mature interest in politics, and political comment left little room for soft blandishments in Lafayette's letters to her. Brief words of affection nevertheless crept in. He still missed her, he now confessed. "My heart counts the days that have passed and the days that remain. They grow longer toward the close of separations, like shadows at the close of day." Politics, however, quickly crowded out sentiment again, and he ended his letter on a note of self-satisfaction. He was proud, he implied, of the hostility he had won from the friends of both Calonne and Brienne. "Those two entries counterbalance each other in the books, but they both agree . . . that I am wrong. It is impossible that any justification of me will come from that [court] circle, and impossible that my conscience will be troubled by it."[64]

Whether or not Mme de Simiane shared Lafayette's enthusiasm for what the future might bring, another to whom Lafayette was dear was somewhat fearful. From Mount Vernon came words of paternal advice, probably far different from

62. Lafayette to [Mme de Simiane], *jeudi soir* (which can be only August 28, 1788, and not August 26 or 27 as suggested by the editors), *Mémoires*, II, 237.

63. *Ibid.*, pp. 237–38. 64. *Ibid.*, p. 238.

those that came from the less Fabian Sage of Monticello. "I do not like the situation of affairs in France," Washington observed. "The bold demands of the parlements and the decisive tone of the king shew that but little more irritation would be necessary to blow up the spark of discontent into a flame that might not easily be quenched. If I were to advise, I would say that great moderation should be used on both sides." Washington did not trouble to hide his apprehension that his young friend might be acting without sufficient discretion. "Let it not, my dear Marquis, be considered as a derogation from the good opinion that I entertain of your prudence when I caution you, as an individual desirous of signalizing yourself in the cause of your country and freedom, against running into extremes and prejudicing your cause." Despite the reasons for believing Louis XVI "really a good-hearted tho' a warm-spirited man," nevertheless, "if thwarted injudiciously in the execution of prerogatives that belonged to the Crown and in plans which he conceives calculated to promote the national good," he might "disclose qualities he had been little thought to possess." Washington did not propose surrender, however, so much as watchful waiting. "Such a spirit seems to be awakened in the Kingdom as, if managed with extreme prudence, may produce a gradual and tacit revolution much in favor of the subjects, by abolishing Lettres de Cachet and defining more accurately the powers of government. It is a wonder to me, there should be found a single monarch who does not realize that his own glory and felicity must depend on the prosperity and happiness of the People. How easy it is for a sovereign to do that which shall not only immortalize his name, but attract the blessings of millions."[65]

Thus, while Lafayette urged a reluctant Washington to put himself at the head of the American government in order to guide a still unfinished revolution to a successful conclusion, Washington urged a willing Lafayette to be careful not to commit himself too hastily in the revolution just begun in France. The younger man, loyally striving to act as he imagined the older man would approve, was eventually to lose control of

65. June 19 [18], 1788, Fitzpatrick, XXIX, 524.

events he had meant to guide and was to be carried much farther much more speedily than he had meant to go. That was to prove true partly because he lacked his idol's understanding of the human mind. But it was also true that the opportunity for "a gradual and tacit revolution" was rapidly passing in France—and others were more to blame than Lafayette that that opportunity was not grasped before it was too late.

BIBLIOGRAPHICAL NOTES

Augustin Cochin, *Les société de pensées et la révolution en Bretagne* (*1788–1789*) (Paris, 1925), gives an account of Brittany's resistance in 1788 that is inaccurate in detail (see esp. I, 124).

The letters of Lafayette to Latour-Maubourg during this period are to be found in the Archives nationales, F⁷4767. They have been reprinted, with negligible changes and omissions by Charles Nauroy in *Le curieux*, I (1884), 91–96 and 123–26.

Jules Cloquet's version of Lafayette's retort to Marie Antoinette (see above, p. 392) in his *Recollections of the private life of General Lafayette* (London, 1835), pp. 14–15, implies that the marquis still visited the court at Versailles during this period. That is highly unlikely. Cloquet learned about this event only many years later.

Ciampini's collection of the letters of Mazzei to Poland make available many details regarding Lafayette's activity that have hitherto been lost.

Jean Bouchary, *Les manieurs d'argent à Paris à la fin du XVIIIᵉ siècle* (Paris, 1939), p. 104, and Philippe Sagnac, *La fin de l'ancien régime et la Révolution américaine* (*1763–1789*) ("Peuples et civilisations," Vol. XII [Paris, 1947]), p. 458, state that Lafayette frequently called at the home of the banker Jean-Gaspard Schweizer. I have found no evidence before 1789 that that was true.

CHAPTER XXV

The End of an Era

Fame is relative. One day in the summer of 1788 Lafayette joined a party of distinguished Frenchmen who took Sir Samuel Romilly to visit a roadhouse outside Paris. The innkeeper was a tenant of Malesherbes, who was also one of the party. Meaning to impress the innkeeper with the greatness of his guests, Malesherbes asked him if he had ever heard of the Marquis de Lafayette. "No, really I can't say I ever have," answered the innkeeper. "Who was he?"[1]

Malesherbes's publican, however, was certainly not typical. This was the day of Lafayette's greatest glory so far, though greater glories were yet to come. He was a leader of the "Americans" in France. That meant that he was not only the outstanding French military hero of the recent war but also one of the most conspicuous political figures in the current crisis. At least one child then in the schools thought he heard his teachers pronounce Lafayette's name, always linked with Washington's, as often as the names of Horace and Cicero,[2] and in a system of education based largely upon classical training, that must have been quite often. On three continents important people were concerned about him. Washington and Madison feared[3] and Catherine II, because she had not yet given up the idea that he might come to Russia, hoped that he might get into trouble.

1. Romilly, I, 97–99.

2. A. V. Arnault, *Souvenirs d'un sexagénaire*, ed. Auguste Dietrich (Paris, n.d.), I, 51; cf. Daniel Mornet, *Origines intellectuelles de la Révolution française 1715–1787* (Paris, 1933), pp. 337 and 398–99.

3. Washington to Lafayette, Sept. 15, 1788, cited in Washington to Lafayette, Nov. 27, Fitzpatrick, XXX, 139; Madison to Jefferson, Oct. 8, *Letters and other writings of Madison*, I, 420.

"Send him to us," the tsarina wrote, "We'll give him something to do."[4] Ledyard, now engaged in exploring Egypt, found that French patriots in Cairo "call on the name of . . . La Fayette . . . as the soldier and the courtier."[5]

Before the end of the summer of 1788 the marquis was able to assure his worried friends that not only tranquillity but also victory for the liberal cause had come to France. The recent crisis, he declared, would only have the effect of hastening the calling of the Estates General.[6] During the time that trigger decisions had had to be made, however, he had daily run the risk of imprisonment for treason. That others had in fact been imprisoned only made his daring all the more real and his popularity, in the eyes of some, all the more deserved. Now it looked as if, under the skilful pilotage of Necker, the ship of state would have smooth sailing and even its most daring passengers would be safe.

The brief calm between crises was filled for Lafayette in part by a new paternal responsibility. During the summer, the son of the late General Nathanael Greene had arrived in Paris in care of Joel Barlow, who had come to France to sell his own literature and the Scioto Land Company's real estate. Greene's coming was in accordance with a plan the Lafayettes had long had to send their own son, a godson of Washington, to America to complete his education, and to bring Greene's son, also a godson of Washington, to France.[7] George Washington Lafayette's voyage was to be deferred by the uncertainties of French politics, but George Washington Greene now became the object of Lafayette's "fatherly attention."

Together with Jefferson, Short, and Barlow, the marquis planned the orphan's education. He placed him in the Pension

4. Catherine to Grimm, Oct. 3, 1788, *Sbornik Istoricheskago Obshchestva*, XXIII (1878), 466.

5. Ledyard to Jefferson, Nov. 15, 1788, Sparks, *Ledyard*, 321–22.

6. Lafayette to Washington, Sept. 5, 1788 (which apparently is not extant), cited in Washington to Lafayette, Jan. 29, 1789, Fitzpatrick, XXX, 184; to the intermediary commission of Auvergne, Sept. 6 and 9, 1788, Archives départementales (Clermont-Ferrand), sér. 4C, cote 8, Nos. 37 and 38.

7. Lafayette to Mrs. Montgomery, Feb. 22, 1786, C. H. Hunt, *Edward Livingston*, pp. 43–44, and see above, p. 161.

Lemoyne, across the street from Jefferson's home, where Crèvecœur's two sons were already enrolled. This school was "the best I ever heard of," Lafayette reported to the boy's mother. There the young man could be expected to learn French faster than if he stayed at Lafayette's home under the guidance of his fellow namesake's tutor, and at the same time he would be close enough to receive the direct attention of his new guardian. "No affair in my life can be more capital," the marquis wrote Mrs. Greene, "no task more pleasing than the one I owe to your confidence and that of the good and great man of whose friendship I was proud and happy."[8] Thus, Lafayette once more exhibited his generosity. It was all the more striking because Greene's estate owed him 24,000 livres, which he preferred not to ask for at this time.[9]

Young Greene joined Lafayette's household just about the time that Lafayette's Indian ward, Peter Otsiquette, returned to America. Peter's knowledge of French, English, and music was to astonish those who met him.[10] Yet neither Peter nor George was destined to be a great consolation to their guardian. Peter reverted to barbarism, became a hard drinker,[11] and died within a few years, and George, though Lafayette found that "his temper, his genius, and his heart seem to combine to make him a very hopeful youth," was to drown in a hunting accident shortly after his return to America.[12]

During these final days of a waning regime, several Frenchmen also were benefited by the marquis's generosity. He indorsed new requests of French officers for admission into the Society of the Cincinnati.[13] He interceded with Congress on behalf of the Basmarein family in their effort to recover some of the fortune that they had invested in privateers during the

8. Lafayette to Mrs. Greene, Sept. 5, 1788, Jackson collection. Cf. Carrington to Jefferson, May 14, *Massachusetts Historical Society proceedings*, 2d ser., XVII (1903), 499; Lafayette to Jefferson, [July 12, 1788?], Chinard, *Lafayette and Jefferson*, p. 123; Robert de Crèvecœur, *Crèvecœur*, pp. 130 and 189.

9. Lafayette to Wadsworth, Sept. 29, 1802, Jackson collection; Chinard, *Lafayette and Jefferson*, p. 310.

10. *Thomas's Massachusetts Spy*, Aug. 7, 1788.

11. See Appen. II below.

12. [G. W. Greene], "The home of Lafayette," *Atlantic monthly*, VIII (1861), 652.

13. Lasseray, I, 153 (on behalf of Paul de Chamillard).

War of Independence.[14] That family held a special interest for him, since it was Pierre de Basmarein who had sold him the ship in which he had first gone to America. When the Comte de Moreton thought himself unjustly deprived of his regiment under the Duc d'Ayen's command, Lafayette supported a petition for the rehearing of his case.[15] Thus the marquis's reputation as a philanthropist and champion of justice continued to flourish.

For a brief interval, political activity proceeded at a more leisurely pace. An epidemic of colds struck Paris late that summer, and Lafayette was among its victims. It was not until September 9, 1788, that he was able to call upon Necker, in company with the Marquis de Lacqueuille, as requested by the Auvergne commission, to congratulate the comptroller-general on his new dignity. Necker was pleased with their visit. They discussed national politics, and Lafayette learned that Necker intended to call the Estates General for January. The minister also urged them to keep in touch with the permanent secretary of his ministry, Joseph-François Coster, regarding Auvergne's local problems.[16]

Lafayette soon found himself charged again with negotiations that necessitated several visits to Necker's and Coster's offices and lengthy reports back to Clermont.[17] One of the problems he and Coster debated dealt with the most desirable method of choosing deputies to the Estates General. That debate was to last until the very end of the year.[18]

14. Basmarein to Lafayette, Apr. 17, 1788, Robert Castex, "Armateur de La Fayette, Pierre de Basmarein," *Revue des questions historiques*, LIII (1925), 125–26.

15. Lafayette to Moreton, *ca.* June, 1788, *Réclamation présentée à l'Assemblée Nationale par J. H. Moreton, contre sa destitution militaire de la charge de colonel du Régiment d'infanterie de La Fère* (Paris, 1790), p. 32.

16. Lafayette to the intermediary commission, Sept. 6 and 9, 1788, *loc. cit.*; Lacqueuille to the intermediary commission, Sept. 9, Francisque Mège, "Les populations de l'Auvergne au début de 1789," *Bulletin historique et scientifique de l'Auvergne*, 2d ser., 1904, p. 210 n.

17. The correspondence of Lafayette and the intermediary commission, Sept. 11–25, 1788, Archives départementales (Clermont-Ferrand), sér. 4C, cote 39, No. 15; cote 8, No. 49; cote 9, No. 2; and cote 1, Nos. 37 and 38. Cf. Rouchon, VI, 222, 227, and 304.

18. Lafayette to Coster, [Sept. 12, 1788], Jackson collection; cf. Lafayette to intermediary commission, Archives départementales (Clermont-Ferrand), sér. 4C, cote 12, No. 41; and Francisque Mège, *Les élections de 1789, la dernière année de la province d'Auvergne* (Clermont-Ferrand, 1904), pp. 15–17 n.

Meanwhile, Necker made good his promise. On September 23, Louis XVI yielded in his quarrel with the Paris parlement. He convoked the Estates General for the next January and permitted the parlement at the same time to resume its traditional functions. Except that he declared his intention to bring the matter of judicial reform before the new Estates General, the king's surrender was complete. Although it was greeted with disorderly demonstrations and minor riots in the streets of Paris, it looked like a decisive victory for the cause of peaceful reform. A few days later Barlow had dinner at Lafayette's house, along with "much company, chiefly American," and found the "Patriots," as Lafayette's party was coming to be called, "very sanguine in their expectations that they shall effect a speedy and complete revolution in the government and establish a free constitution."[19]

An upset in the Patriots' plans developed, however, when the restored parlement of Paris revealed its true colors. In registering the king's decree convoking the Estates General, it insisted that the new body must follow the ancient constitutional tradition. If that view prevailed, the aristocracy would benefit the most from the recent political upheaval, for the old Estates General had been organized along lines that assured the upper classes of domination. In insisting upon tradition, the parlement was betraying its real purpose in its quarrels with the king. It wanted to substitute aristocratic influence for absolute monarchy. Almost overnight parlement lost its popular support.

Necker, while nursing his general reputation as a liberal and a political wizard, hoped also to avoid the hostility of parlement. Resistance to the tribunal would involve an appeal to public opinion, and such an appeal might encourage the more radical writers. Taking advantage of the king's invitation to study the history of the Estates General, such writers had already flooded the country with literature contending that the Third Estate should thenceforth predominate in the Estates General. Necker was not prepared to go that far. Yet he dared not surrender to

19. Barlow's "Journal," Oct. 3, 1788, Todd, p. 83. Cf. Lafayette to the intermediary commission, Sept. 25, Archives départementales (Clermont-Ferrand), sér. 4C, cote 1, No. 38.

parlement either, for thereby he would stultify the royal position and incur popular animosity. In the dilemma he hit upon
the expedient of recalling the Assembly of Notables to handle
the question. The king announced this decision on October 5.
The Notables were to meet on November 3 to consider the
composition of the next Estates General, and meanwhile the
meeting of the provincial assemblies for 1788 was canceled.

Lafayette did not approve of Necker's maneuver. He had expected to go to Auvergne for the forthcoming meeting of the
provincial assembly in order to choose the province's deputies
to the Estates General. He protested against the cancellation.
An Assembly of Notables would delay the opening of the
Estates General, and such a delay, he declared, would not be
helpful to his province. In fact, postponement of the election of
deputies to the winter, when roads would be impassable, might
even be harmful.[20] But Necker simply refused to make any
public decisions before consulting the Notables. Thus, the convocation of the Estates General, which alone Lafayette considered "truly curative," would have to wait until spring. "I do
not believe, *entre nous*," he wrote to a confidant, "that the
Notables are very strong on constitutional matters," and he expected some "pretty strange conferences."[21]

Lafayette's own opinions in the mounting political conflict
were somewhat two-sided, thereby reflecting his paradoxical
loyalty to Tradition and Reason at the same time. He preferred the "constitutional form" for the Estates General although on grounds that were different from parlement's. "Only
the nation has the power to make improvements," he felt. He
apparently did not stop to consider that the old constitutional
forms would make the expression of a truly national opinion
highly unlikely. But he was obviously less concerned with constitutional forms than with constitutional reforms. He envisaged—for Auvergne, at least—"a numerous assembly of all
three orders, which would choose their deputies, give them their

20. Lafayette to the intermediary commission, Oct. 11, 1788, *loc. cit.* Mège, "Auvergne au début de 1789," pp. 211–12, quotes this letter but gives it the date of October
15.

21. Lafayette to [Mme de Simiane?], [Oct. 6, 1788], *Mémoires*, II, 239.

instructions and propose a constitution for our future estates."[22]
He hoped that voting in the forthcoming Estates General would
be "by head." In that event the number of deputies from a province would have real significance, and he suggested that the
intermediary commission of Auvergne take steps to apportion
the province's representation according to population or taxation or a combination of both. He also advocated preparing a
cahier setting forth Auvergne's grievances, particularly the un-
fairness suffered from the tax privileges extended to other provinces.[23] Thus, even before the Notables met, Lafayette committed himself to an electoral procedure for the Estates General
that would have weighed heavily in favor of reform.

To safeguard the interests of the province, Lafayette continued frequently to meet with Beaune, Lacqueuille, and other
influential Auvergnats in the metropolis, as well as with Coster.
The Auvergnats in Paris and Versailles were still being plagued
by the rivalry of Riom and Clermont. The champions of Riom
were again clamorous, demanding that if their city was not to be
considered the official seat of the whole province, Auvergne
should be divided into two parts. Every person of importance in
any way connected with Riom was appealed to in this matter—
Lafayette among them. But he advised against it. Unless a
perfectly even division of the province were effected, he implied, a new injustice and a weakening of the province's
strength would result.[24]

Meanwhile, preparations advanced for the approaching Assembly of Notables. This time the Notables were not the butt of
wags and punsters. They had won great esteem in their last
meeting, and a respectful interest was expressed even abroad.
The forthcoming Assembly became the pretext for another,
though indirect, contact between Lafayette and a crowned
head of Europe. King Stanislaus Augustus Poniatowski of
Poland had long been employing Lafayette's friend Mazzei as

22. Lafayette to Lacqueuille, Oct. 10, 1788; Gardner-Ball collection. Cf. Lafayette to
the intermediary commission, Oct. 11, *loc. cit.*

23. Lafayette to the intermediary commission, Sept. 6 and Oct. 11, 1788, *loc. cit.*
Cf. Mège, "Auvergne au début de 1789," p. 210.

24. Lafayette to the intermediary commission, Oct. 11, 1788, *loc. cit.* Cf. Mège, *Les
élections de 1789*, p. 10.

"intelligencer" in Paris. Mazzei was now instructed to present to the marquis the compliments of the Polish ruler. Lafayette's evident pleasure at this honor caused the intelligencer to remark, somewhat incongruously, that "modesty is one of the most eminent qualities of this young hero." Lafayette, to show his appreciation, promised to let Mazzei know about the proceedings in the Notables,[25] and he kept his word.[26] Thus the king of Poland became better informed than many prominent Frenchmen regarding what was happening in French politics.

Louis XVI's letter summoning Lafayette to join the second Assembly of Notables indicated that he sought advice on "the most just and most fitting" manner to proceed in the formation of the Estates General.[27] And that was the wording in the invitations that were sent to the great majority of others summoned. The invitations to those who were magistrates, however, employed, instead, the phrase "the most regular and most fitting."[28] Perhaps unintentionally, but nonetheless strikingly, the issue thus was joined. Was justice or regularity to be the criterion of the Notables' decisions?

In keeping with the leisurely manner in which an unmechanized age met its crises, it was not until November 6 (three days late) that the Notables held their first meeting. At nine o'clock in the morning the guards took their posts at the Hôtel des Menus Plaisirs, but it was some time before the tiresome etiquette and protocol of court procedure permitted the king formally to open the assembly with a brief speech of welcome. After much putting-on and taking-off of hats and much sitting, standing, kneeling, and bowing of those who were expected to sit, stand, kneel, and bow, the new keeper of the seals, M. de Barentin, made a speech calling upon the Notables to co-operate with the king. He urged them to show a "filial piety," worthy of "the tender effusions of a father" like Louis XVI, in order to bring about "that truly constitutional assembly where,

25. Mazzei to Poniatowski, Oct. 24 and Dec. 19, 1788, Ciampini, I, 41 and 64.

26. [Secretary of?] Mazzei to Poniatowski, Dec. 8, 1788, *ibid.*, p. 61; Mazzei to Poniatowski, Dec. 13 and 18, *ibid.*, pp. 63 and 65.

27. *Procès-verbal de l'Assemblée des Notables tenue à Versailles en l'année MDCCLXXXVIII* (Paris, 1789), p. 35.

28. *Ibid.*, p. 37.

as a result of a happy collaboration, the nation will take on a new vigor and acquire a new luster."[29]

Then Necker presented at length the problems that the Assembly was called upon to resolve. They split into four major questions—how the Estates General should be composed, how they should be convoked, in what order the three estates should be elected, and how the assemblies that were to elect them should be regulated. It became apparent that the issue which bothered Necker the most was what number of deputies to assign to each of the three estates. That was the point most hotly debated in the numerous pamphlets which had recently swept the country. If the three estates were to be equal in number as before, the two privileged orders would be the stronger, whereas, if the lowest house were to be doubled in size, its strength would, in appearance at least, be equal to that of the other two combined. Other questions were more or less subordinate to the "doubling of the Third," since the manner of electing and convoking deputies would be largely contingent upon whether the traditional predominance of the upper orders would be maintained.

When Necker's exposition was done, selected spokesmen of the Notables made brief replies. The Comte de Provence, speaking for the Nobility, and the Archbishop of Narbonne, speaking for the Clergy, formally promised zealous co-operation. The address of the president of the Paris parlement, however, was more pointed. Reminding the king that it was the parlements that had spearheaded the demand for the Estates General, he stressed the importance of *"regularity and fittingness"* in reaching decisions and prayed for unity among all elements of the population.[30] His words sounded more like an omen than a promise. Before the inaugural meeting ended, the Notables were divided into bureaus again. As before, Lafayette found himself in the Second Bureau under the Comte d'Artois.[31]

These ceremonies attendant upon the opening of the Assembly of Notables—all of which Lafayette saw and part of which he was—elicited no adverse comment from him. But his actions

29. *Ibid.*, pp. 49–51.
30. *Ibid.*, pp. 67–69.   31. *Ibid.*, p. 71.

at the time indicate that he was far from impassive. The promise of an Estates General had induced many public minded citizens to take a more direct interest in politics. For months France had been afflicted with a rash of political "clubs." Several were local study groups that now turned to politics, some had evolved from Masonic lodges, others had developed out of philanthropic organizations, still others had grown from the numerous provincial literary and debating societies. They became so active and outspoken that many contemporary observers thought (and have misled later writers into thinking) that they were manipulated by a single group of clever conspirators. They certainly helped to spread the discussion of political questions and to articulate and solidify public opinion. They were, however, as much a symptom and a result of times that were awry as they were a cause. They were created by the provocations that they debated, but at the same time they helped to provoke further debate.

The most famous of these clubs came to be the Society of the Thirty. For some observers the major issue before France was not the royal deficit but constitutional government. One of these observers was the Comte de Mirabeau, already celebrated as a brilliant publicist, with whom Lafayette had been associated in the Society of the Friends of the Negro. Another was Adrien Duport, who was the leader of the liberal faction among the parlement councilors and had long been a member of Mesmer's Order of Harmony. If the representatives to the forthcoming Estates General would be guided by the general well-being rather than by class considerations, these mentors were confident that a new, written, rational constitution would replace the traditional, unwritten one. To that end they agreed upon a "conspiracy of well-intentioned men" to form a "constitutional club" and to push reform "as far as the public welfare, truly understood, would permit."[32]

By the time the Assembly of Notables opened, this "conspiracy" was already well under way. Its meetings took place in Duport's home several times a week and lasted several hours

---

32. Mirabeau to the Duc de Lauzun, Nov. 10, 1788, Montigny, V, 199. Cf. *Mémoires*, II, 360, n. 1.

each time. They were devoted to the discussion of current events, the latest pamphlets, and the members' own political theories. The society also frankly tried to act as a pressure group upon the Assembly of Notables and Necker.[33]

Lafayette from the very start was a member of the group. Before it was many weeks old, other noblemen like La Rochefoucauld, Condorcet, the Vicomte de Noailles, and Latour-Maubourg, clerics like Talleyrand and the Abbé Louis, political writers like Target and the Abbé Sieyès, enlightened officials like Dupont and Lenoir, and several of Duport's colleagues in parlement joined it. Most of them were old friends of Lafayette. Soon the group had enough members to become known as the Society of the Thirty (Société des Trente), though it was often also spoken of as "the Duport Committee." Conspicuous among its members was a group of young liberal lawyers, the so-called "Americans" of the Paris parlement.[34] The Society of the Thirty early committed itself to the doubling of the Third Estate. It soon became apparent, however, that they could not count upon the Assembly of Notables to advance their program.

Lafayette apparently played no leading part in the Notables' debates. Part of the time he was sick again with a new pulmonary attack[35] and was obliged to stay away from some meetings. If he was appointed to any committees, the minutes of his bureau do not indicate it. When he was well and active, part of his attention was directed elsewhere. The old dispute between Upper and Lower Auvergne continued to absorb some of his now diminished time and energy. Division of the province had its champions, and they too sought the ear of Necker and Coster. The matter dragged on beyond the adjournment of the Assembly of Notables. Finally, at a meeting on December 30, a dozen officials and Auvergnat personages, of whom Lafayette was one, met to reach a decision on this and other matters pertaining to the election of deputies from Auvergne. At first, it

33. *Mémoires*, IV, 4.

34. *Ibid.*, pp. 3–4; Michon, pp. 28–29; Chérest, II, 169–71; Paul Filleul, *Le Duc de Montmorency Luxembourg* (Paris, 1939), pp. 90–91 and 306; Georges Lacour-Gayet, *Talleyrand, 1754–1836* (Paris, 1928–31), I, 83.

35. Mazzei to Poniatowski, Dec. 5, 1788, Ciampini, I, 61; Lafayette to [Mme de Simiane], Nov. 19, *Mémoires*, II, 239.

looked as if Riom would establish its claim to being the exclusive capital of the province. In the end, however, it was decided that, in conformity with ancient customs, Clermont and Riom would each serve as the electoral seat for the communities within its jurisdiction.[36] Thus Auvergne was divided, and Lafayette's holdings fell under the jurisdiction of Riom.

Meanwhile, the Assembly of Notables had come to a close. The Notables had early decided that each bureau would examine Necker's questions separately and give tentative answers. The Second Bureau had worked the hardest of all. Its minutes took the form of a report upon Necker's queries.[37] Many of its decisions, being concerned only with ceremonial matters such as honors, precedence, and privileges, occasioned little or no discussion. But on several issues there was some division of opinion. Individual ballots were not recorded, and so it can only be inferred how Lafayette voted. Perhaps he joined with the minority that voted against certain conservative recommendations—such as giving equal representation to all bailiwicks regardless of population, excluding domestic servants who owned no landed property from the right to vote, allowing only those cities which had sent deputies directly to the Estates General of 1614 to do so again in 1789, limiting the newer commercial cities to indirect representation through their bailiwicks, permitting more than one vote to those who owned property in more than one bailiwick, and obliging commoners even when they owned a noble fief to vote with the Third Estate.[38] On the other hand, unless he was absent, he must have voted in favor of the recommendations that in the electoral assemblies the three estates should deliberate separately (which was a victory for the Clergy and the Nobility) and that all taxes be borne proportionately by all (which was a victory for the Third Estate), since these proposals were among the several that passed unanimously.[39]

36. Lafayette to the municipality of Riom, Nov. 26, [1788], Archives communales de Riom, AA22; Boyer, p. 7; Pierre-Victor Malouet to the municipality of Riom, Dec. 31, cited in Mège, Les élections de 1789, pp. 15-17 n.

37. AN, C6, liasses 1 and 3, and C7, liasses 4 and 7; Procès-verbal, pp. 84-85 and 135-99.

38. Procès-verbal, pp. 147, 175, 177, 179, 189, and 190.

39. Ibid., pp. 185 and 199.

On the burning question of the day, Lafayette certainly voted with the minority. That was the question whether the Third Estate should have as many representatives as the other two estates combined. When the vote was taken in the Second Bureau on that question, Lafayette, despite the known disapproval of the Comte d'Artois, voted in favor of double representation.[40] Nevertheless, the bureau, by a vote of sixteen to eight, went on record as favoring equal representation for all three orders in keeping with the ancient practices of the realm.[41]

Lafayette's behavior during the second Assembly of Notables seemed to some to lack commendable vigor and clarity. The reason assigned by the Second Bureau for most of its decisions was that it was acting to preserve "the form established by the laws and customs" of the realm. Maintaining that nothing should be done to delay the convocation of the Estates General unnecessarily, the bureau declared: "It would seem that innovations that may in themselves be useful ought to be the business of the Estates General rather than of an Assembly of Notables."[42] Those words were reminiscent of the opinion that Lafayette had already pronounced on the same subject.

Thus it was possible for Lafayette to reflect loyalty at the same time to both Reason and Tradition—in other words, to be conservative for revolutionary motives. He could satisfactorily explain to himself that it was wise to vote both for the doubling of the Third Estate and for the separation of the orders in the electoral assemblies. Contemporary opinion was confused about his position. Although the parlement of Paris was divided into an aristocratic faction, who wanted to observe the "forms of 1614," and the "Americans," who advocated new forms, among the councilors the reform party was the stronger. They invited Lafayette along with the Duc de La Rochefoucauld, to become an honorary councilor. To some the proffered title seemed no better than an honorarium, since they believed that few parlementarians would have approved if he had stood out boldly as an opponent of regularity.

Among those who had begun to worry whether Lafayette

40. *Mémoires*, II, 184 and 249, and VI, 6.
41. [Dec. 1, 1788], *Procès-verbal*, p. 148.
42. *Ibid.*, pp. 137 and 143. Cf. above, p. 408.

might not go over to the enemy (for to an uncompromising champion of the Third Estate, parlement was no less an enemy than the king) were some of the Society of the Thirty. Before the Assembly of Notables ended, Mirabeau, apprehensive of the predominance of Duport in the society, had begun to fear that it would become only "a reserve corps of parlementarians" and advocated a secession movement.[43] The Abbé Sieyès, on the other hand—if his later account is to be credited—was fearful of noblemen like Lafayette and Mirabeau, in whom he saw only disappointed courtiers driven to intrigue by their jealousy of the queen's more favored friends.[44] But Condorcet was the one most profoundly concerned. Though a nobleman himself, he was more antiaristocratic than Lafayette. Uncompromisingly opposed to any concessions whatsoever to the privileged orders and fearing that parlementarians wished merely to preserve privilege, he was worried lest Lafayette might join the parlementary party. He engaged in an exchange of bantering letters with the hero-worshiping Mazzei on that subject. Not even his humor could hide his distress. "If you go to Lafayette's house," he wrote Mazzei, "try to exorcise the devil of aristocracy that will be there to tempt him in the guise of a councilor of parlement or of a Breton noble. For that purpose take along in your pocket a little vial of Potomac water and a sprinkler made from the wood of a Continental Army rifle and make your prayers in the name of Liberty, Equality, and Reason, which are but a single divinity in three persons."[45]

Mazzei in fact did go to see Lafayette. He soon assured Condorcet that he had found no councilor or Breton noble at the Rue de Bourbon but only the trinity of Liberty, Equality, and Reason. Their mutual friend, he implied, was doing all that could reasonably be expected of him. Perhaps echoing Lafayette, he wrote, "When it is not possible to do all the good that is desired, one must not fail to do what one can." That, he said, was the principle which had guided the Americans in their revolution.[46]

43. Mirabeau to Lauzun, Dec. 4, 1788, Montigny, V, 200.
44. Cf. *Mémoires*, IV, 3.   45. Ciampini, I, 53.
46. *Ibid.*

That soft answer did not turn away Condorcet's wrath. While Mazzei had been looking for the devil of aristocracy, Condorcet rejoined, "the devil, more cunning than he, had slipped behind him and whispered to him that comparison with America." But conditions in France and the United States were obviously not comparable. Compromise had been desirable in America but was not in France. There were no privileges and privileged classes in America. To give to the French nation as a whole only the same representation as the clergy and nobility combined would be little enough. But even if that small concession were won, the Estates General would still be a body in which the privileged classes would control half the members. That would give them "a new sanction," which would "render their destruction impossible."[47] Condorcet thus betrayed a fear that Lafayette might show too much respect for some of the "constitutional forms" like the separation of the orders.

Mazzei's reply to Condorcet's latest rejoinder still breathed the spirit of compromise. It was necessary, he contended, to form an alliance with the aristocrats in order to make any headway against despotism. In the end, he felt certain, the aristocracy would not triumph.[48] How far this reflected Lafayette's opinions, Mazzei did not say, but he was certainly trying to speak in his hero's defense and thereby revealed that in his opinion Lafayette also considered appeasement and alliance on one front a wiser strategy than war on two fronts.

The repartee between Condorcet and Mazzei was cut short when the *philosophe* left town for the summer.[49] Upon learning of their encounter, King Stanislaus shared Mazzei's impatience with those who like Condorcet doubted Lafayette's constancy; "The errors of such people call to mind the opinion of those astronomers who contend that there are stars that become extinguished."[50] Thus philosopher and king disputed regarding the intentions of the marquis. Probably with Condorcet's search for the devil of aristocracy in mind, Lafayette at this time uttered a protestation of his sincerity. "My heart is pure,

47. *Ibid.*, pp. 53–55.   48. *Ibid.*, pp. 55–56.
49. Mazzei to Poniatowski, Nov. 21, 1788, *ibid.*, p. 56. Cf. Mazzei, *Memoirs*, 304.
50. Mazzei, *Memoirs*, p. 304, n. 2.

my spirit free, my character disinterested. My conscience and my public standing are my two supports. If I lose the latter, the former would suffice me."[51] It was hard to be a court noble and a popular leader at the same time.

The "conspiracy of well-intentioned men" in the Society of the Thirty thus developed its inner strains. Lafayette attributed much of these misunderstandings to court intrigue. "You are right," he wrote his confidant, "to think that they have so bad an opinion of me at court that they can poison my relations with the councilors of parlement." But he was not distracted from his major purpose by such disagreements. "One cannot change one's society as often as the king changes ministers."[52] He realized that there were some malcontents among the Thirty, but he knew other members personally as honest men motivated by high patriotic considerations.[53] The same was true of the parlement of Paris. "My acquaintances in that body, and especially M. Duport, to whom I am devoted, are honorable, cultured, and patriotic men. They are less parlementary than many ministers, and no one is less so than I."[54] In the end, nevertheless, Lafayette, admitting that he was "hardly parlementarian"[55] and "anything but parlementariian,"[56] considered it wiser to decline the honor offered him by the councilors of parlement.[57] He continued, however, to remain on a friendly footing with several of them, particularly with Adrien Duport and the "Americans" in the Society of the Thirty.

For one who was as concerned about his public standing as Lafayette, the Assembly of Notables proved singularly unproductive of laurels. Only once during this second session did his

---

51. Lafayette to [Mme de Simiane?], Nov. 19, 1788, *Mémoires*, II, 239–40.

52. *Ibid.*, p. 239.

53. *Ibid*, IV, 4.

54. Lafayette to [Mme de Simiane?], Nov. 19, 1788, *ibid.*, II, 239.

55. Lafayette to [Mme de Simiane], [Aug. 28, 1788], *ibid.*, p. 237.

56. Lafayette to Rabaut-St. Étienne, Dec. 28, 1788, Bibliothèque de la Ville de Nantes, MS 661, No. 133.

57. *Memoirs of the Margravine of Anspach written by herself* (London, 1826), II, 194–98; Weber, pp. 80–81. Cf. Lafayette to [Mme de Simiane?], *ce vendredi* [*ca.* June 23, 1789], *Mémoires*, II, 309.

name get into the papers. That was in connection with a matter which was only indirectly associated with the agenda of the Notables. The Prince de Conti had been greatly disturbed by the radical tone of the numerous writings that had been spread throughout the country. Supported by other princes of the blood, he demanded that "all new systems be proscribed forever, and the ancient constitution and forms be maintained in their entirety." The king, considering Conti's fears irrelevant to the purposes of the Assembly, refused to put the subject on the agenda. But Conti's outburst had already been submitted to the Second Bureau. Blanc de Castillon, of the Aix parlement, indorsed his apprehensions and proposed a royal decree strengthening the censorship. Lafayette rose to denounce this proposal. He was astounded, he said, that a judge should seek by arbitrary authority to inflict a punishment which ought to be imposed only by due process of law. Thus Lafayette contrived to put the country's law on the side of liberty.[58] According to Mazzei, it was generally noted that Lafayette had been much more logical than Castillon, who had exhibited nothing but warmth on the subject.[59]

This forensic victory for the reform party, if victory it was, proved a minor one, however. The important question before the Assembly was double representation, and on that question the Notables were a great disappointment to the "Patriots." Only the First Bureau, presided over by the Comte de Provence, approved double representation for the Third Estate— and that by only a single vote. Lafayette informed Mazzei that he thought the idea might have a better reception when the bureaus met in full session.[60] But the separate bureaus' definitive answers to Necker's queries made quite clear that the marquis was mistaken.

At this juncture, Lafayette's continued faith in the parle-

58. *Gazette de Leyde*, Dec. 12, 1788; Garrett, p. 109; *Procès-verbal*, pp. 91–93; *Mémoire présenté au roi par Mgr Comte d'Artois, M. le Prince de Condé, M. le Duc de Bourbon, M. le Duc d'Enghien, M. le Prince de Conti* (1788); [Gabriel Brizard], *Modestes observations sur le "Mémoire des princes" faites au nom de 23 million de citoyens français* (Dec. 22, 1788), p. 15.

59. Mazzei to Poniatowski, Dec. 5, 1788, Ciampini, I, 60.

60. Mazzei to Poniatowski, Nov. 12, 1788, *ibid.*, p. 56.

mentarians of his acquaintance proved justified. On December 5, 1788, largely because of the daring of the "Americans," parlement experienced a stormy session. It ended in a decision that could be interpreted as favorable to double representation for the Third Estate. By a narrow vote parlement declared its confidence in "the king's wisdom to decide upon the measures necessary to effect the changes that Reason, Liberty, Justice, and public opinion may demand." It was a somewhat ambiguous victory, but since it envisaged the possibility of change, it was decisive enough to allow Necker to take action if he dared.

The final meeting of the Assembly of Notables took place a week later. Unseasonably wintry weather diminished the pomp of the occasion. After the king's brief address, the keeper of the seals and various spokesmen for the three orders made polite, self-satisfied speeches, which, though they breathed a touching loyalty to the throne, showed no inclination to depart from the approved constitutional and legal forms.[61] If the opinions of the Notables were to be binding, Condorcet's worst fears would be realized. The total effect of the Assembly would be only to reinforce the control of the privileged orders and to defeat the trinity of "Liberty, Equality, and Reason."

For Lafayette, the meeting of the Notables had been a grave disappointment. They could never compensate, he declared, for the time they had wasted, although they had won the unique distinction of "being surpassed in philosophy by the parlement of Paris."[62] When he visited Mazzei upon his return to the metropolis, he explained that he had not reported on the Assembly as regularly as he would have liked because it had been "very uninteresting."[63]

Nevertheless, "that accursed Assembly of Notables" had had a significance that Lafayette was better able to understand now that it was over. Necker had made a fortunate tactical error, he felt. In submitting the cause of the Third Estate "to the very ones who would be most opposed to the people among the privileged classes," the misguided minister had opened "a

---

61. *Procès-verbal*, pp. 473–94.
62. Lafayette to "Madame," [*ca.* Dec. 8, 1788], Jackson collection.
63. Mazzei to Poniatowski, Dec. 13, 1788, Ciampini, I, 63–64.

Pandora's Box" that could be closed only if he heeded the handful of liberal Notables.[64] The Assembly had made crystal clear the threefold nature of the struggle then going on in France. Everyone could now see that it was not a battle between the friends of absolutism, on the one hand, and the friends of liberty, on the other, but rather one in which the aristocracy stood halfway between the two major antagonists, ready to side with either against the other in order to serve its own purposes. "From that period," Lafayette wrote about forty years later, "may be dated the fatal conflict between the immovable prejudices of a small group of privileged and the gradual development of public enlightenment."[65]

Some American observers understood the true character of the unrest in France better than some participants in it. "The struggle at present in that kingdom," wrote Madison, "seems to be entirely between the monarchy and aristocracy, and the hopes of the people merely in the competition of their enemies for their favour. It is probable, however, that both the parties contain real friends to liberty, who will make events subservient to their objects." No American could doubt that Lafayette at least was to be numbered among these friends. "The Marquis de La Fayette," Jefferson opined, "is out of favor with the court, but high in favor with the nation. I once feared for his personal liberty, but I hope he is on safe ground at present."[66]

The friends of reform in France had lost a battle but not the war. The issue had been joined on more than one field at the same time. Even while the Notables were in session, Lafayette had won a slight skirmish on the commercial front. At the beginning of the year 1788, Franco-American amity had seemed jeopardized once more. The generous concessions made by the government had excited "a pretty considerable fermentation among some commercial and financeering people" in France.[67] Nevertheless, Lafayette and that "great statesman, zealous

64. Lafayette to Rabaut-St. Étienne, Dec. 28, 1788, *loc. cit.*

65. *Mémoires*, II, 184.

66. Madison to Washington, Oct. 21, 1788, *Letters and other writings of Madison*, I, 429; Jefferson to Washington, Dec. 4, Lipscomb and Bergh, VII, 231.

67. Lafayette to Washington, Feb. 4, 1788, Gottschalk, *Letters*, p. 338.

citizen and amiable friend" Jefferson were sanguine about winning still more favors. Counting on Jefferson's "abilities, virtues, pleasing temper" and statesmanship, and on his "very able, engaging and honest" secretary, William Short, Lafayette hoped to put "American merchants on the same footing with the French" regarding whale oil and then to win advantages for Americans in the West Indian trade.[68]

The change of ministers and the political crises in France, however, had worked against further understandings, and in the fall of 1788 the French government announced that the importation of all foreign whale oil, without exception, would be prohibited. That drastic decree was aimed at English importers, who, taking advantage of the recent Anglo-French commercial treaty, had glutted the French market and had thereby brought on a loud outcry from the fishermen of Dunkirk. Nevertheless, the American whaling industry, though innocent, was once more brought face to face with disaster by this latest development. Jefferson addressed to Montmorin a long letter presenting in detail the hardships this new threat would work on the fisheries of America, the difficulties France would experience from it, and the advantages England would derive. He tried also to appeal to Necker's liberal inclinations "as an economist."[69] Lafayette likewise used his influence with the ministers. On November 16, Jefferson and Lafayette were invited to a conference with Councilor of State Lambert, formerly comptroller-general. When it ended, they were assured that the United States would be exempted from the prohibition on whale oil, provided that shippers could prove they were in fact of American origin.[70] "We are greatly indebted," Jefferson acknowledged, "to the Marquis de La Fayette for his aid on this as on every other occasion."[71]

Ministers who dared defy not only "the commercial and financeering people" but also common fisherman by making concessions to American traders could be considered capable of

68. Lafayette to Washington, May 25, 1788, *ibid.*, p. 344; cf. Lafayette to Wadsworth [*ca.* Aug. 25], Massachusetts State Library, Trumbull collection.

69. Jefferson to Jay, Nov. 19, 1788, Lipscomb and Bergh, VII, 192–93.

70. *Ibid.*, pp. 193–94; cf. Jefferson to Lafayette, Nov. 19, 1788, Chinard, *Lafayette and Jefferson*, p. 124, and to Adams, Dec. 5, Lipscomb and Bergh, VII, 232–33.

71. Jefferson to Adams, Dec. 5, 1788, Lipscomb and Bergh, VII, 234.

defying other powerful elements. The agitation for and against double representation of the Third Estate now became even more vehement than before the meeting of the Notables. Pamphlets and petitions continued to pour from the presses. Lafayette entered this battle of the books by joining with over a hundred other citizens of Paris of all classes in signing a petition to the king. The petition was broken into two parts. The first part raised the question of how delegates from Paris to the Estates General should be chosen, and the second presented an answer by some parlement lawyers to that question. Lafayette signed only the first part. Nevertheless the answer probably represented his point of view. Though in the past deputies to the Estates General had been chosen by the city's officials and selected notables, the petition suggested that now all adult French males, native or naturalized, who paid a capitation (or poll tax) of 6 livres should be allowed to vote. To be sure, those qualifications would take the franchise away from all women, children, foreigners, and poor (who were considered illiterate or irresponsible), and only fifty thousand (out of around seven hundred thousand) inhabitants of Paris would thus get the right to vote. Still the proposal envisaged another conspicuous departure from ancient forms in favor of more representative government. Lafayette's apparent approval of it indicated a change in his previously announced preference for elections by local assemblies.[72]

A few days later the cause of peaceful revolution by monarchical fiat won a resounding victory. Encouraged by what seemed to be the liberal stand of the Paris parlement, Necker insisted that the king defy the Assembly of Notables, nearly all the princes of the blood, most of the nobility, many of the clergy, and some of his own ministers. On December 27, Louis XVI bowed to Necker's judgment and decided in favor of double representation. When the decision was announced to a waiting people, it was immediately dubbed "Necker's New Year's gift to the nation." It was a Greek gift, however. To be sure, it offered as many votes to the Third Estate as to the two privileged orders combined, along with proposals for other reforms. Nevertheless, it reserved decision as to whether voting in

72. Chassin, I, 79–81 and 91. Cf. above, pp. 408–9.

the Estates General was to be "by head" or "by order," thereby making it possible that double representation might still be rendered meaningless. The significance of the king's reservation, however, was not yet apparent. All that the people of France saw in "Necker's New Year's gift" was triumph on the issue of double representation.

Great expectations arose, and some of them hinged upon the stalwart figure of America's "Marquis." Condorcet, his confidence restored, gave voice to them when he explained to Lafayette why he saw no need to take up his pen to sear a recent apologia for slavery: "It is in the Estates General that the cause of the Negroes should be pleaded, and it is to you, the hero of American liberty, the wise and zealous advocate of the noble resolution on behalf of Negroes [forbidding slavery in the American Northwest Territory], the generous man who has devoted part of his fortune and some of his brilliant youth to the search for ways to break the chains that his eyes ought never to see—it is to you that belongs the defense there of Liberty and the Rights of Man, which are the same for all, no matter what their color or their country may be."[73]

BIBLIOGRAPHICAL NOTES

The articles and booklets of Mège and the calendars of the Riom and the Clermont archives by Boyer and Rouchon, respectively, give many details on the affairs of Auvergne during the period. I am indebted to the staffs of the departmental archives in both cities for copies of the relevant documents.

Ciampini has published some of Mazzei's letters to King Stanislaus Poniatowski also in *Un osservatore italiano della Rivoluzione francese: littere inedite de Filippo Mazzei* (Florence, 1934).

The story of the Society of the Thirty has to be pieced together from several inadequate sources. Chérest, Michon, Filleul, and Sagnac give it brief attention, though more than it receives in other secondary works. They exaggerate its importance for 1788, however, imputing to its early career some of its later influence.

Chérest (I, 244–45) gives an account of Lafayette's association with the parlement of Paris, but his dates are inaccurate.

The article by G. W. Greene, grandson of General Nathanael Greene, in the *Atlantic monthly*, VIII (1861), 648–63, has been translated as "Lafayette chez lui (souvenirs d'un Américain)" in the *Revue britannique*, Series I, II (1862), 63–84.

73. Léon Cahen, "La Société des Amis des Noirs et Condorcet," *Révolution française*, L (1906), 503.

CHAPTER XXVI

Great Expectations

LAFAYETTE himself shared the new hopefulness of his countrymen. At the close of the last year of the Old Regime, he gave to Rabaut-St. Étienne a long account of recent events.[1] His remarks revealed that, although he was too much of a nobleman to be a doctrinaire republican, he was nevertheless an apt pupil of American political practices. "We must exploit our victory with moderation, in order to bring to the Estates General a spirit of peace. Rest assured that then ecclesiastical, parlementary, and other abuses will not resist the force of reason and the league of good citizens in the two landed orders—especially if voting is to be by head, as it is entirely right to expect."

The king of France, in Lafayette's opinion, had earned "the affection, gratitude, and confidence" of his people, since all his life he had sought to make them happy. "It is in fact this certainty of the king's justice and goodness that confirms me in the idea that the best monarchs cannot achieve good without the support of the nation." The marquis envisaged a new constitution that would restore to the people their rights, well guarded and carefully limited, and would studiously regulate and separate the legislative, executive, and judicial powers of government. By such a system of rights, checks, and balances, "we shall work for the happiness of a paternal and just king while keeping him from the abuse of his power." Since Lafayette believed that Rabaut-St. Étienne and he would probably both be elected members of the Estates General, he looked forward to the pleasure they would have in working together "for

1. Lafayette to Rabaut-St. Étienne, Dec. 28, 1788, Bibliothèque de la Ville de Nantes, MS 661, No. 133.

the public welfare, the strengthening of our monarchy, and the satisfaction of our monarch." Those ends, he hoped, would be achieved by building them upon "their true foundation, which is national liberty."

If Lafayette's philosophy sounded as if it came right out of Montesquieu's *Esprit des lois*, it was nevertheless from American political practice more directly than from French theory that he had derived it. Peaceful revolution seemed only a matter of good intentions, patience, and moderation in the winter of 1788–89 to the sanguine young leader of France's "Patriots." All that was needed was that the opposing champions of despotism and of aristocracy should yield to the men of good will and that all classes of citizens should co-operate—and never having been tried, such co-operation seemed easy. If it were achieved, "the executive power of the monarchy, the predominance of the nobles, and the rights of property" could within a few months be firmly established upon "a free constitution that would permit all citizens to participate in the advantages which nature has accorded to all men [and] which common sense ought to guarantee to all societies."[2] A liberal constitution for France, therefore, seemed a simple thing—a hereditary monarchy with a hereditary aristocracy in which royal power would be limited by a system of checks and balances and the .common people protected by a declaration of rights. It was to be like the American precedents, with such modifications as the traditional institutions of France would require.

Three thousand miles away, great expectations for France were tempered by doubts. Events had followed each other so fast that Lafayette had written to Washington only once in the last seven months.[3] Still Washington had not forgotten his disciple. The rumor that the marquis had been locked up in the Bastille spread quickly in the United States, alternating with the report that he was heading an open revolt in one of the provinces.[4] Before it was discovered that both reports were false,

2. Lafayette to Rabaut-St. Étienne, Mar. 10, [1789], *ibid.*, MS 667, No. 244.

3. Gottschalk, *Letters*, p. 345 n.

4. A. Iredell to J. Iredell, Aug. 5, 1785 [should be 1788], G. J. McRee, *Life and correspondence of James Iredell, one of the associate justices of the Supreme Court of the United States* (New York, 1858), II, 127; Madison to Jefferson and to Edmund Pendleton, Oct. 8 and 20, 1788, *Letters and other writings of Madison*, I, 420 and 429.

Washington had been "under great anxiety."[5]

Anxiety was not fully dissipated when Brissot de Warville reached Mount Vernon. Among the many things that struck the alert French publicist about the great American was his paternal affection for Lafayette. Washington proudly foresaw that his young friend was going to play an important role in the revolution then beginning in France. Yet the probable outcome of that revolution puzzled him. "If on the one hand, he recognized the ardor of Frenchmen in going to extremes, on the other he recognized their deep veneration for antique governments and monarchs, whose inviolability appeared strange to him." That conflict of emotions in Frenchmen made the issue seem to him uncertain, and hence his pride in Lafayette was "mixed with uneasiness."[6]

The future was to show that Washington had every right to feel uneasy for Lafayette. But for the time being the world seemed far too good for evil ultimately to triumph. In the United States the period of indecision that had begun with the peace of 1783 had ended, and in 1789 a new and lasting government was about to be inaugurated; weakness and decentralization were gradually to give way to strength and union. In France the same six years had been a period of reform and defiance. The defiance, to be sure, had so far come chiefly from nobles and magistrates, but they were emboldened by the moral support they received from the rest of the nation, and the time was already at hand when the nation would speak for itself. Only two men had played and were to continue to play a leading role in both countries—Jefferson and Lafayette—and behind both stood the noble figure of Washington, respected by the one and venerated by the other.

Those years since 1783 had been years of striking changes in the personality of Lafayette. When they began, he was famous as a young aristocratic soldier who had fought overseas— primarily for glory and *revanche*, but incidentally for the Rights of Man as well. As they progressed, he became an advocate of free trade, toleration, emancipation, philanthropy, and popular

5. Washington to Lafayette, Nov. 27, 1788, Fitzpatrick, XXX, 139.

6. J.-P. Brissot, *Nouveau voyage dans les États-Unis d'Amérique septentrionale, fait en 1788* (Paris, 1791), II, 270.

government; an opponent of monopoly, hereditary privilege, oppression, poverty, and abuse of power; a patron of commerce, science, and letters; a symbol of freedom generally respected by patriots in America, Holland, and Ireland and generally distrusted or scorned by oligarchs in France, Germany, and Russia. At the end of those six years he emerged a full-fledged revolutionary leader at home for whom the Rights of Man were no longer slogans but a heartfelt credo. He was ready to sacrifice for them, if need be, even his glory, which was dearer to him than life itself.

The startling implications of such a change were only dimly grasped by some of his contemporaries. It was hard for them to understand why a leading aristocrat, young, rich, popular, influential, and *ministrable*, should wish to be a conspicuous advocate of American, that is, revolutionary, ideas. Some of them thought he was ambitious and dangerous, others that he was silly and insincere. A few understood that he had consciously set out to be a hero, deliberately sculpturing himself after the finest model of his day.

The influence of Washington on his "adoptive son" was to remain great—so great that their resemblance both in behavior and appearance was to be more frequently noted than before,[7] and the influence of Jefferson reinforced Washington's. Yet those six years had shown that Lafayette still lacked some of the heroic qualities. He did not fully understand his own motivations or the implications of his own words and actions. He was unable to remain sternly imperturbable against the guile of less well-intentioned men. His need to be approved was so great that he was unable to develop a decent disrespect for the opinions of mankind. And being essentially self-centered, despite his warm interest in others, he was unprepared to dissociate his personal interests from his causes. Nevertheless he had grown markedly both as a public figure and as a personality, and he was to continue to grow in the trying times that lay ahead.

So far, Americans like Washington and Jefferson, along with

7. See above, p. 349; Bertrand de Molleville, VIII, 126; Dumont, p. 30; Marquis de Clermont-Gallerande, *Mémoires particuliers pour servir à l'histoire de la Révolution qui s'est opérée en France en 1789* (Paris, 1826), III, 295.

Frenchmen like Louis XVI and Necker, Malesherbes and Condorcet, Mirabeau and Brissot, had joined forces to bring about a new France. Even the real Washington, however, might have hesitated before conditions such as "the French Washington" was now to face. Events were soon to turn Jefferson against Washington, Necker against Louis XVI, Condorcet against Malesherbes, Brissot against Mirabeau—and Lafayette, France's "Washington," against Lafayette, America's "Marquis." But that was not yet. Few were the skeptics at the beginning of 1789 who refused to believe that a new era of political peace and social happiness was dawning in France, and Lafayette certainly was not among those few.

APPENDIX I

Legends of the 1784 Journey

A number of anecdotes told about Lafayette's third visit to the United States seem to be legendary. No evidence whatsoever substantiates the tale that he arrived at Mount Vernon just in time to help Washington paper the walls.[1] The hundred books that the colleges at Philadelphia and Williamsburg each received as a gift from Louis XVI[2] are probably more accurately ascribed to the intervention of Chastellux than Lafayette,[3] and there is no testimony that he personally conveyed them to either institution.

The most persistent tradition is that of the Masonic apron which Mme de Lafayette is supposed to have embroidered and which Lafayette is supposed to have presented to Washington at this time.[4] This tradition seems, however, to have arisen some time after 1784 and has no supporting primary testimony. The notes that Mme de Lafayette and her daughter Anastasie wrote to Washington and that Lafayette did actually deliver in August, 1784, say nothing of an apron. Washington's replies are equally silent on the subject. The numerous letters exchanged between Washington and Lafayette, though they speak of other trivial gifts like toys and hams, mention no apron of any kind. Washington would have been far too gallant to fail to acknowledge receipt of such a memento, if he had received it, especially if it had been embroidered by Adrienne's own hand. No other contemporary source speaks of this Masonic apron in or around 1784.

1. *Wallpaper*, XXXVI (1937), 34. Cf. *ibid.*, XXII (1935), 99.

2. Mitchell, pp. 146, n. 31, and 215.

3. Thomas McKean to Chastellux, Oct. 4, 1784, *Gazette de Leyde*, Dec. 28, 1784.

4. See, e.g., C. H. Claudy, *Washington's home and fraternal life* ("Honor to George Washington" series, published under the direction of the George Washington Bicentennial Commission, Pamphlet 14) (Washington, [1932]), pp. 176–77; E. B. Delzell, "Lafayette," *Grand Lodge bulletin, Grand Lodge of Iowa, F. and A.M.*, XXXI (1930), 745; Sidney Hayden, *Washington and his Masonic compeers* (New York, 1867), pp. 106 and 229–30; *Masonic exhibit of the R.W. Grand Lodge of Pennsylvania commemorating the 100th anniversary of the death of its distinguished honorary member Brother Lafayette, Philadelphia, May 21–26* [1934] (Philadelphia, 1934); C. S. Plumb, *Lafayette and his contacts with American Freemasonry* (reprinted from the *Proceedings* of the Grand Lodge of Ohio, 1934), p. 9; P. A. Roth, *Masonry in the formation of our government, 1761–1799* (Milwaukee, 1927), p. 44 n.; J. F. Sachse, *History of Brother General Lafayette's fraternal connections with the R.W. Grand Lodge F. & A.M., of Pennsylvania* (Philadelphia, 1916), p. 5. Mr. R. Baker Harris informs me that the apron was pre-

The chances seem small that the apron was in fact embroidered by Mme de Lafayette and nil that it was presented to Washington by Lafayette in 1784. Although Lafayette was a more active Mason in the 1780's than he had been in the 1770's,[5] there is little reason to believe that he was yet sufficiently enthusiastic about Freemasonry to consider such a gift appropriate and still less to believe that Mme de Lafayette would have thought so.

The story of the chinaware that Lafayette is supposed to have presented to Martha Washington on this occasion is only slightly more substantial.[6] It apparently owes its alleged existence to the silver plate that Washington ordered but canceled too late to prevent purchase and delivery.[7]

Several Boston legends recur from time to time regarding Lafayette's visits there in 1784. For example, he is made sponsor at the baptism of General Knox's son, who in fact was not born until afterward. Though he later became the child's godfather, Lafayette was in France when it was baptized.[8] Again, he is said, on Samuel Breck's authority, to have attended a meeting at Faneuil Hall, where he received an unintended lesson in the shortcomings of democratic debate.[9] While this story is not in itself incredible, it has no contemporary confirmation, and it is hard to avoid the suspicion that it is an embroidery of the facts.

Two other traditions may be true, although there seems to be no contemporary evidence to support them. That Lafayette presented to Patrick Henry an army desk that he had used during the War of Independence is not incredible, though the earliest source for the statement to that effect goes no farther back than 1859 and is at best second hand.[10] That he should have presented a flint musket to Congress seems quite possible but was hardly appropriate and also lacks contemporary confirmation.[11]

---

sented in 1816 by Washington's legatees to the Washington Benevolent Society of Pennsylvania, which in 1819 presented it in turn to the Grand Lodge of Free and Accepted Masons of Pennsylvania, which still has custody of it.

5. See Gottschalk, *Lafayette joins the American Army*, pp. 337–38, and *Lafayette and the close of the American Revolution*, pp. 367–69 and 433–34. See also above, pp. 177 and 335. Delmas (p. 18) states that Lafayette was made a member "honoraire et affilié" of the St. Flour lodge in 1784, but this must be an error for 1787 (see pp. 531–32).

6. Cf., e.g., Léon Chotteau, *La guerre de l'Indépendance (1775–1783): les Français en Amérique* (Paris, 1876), p. 427, n. 1; S. V. Henkels (comp.), *Washington-Madison papers, collected and preserved by James Madison, estate of J. C. McGuire,* catalogue No. 694, sale of Dec. 6–7, 1892, p. 279.

7. See above, pp. 55–56.

8. E. F. Ellet, *The women of the American Revolution* (New York, 1850), III, 44. Cf., however, Lafayette to Knox, May 11, 1785, Massachusetts Historical Society.

9. *Recollections of Samuel Breck*, pp. 39–40.

10. "Diary of Col. William Winston Fontaine," *William and Mary quarterly*, 1st ser., XVI (1908), 158 and 161, n. 2.

11. "Historical relics in Trenton, N.J.," *New England historical and genealogical register and antiquarian journal*, XXVII (1873), 245.

APPENDIX II

Otsiquette and Kayenlaha

One of the marquis's later secretaries and the anonymous *Complete history of Lafayette*[1] are responsible for the belief that George Washington Greene and Peter Otsiquette accompanied Lafayette to France when he returned in January, 1785. As shown above (pp. 141, 284, and 404), young Greene and Otsiquette arrived afterward and at different times.

A young Indian was with Lafayette, however, when he arrived. That this was not Otsiquette is evident from the letters Lafayette afterward wrote to American friends asking them to expedite Peter's voyage to France.[2] The lad who was with Lafayette on the "Nymphe" was apparently twelve years old. It was probably he whom Ledyard saw in 1785–86 and described as an Onondaga.[3] Peter was older and was an Oneida.

In all likelihood, Otsiquette did not reach France before the summer of 1785 and perhaps not until the beginning of 1786. Lafayette's first testimony that Peter had arrived came in a letter to Jefferson in March, 1786, in which he mentioned "my young Indian whom I requested to ask Brant [the pro-British Indian leader] what are his views."[4] Since Otsiquette had once visited Brant at Quebec,[5] this "young Indian" must be he and not the other, who would have been only about thirteen at the time. In any case, Peter was part of the Lafayette household around August, 1786, since Lafayette then mentions him by name. Lafayette called him Otchikeita,[6] but it must be recalled that Indian names were necessarily transliterated differently by English and French. Otchikeita can be no other than Otsiquette.

The letter in which the name Otchikeita occurs also gives us our single clue to the name of the younger Indian in Lafayette's household. It explains to Jefferson that since Otchikeita cannot wait for him (apparently to take him

1. A. Levasseur, *La Fayette en Amérique en 1824 et 1825* (Paris, 1829), II, 459–60 and [Davis], pp. 170–71.

2. Lafayette to Wadsworth, Apr. 16, 1785, Connecticut State Library, Trumbull collection, and to Constable, May 13, 1785, *Magazine of American history*, XI (1884), 546.

3. See above, p. 141 and n. 11.

4. Lafayette to Jefferson, Mar. 18, 1786, Chinard, *Lafayette and Jefferson*, p. 92. See also pp. 108 and 237 above.

5. Lafayette to Wadsworth, Apr. 16, 1785, *loc. cit.*

6. [Lafayette] (not Mme de Lafayette) to Jefferson [*ca.* August, 1786], Chinard, *Lafayette and Jefferson*, p. 104.

to a meeting with some of Lafayette's friends), Kayenlaha would do so.[7] Kayenlaha may, of course, be some other than the thirteen-year-old Onondaga, but the juxtaposition of the two names in such a context makes it somewhat unlikely that any other is meant. Kayenlaha was still in Lafayette's service at the beginning of 1787.[8]

Some confusion arises regarding the length of Otsiquette's stay in France. Beelen's comments on his interview with the Oneidas would seem to place it in September, 1785, but the Indian he encountered in European clothes who spoke French must have been Peter,[9] and so the meeting was probably the one of September, 1788, at which Peter is known to have been present. O. Turner declares in one place that Peter stayed in France four years and in another seven,[10] but the analysis of the best sources indicates no more than three at the most.

That Lafayette's friendliness did not lead to Peter's happiness and may even have been a cause of his early death from drink is indicated by the comments of contemporaries.[11] In 1825, on passing through Utica, New York, Lafayette met an Indian who claimed to be Peter's son and perhaps was, but in that case he would have had to be older than twenty-four years of age, as reported.[12]

7. *Ibid.* Chinard gives the name as Kayenlatra, but see the original in LC, Jefferson papers, p. 42152.

8. See above, pp. 161 and 284. The Indian referred to there may be Otsiquette, but the context seems to designate a younger one.

9. Schlitter, p. 558. The dating of this report may be an editorial error.

10. O. Turner, *History of the pioneer settlement of Phelps and Gorham's Purchase, and Morris' Reserve*, etc. (Rochester, N.Y., 1851), pp. 116 n. and 475.

11. Ternant to the French minister of foreign affairs, Apr. 6, 1792, F. J. Turner (ed.), "Correspondence of the French ministers to the United States, 1791–1797," *Annual report of the American Historical Association*, II (1903), 108; Vanderkemp to Colonel A. G. Mappa, July 27, 1792, "Extracts from the Vanderkemp papers," *Buffalo Historical Society publications*, II (1880), 53. Ternant uses the name "Peter Jacquett."

12. Levasseur, II, 459–60. Levasseur's account of this episode is probably correct, but his knowledge of Otsiquette (whom he calls Ouekchekaeta) leaves much to be desired.

APPENDIX III

The American Citizenship of Lafayette's Descendants

The several American cities and states that made Lafayette an honorary citizen have been enumerated above.[1] It is highly doubtful, however, that this right of citizenship extends to any of his descendants of our day.

Nevertheless, at first sight, the argument in their favor seems almost persuasive. Presumably as a citizen of Maryland (not to mention other places) when the Constitution of the United States was adopted, Lafayette became a citizen of the United States. This right also applied to his male heirs. Therefore, when the Fourteenth Amendment was ratified in 1868, their claim to citizenship in the United States was confirmed by the provision that "all persons born or naturalized in the United States . . . are citizens of the United States and of the State wherein they reside," since they had been naturalized by the special acts of several legislatures (unless, as is possible, the phrase "wherein they reside" is construed to mean that they must previously have resided somewhere in the United States).

No one has ever seriously disputed Lafayette's own right to be considered "an *adopted* citizen of this country,"[2] even though he never renounced his French citizenship. Nor did the question arise during the lifetime of his direct male heirs. Greater doubt exists, however, regarding the claim of his present-day descendants. It must be recalled that the act of Maryland, which was the most generous in this regard of all the acts adopting Lafayette as a citizen, extended that honor only to "his heirs male for ever." Exactly what that phrase meant is subject to varying interpretation. If it meant (as seems unlikely) that all his male descendants were intended to be citizens, then the present male descendants of his daughters and granddaughters may perhaps be regarded as full-fledged citizens of the United States.[3] It is more prob-

1. Pp. 93, 145–47, and 146, n. 25.

2. Washington to La Rochefoucauld, Aug. 8, 1796, Fitzpatrick, XXXV, 168. Cf. *New England historical and genealogical register*, XXIV (1870), 81; S. F. Bemis, "The United States and Lafayette," *Daughters of the American Revolution magazine*, LVIII (1924), 341–42 n. and 346.

3. General de Chambrun, Virginie de Lafayette's great-great-grandson, has contended that this is true (see "Have the male descendants of Lafayette right to American citizenship?" *Légion d'Honneur*, II [1931], 141–42, and "Was Lafayette an American citizen?" *Golden book*, XVI [1932], 83–84).

able, however, that the act of Maryland was intended to apply only to direct male descendants, and, still more probable, to that single heir in each generation who by the prevalent French practice of primogeniture would inherit Lafayette's estate and title. No such descendant survives today, however. Oscar and Edmond, the sons of George Washington Lafayette, had no surviving male heirs, and the name Lafayette has been preserved of late only because the marquis's descendants through collateral lines have assumed it. Should the question arise in the future, it will perhaps require a decision of the American immigration authorities or the courts to settle definitively whether Lafayette's collateral male descendants are entitled to American citizenship without previous residence in the United States.

APPENDIX IV

The Cultivation of the Lafayette Legend (1783–88)

Lafayette early began to guide contemporary historians in the proper appreciation of his role in the American Revolution and subsequent events. In the first place, he wrote his own account of what had happened. Somewhere between 1783 and 1786 he composed parts of what later became known as the "Mémoires de ma main jusqu'en l'année 1780."[1] He also furnished other historians with his views and testimony. Shortly after the war the Rev. William Gordon began to collect data for his study of the American Revolution, which eventually resulted in his *History of the rise, progress, and establishment of the independence of the United States of America.* He apparently approached Lafayette for his testimony when the marquis was touring the United States in 1784. With that "modesty" for which Lafayette became famous, he preferred not to tell his story himself. McHenry undertook to do so for him. In the end, McHenry wrote a memoir on Lafayette, which he sent to Washington, who in turn sent it to Gordon.[2] The reverend historian was cautioned on the "propriety of keeping the Marquis's wishes in this business behind the curtain."[3] About the same time, Lafayette also helped Brissot, Crèvecœur, Mazzei, and perhaps some other writers of the day[4] to give the correct impression of his share in America's glory. All this coaching was done despite the fact that he disclaimed any intention of writing or speaking about his campaigns.[5] Thus he managed to receive what today we should call "a good press" while preserving his reputation for modesty. In all fairness, it must be granted that, although Lafayette entertained a good opinion of his own exploits, although he was easily misled regarding the motives of those who advised him as he wished to be advised, and although his memory sometimes played him tricks, he seems seldom, if ever, deliberately to have lied.

1. *Mémoires*, I, 5–66; cf. *ibid.*, p. vii, nn. 1 and 2, and p. 3.

2. McHenry to Washington, Aug. 1, 1785, Parke-Bernet Galleries, catalogue No. 562, *James McHenry papers* (New York, 1944), Part 1, No. 113; Washington to McHenry, Aug. 22, Fitzpatrick, XXVIII, 227.

3. Washington to Gordon, Aug. 31, 1785, Fitzpatrick, XXVIII, 242; see also Washington to Gordon, Mar. 8 and Dec. 5, *ibid.*, pp. 96 and 345.

4. See above, pp. 20–21, 293, 310, and 368–69.

5. Lafayette to [Mme de Tessé], Aug. 7, 1783, *Mémoires*, II, 129.

INDEX

(Italics indicate bibliographical data.)